The Story of Act 31

THE STORY OF ACT 31

*How Native History Came
to Wisconsin Classrooms*

J P LEARY

WISCONSIN HISTORICAL SOCIETY PRESS

Published by the Wisconsin Historical Society Press
Publishers since 1855

The Wisconsin Historical Society helps people connect to the past by collecting, preserving, and sharing stories. Founded in 1846, the Society is one of the nation's finest historical institutions.
Join the Wisconsin Historical Society: wisconsinhistory.org/membership

Printed in the United States of America
Designed by Tom Heffron

22 21 20 19 18   1 2 3 4 5

Library of Congress Cataloging-in-Publication Data applied for

♾ The paper used in this publication meets the minimum requirements of the American National Standard for Information Sciences—Permanence of Paper for Printed Library Materials, ANSI Z39.48-1992.

Dedicated to the memory of my teachers, mentors, and friends
Ronald N. Satz, Alan J. Caldwell, Dorothy Davids,
Ruth Gudinas, and Veda Stone

To my grandmothers

To those generations yet to come

CONTENTS

INTRODUCTION

In June 1961, a Stockbridge-Munsee tribal member named Elmer L. Davids Sr. spoke at the American Indian Chicago Conference, where he addressed the "white public's" general lack of awareness of American Indian issues. Davids, who was a member of the Stockbridge-Munsee Historical Committee, shared his observations "as a reservation Indian and a citizen living on taxable land."[1]

In a passage that foreshadowed educational reform efforts, Davids argued that the public needed to be "educated to look upon a reservation in the true meaning of the word: something the Indian Tribes have reserved for themselves out of the vast territory of this country which was once their domain and for which, in some cases, they so valiantly resisted the invaders."[2]

Davids wondered whether most white Americans recognized that "many of the products that loom large in our present economy are of Indian origin, like corn, tobacco, etc.?" He asked whether his white peers and neighbors knew "that the early explorers were shown the valleys and water courses that became our highways" or "that the stories of Daniel Boone, Kit Carson, and Lewis and Clark could never have been written were it not for friendly Indians."

Davids challenged the audience with this pivotal question: "Is it fair to the Indian to use the textbooks in our public schools that tend to justify the acts of early settlers and make the poor Indian, resisting in proud self-defense, a culprit and a savage?"[3]

The answers to Davids's questions likely were quite clear to those in the audience that day. However, it would take nearly thirty years for American Indian educators and their allies in Wisconsin to succeed in changing curriculum policy to respond to the kinds of issues raised in Davids's address.

On August 8, 1989, Wisconsin lawmakers enacted 1989 Act 31, the state biennial budget, which included requirements for Wisconsin public schools and teacher education programs to teach about the Native peoples in the state. Act 31, as these requirements are commonly called by educators today, was a huge victory for Indian educators and their allies.[4] The new law contained several provisions that sought to use the public schools to increase understanding of American Indian history, culture, and tribal sovereignty among the state's citizens. One provision required the state superintendent to collaborate with the American Indian Language and Culture Education Board to develop instructional materials on the "Chippewa Indians' treaty-based, off-reservation rights to hunt, fish and gather" by the end of the biennium.[5] Other provisions required Wisconsin school districts to provide students with an "appreciation and understanding of different value systems and cultures" and "an understanding of human relations, particularly with regard to American Indians, Black Americans and Hispanics."[6] Act 31 effectively required those seeking a license to serve as a teacher, administrator, or pupil services professional in Wisconsin to learn about "minority group relations, including instruction in the history, culture and tribal sovereignty of the federally recognized American Indian tribes and bands located in this state."[7] The biennial budget also enacted a provision that required school districts to "provide adequate instructional materials, texts and library services which reflect the cultural diversity and pluralistic nature of American society."[8] These policy changes reflected a multifaceted approach to transforming students' understanding of critical issues around culture, race, and identity.

Another provision, which was widely considered the heart of Act 31, required Wisconsin public schools to "include instruction in the history, culture and tribal sovereignty of the federally recognized American Indian tribes and bands located in this state at least twice in the elementary grades and at least once in the high school grades." This instruction would be folded into social studies curricula and would begin the first school day of the following biennium, September 1, 1991.[9]

Wisconsin is a state that prides itself on local control of education and grants broad authority to locally elected school boards. Yet advocates for curriculum policy reform had succeeded in securing specific instructional requirements that applied to every public school in the state. In Indian education circles, the budget act lent its name to the instructional requirements themselves, and the passage of Act 31 was a point of pride.

It has been more than twenty-five years since Act 31 became law. Yet, disconcertingly, the origins and rationale behind the law seem to be largely unknown—to the educators responsible for implementing the law, as well as to the parents across the state whose children's classrooms were affected by its requirements. For fifteen years, I worked with the American Indian Studies program at the Wisconsin Department of Public Instruction, the unit created through the 1989–1991 biennial budget to support instruction in the required areas. During my time there, I learned that Act 31 was widely viewed as yet another example of using education policy to address broader societal issues. Those who understood the law correctly traced its origins to the spearfishing controversy of the 1980s, which grew from the violent protests following federal court decisions affirming the continued validity of the Ojibwe people's treaty-based right to hunt, fish, and gather in northern Wisconsin. Importantly, however, most people failed to recognize that the public outcry, controversy, and violence that accompanied the reassertion of treaty rights were the result of policies that for generations had denied Wisconsin students authentic knowledge about American Indians and had excluded the American Indian story from the domain of official knowledge. The policy had become disconnected from its purpose.

Existing scholarship addresses the treaty rights controversy quite well.[10] *The Story of Act 31* draws critical insights from this existing research and builds on it by examining the origins of this groundbreaking law and the ways in which changes to educational policy formed a solution to the problems identified by earlier researchers. Doing so challenges the common, and simplistic, understanding of Act 31's origins and purpose by telling the story of how Indian educators and their allies successfully challenged an instructional and political system that excluded accurate information about American Indians from the classrooms across Wisconsin.

Today, many contemporary advocates for American Indian Studies have become disillusioned with what they view as a failure to implement the law at the state and local levels, especially as federal policies have promoted standards-based reforms focused on reading and mathematics. While historical analysis alone cannot provide a road map for where educators and lawmakers should go from here, in part because relationships between Native and non-Native communities have changed since Act 31 was passed and the broader policy context is now vastly different, contemporary advocates can redefine the current problem by studying how an earlier generation struggled with similar issues.[11]

The Story of Act 31 considers the many interrelated factors that inspired Wisconsin lawmakers to enact a groundbreaking law that not only required instruction about American Indians, but did so with an unprecedented degree of specificity that challenged cherished traditions of local control. The book is organized into five major sections. We begin in Part 1, The Battle for Treaty Rights, by exploring the history of federal Indian policy and the practice of treaty making. It further explores how the reassertion of treaty rights by the Lake Superior Bands of Chippewa Indians set off a chain of litigation from 1983 to 1991, which affirmed tribal rights defined in treaties with the US government in 1837 and 1842.

The first of these landmark decisions, 1983's *Voigt* decision, ignited a dramatic public outcry, examined in Part 2, The Backlash against Treaty Rights. Widespread public ignorance about treaty rights and Native culture turned into protests marked by incidents of actual and symbolic violence. These protests led to a sociopolitical crisis that threatened public safety, as well as a potential economic crisis that threatened the state's image as a tranquil tourist destination. Although the crisis itself happened outside the schoolyard, the tendency of lawmakers to look to education policy rather than social policy paved the way for Act 31.[12]

Part 3, Social Studies on the National Stage, examines why there was such widespread public ignorance about American Indian history and culture to begin with, tracing it back to past curriculum policy decisions. For example, broad trends in social studies curricula often redefined classroom content to reflect sociopolitical crises related to World War II, the Cold War, the civil rights movement, and national economic anxieties. Efforts to redefine "official knowledge" often created curricular absences or problematic presences for Native peoples. These shifts limited students' opportunities to learn about Native peoples and their history.[13]

Part 4, Official Knowledge and the State of Wisconsin, shows how efforts at the local and state level in Wisconsin affected learning opportunities related to American Indians—from the locally elected school boards that exercise primary authority in educational decision making, to the state Department of Public Instruction, which provides support to local districts, to the commonly used textbooks that change over time to reflect variations in official knowledge at the local level.[14]

Part 5, Passing Act 31, places the legislative history of Act 31 in the broader context of Native people's efforts to transform curriculum policy throughout the twentieth century. Efforts in Wisconsin to redefine official knowledge to include the history, culture, and tribal sovereignty of federally recognized tribes had many precedents at the national and state level. Advocates for Act 31 viewed their work as more than a simple reform prompted by the backlash to *Voigt*. The struggle over how to implement the law underscores the difficulties of creating meaningful changes in curriculum policy.

As a whole, *The Story of Act 31* places the law in the multiple contexts from which it emerged, showing how it was both a response to a crisis external to schooling and a critical solution to a problem in classrooms in every corner of the state. This historical analysis explains why this often overlooked and misunderstood policy exists, challenges the simplistic view that it is merely a response to the spearfishing controversy of the late 1980s, and illustrates why it remains relevant today.

A Note on Terminology

The terms "Indian," "American Indian," "Native American," and "Native," among others, can be problematic in that they ignore the vast cultural and linguistic differences among Indigenous peoples in the Americas and instead create a single category based on the shared experience with colonialism. Furthermore, there is no consensus regarding preferred terminology among those described by these terms nor among contemporary scholars.

In the legal realm, "Indian" is a term of art, but it is also fraught with baggage related to simplistic stereotypes outside of that specific context. To avoid privileging any particular problematic term over any other, *The Story of Act 31* uses them interchangeably.[15]

Contemporary preferred names are used to refer to specific Indigenous nations except in quoted material. For example, *Ojibwe* will be used in discussion, while *Chippewa* will generally appear in quoted material according to its historical context.

PART 1

THE BATTLE FOR
TREATY RIGHTS

CHAPTER 1

Sovereignty, Treatymaking, and State Law

At a treaty council at the St. Peters Indian Agency on July 27, 1837, near present-day Minneapolis, two sovereign nations met across the negotiating table. The United States, represented by Wisconsin Territorial Governor Henry Dodge, sought to secure access to the vast stands of timber stretching across the new Wisconsin Territory. The Ojibwe Nation, represented by Magegawbaw, sought to retain its rights to the land's life-giving resources: its trees, water, fish, and wildlife. Addressing US government officials through interpreters, Magegawbaw, also known as La Trappe, explained that while representatives of the Ojibwe bands from Leech Lake and the Upper Mississippi region were willing to cede land to the United States, "we wish to hold on to a tree where we get our living, and to reserve the streams where we drink the waters that give us life."[1] Magegawbaw pressed the point by placing an oak sprig on the table where Governor Dodge sat looking at a map of the cession Dodge had proposed. The Ojibwe leaders were willing to discuss leasing their Wisconsin pinelands, but they were not willing to sell the hardwood forests across the river. After Dodge rejected this proposal, Magegawbaw again sought to clarify: "If I have rightly understood you, we can remain on the lands and hunt there."[2]

Flat Mouth, a chief of the Pillager Bands of Ojibwe, also spoke on behalf of the assembled chiefs. "My Father," he told Dodge, "your children are willing to let you have their lands, but they wish to reserve the privilege of making sugar from the trees, and getting their living from the Lakes and

3

Rivers, as they have done heretofore, and of remaining in this Country." Flat Mouth described his people's strong connection to the land and waters, which was not only economic but also spiritual: "The Great Spirit above made the Earth and causes it to produce, which enables us to live."[3]

Dodge, claiming to speak for US President Martin Van Buren, assured the Ojibwe chiefs they would enjoy "free use of the rivers and the privilege of hunting upon the lands you are to sell to the United States, during his pleasure."[4] Perhaps attempting to provide further reassurance, Dodge noted, "it will probably be many years before your Great Father will want all these lands for the use of his white Children."[5]

Regardless of whether Dodge was speaking in good faith, the new territory flourished, and by 1848—just eleven years later—Wisconsin had become the thirtieth state. As white settlement increased, the government initiated or continued efforts to remove the Ojibwe, Menominee, Stockbridge-Munsee, Potawatomi, and Ho-Chunk peoples. When those efforts failed—as nation after nation signed treaties or secured legislation that ensured the continued existence of their Wisconsin homelands—state officials instead began to assert jurisdiction over indigenous lands and peoples. State enforcement of the conservation code meant that Ojibwe people who were exercising their legally reserved rights to hunt, fish, and gather faced arrest, jail, fines, confiscation of the fish and game they had harvested, and seizure of the equipment used. For the Ojibwe people, this interference lasted well over a century.

Treaty Making and the US Constitution

In 1991, legal scholar Rennard Strickland observed, "Perhaps more than any other field of American jurisprudence, American Indian rights are deeply rooted in ancient ways and historical bargains. The aboriginal inhabitants of the American continents are the original sovereigns. As such, they retain rights that long predate the coming of more recent sovereigns such as our modern national or individual states."[6]

These rights as "sovereigns" are reflected in the "special federal relationship" that the United States has with Indian tribes, as defined in the US Constitution.[7] Historian David Wrone characterizes this unique relationship as a reflection of the nation's democratic ideals and argues that it was originally intended to serve as "a means of protecting the tribes from the states and unscrupulous citizens, thereby avoiding Indian wars."[8]

For nearly the first century of its existence, the United States continued the European tradition of recognizing Indian tribes as independent nations, engaging in nation-to-nation negotiations and relying on treaties as the primary legal instrument of diplomacy. Between 1778 and 1871, the US government ratified 367 treaties with Indian tribes.[9] The Constitution's Supremacy Clause—Article VI, Clause 2—recognizes "all Treaties made, or which shall be made," along with "Constitution, and the Laws of the United States," as the "Supreme Law of the land."[10] The Supremacy Clause "makes treaties superior to any conflicting state law or constitutional provision, in effect becoming amendments to the constitution."[11]

The diplomatic act of treatymaking emerged as the most efficient means of acquiring land and advancing non-Indian settlement. Many considered warfare with tribal nations to be too costly in terms of blood and treasure.[12] This view is reflected in the Northwest Ordinance, through which the United States claimed and organized lands in present-day Wisconsin, and its admonition that the United States was bound to show "utmost good faith" in its dealings with Indians.[13] This view was further solidified after the United States was militarily defeated by the "victorious tribes of the Old Northwest," leading the government to abandon any goals of conquest and instead embrace "the democratic idea as the path to follow with Indians."[14]

The federal government's intent was often simply to "open up Indian lands for non-Indian settlement and the capitalist exploitation and development of natural resources" as well as to "remove the cloud of Indian sovereign control from most of the West so that new states could govern most land within their boundaries free of complications from Indians."[15] The political question in the United States was never whether to acquire Native lands, but simply how to do so. As US settlement grew, "whites frequently enough disregarded Indian rights."[16]

Treatymaking "rested upon a concept of Indian sovereignty or quasi sovereignty," served in part to help shape and define the doctrine of tribal sovereignty, and established a "protected existence" for Indian nations that has developed into the doctrine of trust responsibility.[17] Tribal sovereignty "guarantees that Indian tribes are domestic nations with a substantial degree of independence," and trust responsibility defines the obligation of the United States "to serve as a trustee to protect a beneficiary, the Indian peoples." Together, these doctrines formed the foundation of federal Indian law.[18]

Beginning in the 1820s, Chief Justice John Marshall first defined the nature and scope of tribal sovereignty in the landmark Supreme Court cases known collectively as the Marshall Trilogy. The Marshall court recognized "the several Indian nations as distinct political communities, having territorial boundaries, within which their authority is exclusive, and having a right to all the lands within those boundaries, which is not only acknowledged, but guaranteed by the United States."[19] These tribal rights included the right to hunt, fish, and reside on their aboriginal lands—though the Marshall court held that these rights were shared with the federal government of the United States.[20] Congressional acts to regulate Indian relations must, according to the court, "treat them as nations, respect their rights, and manifest a firm purpose to afford that protection which treaties stipulate."[21] The court viewed treaties as instruments of diplomacy. In considering the treaties through which the United States secured title to tribal lands, the court ruled that the words "treaty" and "nation" should apply to "Indians as we have applied them to the other nations of the earth."[22]

While subsequent court decisions would develop and modify these principles in sometimes contradictory ways, the Marshall Trilogy created the legal foundation for understanding tribal sovereignty and the government-to-government relationship between tribal nations and the federal government of the United States. More recently, the courts have held that "tribes still possess those aspects of sovereignty not withdrawn by treaty or statute, or by implication as a necessary result of their dependent status."[23] Still, the concept of tribal sovereignty, the seemingly contradictory legal precedents governing Indian relations, and the status of treaties between the US government and Native peoples would become widely misunderstood and hotly contested issues in Wisconsin during the 1980s and early 1990s.[24]

TREATY NEGOTIATIONS

Since time immemorial, the traditional way of life for the Ojibwe people in present-day Wisconsin centered on the seasonal practices of hunting, fishing, trapping, harvesting wild rice, and making maple sugar.[25] The Ojibwe made use of virtually all natural resources available—plants, animals, and minerals—a relationship with the landscape that was as much social and spiritual as it was economic.[26]

Judge James Doyle acknowledged this fact during the treaty rights litigation. In 1987, he held that the Ojibwe "had some use or uses for all the flora and fauna in their environment, whether for food, clothing, shelter, religious, commercial, or other purposes."[27] But as non-Indians encroached on the landscape, trade between the Ojibwe and the British and the French began to transform that traditional economy. Manufactured European goods began to replace handmade items of bone, stone, wood, and clay. Indians traded furs for these goods, which led to an increased focus on trapping.[28] Despite their involvement in commercial activity, they did not "strive for more than a 'moderate, satisfactory living.'"[29] Another change loomed on the horizon after their homelands became part of a parcel claimed by the United States when it founded the Northwest Territory in 1787 and began to establish a presence in the region after the War of 1812.[30]

In 1825, the Lake Superior Chippewa, the legal name the US government used in reference to several bands of Ojibwe people, were parties to the Treaty of Prairie du Chien. Through this treaty, the United States hoped to shift the tribes' allegiance from the British and establish boundaries for future land cessions as US settlement expanded westward.[31] At Prairie du Chien, the federal government sought to extinguish Dakota title to lands east of the Mississippi River and recognized Ojibwe title to lands historically claimed by both peoples. By the mid-1830s, the United States sought nearly ten million acres of abundant pine timber in northern Wisconsin to serve the needs of the growing states of Illinois and Missouri and the newly established Wisconsin Territory.[32]

The Treaty of 1837 and Reserved Rights

When Ojibwe leaders from around the region arrived at the St. Peters Agency for the July 1837 treaty council, Governor Dodge, presiding as treaty commissioner, explained the federal government's intent to buy a portion of the tribe's 27 million acres in Wisconsin, Minnesota, and the Upper Peninsula of Michigan.[33] Dodge described the region as "barren of game and not good for agriculture." He explained that the parcel "abounded in pine timber, for which their Great Father the President of the United States wished to buy it from them, for the use of his white children."[34] Not communicated to the Ojibwe was the fact that the federal government also sought to open that land to white settlement.

The Ojibwe leaders "came to the bargaining table with considerable sophistication."[35] Their traditional culture, which recognized several distinct, self-governing societies, was "mostly intact despite early contact with whites," and they were confident their skills as hunters and trappers would allow them to get what they wanted through commercial trade.[36] They also possessed a strong grasp of economics, including "the principles of the Euro-American market economy," yet they remained unmotivated "by the hopes of profits and the accumulation of material goods."[37] As such, they proved to be formidable negotiators.

Magegawbaw, Flat Mouth, and other tribal leaders made their case with the help of interpreters. Yet Verplanck Van Antwerp, secretary to the US Commissioner of Indian Affairs, lamented the "nonsense" that resulted from the efforts of interpreters "unfit to act in that capacity" and noted in his transcript of the proceedings: "I presume it to mean that the Indians wish to reserve the privilege of hunting and fishing on the lands and making sugar from the Maple."[38] In the treaty discussions, including failed attempts to negotiate what amounted to a lease, the Ojibwe leaders made several references to their people's desire to reserve the right to access and use the resources within the ceded territory.[39]

The final version of the treaty included the guarantee that "the privilege of hunting, fishing, and gathering the wild rice, upon the lands, the rivers and the lakes included in the territory ceded, is guaranteed to the Indians, during the pleasure of the President of the United States."[40] Governor Dodge had added the final clause, and Ojibwe leaders agreed to it only because they understood they could thus remain in their villages and maintain their way of life as long as peace persisted.[41]

The Ojibwe leaders' intent and understanding of this agreement would become a pivotal issue in legal proceedings that would happen generations later.[42]

THE TREATY OF 1842 AND RESERVED RIGHTS

A few years after the treaty at the St. Peters Agency, the US government learned of extensive copper deposits along the Lake Superior shoreline. Robert Stuart, superintendent of the Michigan Indian Agency, traveled to the subagency at La Pointe, Wisconsin, to negotiate a land cession with the Ojibwe in which the United States would acquire the minerals and lands along the lake's south shore.[43]

These negotiations for what would become the Treaty of 1842 again included discussions of the tribe's continued access and use of ceded territory in their customary ways. Ojibwe leaders who gathered at the treaty council once again received assurances that their people could remain in their homelands provided they "behaved well and are peaceable with our grandfather [in Washington] and his white children."[44] Federal officials suggested it could be fifty or one hundred years before the tribes would need to move, if ever.[45]

Article 2 of the Treaty of 1842 reflected these discussions: "The Indians stipulate for the right of hunting on the ceded territory, with the other usual privileges of occupancy, until required to remove by the President of the United States, and the laws of the United States shall be continued in force, in respect to their trade and inter course [sic] with the whites, until otherwise ordered by Congress."[46] Indeed, during the 1842 negotiations, the Ojibwe "supposed they were simply selling the pine and minerals," just as they understood they were selling timber in 1837.[47] Again, the intent and understanding of the Ojibwe leaders gathered at La Pointe would become one of the central questions before the courts in the 1970s and 1980s.

LIFE UNDER THREAT OF REMOVAL

Following the cessions in 1837 and 1842, the Ojibwe people continued to live off the land. They also became more directly involved in the region's economy, as trading partners; as laborers in commercial industries such as fishing, mining, and lumbering; and as providers of various goods and services to non-Indian workers in these industries.[48] Nonetheless, discussions related to their removal were already beginning.

In 1846, as Congress enacted a law authorizing the Wisconsin Territory to establish a state government, Commissioner of Indian Affairs William Medill began to recommend Indian removal in order to give the Ojibwe people "the benefit of the benevolent policy of the government for the improvement of the Indian race."[49] In response, the Ojibwe people "began to hold councils and to ask each [other] as to how they had understood the treaties, and all understood them the same, that was: that they were never to be disturbed if they behaved themselves."[50] They submitted a pictorial and written petition to Congress on February 7, 1849, requesting "a donation of 24 sections of land, covering the graves of our fathers, our sugar orchards, and our rice lakes and rivers, at seven different places now occupied by us as villages," including "LCotore [Lac Courte Oreilles]" and La Point.[51] Instead of promises that removal was merely a remote possibility in a distant future, the Ojibwe leaders now sought a clearer guarantee that they would be secure in their homeland.

That fall, pressure to leave their homeland increased when Alexander Ramsey, a Whig, became governor of the newly formed Minnesota Territory. Ramsey immediately sought to create additional patronage positions in the new territory by convincing President Zachary Taylor, a fellow Whig, to transfer them from Democratic Wisconsin. Despite clear objections from the Ojibwe people, and with no acts of violence that would merit their expulsion under the treaties, Ramsey pushed on with his removal efforts. The issue had little to do with the Ojibwe people themselves and everything to do with financial gain and partisan politics.[52]

In early 1850, both the commissioner of Indian affairs and the secretary of the interior recommended a removal order, without explanation, which Taylor approved on February 6, 1850. The order directed the removal of the Ojibwe people from Wisconsin and canceled their usufructuary rights, that is, their reserved right to use land that now belongs to the United States, in Wisconsin and Michigan. The Ojibwe were "surprised and dismayed" by the order, which was a clear violation of how they had understood the treaty negotiations of 1837 and 1842. Their leaders had understood that they would remain secure in their homes as long as peace prevailed, and they held that they had not agreed to any scenario in which removal was likely.[53]

After conferring with one another once again, Ojibwe leaders organized support among their allies—white missionaries, civic leaders, mine owners, and others who relied on their labor.[54] They also enjoyed significant support from several regional and national newspapers, including the *Detroit Free Press* and the *New York Times*, many of which printed letters from Ojibwe Chief Hole-in-the-Day and others arguing that Ojibwe leaders never would have signed the treaties of 1837 or 1842 without assurances they could remain in their homeland.[55]

Hole-in-the-Day's account was corroborated by Selah B. Treat, the secretary of the American Board of Commissioners for Foreign Missions, who had witnessed the 1842 treaty negotiations. Treat reported that federal officials had promised the Ojibwe people would "never see the day when your Great Father will ask you to remove." He further noted "the treaty never would have been consummated" without such assurances.[56] Other witnesses provided similar testimony that validated the Ojibwe's account of the treaty proceedings that they "would not be removed during the term of their annuity, and probably never," and reiterating that without such assurances, there would have been no agreement.[57]

Opposition to the tribe's removal grew even further following Ramsey's attempt in October of 1850 to lure the Ojibwe to Minnesota by moving the payment of treaty annuities to Sandy Lake, a remote location in Minnesota. Neither the territorial nor federal government had made arrangements for food or shelter at Sandy Lake, and while they waited for payments to arrive, the Ojibwe people were badly exploited by local merchants who sold spoiled food at inflated prices. After learning that Congress had yet to make the necessary appropriations for the payments, many Ojibwe attempted to return to their villages in Wisconsin before winter set in. Observers estimated that four hundred people died of illness, hunger, or exposure at Sandy Lake or on their way home.[58] Despite these horrific occurrences, federal officials again attempted to remove the Ojibwe people from Wisconsin in 1851, this time to another location in Minnesota.[59]

By June of 1851, the federal government had begun to receive "communications from sources of the highest consideration," including the Wisconsin legislature, missionaries, and the Ojibwe people themselves, "remonstrating in strong terms" against removal.[60] Chief Buffalo of La Pointe, nearly ninety years old in summer 1852, led a delegation that traveled by canoe and train to Washington to petition directly against their removal. Through the fortuitous intervention of Whig Congressman George Briggs of New York, the delegates were able to meet with President Millard Fillmore, Taylor's successor. At the conclusion of the meeting, Fillmore agreed to rescind the removal order, to end all removal efforts, and to pay back current and future annuities at La Pointe.[61] The delegation returned home with "a written instrument" that explained the president's promise. However, Fillmore did not follow through on his promises; Taylor's removal order and Fillmore's alleged revocation would prove to be a contentious point many years later in the wake of the *Voigt* decision and a major component of the legal case raised by the State of Wisconsin.[62]

On February 27, 1854, the Wisconsin legislature petitioned the president and Congress, noting that the Ojibwe were "a peaceable, quiet, and inoffensive people, rapidly improving in the arts and sciences," who had intermarried with local whites and were "becoming generally anxious to become educated and adopt the habits of the 'white man.'"[63] Although state legislators noted the ongoing importance of hunting, fishing, and gathering, they asked the president to "rescind the orders heretofore given for the removal of said Indians," to pay annuities at La Pointe, and to "encourage permanent settlement of those Indians as shall adopt the habits of the citizens of the United States."[64]

By the fall of 1854, federal officials abandoned the idea of removal altogether. The commissioner of Indian affairs noted in his annual report that several Ojibwe bands "still occupy their former locations on lands ceded by treaties of 1837 and 1842" because "it has not been found necessary or practicable to remove them."[65] He noted that the government might allow them to remain in the ceded territory on small reservations in order to secure additional mineral-rich lands and to facilitate the Ojibwe people's "improvement."[66]

In September 1854, Ojibwe leaders succeeded in securing reservations in Wisconsin at Bad River, Red Cliff, Lac Courte Oreilles, and Lac du Flambeau through treaty negotiations at La Pointe.[67] At the treaty council, Commissioner Henry Gilbert noted that "it was idle for us to talk about a treaty" until the "points most strenuously insisted upon," including the "privilege of remaining in the country where they reside" and the "appropriation of land for their future homes," were settled.[68]

Because they had previously secured the right to hunt, fish, and gather in territory ceded to the United States, the bands in Wisconsin chose permanent reservation lands in the area, often near existing village sites where there were wild rice beds and maple groves.[69] In exchange, the bands ceded new territory, this time located in Minnesota. Once again, the treaty included a provision wherein the signatory bands reserved the right to hunt, fish, and gather within the ceded territory.[70]

Even after securing reservations, it was common for Ojibwe people in Wisconsin to continue to live elsewhere in the ceded territory for most of the year. Federal officials indicated that many were living on the reservations only in the winter as late as 1869, and a majority were not "permanent reservation residents" until 1892.[71] The Treaty of 1854, in effect, meant that the reserved rights to hunt, fish, and gather remained the basis for the Ojibwe way of life for decades before the Ojibwe came to live permanently on the reservations it established.

These ambiguities raised fundamental questions. What rights did the Ojibwe retain on ceded lands as compared to the new reservation lands? What were the broader implications for usufructuary rights without a provision specifically re-affirming their continued existence? These would be critical issues in the *Voigt* litigation. A comparison of the treaty council documents shows that the Ojibwe people "knew that they were ceding away full title to their land" in 1854, but because the concept of land ownership was "utterly foreign to their belief system," they held no such understanding in 1837 and 1842.[72]

Through the treaties of 1837, 1842, and 1854, the Ojibwe ceded 98 percent of their lands in Wisconsin, Minnesota, and the Upper Peninsula of Michigan.[73] Historian David Wrone observes that "in terms of business transactions the treaties constituted an unbelievable bargain for the United States." In that ceded territory, the United States received 100 billion board feet of timber, 150 billion tons of iron ore, 13.5 billion pounds of copper, 19 million acres of land, plus ports, power sites, and quarries, in addition to the billions of fish, fowl, game, and 11,200 lakes. For all of this, the Ojibwe received "only a few thousand dollars, some odds and ends of equipment, and a few thousand acres of reservation lands."[74] The economic benefits to the new Wisconsin Territory were clear.

STATE INTERFERENCE WITH THE EXERCISE OF RESERVED RIGHTS

The important role the Ojibwe people played in the local economy had been crucial to their efforts to garner support for staying in Wisconsin. By the late nineteenth century, however, the state's economy began to change. Most of the standing timber had been clear-cut, and tourism, especially in northern Wisconsin, was on the rise. Ojibwe and other Native fishers and hunters in Wisconsin began to face competition from non-Indian "pleasure seekers," tourists who traveled the railroads to Ashland, Bayfield, and elsewhere to hunt and fish for sport.[75]

The tourism economy prompted state regulations that restricted the Ojibwe's access to lands and waters.[76] Near the turn of the twentieth century, the state began vigorous enforcement of the conservation code, particularly "as rural Wisconsin began to fill up with non-Indians who were not happy with the competition from Indian rifles, weirs, nets, and spears."[77] The state had come to view northern Wisconsin's natural resources "as a springboard for a tourist industry and as a form of income for itself," and "grew less and less tolerant of Indians hunting, fishing, and gathering off the reservation."[78] The Great Father's "white children" were now aggressively asserting their own claim to the land.

Nearly a century later, as part of the *Voigt* case, federal courts would weigh these competing claims, considering the degree to which treaty-based, reserved rights could coexist with the state's authority over the lands within its borders.[79] "Far from acknowledging treaty-reserved rights within the ceded territory, the Supreme Court of Wisconsin, from 1879 until 1931, took the position that State law applied even within Indian reservations," wrote Brian Pierson, one of the attorneys representing the Lake Superior Bands of Chippewa in the *Voigt* litigation.[80] Among the

Ojibwe, "firsthand recollection of treaty rights lasted into the twentieth century," and as a result, a "culturally distinct form of illegal hunting called 'violating' emerged at Lac du Flambeau and elsewhere."[81] Traditional hunting and fishing, exercised based on "unbroken . . . memories of off-reservation rights," persisted "clandestinely" and were "revalued as resistant symbols of ethnicity by virtue of their being contested, if not criminalized, by the dominant society even as engagement with that society deepened."[82]

Wisconsin courts would continue to crack down on the exercise of treaty rights throughout most of the twentieth century. Despite repeated denials of their rights, Ojibwe hunters, fishers, and gatherers engaged in "practical struggle" as they continued to pursue resources off the reservation "with increased furtiveness," and many suffered the legal consequences.[83]

The state's efforts to regulate all hunting and fishing within its borders escalated in the closing decades of the nineteenth century. In 1879, the Wisconsin Supreme Court, "apparently without reference to treaties," determined that Indian reservations were subject to state conservation laws.[84] By the early 1880s, the state was implementing closed seasons on game fish and imposing bag and size limits on specific species, limiting the length of the hunting season, and prohibiting hunting at night. Wisconsin hired its first game wardens in 1891 and began to require hunting and fishing licenses; by 1893, no hunting at all could take place without a license. These efforts imposed state authority both on and off Indian reservations. As part of an "overall effort to redefine the northern third of the state as a recreational playground," the state sought to declare that "Indians did not have treaty rights on navigable water on their reservations."[85] In effect, state officials had declared that recognition of treaty rights was incompatible with northern Wisconsin's emerging political economy.

At the turn of the century, those Ojibwe who continued to exercise treaty rights began to face criminal prosecution. In 1897, for example, two elderly Ojibwe men from Lac du Flambeau were arrested for hunting deer off-reservation. The official at the reservation, writing to the Indian agent at Ashland, explained that although he believed "in enforcing the game law on white men as well as Indians," he found the arrest to be "out of proportion to the offence [sic]" because "these old men who were told when the treatys [sic] were made with them that the game belonged to them and they should have the privilege of hunting any where they pleased."[86] No such leniency was forthcoming.

In 1901, Bad River Ojibwe tribal member John Blackbird was convicted of fishing with a net on the reservation and sentenced to thirty days of imprisonment and hard labor, though his conviction would later be overturned on appeal as "not justifiable in law."[87] In ordering Blackbird's release, the judge argued that "after taking from them the great body of their lands" and "allowing them to reserve certain portions for reservations, and stipulating that they should always have the right to hunt and fish upon all lands so ceded," it was "adding injustice to deprive them of the poor privilege of fishing with a seine."[88] Despite Blackbird's release, the State of Wisconsin routinely ignored the case as precedent and continued to treat the exercise of treaty rights as a criminal act.

Perhaps the most dramatic example of conflict between state officials and the Ojibwe people was the murder of Joe White in 1894, a few years before Blackbird's arrest. White, whose Ojibwe name was Giishkitawag, was a prominent leader of an Ojibwe community near Rice Lake, Wisconsin, within ceded territory about fifty miles southwest of the Lac Courte Oreilles reservation, which had been established by treaty in 1854. White's community had resisted removal to Lac Courte Oreilles and instead relied on hunting, fishing, and gathering, supplemented by wage labor in nearby logging camps. On December 13, 1894, two wardens encountered White at the logging camp where he was working and attempted to arrest him for hunting deer off-reservation and out of season. During the course of the arrest, the wardens beat and fatally shot him. Although the wardens were tried for murder, area newspapers celebrated their acquittal the following spring.[89]

Wisconsin again attempted to assert jurisdiction over Ojibwe usufructuary rights in 1907. Michael Morrin was an Ojibwe and a US citizen with full rights to his land allotment. He was arrested and convicted of using a gill net on Lake Superior, a location off the reservation but within the ceded territory.[90] In what Wisconsin Attorney General Don Hanaway would describe in 1989 as "an incident foreshadowing today's legal battle," Morrin argued that "he was immune from state conservation laws because the Ojibwe reserved hunting, fishing, and gathering rights in the land cession treaties of 1842 and 1854."[91] On appeal, the Wisconsin

Supreme Court upheld Morrin's conviction, holding that "the stipulations in the treaty with the Chippewa Indians respecting their right to hunt and fish within the borders of this state were abrogated by the act of Congress admitting the state into the Union and making no reservation as to such rights."[92] Furthermore, the court ruled that exempting Indians from state fish and game laws "would deprive the state of its sovereign power to regulate the rights of hunting and fishing," thereby denying it equal standing with other states in the Union. Legal scholars would later note that the court made a critical error in refusing to cite relevant precedents.[93] *Morrin* would stand until 1983, when it was reversed by the federal Court of Appeals in *Voigt*.[94] As the Seventh Circuit held in *Voigt*, the state, in the *Morrin* decision, had "in effect . . . seized private property," and "harassed" those people who attempted to exercise their reserved treaty rights.[95]

In 1927, the Wisconsin Supreme Court went even further, ruling in *Lemieux v. Agate Land Co.* that the 1850 removal order had terminated the Ojibwe people's "right of occupancy" in Wisconsin, contravening earlier US Supreme Court rulings that no such action had occurred.[96] In the wake of this decision, state officials escalated their enforcement actions against Ojibwe hunting and fishing within the ceded territory, fining or jailing those arrested, impounding cars, and confiscating equipment.[97] Such actions increased during the Great Depression when the state began to advertise tourist destinations in northern Wisconsin, leading to further deterioration in the Ojibwe's already precarious standard of living.[98]

Despite these repeated losses in the courts, Ojibwe leaders continued to press their case. In 1933, Thomas L. St. Germaine, a Lac du Flambeau Ojibwe tribal member and an attorney, used reserved treaty rights as an affirmative defense in *State v. Johnson*.[99] St. Germaine argued before the Wisconsin Supreme Court that the state could not prosecute Ojibwe tribal members for hunting or fishing off-reservation within the ceded territory because of the terms of the treaties of 1837, 1842, and 1854.[100] In 1933, and again in 1940, the court held that although the Ojibwe retained their right to hunt and fish on the reservation without state interference, state jurisdiction otherwise prevailed, including on lands owned by Indians who, as American citizens, had private ownership of their land within the reservation boundaries.[101] St. Germaine's efforts represented an attempt to rebut the "take-for-granted belief in state-centrism—the assumption that state sovereignty was homologous with its territory and that state government, alone, controlled natural resources within this territory."[102]

In 1947, as Bad River Tribal Council Chairman Gus Whitebird argued in a letter to Great Lakes Agency Superintendent J. C. Cavill, "When the Indians ceded these lands to the United States they reserved the right to hunt and fish and safeguard the interests of the future generations. They had implicit faith that the promises held out to them by the representative of the government would be carried out, but it seems that the United States has failed in its duty."[103] Community memory of reserved rights remained strong, as did the Ojibwe people's will to continue to exercise them even in the face of increasing legal pressure from the state.[104]

After World War II, automobile-based tourism increasingly became a major part of the Wisconsin economy. Over the next several decades, as many local economies became dependent on visitors traveling north, conflict with the Ojibwe became more frequent.[105] In the early 1950s, the state "accelerated its crackdown on Indian hunting and fishing" after the enactment of Public Law 83-280, which transformed the federal relationship with tribes by granting Wisconsin and six other states jurisdiction over tribal lands within state boundaries.[106] The state attorney general declared that PL 280 "extinguished any federal immunity on the part of the Chippewas."[107] With that declaration, the State of Wisconsin essentially terminated the rights the Ojibwe had reserved in the treaties of 1837 and 1842.

State interference with Ojibwe treaty rights imposed a heavy economic, psychological, and spiritual burden. Non-Indian residents "seemed oblivious of the fact that state restrictions of Indian hunting, fishing, and gathering had deprived several generations of Chippewas of major sources of food and income."[108] Enforcement of state conservation laws, including jail time, confiscation of guns and cars, along with fines that ran eight hundred dollars in the 1960s, "often devastate a family's ability to sustain itself."[109] Billy Big Thunder, an alias given to an Ojibwe man interviewed by researchers from Michigan State University, remembered, "It was a shameful and humiliating thing [to have your dad thrown in jail for hunting]."[110] Big Thunder continued, "While Dad was in jail, Mom and the kids would have to go down to Bayfield to welfare and kiss ass to get a few bucks. Mom had to beg to get the money to feed seven or eight kids."[111]

By the late 1950s, state actions so enraged the Bad River Band that they declared a "state of cold war" with Wisconsin's Department of Conservation and stated, "State conservation officials shall be denied access to all tribal and restricted lands within the boundaries of this reservation."[112] Hunting and fishing were essential to survival, and in both real and symbolic ways, the Ojibwe people struck back at state actions that threatened their people.

—ıı—

As the legal scholar Charles Wilkinson wrote in 1991:

> For American Indians, their survival as a people—mark down those words, survival as a people—ultimately depends on 19th century treaties recognizing a range of special prerogatives, including hunting, fishing, and water rights; a special trust relationship with the United States; and ultimately, the principle of tribal sovereignty, the right of tribal members to be governed on many key issues by their own tribal governments, not by the states.[113]

This was the central issue in the Ojibwe people's struggle to reassert their reserved rights under the treaties signed in 1836, 1837, 1842, and 1854. Principles of justice require that the American people, both the general public and those in government, recognize and understand these concepts, yet most have had few opportunities to learn about them in any meaningful way. It is this issue of opportunity to learn that led American Indian educators and their allies to pursue changes in curriculum policy through the passage of Act 31.

CHAPTER 2

CULTURAL RESURGENCE AND THE FIGHT FOR TREATY RIGHTS

I n the early 1970s, Fred and Mike Tribble, brothers from the Lac Courte Oreilles reservation in northwestern Wisconsin, were students at the College of St. Scholastica, in Duluth, Minnesota. The Tribble brothers had grown up hearing family and community members tell stories of getting arrested for exercising their treaty rights to hunt and fish. Their instructor, Minneapolis attorney Larry Leventhal, confirmed a key part of those stories: the Ojibwe people had retained the right to hunt, fish, and gather off the reservation within the territory ceded to the United States through treaties signed in 1837 and 1842. Fred Tribble, in the documentary film, *Lighting the Seventh Fire*, said, "When I was young, I'd hear about our elders that would go off the reservation to hunt and fish, and then they would get arrested, and their fish and their equipment would get confiscated and then they'd be taken to jail."[1]

In 1974, Larry Leventhal, a lawyer who had frequently defended members of the American Indian Movement (AIM), encouraged them to challenge the state's refusal to honor treaty rights. He was looking for a test case. Later that year, the Tribble brothers got arrested and were convicted.[2] The story of their arrest, conviction, and appeal imparts important lessons about politics, race relations, and natural resources—and education reform.

A key portion of Act 31 stems from the educational experiences of the Tribble brothers.[3] Their actions, based at least in part on what they had learned in a college classroom, ultimately led to a decision by the federal courts affirming the Lake Superior Chippewa's rights to hunt, fish, and gather within the territory ceded through nineteenth-century treaties. (The Lac Courte Oreilles would join the case in 1978, and by 1983, the other five Ojibwe bands in Wisconsin would also join.) In deciding the case, which spanned seventeen years, judges drew on historical accounts, ethnographic evidence, and a body of federal statute and case law defining the relationship between the federal government and tribal nations. The Tribble brothers' actions led to the legal recognition of treaty rights and inspired their opponents to an often-violent backlash. Their case—*Lac Courte Oreilles Band of Lake Superior Chippewa Indians, et al., v. Lester P. Voigt, et al.*, popularly known as the *Voigt* decision—and the general public's reaction, highlight gaps in public understanding of tribal history, culture, and sovereignty and show how educational policy was implicated in both the problem and the solution.[4]

On March 8, 1974, the Tribble brothers challenged decades of enforcement of state laws that prohibited their people from spearing fish on Chief Lake, located off the reservation in Sawyer County. The brothers alerted the Sawyer County sheriff of their intentions in advance. When Department of Natural Resources (DNR) wardens Milton Dieckman and Larry Miller arrived, Fred Tribble produced a copy of the treaty of 1837.[5] Fred recalled, in *Lighting the Seventh Fire*, "The wardens came on us right away, and I had a treaty in my pocket, and when they said I was doing it illegally, I took the treaty out of my back pocket and I said, 'No, I'm doing this under treaty rights.'"[6] In most tellings of the story, the arresting warden responded with "that doesn't matter," and in others, he adds, "I don't know anything about that."[7] The brothers were arrested, charged, and found guilty of possessing a spear for fishing on inland waters and of failure to have a proper tag for their fish shanty; their fine was stayed, pending appeal.[8]

In response to their conviction, their tribal government, the Lac Courte Oreilles Band of Lake Superior Chippewa, filed suit against Lester P. Voigt, secretary of the Wisconsin DNR, as well as the wardens who arrested them, the county sheriff, and the district attorney.[9] Wisconsin Attorney General Donald J. Hanaway later called the Tribbles' arrest "the most important fishing citations ever issued in Wisconsin."[10] Their arrest touched off a series of court cases that began in 1978 with the Lac Courte Oreilles Band's assertion of reserved rights and culminated in 1983 with *Lac Courte Oreilles*

Band of Lake Superior Chippewa Indians, et al., v. Lester P. Voigt, et al., which affirmed their contemporary validity. The *Voigt* decision was the first decision in a multiyear case that was finally settled in 1991 after subsequent trials defined the scope of those rights.[11]

The Tribble Brothers, Cultural Resurgence, and the Reassertion of Treaty Rights

Ojibwe people from across Wisconsin referred to off-reservation hunting and fishing as "violating," an ironic term that reflects the state's refusal to recognize their reserved rights.

The hunting and fishing practices were both routine and essential for feeding families. The Tribble brothers sought to challenge the legal basis for defining these acts as illegal. Their actions reflected a broader trend in Indian Country, an assertion that "in defiance of all odds, the old cultures still had vitality" and that "at some undefinable point in the 1960s the moccasin grapevine built up a consensus that the terrible descent since the treaties and allotment must be halted and reversed."[12] Ojibwe communities, like other Native communities across the United States, were reasserting their unique cultural and legal status, and they began to openly and actively practice cultural ways that had quietly continued, often at significant personal risk.

Indeed, the actions of the Tribble brothers were part of a greater social, cultural, and political revitalization sweeping Indian Country—that is, reservation land and urban areas Native people call home—during the 1960s and 1970s. Pan-Indian movements were organizing nationwide, represented by groups such as the American Indian Chicago Conference, National Indian Youth Council, United Indians of All Tribes, and AIM. Similar smaller movements were happening on reservations across the country, as well.

In Wisconsin in the early 1960s, the Ho-Chunk people were reorganizing politically as the Wisconsin Winnebago Tribe. In 1971, the Lac Courte Oreilles Ojibwe people, with support from AIM, seized Winter Dam in Winter, Wisconsin, drawing attention to the destruction of their lands at the hands of Northern States Power and the Army Corps of Engineers. In 1972, the Red Cliff and Bad River Ojibwe people used the federal courts to secure their treaty rights to fish on Lake Superior. By 1974, the Menominee people, organized as Determination of Rights and Unity for Menominee Shareholders, or DRUMS, had successfully overturned the federal termination policy and were pursuing restoration of their treaty rights to hunt and fish.[13] All of these movements formed the historical backdrop for the Tribbles' actions.

The non-Native public had, at best, a partial understanding of these developments. They occasionally became aware of the more spectacular efforts, such as the Indian takeovers of Alcatraz; the Bureau of Indian Affairs building in Washington, DC; the Alexian Brothers Novitiate in Gresham, Wisconsin; and the Milwaukee Coast Guard Station.[14] Other efforts were typically less visible to outsiders, including those to revive tribal languages and traditional spiritual practices and those to found schools, including Red School House and Heart of the Earth Survival School in the Twin Cities, Indian Community School in Milwaukee, Lac Courte Oreilles Ojibwe School near Hayward, the Oneida Nation School System, and the Menominee Indian School District.[15] As a result, changing realities in Indian Country went mostly unnoticed by the non-Native public and likely had minimal impact on public knowledge about Native peoples.

In the late 1960s, the development of legal services programs for Indians proved to be a crucial step that enabled the Ojibwe and other nations across the United States to "litigate their hunting and fishing rights and other pressing issues."[16] Wisconsin Judicare, the Indian Law Center, and private attorneys who had been affiliated with those or other legal services programs began to assist tribes in reasserting their rights.[17] Native people finally had the resources necessary to defend their legal rights.

The tide began to turn in the 1970s. In 1971, the Red Cliff and Bad River bands, with the assistance of Wisconsin Judicare, sought to assert their fishing rights on Lake Superior. In *State v. Gurnoe*, the Bad River and Red Cliff bands brought a test case to determine whether they held fishing rights on Lake Superior based on the establishment of their reservations along its shores under the Treaty of 1854. In its decision, the Wisconsin Supreme Court recognized these tribes' rights to fish on Lake Superior. The majority held that the state had a right to "reasonable and necessary"

regulations to protect the fish population and stated that the means of
harvest must "reasonably conform to the aboriginal methods" used circa
1854 or "such modern types and methods as are reasonably consistent with
those used at the time of the treaty." (This requirement was later invali-
dated in *Peterson v. Christensen*.[18]) Concurring justice E. Harold Hallows
disagreed with the majority on both points, arguing that the state "who
did not grant you those rights in the first place" cannot regulate them nor
proscribe particular methods of harvest without unlawfully reducing the
tribe's fishing rights to the level of the privileges enjoyed by other citizens.[19] The reasoning in these decisions would prove critical to *Voigt* as
the court reexamined these issues relative to inland waters.

The Tribble brothers' challenge to state fishing regulations came just
three years after *Gurnoe*, and coincided with a major treaty rights victory
in the *Boldt* decision, which upheld the reserved fishing rights of fourteen tribes in Washington state.[20] In 1978, four years after their initial
convictions, and seven years after the victory in *Gurnoe*, the Tribbles' case
came before Judge James Doyle in the US District Court for the Western
District of Wisconsin, consolidated as part of *U.S. v. Bouchard*. Wisconsin
Judicare, attorneys for the plaintiffs, the Lac Courte Oreilles Band, were
"suing on behalf of itself and its members; a member of the band who is
being prosecuted for exercising his alleged treaty rights; [and] a member
of the band who is being threatened with prosecution for exercising his
alleged treaty rights" reserved under the treaties of 1837 and 1842, and
sought a declaratory judgment upholding usufructuary rights (i.e., the
right to use land you do not otherwise legally own) within the ceded territory. The defendants, the secretary of the Wisconsin DNR, along with state
and county officials "charged with the duty of enforcing and prosecuting
state fish and game laws," countered that those rights were affirmatively
extinguished by the 1850 Removal Order or by implication through the
Treaty of 1854.[21] Both sides sought summary judgment.

In reaching his decision in *U.S. v. Bouchard*, Doyle scrutinized the
historical record, paying particular attention to the 1850 Removal Order
and the Treaty of 1854. Doyle held that the 1850 Removal Order was "not
authorized by the treaties of 1837 and 1842" and thus it was "without
legal effect," because there was no evidence of "misbehavior" that would
have triggered removal, according to the Ojibwe understanding that was

reflected in the minutes of the treaty council.[22] In examining the Treaty of 1854, Doyle ruled that

> when the boundaries of the Lac Courte Oreilles reservation were finally determined pursuant to the 1854 treaty, the general right of the Lac Courte Oreilles Band and its individual members to hunt, fish, and gather wild rice and maple sap in the area ceded by the treaties of 1837 and 1842, free of regulation by state government, was extinguished, except as to reservation lands, and except as to special hunting and fishing rights on limited parts of the ceded territory adjacent to treaty reservations which might properly be inferred from the language of the 1854 treaty setting apart the reservations "for the use of" the Chippewa.[23]

Doyle found that both parties understood the treaty as "extinguishing Chippewa rights to occupy lands outside the reservation."[24]

Essentially, Doyle ruled that the 1854 treaty implicitly terminated the usufructuary rights because "had the parties intended the 1854 treaty to continue to preserve those rights . . . it is reasonable to believe that they would have made it explicit in 1854."[25] Therefore, "the Chippewa surrendered their rights of permissive occupation in the territory ceded in 1837 and 1842, except to the extent that portions of the territory so ceded were to become parts of the reservations provided for in the treaty of 1854."[26] Similarly, reasoning from *Gurnoe*, Doyle concluded that only "particularized" rights could be claimed; therefore, the plaintiff's claim to an unabrogated "general right" within territory ceded in 1837 and 1842 was without merit.[27]

Both parties filed an appeal with the US Court of Appeals for the Seventh Circuit.[28]

THE *VOIGT* DECISION

On September 14, 1982, a three-judge panel, representing the Seventh Circuit Court of Appeals, heard oral arguments and weighed ethnographic and historical evidence to examine three key issues. The court considered the nature of the usufructuary rights under the treaties of 1837 and 1842 as well as "two arguable abrogations" (that is, unilateral federal withdrawals) of the relevant sections that reserved the right to hunt, fish, and gather within the ceded territory; the Removal Order of 1850; and the Treaty of 1854.[29] The court's analysis distinguished between Aboriginal title, understood as "the right of native people in the new world to occupy and use their native area," which could be extinguished by implication, and a treaty-recognized "right permanently to occupy land," which cannot be extinguished without compensation.[30] The appeals court held that the reserved rights in question were treaty-recognized rights, that they were independent of any right to permanent occupancy, and that any action or intent to extinguish them must be explicit.[31]

The appeals court reviewed the clauses guaranteeing the rights "during the pleasure of the President of the United States," and found this language to be understood to mean that "the rights would endure until the tribe 'misbehaved,' at which point the president could revoke them."[32] The justices examined the historical record, including the annual reports of the agent at La Pointe, and found no evidence of "misbehavior" between the signing of the treaties and the issuance of the Executive Order. The court noted that as late as 1854, the Wisconsin Legislature had remained actively involved in pressing for the Ojibwe, "a peaceful, quiet, and inoffensive people," to stay in Wisconsin.[33] The court thus ruled that Taylor's 1850 removal order "exceeded the scope of presidential authority under the 1837 and 1842 treaties and was therefore invalid" because it did not reference any alleged depredations.[34]

The Seventh Circuit also analyzed the implications of the 1854 treaty using the canons of construction of Indian law (that is, the legal doctrine that reflects precedent in federal Indian law cases). It held that the Lake Superior Ojibwe's usufructuary rights had not been abrogated because the treaty "made no reference to hunting, fishing, and gathering rights on ceded lands."[35] The treaty was silent on the issue, the court found, because the Ojibwe were confident that they had reserved the rights in earlier treaties, continued to rely on them for subsistence, believed the events leading up to the rescinding of the 1850 removal order "vindicated their presence in Wisconsin," and saw "no need to set out additional protections for off-reservation rights" which were understood to be "secure and unaffected by the 1854 treaty."[36]

In its decision, the Seventh Circuit held that because neither the 1850 Removal Order nor the Treaty of 1854 specifically revoked usufructuary rights, the rights remained in force.[37] As a result, the court reversed Doyle and on January 25, 1983, affirmed "the sanctity of the treaties and the right of the Indians to hunt, fish, and gather on and off their reservations on public lands in ceded territory."[38] In remanding the case back to Judge Doyle, the US Court of Appeals instructed him to "enter judgment for the LCO [Lac Courte Oreilles] band . . . and for further consideration as to the permissible scope of State regulation over the LCO's exercise of their usufructuary rights."[39] The decision became known as the *Voigt* decision after named defendant Lester P. Voigt, secretary of the DNR (some also call this decision *LCO I*, after Lac Courte Oreilles and because it was the first decision in a multiyear case). The decision "effectively reversed the district court's decision in *Bouchard*" and upheld the "traditional Indian right to use traditional methods to harvest fish" when "no one had been permitted to spear game fish in Wisconsin for over a century before that decision."[40] Voigt's dubious honor of serving as the named defendant would carry over to the ensuing phases of the case, ongoing litigation that would yield a series of published and unpublished orders and opinions until its conclusion in 1991.[41]

The *Voigt* decision was immediately controversial. Within days, the Wisconsin Department of Justice filed an appeal, claiming that usufructuary rights could not be exercised on any lands that were or had been privately owned.[42] Attorney General Bronson La Follette secured a stay of the decision, pending an appeal to the Seventh Circuit for rehearing as well as an appeal to the US Supreme Court. The stay was to take effect on February 19, 1983, and continue until the tribes and state could negotiate an off-reservation deer season.[43] The state, in its attempt to secure a hearing before the full Seventh Circuit Court of Appeals, raised a new question of whether usufructuary rights could be exercised on private lands. On March 8, 1983, the Seventh Circuit denied the state's request for a rehearing, determining that Lac Courte Oreilles was not claiming rights to private lands and that such a request would not be consistent with the historical record. The court then amended the initial opinion to indicate that "the exercise of these rights is limited to those portions of the ceded lands that are not privately owned."[44] The case was again remanded to district court.

Judge Doyle chose not to mediate the issues that were emerging from the decision, thereby forcing the state to negotiate with the tribes. As anthropologist Larry Nesper explains, "For the first time, the state of Wisconsin had to confront realistically the implications of tribal sovereignty and accept that it did not fully control what went on within its borders."[45] Throughout the litigation, the state repeatedly sought to limit the Ojibwe's exercise of reserved rights in court. The state also sought to limit the exercise of treaty rights in negotiations for interim agreements governing the exercise of usufructuary rights.

The political context for these negotiations changed further when, in October 1983, the US Supreme Court determined it would not review the circuit court's judgment. This refusal to hear the state's appeal on *Voigt* thereby upheld the ruling of the Seventh Circuit. Soon after, the other five bands who were signatories to the 1837 and 1842 treaties—Red Cliff, Bad River, St. Croix, Lac du Flambeau, and Sakaogon/Mole Lake—joined Lac Courte Oreilles as plaintiffs in the subsequent lawsuits.[46]

The case was then remanded to Judge Doyle. The plaintiffs, now six bands strong, sought clarification of their rights and submitted four issues to the court on January 13, 1984. They sought to delineate the activities they could engage in under the treaties, to determine the permissible uses of natural resources, to declare the boundaries within which their rights could be exercised, to allocate the resource base between Ojibwe tribal members and the general public, and to determine the degree to which the state could regulate the Ojibwe tribal members' exercise of treaty rights. On November 13, 1984, the court responded that it would address these issues in a trial to begin the following year.[47]

On March 6, 1984, Judge Doyle entered partial judgment for the plaintiffs, as directed by the Seventh Circuit Court of Appeals in their order to remand in *Voigt*. Doyle ruled that the Lake Superior Band of Chippewa Indians had reserved usufructuary rights under the treaties of 1837 and 1842; that those rights were not extinguished by the 1850 Removal Order nor the Treaty of 1854; that they could be exercised on lands "not privately owned as of March 8, 1983"; and that the court retained the jurisdiction necessary to define those rights and to determine the extent to which state regulation was permissible.[48] Lac Courte Oreilles and its co-plaintiffs supported the opinion. The state filed an appeal to the Seventh Circuit, arguing that treaty rights were invalid on lands that had been privately owned.[49]

In what would become known as *LCO II*, a three-judge panel for the Seventh Circuit Court of Appeals stated that "the whole thrust of *LCO I* was that the usufructuary rights survived after the Treaty of 1854 and that those rights must be interpreted as the Indians understood them in 1837 and 1842."[50] The court held that a reading of its previous ruling that held to the March 8, 1983, date was in error because it would suggest that "passing to private ownership is a laundering process" that could be used to extinguish usufructuary rights in perpetuity.[51] To clarify its position, the Seventh Circuit wrote, "Wisconsin's obligation to honor the usufructuary rights of the Indians is no more or less than was the federal government's obligation prior to Wisconsin's statehood."[52] The court recognized that the exercise of treaty rights was exempt from state licensing "and no doubt from other restrictions," but also noted "public policy which would benefit the Indians as well as all others might well enter into the picture."[53] The justices again remanded the case to the district court.

After *LCO II*, the court divided the issues to be addressed into three phases that would answer key questions relating to the "level of permissible tribal harvest and the extent of tribal and state regulatory powers."[54] Phase I, the declaratory phase, was to determine the nature and scope of treaty rights. Judge Doyle would consider what types of activities the Ojibwe were engaged in at the time of the treaties, what their current usufructuary rights were, and whether there was a basis for state regulation. Phase II, the regulatory phase, was to determine the allowable degree of state regulation. Phase III, the damages phase, was to ascertain the amount of damages, if any, that were to be awarded to the Ojibwe based on past state interference.[55]

As the legal case dragged on, the Ojibwe bands were organizing their own response, to ensure that the newly reaffirmed rights would be recognized as belonging to the tribes collectively rather than to individuals. Gordon Thayer, tribal chairman at Lac Courte Oreilles, invited leaders from the other five bands to a meeting at Mount Telemark in February 1983.[56] This began a series of meetings that led to the formation of the Voigt Intertribal Task Force, an organization developed to manage the resources and oversee the exercise of off-reservation harvests as collectively held rights. It later merged with the Great Lakes Indian Fisheries Commission to form the Great Lakes Indian Fish and Wildlife Commission (GLIFWC), an organization created to assist the thirteen Ojibwe bands in Minnesota, Wisconsin, and Michigan with matters related to conservation and management of natural resources, regulation and enforcement of off-reservation harvests, and "traditional pursuits of the Ojibwes."[57]

The Voigt Intertribal Task Force and its successor organizations began the process of negotiating interim agreements with the State of Wisconsin to govern the harvest of game fish, deer, small game, migratory birds, bear, and wild rice while the exact scope of these rights were still being determined in the courts. The first agreement, which addressed deer hunting, went into effect in 1983, and the two sides reached a second agreement, governing spearfishing, in 1985.[58] Between 1983 and 1991, the state and Ojibwe bands entered into more than thirty agreements that governed the harvest until the court made its final determinations.[59] These agreements defined the time, place, and manner for exercising off-reservation rights, set size and bag limits, and defined monitoring and enforcement practices.[60] Through these agreements, the Ojibwe people effectively "circumscribed their rights in order to accommodate state concerns."[61]

Judge Doyle, to whom the Seventh Circuit had once again remanded the case as part of its order in *LCO II*, ended Phase I of the *Voigt* litigation with his ruling in *LCO III*, issued on February 18, 1987. In a trial that began in December 1985, the court addressed several contentious issues. Judge Doyle held, consistent with the canons of construction of federal Indian law, that the treaties "must be construed as the Indians understood them" based on all circumstances and that all "ambiguities are to be resolved in the favor of the Indians."[62] In order to determine what the Ojibwe signatories understood, Doyle reviewed extensive testimony featuring historical and ethnographic evidence of treaty-era hunting, fishing, gathering, and trade practices of the Ojibwe; the historical context of the treaty negotiations; and related issues.

Doyle determined "the off-reservation usufructuary rights reserved by the Chippewa in the treaties of 1837 and 1842 continue to be effective today." The court found that the tribe understood that they would retain their right to hunt, fish, and gather within the ceded territory in the usual and customary manner unless they "misbehaved," which would have triggered removal. Previous phases had already determined that the Removal Order of 1850 was invalid and therefore did not extinguish rights that the state continued to argue were "temporary" and "conditional," yet the state continued to press this point.[63]

The evidence regarding treaty negotiations in both 1837 and 1842 indicated that the Ojibwe "enjoy[ed] greater rights to hunt, fish, and gather within the ceded territory than do non-Indians."[64] To conclude otherwise, Doyle held, would mean that the Ojibwe people would merely be able to hunt, fish, and gather as any other Wisconsin citizen. Such a conclusion would essentially nullify any reserved rights, which would be "an impotent outcome to negotiations and a convention, which seemed to promise more and give the word of the Nation for more," and thus would not have reflected the Ojibwe leaders' intentions nor their understanding of the treaty provisions.[65]

The court considered extensive testimony on the Ojibwe people's relationship with and use of the resources in their homeland and concluded that, by virtue of the treaty provisions, the Ojibwe "have the right to exploit virtually all the natural resources in the ceded territory, as they did at treaty time," which they may exploit at any time, subject to agreements with the State of Wisconsin or congressional action. Because treaty-era harvest methods depended on both items of Native manufacture and trade goods, the court considered this evidence of technological adaptation, which meant the "method of the exercise is not static." The opportunity to continue to adapt technological advances meant that the Ojibwe were "not confined to the hunting and fishing methods their ancestors relied upon at treaty time" and could therefore "take advantage of improvements in the hunting and fishing techniques they employed in 1842." This was a rejection of the arguments raised by the State of Wisconsin and treaty rights opponents that the means of harvest should essentially be frozen in time.[66] Similarly, based on testimony about historical trade relationships, Judge Doyle further held that because the Ojibwe people "were clearly engaged in commerce throughout the treaty era," they retained the right to "trade and sell to non-Indians, in the modern manner, from their current harvests."[67] This was yet another rejection of the state's assertion that such rights had been extinguished.

The court considered whether certain types of public lands were not "compatible with the exercise of treaty usufructuary rights" because of the nature of their use, whether the exercise of treaty rights on public lands that had previously been privately held has been "extinguished," and whether any privately owned lands might be subject to the exercise of treaty rights. The State of Wisconsin had repeatedly argued that these "temporary" and "conditional" rights were extinguished by the Removal Order, but now added the argument that settlement had extinguished the right to harvest off-reservation on lands that were privately held by non-Indians. The Ojibwe themselves did not assert such a right, but the parties were in dispute as to whether private title itself extinguished treaty rights. Doyle ruled that the central issue was whether a specific parcel was privately or publicly held at the time of the exercise of off-reservation treaty rights, not whether it had ever been privately held. If private owners opened their lands for hunting, fishing, and gathering by the general public, then the Ojibwe could exercise their rights on those lands.[68]

The tribes continued to seek an allocation of the resources "to the extent required to provide them with a livelihood of moderate living," and the State of Wisconsin continued to dispute the tribes' assertion that they were entitled "to any permanent share of the resource," as it continued to hold that such a right had been extinguished by the Treaty of 1854. The court found that the Ojibwe people had historically "harvested virtually everything on the landscape," and it affirmed the right to "harvest nearly all varieties of fish, animal, and plant life available in ceded territory necessary to maintain a 'modest living' free from state interference."[69] The concept of a "modest living" was critical to Doyle's reasoning in *LCO III*, as it related both to the Ojibwe people's right to sell or trade harvested plant and animal materials, as well as the right to exercise their rights on private lands. Doyle found that if public lands were to be found to be insufficient to meet the "modest living" standard, "appropriate arrangements" must be made for "access to private lands." He found that state regulations, which would be considered and further defined in future litigation, would be permissible so long as they were "reasonable and necessary to conserve a particular resource."[70]

Opponents of treaty rights immediately referred to *LCO III* as "Doomsday for Wisconsin," and Governor Tommy Thompson announced the state's plans to appeal the decision.[71] Despite the support of the federal courts, the social legitimacy of these rights would remain contested, and the Ojibwe people would continue to experience significant resistance to the lawful exercise of their rights.

THE REGULATORY PHASE

Following Judge Doyle's death in June 1987, Judge Barbara Crabb took over the case, and Phase II, which had been termed the Regulatory Phase, began in her courtroom. Judge Crabb considered the applicable legal standards for state regulation; whether the state could regulate for "any legitimate purpose," specifically including health and safety purposes, or solely in the interest of conservation; the applicable legal standards for other legitimate state concerns; the state's right to regulate and enforce the moderate living standard; and whether tribal self-regulation would rule out concurrent state regulation. In *LCO IV*, issued in August 1987, the court found broad agreement about the importance of conservation regulations, but clear disputes existed about their nature and scope, as well as the matter of who would enforce them. The tribe had claimed the right to self-regulation for conservation purposes and opposed other state regulations. The state had repeatedly cited tourism-related interests in opposing self-regulation and seeking broader regulation, but Judge Crabb dismissed this claim. The court ruled that while regulations adopted to protect tourism would reflect legitimate state interest, "the state may not qualify the federal right by subordinating it to some other state objective or policy." Ultimately, Judge Crabb held that the state had the right to regulate the exercise of off-reservation usufructuary rights provided such regulations were in the interest of "conservation, public health and safety," were "reasonable and necessary to conserve a particular species," were not discriminatory, and used the least restrictive available means.[72]

Judge Crabb deemed it unnecessary to determine a specific allocation of resources because the state was unable to demonstrate that a scarcity existed. Still, she held "the plaintiffs rights were paramount but not exclusive."[73] The State of Wisconsin sought to regulate the tribal harvest to ensure compliance with the "moderate standard of living" established by Doyle, but Judge Crabb held that "so long as a resource is abundant for treaty and non-treaty harvesters alike, there is no need to limit the tribes' use to the moderate living standard." Similarly, any wealth beyond that standard did not violate treaty terms, provided the resources remained abundant for all, because the modest living standard established by her predecessor was intended to set a minimum treaty harvest, not to restrict the Ojibwe harvest to an upper limit. Judge Crabb denied the state's asserted right to regulate the exercise of treaty rights to ensure adherence to a moderate living standard.[74]

In *LCO IV*, Judge Crabb held that the tribes "possess the authority to regulate their members in the exercise of treaty usufructuary rights off the reservation," as such rights remained an internal matter. Effective tribal self-regulation would preclude state regulation, but in its absence, the state could regulate the off-reservation harvest itself, provided those regulations met the criteria defined in the decision. Self-regulation required adequate enforcement personnel, official tribal identification for those exercising treaty rights, and exchange of scientific, management, and harvest information with the state.[75]

The State of Wisconsin also filed an immediate appeal to Doyle's decision in *LCO III*.[76] The US Court of Appeals for the Seventh Circuit viewed the state's appeal as politically motivated and dismissed the "frivolous" appeal on August 31, 1987. It also imposed sanctions related to the state's "inexcusable" errors in filing that they said showed "serious lack of understanding of the basic principles of federal appellate review."[77] Once again, federal courts had issued a stinging rebuke to the state.

The State of Wisconsin was undeterred by the court's rebuke and was emboldened by what it viewed as the court's declaration that treaty rights were nonexclusive rights to the resources and that it had a right to regulate the harvest under certain circumstances. The state sought to negotiate settlements with each of the bands to end the treaty harvest by leasing or relinquishing their rights.[78] Wisconsin Attorney General Don Hanaway had been advocating for a negotiated, out-of-court settlement, and he worked to secure such an agreement. He believed a settlement would quickly and cheaply resolve the issue rather than "prolong frustration and anger in the north." Hanaway sought to settle the controversy "once and for all" in order to provide "clarity," as well as to address "other state/tribal concerns like reservation gambling and law enforcement issues."

He argued that a settlement would "strengthen" relationships between the state and tribes. Given that the parties were already negotiating one-year interim agreements, which represented "willingness to reach agreements with the state to protect northern Wisconsin's resources," Hanaway believed the tribes would be willing to do so again on a broader scale, despite clear evidence to the contrary.[79]

After discussions with the six Ojibwe bands, Hanaway reported that "they view their ability to hunt, fish, and gather resources as vital to their well-being" and are "unwilling to permanently sign away the resource rights the federal courts have said they retained in the 19th century treaties." It was clear, Hanaway wrote in 1989, that "today's Chippewa do not want to make the kind of decisions for future generations that their grandfathers made for them." He acknowledged state efforts to negotiate a settlement with Mole Lake and noted that "members of the band overwhelmingly voted against the proposal."[80] The state would continue to press such negotiations nonetheless, and indeed it was in discussions with Lac du Flambeau when Mole Lake rejected the proposal.[81] Hanaway admitted, "I remain only marginally hopeful that out-of-court settlement with the tribe can be reached before the next spearfishing season begins."[82] As lease negotiations continued, the parties reached another interim agreement to govern the harvest for the 1988 spearing season. The provisions affecting the harvest itself were substantially similar to the previous year's regulations, but changes made to law enforcement activities would involve the use of canine units on shore, National Guard helicopters in the air over the lakes themselves, and additional police officers on standby at National Guard armories.[83]

Litigation continued even as the parties continued their lease negotiations. The purpose of the next phase, known to the parties as *LCO V*, was to define harvest rights and to elaborate further on the "modest living" standard. Judge Crabb had assigned the tribes the task of quantifying the modest living standard and the potential commercial value of the resources in the ceded territory.[84] The tribes offered only one expert witness, University of New Mexico economist Ronald Cummings, who defined a modest standard of living as a zero-savings level of income of approximately twenty thousand dollars per household. Cummings then calculated the commercial value of the harvestable resources within the ceded territory and concluded that it would not be possible for members of the Lake Superior Bands of Chippewa to attain a modest standard of living by exercising their treaty rights to the land.

Judge Crabb found Cummings's testimony to be "persuasive and credible" and held that the state, who offered no testimony of its own, failed to provide proof to support its challenges to his expert testimony. Within this context, the state again sought to define an allocation for the treaty harvest; while the court found the state's arguments compelling, it again held that there was no legal basis for such a court-imposed division. As a result, the court ruled on June 3, 1988, that it was not possible to earn a modest living from the available harvest within the ceded territory. Judge Crabb declared that questions related to the permanent division of resources of allocation would be addressed in future litigation "when and if a need for allocation of the resources is required."[85] The modest living standard prevailed over any consideration of allocation.

One of the primary concerns reflected in the interim agreements was focused on game fish in inland lakes, primarily muskellunge and walleye, which Judge Crabb described as "probably the most-highly prized in the entire ceded territory," and which both sides recognized as critical to northern Wisconsin's tourism-dependent economy. The tribes had voluntarily limited their harvest in previous years, but a March 3, 1989, decision from the District Court, *LCO VI*, created new regulations to govern spring spearing and netting practices.[86] During a fourteen-day trial featuring extensive expert testimony from fisheries and wildlife biologists, the court weighed tribal plans for self-regulation, state concerns about the adequacy of those plans, and state assertions that additional state-enforced regulations were both reasonable and necessary.

In her opinion, Judge Crabb praised both parties, declaring, "What the parties in this case have done to give practical effect to plaintiffs' judicially recognized treaty rights is a remarkable story." She specifically praised the Wisconsin Department of Natural Resources for working with GLIFWC and state and local law enforcement to cooperatively enforce the interim agreements with only minimal federal funding or assistance. Judge Crabb had similar praise for the cooperative stance adopted by the tribes, particularly given that "their members had been subjected to physical and verbal abuse" while exercising their treaty rights to the extent that "harassment has become a fact of life for them."

The court weighed the concerns raised by the state about the robustness of the tribes' proposed management plan and concluded that with modifications to address the state's concerns, adequate self-regulation was still appropriate.[87]

Ultimately, Judge Crabb accepted the detailed plan to manage the muskellunge and walleye populations proposed by GLIFWC after modifications to incorporate a "safe harvest" calculation provided by the Wisconsin Department of Natural Resources.[88] Addressing the state's ongoing contention that a defined allocation was necessary, Judge Crabb held that Ojibwe fishers "had the right to take the full safe harvest of walleye and muskellunge from any lake they selected for fishing."[89] Furthermore, the court enjoined state officials from interfering with the harvest, except as stipulated by the tribes, and determined that GLIFWC was capable of handling management and enforcement, unless the amended plan submitted by the tribes failed to meet the criteria specified in the order.[90]

The State of Wisconsin and the Lake Superior Band of Chippewa continued their negotiations of off-reservation harvest and management issues, often reaching agreements outside of the federal courts. The next phase of the case, known as *LCO VII*, addressed rights to hunt deer and small game within the ceded territory in the broader context of all disputed resources. The tribes agreed to accept the state's deer management program and incorporated several health- and safety-related provisions in state law into their own regulatory structure. Further, the tribes came to general agreement on fur bearers. In *LCO VII*, the courts considered "[w]hether there is a need for a judicially-determined allocation of the deer harvest," and if necessary, what the allocation should be; whether treaty rights could be exercised on private lands within the ceded territory with the owner's consent; whether the state could prohibit deer hunting in summer; whether the state could prohibit treaty-based deer hunting immediately prior to state hunting seasons; and whether the state could prohibit the practice of shining deer—that is, using bright lights while hunting at night to temporarily blind the deer, causing it to freeze.[91]

On May 9, 1990, Judge Crabb issued her decision in *LCO VII*, ruling that the resources were to be allocated evenly among Indians and non-Indians because there is "heavy competition for the most desirable species," despite the fact that current harvest levels were only a small fraction of the non-Indian harvest, and because harvest capacity would no longer be an adequate cap as tribes increased their capability.[92] In setting the allocation, Judge Crabb revisited Judge Doyle's finding in *LCO III* that the rights were nonexclusive because "the bargain between the parties included competition for the harvest."[93] As a result, she ruled that "[the tribes'] needs for a moderate standard of living dictate their right to a full share of the harvest, subject to a ceiling set at 50 percent to prevent the frustration of the non-Indian treaty right."[94] In order to attain that equal share, she held that harvest rights might be expanded to include private lands if both need and capacity exist, but that at present (in 1990), state regulations would apply on private lands.[95]

Judge Crabb ruled once again that the state had authority to regulate off-reservation hunting and fishing "on a narrowly-defined basis for resource conservation and public safety concerns," and she prohibited hunting in the evenings and during summer on that basis.[96] She recognized the safety concerns raised by the state, and Attorney General Hanaway lauded the decision as "equal rights for everyone." However, anti-treaty protest leader Dean Crist of Stop Treaty Abuse lamented that "the bad thing is you still have less than 1 percent of the population with 50 percent of the resource."[97] Although the State of Wisconsin counted this as a victory, treaty rights opponents disagreed vehemently with the decision.

THE DAMAGES PHASE

The third phase of the *Voigt* decision, as defined by the parties under Judge Doyle, was the damages phase. The Lake Superior Band of Chippewa sought to collect an estimated $300 million in damages from the State of Wisconsin for past abrogation of treaty rights.[98] On October 11, 1990, Judge Crabb issued her ruling in *LCO VIII*, granting partial summary judgment against the tribes. The court held that recent case law determined that the Eleventh Amendment provided states with sovereign immunity from suits by tribes. Judge Crabb observed, "After more than sixteen years of litigation during which this court and the Court of Appeals for the Seventh Circuit have determined that the State of Wisconsin has violated plaintiffs' treaty rights for over 130 years, plaintiffs are left with no means of recovering monetary damages from the state except in the unlikely event that the United States joins this suit on their behalf."[99] The decision was a significant victory for the State of Wisconsin, and it "brought loud cheers from the Thompson administration and anti-treaty spokespersons" while disappointing treaty rights supporters.[100] As expected, the federal government did not bring suit on behalf of the tribes.

One of the remaining issues to be addressed in the courts was whether there was a treaty-derived right to harvest and sell timber. Judge Crabb had previously enjoined the state and counties from challenging timber rights, which were a major source of revenue for many counties. Among the Ojibwe, timber rights also represented a means to address the 50 percent unemployment rates on Ojibwe reservations.[101] On February 21, 1991, after a four-week trial, Judge Crabb declared that timber harvest and sales were not among the "usual and customary activities" referenced in the treaties and that logging was not a modern adaptation of a traditional practice despite the fact that the Ojibwe "never understood that they were selling timber resources other than pine" and presumably could assert timber rights to other species.[102] Examining the historical record, Judge Crabb determined that treaty-era Ojibwe forestry practices left the trees alive while making use of the "sap, bark, branches, leaves, needles and roots."[103] The court held that cities and counties could regulate timber harvest by Ojibwe tribal members as with non-Indians, and that with regard to the gathering of these other "miscellaneous forest products," the rights to which were not in dispute, they could regulate as "reasonable and necessary" in the interest of conservation.

On March 19, 1991, Judge Crabb issued the final judgment in the case, summarizing all of the court's opinions in the *Voigt* litigation and advising all parties that they had two months to conduct a review and determine whether to file for appeal. Unless either side had further appeals or raised additional issues, Judge Crabb declared that all of the issues dating back to *Voigt* had been resolved.[104] On May 20, 1991, both parties indicated that they would not appeal the court's decisions.[105]

—‖—

As the litigation was reaching its conclusion, legal scholar Rennard Strickland observed, "There is no longer a serious legal question about these Indian rights. The legal status of Chippewa reserved rights is clearly established. . . . As the courts have recognized, the treaties did not create Chippewa hunting, fishing, and gathering rights. These rights have always belonged to the Chippewas, who reserved them in their treaties with the United States."[106] The usufructuary rights reserved by the Lake Superior Band of Chippewa in the treaties of 1837 and 1842 had become a matter of settled law.

Wisconsin citizens struggled to understand these complex issues throughout the legal proceedings and afterward. Indian scholar Patty Loew, Bad River Ojibwe, observes, "The battle over Chippewa treaty rights lasted seventeen years and cost the state more than ten million dollars. [The controversy] polarized the people of Wisconsin as no other issue had in recent history, and united the previously disparate Chippewa bands who came together to defend their treaty rights and sovereignty."[107]

Throughout the *Voigt* litigation, there was significant lack of public understanding and awareness of essential issues and concepts, including the nature of the unique relationship between federally recognized tribes and the federal government of the United States, as well as the State of Wisconsin's place and limits of authority in that relationship. These concepts were foundational to understanding treaty rights and the *Voigt* decision that upheld and defined them in the modern era. Although the legal process concluded in 1991, the social and moral legitimacy of treaty rights remained contested.

New developments continued to emerge as the legal process unfolded. Opponents of treaty rights had been engaging in activities intended to disrupt Ojibwe spearfishing, seeking to intimidate spearers through violence and threats of violence, and their efforts reached new levels of intensity in 1989, just as proponents of treaty rights were organizing countermeasures.[108] Public information campaigns and other efforts to inform, educate, and persuade Wisconsin citizens on issues related to treaty rights and tribal sovereignty represented a variety of competing perspectives.[109] The cacophony of voices on these issues and the attention protestors' activities were receiving in the local, state, and national media generated interest in a variety of political solutions, including legislative abrogation of treaty rights, many of which were counter to tribal interests.

Many educators and activists continued to advocate for a school-based solution to the fear, ignorance, and violence surrounding the exercise of treaty rights, arguing that schools must be involved in any policy solution because failures in curriculum policy had contributed to the situation. By August 1989, consensus among the various groups was sufficient to enact statutory provisions into the state biennial budget bill, 1989 Act 31, a bill that continues to provide the resulting instructional requirements with its name.

PART 2

THE BACKLASH AGAINST TREATY RIGHTS

CHAPTER 3

"SPEAR THIS!":
THE BACKLASH AGAINST TREATY RIGHTS

"What do you think it means? Maybe it means I don't like Indians. Maybe it means I do like Indians. Maybe it means I don't like them spearing fish," an anonymous protestor carrying a spear with a severed Indian head effigy said to CNN's Jonathan Tower in May 1989.[1] The story on cable news captured what had become a common scene in early spring in Wisconsin: angry mobs confronting Ojibwe tribal members exercising their court-affirmed rights to spear spawning walleye within the ceded territory. The camouflage- and blaze-orange-clad protestors formed gauntlets that spearers had to pass through on their way to designated boat landings on designated lakes, challenging and harassing Ojibwe people, their supporters, and occasionally law enforcement officers on hand to keep the peace. One Ojibwe spearer described the protests as a "war-like, siege-like occupation."[2] The protestors, like the man appearing to national audiences on cable news, were often coy about their aims and motives. Typically, they claimed they were simply for "equal rights" or "protecting the resource." Their loud whistles, chants, and signs, carrying epithets like "timber nigger" and slogans like "Save a Fish, Spear an Indian!" clearly suggested there was more to the story.[3]

Similar scenes had been taking place in northern Wisconsin since 1985, but it was not until April and May 1989 that they received national attention on television, on the radio, and in newspapers. In Wisconsin and across the region, these scenes had become a familiar, unsettling sight following the Seventh Circuit Court of Appeals' ruling in the *Voigt* decision in 1983.

The public uproar over *Voigt* was "like a train hitting a wall," according to George Meyer, head of the Wisconsin Department of Natural Resources Division of Enforcement.[4] The protests, led by organizations such as Equal Rights for Everyone (ERFE), Protect Americans' Rights and Resources (PARR), and Stop Treaty Abuse (STA), featured "some of the most violent and hateful racial confrontations this country has seen since the height of the civil rights movement."[5] Indeed, eyewitnesses frequently made comparisons to anti-black violence in Milwaukee in the 1960s.[6]

Anti-treaty protestors, fueled by ignorance and racism, became one of the proximate causes of the educational policy response that led to Act 31. Anti-treaty organizing coalesced in the 1970s in the wake of the *Gurnoe* decision, which affirmed treaty-based fishing rights on Lake Superior. Racial hostility and harassment lived on in the cities and towns in the ceded territory, including the school systems. The combination of ongoing patterns of hostility and discrimination, punctuated by acute episodes of racist violence, led policy makers to define the treaty rights controversy as a sociopolitical crisis to be addressed by public schools.

THE FIRST WAVE:
ANTI-TREATY RIGHTS ORGANIZING VS. *GURNOE*

Anti-treaty protests after the *Voigt* decision represented a second wave of anti-treaty rights organizing, and their pro-treaty counterparts included many veterans of antiwar organizing. The roots of the anti-treaty protest movement in Wisconsin date back to the early 1970s when six hundred sport fishers formed Concerned Sportsmen for Lake Superior immediately following the *Gurnoe* decision. Group members feared the exercise of the Lake Superior Chippewa's fishing rights would deplete the stocks of commercially valuable trout, walleye, and whitefish. Similarly, the attempts by state Senator Reuben LaFave (R-Oconto) to "purchase" the fishing rights recognized through *Gurnoe*, ostensibly out of concern for the tribe's' "welfare," is echoed in the relationship between Governor Tommy Thompson (a Republican) and anti-treaty rights activists. As the *Capital Times* observed in 1973, "anytime the whites profess interest in the Indians it is time for these native Americans to keep their backs against the white pine and their peace pipes hidden."[7] The scope of the rights, the size of the ceded territory affected, and changes in the media exemplified by CNN and its twenty-four-hour news cycle, made the 1980s dramatically different.

In the late 1970s, both the Senate Select Committee on Indian Affairs and the American Indian Policy Review Commission documented anti-Indian racism in the years between *Gurnoe* and *Voigt*. A witness testifying before the Senate in 1977 attributed the "backlash coming from the common citizens" to "ignorance, because of the lack of educational systems to teach anything about Indians, about treaties." He continued, "When the population really doesn't know what the rights are and what the laws say, they have to make judgment decisions based on what the media puts out to them or what a politician [says]." The American Indian Policy Review Commission reached a similar conclusion, that "one of the greatest obstacles" American Indians faced was "the American public's ignorance of the historical relationship" between the federal government and tribal nations and the "lack of general awareness of the status of the American Indian in our society today."[8] In Wisconsin, as elsewhere, ignorance-fueled racism, exacerbated by economic anxieties, sometimes erupted into violence.

SPEARFISHING

While *Gurnoe* primarily involved the use of nets on Lake Superior, the typical practice associated with the exercise of treaty rights after *Voigt* was spearfishing on inland waters. Spearfishing was controversial because its efficient, intensive harvest methods directly conflicted with the outdoor ethic of those who fish for sport. For more than one hundred years, Wisconsin state law had expressly prohibited spearing game fish, but for generations Ojibwe men had engaged in nighttime harvests of walleye spawning in shallow inland waters, originally using birch bark torches of flaming pine pitch to illuminate the eyes of the fish, which they harvested with wooden spears.[9] In the post-*Voigt* era, Ojibwe spearing practices typically involved small groups of men, and sometimes women, using watercraft ranging from aluminum canoes to fishing boats with outboard motors.

Relevant regulations established through the *Voigt* litigation required those exercising treaty rights to do on lakes designated by GLIFWC. Spearers could use only those boat landings monitored by GLIFWC wardens, many of which were "out of town where rural county roads snake down to small parking lots by scenic inland waters," located next to non-Indians' vacation homes, or simply small driveways in the woods.[10] Spearers wore halogen car headlights powered by six-volt car batteries and taped to construction helmets, a modern innovation that had replaced pine pitch torches, and they used metal spears, typically custom made by local tribal members (not made in Korea, as treaty rights opponents asserted), which had replaced wooden spears.[11] Some of the bands began spearing at the landings, while other spearers, particularly those from Lac du Flambeau, raced "to beat hell" across the lake toward rock bars and other spawning grounds.[12] Such technological innovations, while controversial among treaty rights opponents, were held to be lawful, as Judge Doyle had ruled that the Ojibwe bands had the right to use any method of harvest they might choose, whether it resembled the means used at the time of treaty negotiation or any method developed since then.[13]

Spearing was often a family affair, with various members engaged in every part of the process, from preparing and maintaining the equipment and processing the harvested fish, to preparing the catch to be eaten and distributing shares to family members and elders in the community. Often family members were eagerly waiting at the landings, having created what Nesper describes as "very temporary villages for all practical and cultural reasons."[14] Families were on hand to process the evening's harvest and, in some cases, were listening to recorded pow-wow music over speakers set to project out onto the lakes.[15] At Lac du Flambeau, it was common practice to filet the fish on-site and then dump the head, spine, and tail in the woods or back into the lakes, a traditional practice among many Ojibwe that may well be the basis for treaty rights opponents' claims that spearers were "wasting the resource" because they mistook carcasses for whole fish. Over the years, as the level of protest grew, the presence of family members took on a more defensive nature, reflecting a mix of joy and apprehension.[16]

Anti–Treaty Rights Organizations

Hunting and fishing groups in northern Wisconsin responded almost immediately after the *Voigt* decision upheld the Ojibwe people's treaty-based rights to hunt, fish, and gather within the ceded territory. These groups claimed the traditional hunting and fishing practices would allow the Ojibwe to "wantonly wipe out all fish and game."[17] Opponents of treaty rights particularly objected to, and actively sought to disrupt, such traditional and legally protected practices as spearing, gill netting, and shining, methods of harvest oriented toward efficiency rather than sport, because they viewed these practices as examples of "special privileges" based on "old treaties" that were "relics of the past."[18]

In the decade following the *Voigt* decision, several anti-treaty groups emerged, including Hayward-based Equal Rights for Everyone (ERFE), Superior-based Wisconsin Alliance for Rights and Resources (WARR), Butternut-based Butternut Lake Concerned Citizens, Minocqua-Park Falls–based Protect Americans Rights and Resources (PARR), and Minocqua-based Stop Treaty Abuse (STA), each with names "carefully selected to deflect charges of racism," though they are better known by their acronyms.[19] Historian Ronald N. Satz explains that "the agendas of these organizations [were] blatantly anti-Indian" and they "[sought] nothing less than the restoration of the termination and relocation policies of the 1950s."[20] Their efforts included lobbying for the abrogation of treaties, termination of the government-to-government relationship between tribes and the federal government, and public information campaigns. Their most frequent and visible efforts, however, involved protests and other activities designed to interfere with the lawful exercise of treaty rights. These efforts drew significant public attention to their cause and prompted widespread concern for public safety.

James Schlender, executive director of GLIFWC, testifying in 1988 before the Subcommittee on Civil and Constitutional Rights, said, "When the *Voigt* decision came down, then all Indians became rapers of the resources and a general caste was put upon all."[21] The threat of racial violence was very real, and Native people in northern Wisconsin faced violence not only as "direct victimization" but also as "the daily knowledge . . . that they are *liable* to violation, solely on account of their group identity."[22] Because of the protestors' actions, the State of Wisconsin had to spend "millions of dollars on law enforcement," and the "social fabric of northern Wisconsin became torn along racial lines through numerous acts of overt hostility and violence between tribal members and non-Indians."[23] The protestors' concerns for the environment and the local economy were tainted by the racism they displayed in public discourse and at the lakes where Ojibwe people spearfished.[24]

Protestors engaged in a wide variety of activities to harass spearers and disrupt their harvest, and hundreds were arrested between 1985 and 1991 for what they viewed as "acts of civil disobedience."[25] Rennard Strickland, writing in 1991 as the violent controversy continued to rage on in Wisconsin, noted, "The peaceful harvest of fish by the Chippewas is threatened by non-Indians who barrage the peaceful fishers with rocks and insults, and who use large motorboats with trolling anchors to capsize the boats of the fishers."[26] On many boat landings, protestors openly proclaimed their hostility to treaty rights as well as the Native people exercising them. One protestor complained, "I'm paying taxes to support them every week—to support this, to send them welfare checks, to give them all different kinds of aid. That wasn't in the treaty."[27] Protesters often arrived at boat landings in vehicles with bumper stickers carrying such messages as "Save a Deer, Shoot an Indian," and "Spear an Indian, Save a Muskie."[28] The protestors shouted "timber nigger" and other racially charged insults, threw rocks, and mocked Native songs with chants of "hi how are ya, hi how are ya!" They carried effigies of speared Indian heads and signs with messages like "Save Two Walleye, Spear A Pregnant Squaw."[29] Women standing at the landings singing traditional songs in support of their relatives out on the lakes faced protestors who would "jeer and shout vicious taunts, racial slurs, and threats while others blow whistles in continuous shrill blasts in their ears" and vandalize their vehicles.[30] On the water, protestors used motorboats to create disruptive wakes, dragged anchors to cloud the water, and tried to use concrete fish decoys to break the spears, a ploy Nesper explains is "transparent to an experienced spearer."[31] On the lakes or on the shore, the nature of their actions is reflected in an October 1984 Milwaukee Journal headline: "North Woods Steaming with Racial Hostility."[32]

The earliest of the anti-treaty organizations of the post-Voigt era were relatively short-lived and most notable for their violent rhetoric. ERFE, founded in Hayward by Paul A. Mullaly shortly after the Voigt decision was issued, was, as Gaiashkibos, chair of the Lac Courte Oreilles Tribal Governing Board, explained, "the first racist organization that existed" to oppose treaty rights.[33] ERFE objected to the very idea of treaty rights or spearfishing, and the organization struggled to reconcile the practices and the people engaging in them with their pre-existing ideas about "Indians."

In 1985, Larry Peterson, a paper mill worker from Park Falls, founded one of the most active and enduring anti–treaty rights organizations, PARR. Alarmed by Mullaly's escalating rhetoric, Peterson had left ERFE to found WARR in 1984. After the Ad Hoc Commission on Racism denounced both groups as racist, Peterson sought to distance himself from the charges by founding PARR for the stated purpose of uniting sportspeople, business owners, farmers, and others to oppose "Chippewa special rights."[34] PARR promoted protests at boat landings and "put out a newsletter, and a lot of misinformation" as part of their efforts to disrupt spearing and other forms of exercising treaty rights.[35] It grew quickly, and by 1987, PARR had sixteen chapters in Wisconsin and had absorbed WARR's mailing list and treasury, along with most members of the now-defunct ERFE.[36]

In 1987, a Minocqua pizza parlor owner named Dean Crist founded STA as a more action-oriented alternative to PARR.[37] He told the *Wisconsin State Journal*'s George Hesselberg, "I watched PARR founder for years, even supported them with pizza and beer . . . but I saw they were not able to find their butt with both hands."[38] He told Hesselberg that he founded STA to market Treaty Beer and another organization, Stop Treaty Abuse/Wisconsin, to solicit donations for anti-spearfishing activities ultimately focused on the abrogation of treaties.[39] According to Crist, his organization's fund-raiser, Treaty Beer, marketed as the "True Brew of the Working Man," was an "educational" endeavor to teach "people downstate," as well as nationally, about the "treaty rights problem" by using the slogan "Treaty Beer: Tastes Bitter, Hard to Swallow."[40] Many bars and bait shops in northern Wisconsin sold Treaty Beer, and Crist hoped to use sales figures to demonstrate political clout for anti-Indian legislation in Wisconsin and elsewhere.[41]

Anti–treaty rights protestors featured Treaty Beer at rallies in Washington State, which was still stung by a treaty rights case from the 1970s; at an anti–treaty rights protest on the steps of the Wisconsin capitol, STA leaders "poured the beer into a pink toilet bowl."[42] Critics dismissed the product as "racism in a can," and pro-treaty organizations used their opposition to this commodification of hate as a point of unity.[43] Treaty rights supporters successfully petitioned liquor stores in Illinois and

Oregon not to carry the product, and boycott efforts against the breweries in Wisconsin, Ohio, and Louisiana that canned Treaty Beer ultimately led Crist to abandon the product.[44]

Crist, whom Tom Maulson a spearfishing leader from Lac du Flambeau had nicknamed "the Grand Wizard," dismissed allegations of racism, claiming that "he considers himself 'part Indian'" after learning through genealogical research that he is "a small part" Canadian Iroquois.[45] He similarly denied connections to racist organizations, yet Treaty Beer was profiled in *Skin Head News*, and Crist himself often praised Ku Klux Klan leader David Duke, noting that it was as if Duke "might have been reading from STA literature."[46] He expressed the concern that "people coming from the other side" would frame STA by infiltrating the organization and "showing up at the landings and spouting a whole bunch of racist stuff."[47] In an interview with the *Wisconsin State Journal*, Crist alleged there was a "serious threat" from the American Indian Movement to kill one of their own members at the boat landings in order to pin the murder on STA.[48] There was no evidence to back his claim.

Just weeks before the 1987 spearing season was to open, PARR held its national conference in Wausau, Wisconsin, where more than five hundred people from thirteen states and two Canadian provinces gathered to pursue abrogation of treaties, termination of tribal governments, and an end to "special privileges" held by Native people.[49] At the conference, anti-treaty organizations in Wisconsin "became allied with national anti-Indian organizations in order to oppose the local Indian exercise of treaty rights," and together they formed a new organization, the Citizens Equal Rights Alliance. The formation of CERA quickly transformed what began as a state, local, and perhaps regional issue into a national dispute.[50] Thereafter, the individual organizations themselves often came to function as local CERA chapters.[51]

TREATY RIGHTS–SUPPORT ORGANIZATIONS

An important ally in the struggle to assert treaty rights, Witness for Non-Violence, formed in Milwaukee in early 1987, and the group began to make its presence known at boat landings that spring. Red Cliff Ojibwe activist and educator Walt Bresette had called on peace activists in Milwaukee and

Madison to come north, redirecting their focus on injustices in Nicaragua or elsewhere in Central America.[52] Witness for Non-Violence members "diffuse[d] violent situations and protect[ed] the rights and dignity of people under attack" by engaging in "peaceful, non-confrontational observation of the situation."[53] The organization sought to "lessen the chance of harassment and violence, and to document and testify to any and all violations of the law that we see."[54] Witnesses worked to "shine a witnessing light" as they kept watch on the boat landings while wearing white armbands, adhering to a pledge to nonviolently observe what transpired and to document civil rights violations through audio and video recordings as well as detailed personal notes.[55]

Witness for Non-Violence began to hold nonviolence trainings in early 1987 for those interested in working to "convey calm in the midst of tension" in order to prepare them to "stand with the Chippewa and their families as a supportive presence and to stand between people in a potentially confrontational circumstance" and to "document alleged criminal offenses."[56] The organization required potential witnesses to receive training to prepare them for hostile encounters, which Nesper describes as "a rite of passage that purported to create identification with the Indian spearfishers."[57] Witnesses learned not to dress or identify their vehicles in ways that might "needlessly identify yourself or others as treaty supporters" because their reports likely would be viewed more credibly if they "submerged their support for the movement in favor of documenting what happened routinely on the landings."[58] Witness members frequently served food and hot beverages to protestors, believing that "food is great for bonding" and that people "felt a little differently" with "muffins in their mouths."[59] While their training instructed them not to "use the 'silent treatment' on protestors talking rationally to you," witnesses were not otherwise to attempt to debate or persuade protestors.[60]

Witness for Non-Violence became an increasingly important and controversial presence on the boat landings throughout the 1980s and early 1990s.[61] Andrew Gokee, an active spearer from the Red Cliff Reservation, noted, "The more Witnesses on a given night, the more peaceful the lake will be."[62] Locals, including both protestors and law enforcement personnel, were wary of cities like Madison, Milwaukee, and Chicago, and tended to view witnesses as interfering outsiders, "traitors," and "white niggers."[63] Although their numbers were small initially, anxious state officials and local law enforcement were concerned that the presence of "hundreds of outside supporters" at the boat landings increased the "chance of direct confrontation that will get out of control."[64]

Treaty rights supporters formed a new organization, Honor Our Neighbors Origins and Rights (HONOR), in Wausau in February of 1988. HONOR was a "coalition of individuals, human rights groups, church organizations, and other groups" concerned with the "increasing intensity of anti-Indian rhetoric and activity."[65] The organization viewed treaties as a matter of national honor, and the founders selected their name for that purpose. They sought to counter the treaty abrogation and termination efforts of PARR and STA by working to affirm and build public support for the government-to-government relationship embodied in the treaties. Its executive director, former state Representative Sharon Metz of the Milwaukee-based Lutheran Human Relations Association of America, focused the organization's efforts on educating and lobbying elected officials, providing quality instructional materials to educators, monitoring anti–treaty rights organizations, working with tribal governments, and educating the public through its newsletter.[66]

Local Controversy

Anti-Indian sentiment was also present away from the boat landings, in cities and towns across northern Wisconsin, and elsewhere in the state. Native families commonly experienced harassment in off-reservation towns, particularly during spearing season.[67] Indian children were "ostracized" from Little League in Minocqua and adults were excluded from the recreational league.[68] In Eau Claire, a store displayed a "cap depicting a speared Indian with food stamps."[69] Restaurants and taverns commonly displayed literature attacking spearfishing and advocating for the abrogation of treaties.[70] Many bars and other businesses in the area prominently placed a poster of a revolver pointed directly at the viewer and carrying the caption "Spear This."[71] Public sentiment had clearly grown quite hostile, and while incidents at boat landings were confined to the spring harvest, the deteriorating racial climate knew no season.

Local governments were themselves often quite hostile.[72] The Ashland city council adopted a resolution calling for the abrogation of treaties, and many other local and county governments took up similar resolutions opposing the exercise of treaty rights.[73] In early 1984, a mock flyer for "open season" on "'Smokes,' also known as Injuns, Shenaubees, Chemukamons, Bow and Arrows, and War Hoops" appeared in employees' mailboxes at the Ashland County Courthouse, near the Bad River Reservation. It contained numerous references to welfare, "government housing," "government beef," "government checks," "wacky tobaccy," and "firewater bottles," thereby invoking nearly every negative stereotype of Native people in a single document.[74]

Native children faced increased racial harassment in schools. In Boulder Junction, a K–8 school district near the Lac du Flambeau Reservation, a non-Indian student drew a series of anti-Indian images, including a picture of a giant fish spearing an Indian through the head, that was captioned "Walleye Warrior." Students in Crandon, near the Mole Lake Reservation, displayed racist anti-spearfishing messages on T-shirts. At Lakeland Union High School, in Minocqua, just outside the Lac du Flambeau Reservation, students scrawled racist graffiti and "eight to ten non-Indian students" wrote, photocopied, and distributed a racist, profanity-filled poem called "The Flambeau Shuffle." According to the *Wausau Daily Herald*, the poem opened with the line, "Spear them walleyes, poach them deer." Of the rest of the poem, the paper noted only that "the next line ends with 'beer.'" Kathryn Tierney, an attorney for the Lac du Flambeau band, noted that in years previous, active racial harassment in schools and the community typically subsided after the spearing season ended, but by 1987, the abuse continued year-round.[75] Both Lakeland Union High School and Crandon High School also experienced multiple bomb threats.[76]

The intensity of protests and perceived complicity from local officials gave rise to nicknames for certain locations. Spearers gave Vilas County, adjacent to Lac du Flambeau and home to leading anti–treaty rights organizations, the nickname "Violence County," and the nearby town of Park Falls became known as "PARR Falls."[77] Vilas County Sheriff James Williquette estimated that 90 percent of county residents opposed treaty rights, but he denied any racist motives, claiming that similar actions by various European ethnicities would prompt the same response.[78]

George Meyer, head of enforcement for the Wisconsin Department of Natural Resources, identified "leniency" in prosecution and adjudication of anti-treaty-related offenses as a factor contributing to law enforcement concerns, and he acknowledged Vilas County in particular as an area that "needs improvement."[79] Patrick Ragsdale, an official with the US Department of the Interior, was less euphemistic when he told the *Milwaukee Sentinel* that he was "appalled" and "disgusted" by protestors' language at the boat landings.[80]

Tom Maulson explained that the season was supposed to be year-round, "ice in or ice out or ice out to ice in," but "because of the things that Indian fishermen went through," the season was only two to three weeks "because things were so violent and you had to take that number of fish in that short time."[81] He said the spearers "had to make sure we took our numbers off that lake" because if they were to return, "something drastic could happen."[82] In his address at the Minwaajimo Conference held at Bad River in July 2009, Maulson described dealing with hundreds of protestors who "were drunk, running their little kids back and forth going getting more and more beer and calling names that shouldn't even be repeated here," yet he would often go into the hostile crowds, "just joking with them, laughing with them, getting them settled down" to reduce the level of hostility.[83] Despite his jocular approach, Maulson "had a bounty on his head" during the height of the crisis and had to be accompanied by an undercover FBI agent at all times.[84]

Local churches engaged in the struggle, and many faith communities were deeply divided by the controversy. Archbishop William Wantland of the Episcopalian Diocese of Eau Claire, himself a citizen of the Seminole Nation of Oklahoma, explained that he felt like he was "caught in a time warp" that reminded him of "Selma and Little Rock and Montgomery" in the 1950s and 1960s.[85] During the protests in the spring of 1990, Wantland argued, "Of all the states I've lived in in this union, Wisconsin is the most racist. I grew up in the South. And I said that before the *Voigt* decision was handed down. It's obvious—the racism, the hatred, the bitterness, the prejudice."[86] Wantland attributed the climate to "ignorance of ignorance," the failure to recognize the misconceptions that "breed racist sentiments."[87] Minocqua-area pastor Chomingwen Pond agreed that "ignorance of cultural differences" was a central issue, in part because of an influx of new residents from Milwaukee, Chicago, and elsewhere.[88] As in the South, many churches in Wisconsin sought to promote reconciliation and understanding.[89]

The Role of Law Enforcement

Law enforcement personnel, from wardens employed by the Wisconsin Department of Natural Resources, to county sheriffs and deputies, to local police, were yet another important presence on the boat landings. The DNR's George Meyer was often personally present, leading state enforcement efforts and coordinating with other law enforcement authorities. By contrast, Vilas County Sheriff James Williquette generally preferred to respond to incidents at the landings only when called. He opposed stationing officers on-site as ordered by the federal courts, but feared charges of misconduct in office if he did not comply.[90]

Spearers and treaty rights supporters had little confidence in the police's willingness to provide protection or act upon reports of violence or harassment, especially in areas with large PARR and STA memberships.[91] Instead, spearers and their supporters generally viewed police as allies of the protestors, alleging police chose to "look the other way," were "intentionally failing to protect their safety," provided protection that was "half-hearted at best," or were even "actually being manipulated by the anti-Indian groups."[92] Treaty rights supporters claimed to have heard that "a cop or a sheriff or something said 'If I didn't have this uniform on, I'd be there with them [protestors]'"; whether the story was literally true, it clearly resonated with their experiences.[93] On those occasions when protestors were arrested, treaty rights advocates claimed local prosecutors and judges often reduced or dropped charges.[94] In a 1989 interview, the DNR's Meyer acknowledged his own concerns about law enforcement practices, giving credence to the protestors' claims.[95] Sharon Metz, a founder of HONOR, recalled at the Minwaajimo Conference in 2009 that during the spearfishing protests, the State of Wisconsin "spent eight million dollars just on law enforcement; not on education, not on anything else."[96] Concerns over the use of state resources proved to be one factor among many in marshaling support for a public policy solution to address the social costs of protests.

—⊣⊦—

Organized opposition to the *Voigt* decision emerged almost immediately after the court's ruling. Many of the organizations opposed to it masked strong anti-Indian sentiment with names that conveyed patriotism and environmental concerns, like Equal Rights for Everyone and Protect Americans Rights and Resources. While some protestors may have been concerned about the uncertain environmental impact of spearfishing or perceived unfairness of what they understood to be "special privileges," slogans like "Spear an Indian, Save a Muskie" reveal more of the story.[97] Public ignorance of the legal, cultural, and historical aspects of the reserved rights to hunt, fish, and gather meant that opponents' arguments gained significant political traction. This was particularly true within the ceded territory, as public institutions, including the mass media, schools, churches, law enforcement, and the government itself became embroiled in controversy. Communities in the North Woods were especially affected by the conflict between groups opposed to treaty rights, such as PARR and STA, and those in support, like HONOR and Witness for Non-Violence.

Even as the sides appeared to be solidifying, there was growing consensus that an education policy solution might restore the social fabric, heal existing wounds, and re-establish the state's positive reputation and business climate. Advocates recognized that graduates of Wisconsin schools had little knowledge or awareness of historical or contemporary American Indian issues, and advocates viewed this ignorance as a major contributing factor to racism and violence. The violence and controversy surrounding the affirmation of treaty rights was an important factor in Act 31's passage.

CHAPTER 4

The Boat Landings
and Beyond

In 1984, less than one year after *Voigt*, Paul Mullaly, founder of the group Equal Rights for Everyone, was already likening the court-affirmed right to hunt deer off-reservation within the ceded territory to "rape," and he "openly threatened Indian hunters."[1] The organization's threats "to kill Indians if they came to certain lakes" even drew the attention of the Federal Bureau of Investigation.[2] Lac Courte Oreilles tribal chairman Gaiashkibos credited white resort owners and businesspeople for ERFE's struggle to gain traction locally. He praised the actions of local business leaders to "cut them off" and show "those folks for what they were."[3] The positive relationships and mutual respect between the Lac Courte Oreilles Band and the Hayward-area business community left boat landings and towns near Lac Courte Oreilles and St. Croix relatively peaceful.[4] Eventually ERFE's more committed members joined other organizations that shared its concerns but not Mullaly's open call for vigilantism.

As this episode illustrates, and as the Ad Hoc Commission on Racism confirmed, a level of hostility was already present year-round in many local communities. After *Voigt*, latent hostility erupted into open conflict, and the racial climate seemingly grew worse each year. These changes are best understood through a chronological examination of the efforts of the state and tribes to negotiate successful harvests governed by interim agreements, the escalating efforts of treaty rights opponents to disrupt those activities, and the emerging response of treaty rights advocates seeking to ensure the Ojibwe people's harvest. Racism and antagonism were most acute at the boat landings, and it was these events that received the most law enforcement attention and media coverage. The negative publicity these incidents attracted, including national news coverage, reflected poorly on northern Wisconsin as a potential tourist destination, threatening the local economy. Out of this political crisis, a bipartisan coalition emerged in support of a public policy solution that relied upon public schools to raise awareness, leading to the passage of Act 31 in 1989.

1985: LEGAL SPEARFISHING BEGINS

The first legal spearfishing season took place in 1985. The harvest was conducted under an interim agreement negotiated between the Voigt Intertribal Task Force, a new organization representing the Wisconsin bands of the Lake Superior Chippewa, and the Wisconsin Department of Natural Resources. The season was to last from dusk to dawn for seven consecutive days between "ice out" and the opening day of the state fishing season for anglers. Under the agreement, spearers were subject to enforcement efforts from tribal, GLIFWC, and DNR wardens and could face fines imposed by tribal courts where they existed and state courts where they did not.[5] Lac du Flambeau tribal member Don Smith relates, "We pulled into the parking lot there at the landing and there must have been sixty law enforcement and DNR people there and there was only three of us going to spear! There wasn't anybody there on the landings watching us."[6] The number of spearers would grow dramatically in subsequent years, as would the number of law enforcement officers, protestors, and treaty rights advocates.

Protestors objected to displays and practices that did not match their ideas of legitimate Native identities or cultural expressions. Observers complained about the perceived inappropriateness and inauthenticity of "fish frys [sic] and tribal music on boomboxes."[7] Anthropologist Larry Nesper explains, "Seeing multiple tubs of walleye as well as an occasional large female full of spawn soon turned the curious into critics."[8] Despite numerous allegations of violations of the interim harvest agreement, during the 1985 harvest, only a few minor citations were handed out, some for possessing a fish over the twenty-inch size limit, two for being over the bag limit, and others for infractions such as boat light violations.[9]

At Big Twin Lake in Langlade County, on the last night of the 1985 spearing season, nearly one hundred protestors blocked the spearers' access to the lake, and protestors reportedly fired five shots.[10] Tom Maulson, a Lac du Flambeau tribal member who would soon become a leader among the most active spearers, remembered that the protestors "would say to us, 'Wait 'til it gets dark. We're going to kill you fuckers.'"[11] Although Twin Lake was a sign of things to come in later years, spearers would generally recall 1985 as a relatively calm year.

1986: CONFRONTATION AT STAR LAKE

The interim agreement governing the 1986 spearing season specified a nine-day season to be completed before the state fishing season for anglers began on May 2. The regulations allowed each spearer a twenty-five-fish bag limit per night and authorized spearing until 1 a.m. on weeknights and 2 a.m. on weekends. The bands could designate three lakes per night, and they could not fish the same lake on consecutive nights. An important change from 1985 was that, in order to avoid violence at the boat landings, the DNR would not publicly announce which lakes the bands had designated for spearing.[12]

On April 26, 1986, just before the start of the spearing season, PARR held a rally in Minocqua that attracted nearly twelve hundred people, many of whom were encouraged by the Minocqua-based *Lakeland Times* to "get your message across."[13] One of the speakers, Vera Lawrence, was a Sault Ste. Marie Chippewa tribal member who "called for abrogation of Indian treaties on the grounds that the treaties were made with full-bloods, who now numbered very few at Flambeau."[14] PARR and allied organizations would continue this line of rhetoric, and they would often call upon Lawrence and Chuck Valliere, a Lac du Flambeau Ojibwe, to advance this misunderstanding of the nature of the relationship between tribes and the federal government. PARR's use of Lawrence and Valliere helped to deflect charges of racism and allowed them to attempt to frame the issue in terms of unfair special rights.

Tom Maulson, along with nearly one hundred others from Lac du Flambeau, also attended the first PARR rally in Minocqua. They brought a drum, a descendent of the Drum Dance drum brought to Lac du Flambeau, and they sang four songs taught to them by a spiritual leader from Grand Portage. The songs were an assertion of the cultural as well as legal basis for treaty rights and a sign of resistance intended to show the resilience of the Ojibwe people in the face of an effort designed to intimidate them.[15] Wayne Valliere recalled that "all of the scowling protestors, adorned in blaze orange jackets (a symbol of anti-treaty sentiments), hats, and anti-Indian buttons, turned to look at him" as he began to sing the first song.[16] As they sang, an eagle, understood by the Ojibwe people as a messenger from the Creator, appeared and began to circle overhead. The eagle flew overhead "through the whole song, four times through," and it continued to fly over through the other three songs. Its presence quieted the protestors.[17] Even the *Lakeland Times*'s coverage, which was often inflammatory and anti-treaty, noted the eagle.[18] Nesper explains that the eagle's presence and the absence of violence "helped consolidate the moral superiority of the Indian people who brought the drum to the rally," which they attributed to the drum itself.[19] The Ojibwe people at the rally asserted the legitimacy of their cultural practices, including spearfishing, and they saw the eagle as vindication.

Another incident at the rally was a point of ongoing controversy. During the Pledge of Allegiance that opened the PARR rally, Tom and Jerry Maulson, brothers and Lac du Flambeau tribal members, chose to turn their backs. Despite their explanation that they were turning away from the protestors themselves rather than the flag, this incident continued to appear in the *Lakeland Times* as a symbol of the incompatibility between "an emerging Indian sovereignty and loyalty to the United States." Tribal members, meanwhile, recognized the gesture "and saw the criticism as yet another attempt by outsiders to define their identity, this time by impugning Indian patriotism."[20] Protestors would later refer to the incident frequently as part of a broader effort to portray their own efforts and motives in patriotic terms.

On the last night of the 1986 spearing season, seventy spearers arrived at Star Lake, which, under the interim agreement that governed the harvest, was a site without regulations limiting access or limiting the number of spearers. As George Meyer, the chief enforcement officer for the DNR, was trying to prevent additional boats from entering the lake, he and Tom Maulson "got into a very heated argument about the number of spearers arriving on the asphalt boat landing ramp that led into the water." Meyer had pleaded with Maulson as he tried to keep a trailer away from the landing, and Maulson refused to intervene, recognizing his leadership role in traditional, noncoercive terms. Maulson had no authority to prevent the boats from entering the water, and, in any case, he chose not to assist the state with its enforcement concerns.[21]

Maulson instead proposed an alternative, that the Ojibwe would conduct their harvest on North Twin Lake, where they had speared the night before and taken only a portion of the quota. Meyer denied this request, holding fast to the negotiated agreement that governed the exercise of treaty rights for that year, which specified that spearers could not harvest the same lake on consecutive nights. As the argument grew increasingly heated, Maulson noted the inconsistencies in enforcement practices, pointing out that the DNR had allowed spearing on consecutive nights on the Flambeau Flowage earlier in the week. The argument continued to escalate and ended with Maulson saying, "Get out of the weeds, George, we're going to run you over!" Both men had to move out of the way as Ben Chosa continued to back his trailer into the water, lowering his boat to exercise the rights his people had reserved.[22]

That night on Star Lake, forty-eight spearers harvested nearly eight hundred walleyes. The DNR and local media characterized the situation as an "overharvest," and they held Tom Maulson responsible.[23] Protestors likened the incident to a "rape," and gendered language connoting sexual violence quickly became a common trope in anti-treaty rhetoric.[24] In response to reporters' questions about the alleged violation of the negotiated agreement not to take more than 10 percent of the total allowable catch, Maulson attempted to place the conflict in a broader context and raised "general concerns about how whites use resources and abuse Indians."[25] He spoke of how non-Indians are the primary users of reservation lakes, how spearers are often shot at, and how they had been witnesses to hundreds calling for treaty abrogation and tribal termination in Minocqua. Star Lake attracted regional media attention, including front-page articles and editorials that often "condensed and simplified" these issues to conclude that Star Lake was in retaliation for the PARR rally.[26] Some news outlets, such as the *Milwaukee Journal*, echoed Maulson's comments and further angered non-Indians in the

Lakeland area who already held some antipathy to outsiders from places like Madison, Milwaukee, and Chicago.[27]

The political fallout from Star Lake was intense at the tribal, state, and federal levels. On May 6, 1986, more than one hundred people attended the Lac du Flambeau Tribal Council meeting, where attendees advocated a variety of positions relative to the relationship with "surrounding communities" and discussed the resulting impact on tribal businesses as well as internal strife on the reservation.[28] The Ojibwe bands condemned the DNR for not assuming shared responsibility for the harvest at Star Lake given the state regulations involved.[29] The secretary of the DNR responded with a written protest delivered to Maulson, the Lac du Flambeau tribal government, and GLIFWC, arguing the incident at Star Lake proved that the tribes were unable to self-regulate and that state regulation was therefore necessary.[30] PARR members viewed the incident as an example of the state's failure to protect the natural resources, and its members threatened to boycott hunting and fishing licenses until the state satisfactorily addressed treaty rights.[31]

The events at Star Lake also had political ramifications. In a letter sent to the Lac du Flambeau Tribal Council, Congressman David Obey denounced spearfishing and announced that he was withdrawing his support for federal funding for the Lac du Flambeau fish hatchery. Obey also sent letters congratulating the other bands for what he viewed as more responsible harvest. Despite the attempts of Obey and others to divide the bands, *Masinaigan*, GLIFWC's quarterly newspaper, defended Lac du Flambeau and Maulson and called for the resignation of the DNR's chief negotiator on the interim agreements. The bands also took collective responsibility for Star Lake and announced a united response to Obey's threats would be forthcoming.[32]

After Star Lake, the focus of the controversy shifted from Lac Courte Oreilles, where band members Fred and Mike Tribble's actions had touched off the initial controversy, to Lac du Flambeau.[33] Differences between the two regions influenced how the tribe and the non-Indian community responded to the treaty rights controversy. Nesper describes the ceded territory near Lac du Flambeau as "the politically conservative north-central area of Wisconsin" where many non-Indians feared that spearfishing would destroy the local tourism-dependent economy by destroying the fish populations.[34]

In northwestern Wisconsin, where the Lac Courte Oreilles reservation is located, Ojibwe people still confronted racism—a 1975 school walkout at Hayward was an important flashpoint—but there were also positive relationships in schools and in the business community.[35] There was a well-organized business community on and around Lac Courte Oreilles, including several on-reservation resort properties owned by non-Indians, and they generally had a positive working relationship with the tribe.[36] By contrast, the business community in the Minocqua area was "slow to organize" and had a less collaborative relationship with Lac du Flambeau.[37]

The Lac Courte Oreilles Band had demonstrated its commitment to treaty rights by initiating the court cases, but "because of their traditions and because of their respect for the rest of the community," its members speared less aggressively than their relatives at Lac du Flambeau, whose practices similarly reflected the overall tenor of relationships with neighboring towns.[38] After 1986, Lac du Flambeau, whose name means "Lake of the Torches," would become nearly synonymous with spearfishing once again, this time reflecting public controversy as much as tribal tradition.

1987: LAKE OF THE TORCHES

The Wisconsin DNR and GLIFWC negotiated another interim agreement to govern the 1987 spearfishing season, in which each band could declare a fifteen-day season on forty-eight hours' notice to the state. For the first time, the agreement required all spearers to have permits, which were available at tribal offices and at named lakes. Overall bag limits of twenty-five fish per night remained in place, slightly higher on lakes larger than five hundred acres; no more than one fish could be between twenty and twenty-four inches long, while a second fish could be of any size.[39] The DNR sought to involve its own wardens and local law enforcement personnel at the boat landings; as George Meyer remembers, "you should have heard the language at the first meeting about protecting Indians, but they agreed to do it."[40] Police ambivalence toward protecting the rights of those engaging in spearfishing would remain an issue in the coming years as well.

Butternut Lake, located near Park Falls roughly halfway between Lac Courte Oreilles and Lac du Flambeau, became "one of the most important symbols in the Walleye War and escalated the militarization of spearfishing."[41] On April 26, 1987, the anniversary of Star Lake and the day after a PARR rally drew two thousand people in Minocqua, Lac du Flambeau spearers arrived to fish at Butternut Lake, recognizing that protestors had been waiting for several days since the bands had selected the lake for spearing.[42] By dusk, a crowd of protestors had gathered at the landings, including Larry Peterson, one of the leaders of PARR. By 11 p.m., the crowd grew to an estimated 250 to 500 people, many of whom had come through the woods to avoid the police blockade.[43] The crowd was largely "anti-Indian types from Park Falls," according to Meyer, "many apparently recruited from local bars."[44] The protestors greatly outnumbered the one sheriff's deputy and ten conservation wardens on-site, and as the crowd grew, the protestors became "angrier and bolder," hurling taunts, racial slurs, and "dangerously large" rocks.[45] Meyer recalls that as spearers were putting their boats into the water, his wardens were moving through the crowd "to calm them down" and "to get them to clean up their act because there were young children [present]."[46] Meyer vividly recalls a child whose father "had been spouting some of the most evil rhetoric you'd ever want to hear," and when the child pulled on his father's pants leg begging him to stop, the man simply told his wife to "get the kid out of here."[47] Anti-treaty protests had apparently become a family affair, with young children receiving direct instruction about Native people down at the boat landings.

Spearers also vividly remember the night. Maulson, the spearing coordinator for Lac du Flambeau, and other tribal members gradually moved onto the peninsula, away from the boat landing, because as Neil Kmiecik recalls, "the force of the non-Indians' anger caused people to move away from them."[48] Spearers who were able to get out of their boats were similarly trapped on the peninsula, but according to Meyer, "the eleven law enforcement officers and I put our bodies in the way [when protestors approached the breakwater] to prevent the non-Indians from going at the Indians."[49] Kmiecik spoke of how he was "bending over to count fish and a rock came over my head and hit the boat that was next to me."[50] Ed Chosa related that he "was afraid for the first time at Butternut" because "the police were egging the crowd on."[51] The angry mob pulled two Ojibwe elders, Maggie Johnson and Shirley Miller, out of the back of a truck and threw them to the ground.[52] Chosa reportedly told George Meyer "somebody was going to get killed any moment. . . . It was bad until the boats came in, and then it was worse."[53] No charges were filed related to any of these incidents.[54]

Maulson describes how, as they were backed up against the water, the "cop from town," who was trying to tell the protestors theirs was an illegal gathering, was told by the protestors "to get fucked and that they were going to kill us."[55] "All we had was rocks that we picked up," he told Nesper, and "the rocks they had were flying over our heads. I figured we were going to be killed. I was just looking at those guys wondering which one I was gonna take with me."[56] In that moment, Maulson recalls hearing the voice of his late grandmother reassuring him, saying, "It's going to be all right, Sonny."[57] Family members on the shore had to try to maneuver vehicles and trailers out of the area to get to other landings to allow the spearers to come in off the lake in relative safety.[58] By 2 a.m. police from four counties, along with canine units from Superior, arrived and managed to clear the landing.[59]

The Lac du Flambeau Tribal Council described the scene at Butternut Lake as "fanning the flames of racial hatred" and "as racism in its rawest, ugliest form." They described it as "especially sad" that "many in the mob had brought their children to the scene, as if it was a sporting event." The council compared the protestors to those who "wore brown shirts and swastikas or hid behind white sheets and burnt crosses." They wrote, "In this way, racial hatred is transmitted to a new generation," and they vowed, "We will return to Butternut."[60] Before Butternut Lake, few had described opposition to spearing as racist, but after that incident, "nearly everyone did."[61] The controversy had reached another turning point.

On April 30, 1987, spearers from Lac du Flambeau indeed returned to Butternut Lake, where they found more than 150 police officers on hand, limiting access to only those with tribal identification. More than two hundred Ojibwe people from three states arrived, including drum groups from Lac du Flambeau, Lac Courte Oreilles, and Mole Lake. In an assertion of a distinctly Ojibwe cultural context for treaty rights, an Elder led a pipe ceremony at the lake, placed tobacco in the water, and sent four boats out, each of which returned with one fish. According to GLIFWC's *Masinaigan*, two eagles flew over the landing during the ceremony.[62]

Several speeches that day describe what the return to Butternut meant to spearers from Lac du Flambeau. Maulson praised his people as being "strong as a nation" on the landing, proclaiming, "They wanted to kill us. There's no way they are going to do that. We're back."[63] Lac du Flambeau tribal chairman Mike Allen similarly proclaimed that Ojibwe people "can't allow ourselves to be robbed of our heritage and future by vigilantes" and explained that they were returning "to the scene of such things to show unity."[64] Chosa explicitly invoked the treaties, explaining that "our chiefs reserved that right for us" and those exercising those rights "are all their descendants." He argued that "spearing is traditional, . . . over thousands of years old" and practiced "all over, not just on reservation lakes."[65] The Ojibwe people had made their point: they refused to be intimidated into relinquishing their rights.

Butternut Lake would remain symbolically important in later years. As GLIFWC's Jim St. Arnold explained, high mercury levels meant that the fish harvested there were inedible, "so each of the spearers would go get one fish and turn it over to the biologist," yet both spearers and protestors would wait for Butternut to be selected for spearing. St. Arnold describes a night when Butternut was among the lakes chosen, but Maulson instead led the spearers to Minocqua Lake, leaving "a few hundred protestors at Butternut Lake getting very irritated at us because we weren't there." By the time the protestors realized which lake they were spearing, the Ojibwe had finished their harvest on Minocqua Lake.[66]

Maulson and his fellow spearers from Lac du Flambeau were the most active and most aggressive in exercising the right to spear on off-reservation lakes. They began to wear hats emblazoned with the image of a walleye, along with the words "Walleye Warriors" and "Lac du Flambeau, Wisconsin." Maulson gave out the hats at his store, "the headdress of a contemporary Ojibwe warrior society," as gifts to his fellow spearers, "further strengthening his position as a modern traditional leader."[67] Another Lac du Flambeau spearer, Gibby Chapman, antagonized treaty opponents with the slogan, "Chippewa and Proud: FUCK PARR" on posters prominently displayed on his van as well as on a T-shirt.[68] After Lac Courte Oreilles requested that Lac du Flambeau members refrain from spearing the Chippewa Flowage out of respect for the tribe's relationship with the local business community, thirty-six spearers from Lac du Flambeau nevertheless arrived on April 29, 1988, and took more than one thousand walleye in two nights.[69] During the 1987 spearing season, 266 spearers from Lac du Flambeau harvested more than fifteen thousand walleye, more than 70 percent of the total number of fish speared by all the bands. As a result, Lac du Flambeau tribal members ate more fish from off-reservation lakes than they had in a century.[70]

1988: THE WALLEYE WARS ESCALATE

The harvest parameters adopted under the interim agreement for the 1988 spearing season were substantially similar to the previous year's regulations. The only significant changes had to do with law enforcement. Because the DNR feared a repeat of the chaos and violence at Butternut Lake the year before, the updated agreement prohibited drinking at boat landings, and canine units now patrolled the shores while National Guard helicopters watched the lakes. Police at the landings wore riot gear, set up high-powered lights, and established police lines to separate protestors and spearers.[71] Additional officers were on standby at National Guard armories as the state prepared to enact a "war plan" should the need for law enforcement at boat landings exceed the capacity of local and county police.[72]

Tensions ran high as the start of the 1988 spearing season approached, and local media reflected the hostility in many northern Wisconsin communities. A letter appeared in the *Lakeland Times*, headlined "Stop Sucking Your Thumbs and Act," urging direct action. Its author suggested readers "go to the landings and scream." Those able to get boats on the water were encouraged to "run it at half throttle and stay a few hundred feet away from the Native Americans exercising their rights. They will welcome your presence because it creates more of a challenge when the water is high."[73] The *Lakeland Times*'s rhetoric had been hostile to treaty rights, and now the paper was printing incitement to violence at the boat landings.

Many protestors answered the *Times*'s call to arms or responded to STA's recruitment and organization efforts, and as a result, the crowds at the boat landings during the 1988 spearing were the largest yet.[74] Hostile crowds of protestors grew as the conflict escalated, with many now using the slogan "Save a Walleye . . . Spear an Indian," along with many variations.[75] The threats of violence heightened and the "level of violence increased markedly."[76] Protestors using their own watercraft "rammed, swamped, and blockaded" spearers' boats out on the lakes, and in some cases, five or more protestors' boats would converge on one boat of spearers.[77] On the roads, STA members attacked tribal members' vehicles, attempting to slash their tires or run them off the road.[78] At the landings, protestors chanted mock drum songs and used whistles to harass spearers' family members and supporters. Some protestors used high-powered slingshots and rifles to shoot at spearers from shore, and the presence of exploding pipe bombs made the death threats that spearers faced that much more realistic.[79] The situation was becoming increasingly dangerous.

Despite the escalation of threats to their safety, many of the spearers grew more determined than ever. The size of spearing parties, which included the spearers themselves as well as family members and supporters at the landings, increased in an attempt to provide protection.[80] Nesper reports that Wayne Valliere described how he would "find the loudest [protestor] and walk right up to him and let him know that I wasn't afraid of him. They would think, 'This guy is crazy,' and they would quiet down."[81] Valliere, like many other spearers, went out on the lakes despite pleas from wives and mothers fearing for their safety and their lives. Valliere said he "didn't want [his] children to take over this fight" and was guided by the belief that "if you are going to die, that's it."[82] By contrast, Nesper reports, "whites in the Walleye War did not give the impression that they were willing to die for the fish, despite occasional dramatic displays."[83] Although both spearers and protestors had strong convictions about the issue, the Ojibwe people were drawing strength from what they recognized as a long-standing cultural tradition.

Spearers returned to Butternut Lake on April 18, 1988, the opening night of the spearing season.[84] One hundred police officers were present, and they had closed the landing with yellow tape, set up a giant spotlight in the parking lot, and refused to allow any vehicles other than their own to remain in the lot.[85] The night was replete with protestors' boats on the lake and racial taunts from protestors at the landings.[86] While leaving the area in his pickup, STA leader Dean Crist struck a tribal member's van, breaking off the sideview mirror, and nearly hit two teenage girls, resulting in charges of disorderly conduct, hit-and-run property damage, and reckless driving.[87] Another protestor hit a sheriff's deputy with his car and was charged with disorderly conduct.[88] Forty members of Witness for Non-Violence also made their first appearances at the boat landings that spring.[89]

Ojibwe people exercising their treaty rights on other lakes also faced violence and the threat of violence from protestors on the water and on the shore. On April 21, 1988, spearers on Little St. Germaine heard gunshots and those on Big St. Germaine had to deal with protestors using motorboats to create wakes to unbalance spearers' vessels and disturb spawning beds.[90] Despite pleas from spearers, George Meyer defended the legality of the protestors' actions. Nevertheless, the DNR increased the law enforcement presence and issued a limited number of citations to protestors using boats.[91]

On April 24, 1988, as the spearing season was winding down, PARR held a rally at a tavern near Big Arbor Vitae Lake. The speakers included PARR leaders, special guest STA leader Crist, and former Iran hostage and Republican congressional candidate Kevin Hermening. After the rally, Hermening joined Crist in a boat to confront and harass spearers.[92] It had become not only politically safe, but perhaps even politically advantageous to actively and violently oppose treaty rights.

1989: SCAPEGOATING THE OJIBWE

Tensions escalated even further in 1989 with new developments in negotiations, new decisions from the federal court, and the emergence of several new organizations that supported treaty rights. The year began with an announcement that the State of Wisconsin had successfully negotiated an agreement with the leadership of the Mole Lake band, pending a vote among tribal members, to buy out the band's right to spear fish on off-reservation lakes and withdraw from the remaining phases of the case, which included timber rights and damages. The state had long sought to extinguish treaty rights, and Attorney General Hanaway claimed the agreement was a model for negotiating "leases" with the other Ojibwe bands in the state. Contrary to expectations from state and tribal leaders, Mole Lake tribal members "voted overwhelmingly to reject" the offer. With the offer to Mole Lake now off the table, the state would soon direct its attention to Lac du Flambeau.[93]

The state's failure to reach a settlement with the Mole Lake band led a very frustrated STA to pledge to shut down spearing. Leaders Crist and Al Soik announced on February 21, 1989: "It is the intention of STA to encourage all its members, as well as all citizens, to use every available means to minimize the slaughter of spawning Wisconsin sport fish by nontraditional Chippewa spearing."[94] They exhorted their members to disrupt the spearing season by forming large crowds on the landings; to block landings through sit-ins or other forms of civil disobedience; to put boats in the water to "disrupt the slaughter"; to form lake watch groups to warn residents when lakes were to be speared; to start a legal defense fund for members; and to form a board to determine how funds should be allotted.[95]

The *Wisconsin State Journal* proclaimed that Judge Barbara Crabb's March 3, 1989, ruling in *LCO VI* "set into motion the latest escalation in the case."[96] Protestors particularly objected to the court's ruling that the tribes could regulate the harvest themselves and had the right to the full safe harvest of walleye and muskellunge in any selected lake.[97] The ensuing action by the DNR to lower bag limits for anglers on speared lakes, announced on April 27, 1989, during spearing season, fueled public perception of a causal relationship with the most recent court decision.[98] Nesper explains this "shifted the political cost of this conservation measure by the DNR to the Indian spearers" even though the agency had already been releasing information about an upcoming policy change.[99] Protestors viewed this action, best described as scapegoating the Ojibwe spearers, as a further provocation. In 1989, more protestors converged on boat landings than in any previous year. Wary law enforcement authorities pleaded with only limited success for a mutual aid agreement to help cover costs and to ensure police reinforcements or National Guard troops were available when shots were fired.[100]

Lac du Flambeau was home to the most active spearers. A new organization, the Wa-Swa-Gon Treaty Association, formed at Lac du Flambeau during early spring 1989. Wa-Swa-Gon actively opposed the State of Wisconsin's efforts to negotiate an end to the off-reservation harvest. The organization's members followed traditional, noncoercive leadership styles, and recognized cofounder Tom Maulson as their leader. Other key figures in Wa-Swa-Gon include cofounder Gibby Chapman,

Nick and Charlotte Hockings, Jerry Maulson, Anita Koser, and Dorothy Thoms. Critics often characterized them as "militant" for their active assertion and exercise of their treaty rights.[101] Wa-Swa-Gon members generally supported the efforts of Witness for Non-Violence, and several Lac du Flambeau families provided food and housing for witnesses. Three women from Lac du Flambeau, Maggie Johnson, Dorothy Thoms, and Anita Koser—all members of Wa-Swa-Gon—served as liaisons between Wa-Swa-Gon and Witness for Non-Violence.[102]

That spring, family members standing on shore in support of spearers were joined by educators, law students, clergy, retirees, and other members of the various pro-treaty rights efforts that had begun to organize in response to violent anti-treaty protests. These new organizations were composed of members who were mostly non-Native.[103] A new umbrella organization, Madison-based Midwest Treaty Network, worked to counter PARR and STA by organizing counterdemonstrations, bringing a supportive non-Native presence to the landings and collaborating with reservation-based organizations. By 1989, Midwest Treaty Network became the lead organizer for Witness for Non-Violence, perhaps its most visible effort, and by the following year, it had grown to include thirty grassroots organizations and nearly twenty-five hundred active members.[104]

In early spring 1989, a bulletin board at the Tombstone Pizza plant in Medford, Wisconsin, whose high school teams proudly used the old Milwaukee Braves logo and called themselves the "Red Raiders," had a poster advertising a mock hunting competition titled "The First Annual Indian Shoot."[105] The "competition" offered such scoring opportunities as five points for a "Plain Indian," ten points for "Indian with Walleyes," twenty points for "Indian with Boat Newer than Yours," thirty points for "Indian using Pitchfork," fifty points for "Indian with High School Diploma," seventy-five points for a "Sober Indian," and one hundred points for "Indian Tribal Lawyer (Does not have to be spearing)."[106] Like the flyer found in Ashland, it explicitly invoked numerous racist stereotypes, even extending its animosity stating, "residents that are BLACK, HMONG, CUBAN, or those on WELFARE, A.D.C., FOOD STAMPS, or any other GOVERNMENT GIVE-A-WAY program are not eligible."[107] The flyer solicited funds for state Senator Marvin J. Roshell, a Democrat from Chippewa County, through direct donations as well as the sale of bumper stickers reading "Save a Fish, Spear an Indian."[108] Open displays of racism had become a fund-raising tool for anti-treaty organizations and the political candidates they supported.

A flyer titled "How to Resolve the Spearfishing Issue" was found at Eagle Lanes Bowling Alley in Eagle River, Wisconsin. It openly advocated for the creation of a "crisis" and warned that distributing the document "is probably a federal offense." The flyer called upon protestors to create an "incident" that would be covered by the national news media in order to "get Federal attention by getting national attention." They hoped to "force Governor Thompson to declare an emergency and/or call out the National Guard." It called upon protestors to "raise the stakes by bringing in firearms," noting that "shots fired in the air in the dark will scare any brave." The flyer urged protestors to identify spearers' vehicles and to "take it home to them," by escalating the violence such that they must "secure the roads, travel in convoys, and turn the landings into an armed camp." It expressly warned against shooting spearers, because it would "only get more sympathy for them," and recommended that protestors instead shoot out tires and shoot holes in boats and other "poaching instruments." The flyer urged protestors to "stop spearers on several lakes, spread enforcement thin, force confrontation and overreaction, [and] escalate" in order to create an "emergency."[109]

On April 15, 1989, PARR held a rally in Minocqua that drew nearly two thousand blaze-orange-clad protestors.[110] PARR declared its intention to recall Congress members who were not sufficiently responsive to its concerns, identifying Jim Sensenbrenner as the only member they continued to support.[111] Among the protestors was Vera Lawrence, who once again incorrectly claimed only full-blood Indians could exercise treaty rights. Approximately fifty tribal members from Lac du Flambeau also attended the rally. The Valliere brothers had brought their drum, and Migizikwe, who had brought her pipe, said, "God bless you" to each of the protestors as they left the park to march in the streets.[112]

Before the start of the 1989 spearing season, elected officials representing the State of Wisconsin and the six Ojibwe bands, feeling significant local and federal pressure, met to negotiate the treaty harvest for that year. The bands agreed to reduce their harvest level to 60 percent of the safe catch on fifteen northern lakes in exchange for specific safety-related guarantees. The governor agreed to provide separate areas for Ojibwe families at the landings, to allow spearers to launch their boats and park their trailers at the landings, to urge protestors to stay away from the lakes and landings, and to ensure the availability of police officers to provide backup. Despite the agreement, both Dean Crist and Oneida County Sheriff Charles Crofoot "announced to the press that they would not be able to go along with such an agreement."[113] The situation worsened further after the DNR implicitly blamed Ojibwe spearers for the announced reductions in bag limits.

Due to heightened tensions, and the state's inability or unwillingness to guarantee spearers' safety, St. Croix tribal chairman Lewis Taylor asked the American Indian Movement (AIM) to provide assistance and support at the boat landings.[114] At Lac du Flambeau, the Wa-Swa-Gon Treaty Association, headed by Maulson, supported this decision, while the Lac du Flambeau Tribal Council, led by chairman Michael Allen Jr., opposed it, believing it would only further increase tensions.[115] When they arrived at the landings, AIM members brought a drum and what was commonly known as the "AIM flag," an American flag with a printed image of a plains Indian warrior that is "simultaneously patriotic and, from a non-Indian anti-treaty perspective, a desecration."[116] The presence of the drum "calmed people down, Indian people, and it frightened the ones who didn't understand it, mostly non-Indians."[117] AIM would continue to play a role throughout the 1989 spearing season, serving as a peaceful presence, albeit one that protestors often found to be intimidating.

That spring, anti-treaty protestors outnumbered previous years' crowds nearly ten to one, and they routinely broke through the police lines that separated the Chippewas on the lakes from the protestors on the boat landings.[118] There were more protestors than ever that year, at least 250 per night, in part because of the coordinated efforts of homeowner's associations and STA-sponsored "lake watch groups" that rapidly spread information about spearing activity.[119] On the lakes, protestors made what they called "observation runs" in their own boats, intentionally creating wakes to disrupt spearing and often swamping or ramming spearers' boats.[120] The DNR wardens were too badly outnumbered to provide effective protection, and one spearer reported being shot at on two separate occasions that spring.[121]

Protestors at boat landings in the spring of 1989 became even more aggressive than in past years, even as law enforcement efforts escalated to include the routine presence of National Guard helicopters. Members of PARR and STA sought to portray themselves as the successors of the civil rights movement, and they described their behaviors as acts of civil disobedience.[122] They frequently crossed police lines and were arrested for disorderly conduct or obstruction. On the first day of spearing season, April 23, 1989, protestors were at the landings throwing rocks, shouting racial slurs, issuing threats, and again carrying signs with racist, anti-Indian, and anti-treaty slogans; more than two hundred protestors were arrested that day.[123] Later that week, thirty-five protestors were arrested for crossing police lines and interfering with law enforcement's efforts to ensure safe harvest.[124]

A news story broke on April 28, 1989, that anti-treaty forces had placed thirty-thousand-dollar bounties on both Tom Maulson and Mike Allen. That night at Big Arbor Vitae Lake, police struggled to hold back surging crowds of protestors who alternately shouted "KGB" at spearers and recited the Pledge of Allegiance.[125] Eventually police ordered everyone from the landings, informing the crowd that the spearers had already left the lake via another landing. Instead, as members of Witness for Non-Violence learned the next day, the spearers remained on the lake only to be confronted by an angry, restless mob as they attempted to come in. Gibby Chapman's car, boat, and trailer were run off the road on the way back to the reservation, and although an arrest was made, no charges were filed.[126]

At North Twin Lake the next night, April 29, 1989, between six hundred and a thousand protestors converged at the landings, where they threw rocks and used high-powered slingshots to fire shots at spearers.[127] An estimated eight hundred protestors gathered at Plum Lake, where they shouted that "the only good Indian is a dead Indian," threw stones at spearers, and damaged some of their vehicles, while at other landings, protestors attacked police and were later charged with felonies.[128]

On the night of April 30, 1989, spearers and witnesses withdrew from Lake Tomahawk without spearing and went instead to Lake Minocqua, using a downtown landing. The police failed to keep the protestors, who outnumbered the spearers and their supporters eight to one, cordoned off in a separate area. They also failed to keep individual protestors from surging past their lines to taunt spearers, particularly Tom Maulson, at close range. The threat of violence was in the air, and protestors directed racial, gender-related, and personal taunts and threats at spearers and Witness members.[129] That evening, shots were fired at spearers on Lower Eau Claire Lake, and spearers on Catfish Lake encountered a heavy hail of rocks as they came off the lake.[130]

On May 2, 1989, an exasperated Mike Allen threatened to increase his band's catch to the full safe harvest level, the maximum allowed by the courts for conservation purposes, if the state continued to fail to provide adequate protection for spearers, their families, and their vehicles, including providing police escort from the landings.[131] "My people are suffering. We are under incredible physical and verbal attack," Allen said.[132] Spearers and treaty rights supporters had long been arguing that the administration needed to earmark funds for law enforcement to be able "to protect Chippewa spearfishers and to arrest, prosecute, and incarcerate those who would deny them their rights."[133] Undaunted by Lac du Flambeau's renewed determination and the claims of their allies, Dean Crist of STA indicated that he intended to close down spearing for a weekend, even if it meant more arrests. This comment, made to 150 supporters, was repeated by the media, further raising tensions for the upcoming weekend by essentially daring the Lac du Flambeau to spear.[134]

The official position of the State of Wisconsin was one of grave concern. Governor Thompson again seemingly sided with the protestors as he asked the tribes to end the spearing season early before the sport fishing season began.[135] When they refused, the state Republican Party chair, Donald K. Stitt of Port Washington, called upon Thompson to declare a state of emergency and close northern lakes to fishing of all forms.[136] Thompson responded by directing the attorney general to file two motions in federal court, one to stop Lac du Flambeau from taking 100 percent of the safe harvest and another to secure an injunction against spearing after midnight on May 5, the night before the fishing season opened for anglers.[137] Thompson alleged that "public safety was at risk" and explained that "the state lacks the capacity to provide an adequate level of on-water enforcement and protection."[138] It was preferable, the governor proclaimed, to halt spearing rather than to call out the National Guard.

Concerns for public safety were among several justifications the state provided for its efforts to seek an injunction against the exercise of treaty rights, including off-reservation spearfishing. Although ostensibly intended in the interest of public safety, an assistant attorney general explained the intent was "to protect fish resources," suggesting a political as well as a legal aspect to the maneuver.[139] James Klauser, secretary of administration, indicated that if Judge Barbara Crabb ruled against the state, Thompson "would do everything within his constitutional authority to stop spearfishing."[140] The state's statements and actions continued to send mixed messages to the public, but many strongly believed its allegiances were with the protestors.

When the state's request for an injunction came before Judge Crabb on Friday, May 5, 1989, Thompson took the witness stand himself to explain that public safety was at serious risk because state law enforcement officers were "unable and in some cases, unwilling, to guarantee the protection of the tribes in the exercise of their lawful rights."[141] As attorney Brian Pierson who represented the tribes explains, instead of seeking to enjoin those seeking to interfere with lawful activities, the governor "actually went into court with a straight face and said, 'Your Honor, we have a crisis situation here, someone is going to get killed. Here's what we think you ought to do, prohibit the tribal members from going off and exercising their rights.'"[142]

Judge Crabb explained that it was her responsibility "to enforce the law and the rights of all people under the law."[143] She responded to the protestors' charge, implicitly endorsed by the state, that the Ojibwe people had "unequal rights" by explaining, "They have the same rights as any other resident of the United States to enter into contractual agreements and to go to court to enforce their rights under those contracts." She noted the court had previously ruled that the Lake Superior Band of Chippewa had retained rights to hunt, fish, and gather when they signed land cession treaties. She also noted the rights to spear walleyes were limited by the DNR's own determination of safe harvest. Judge Crabb stressed that the Chippewas "have the same rights as any other resident of this state to seek the state's protection in exercising their lawful rights."[144] Addressing the protestors directly, Judge Crabb argued "the fact that some are acting illegally and creating unjustified fears of violence does not justify abridging the rights of those who have done nothing illegal or improper."[145] She refused to allow "violent and lawless protests" to proscribe the ability to exercise reserved rights, asking, "What kind of country would we have if brave people had not faced down the prejudiced, the violent, and the lawless in the 1960s? What kind will we become if we do not do the same today?"[146] With these admonitions, the court refused the injunction.

The night of the court's refusal was cold and windy, with falling snow and wind chills below zero, creating poor conditions for spearing.[147] Members of the Wa-Swa-Gon Treaty Association and elected officials within tribal government at Lac du Flambeau, including Chairman Mike Allen, had met earlier in the week and decided to declare their intention to spear on nine off-reservation lakes.[148] Nick Hockings explained that they would not normally spear under such difficult weather conditions, but they were determined to do so on Friday night largely in response to STA's pledge to prevent spearing for a weekend.[149] Crist had reiterated that pledge that afternoon before approximately five hundred people at a rally in Arbor Vitae, intending to close down spearing by breaking through police lines and occupying the landing.[150] As a result, Trout Lake, one of the nine named lakes, became the scene of the most violent conflict to date.

Tom Maulson would remember that night on Trout Lake, May 5, 1989, as the most dangerous night on the lakes of any spearing season.[151] In response to Crist's call to arms, an estimated fifteen hundred protestors arrived at the boat landing, and the initial police presence of 90 officers needed to be increased to a force of between 250 and 350.[152] The crowd was "barely contained by snow fences, screaming usually from the dark of trees enclosing the strips of concrete that stretched into the shallow water of Trout Lake," throwing rocks and shouting racial epithets. The protestors chanted "bullshit" increasingly loudly, and "the police grew more vigilant and visibly nervous."[153] Many protestors, in response to the court's ruling from earlier that day, carried signs with the new slogan, "Save a Walleye, Spear a Crabb."[154]

Nesper recalls that "the night oscillated wildly between the boredom of standing around without focus for long periods of time in the early spring cold and the sudden fear of not knowing that would happen when half a dozen police would suddenly erupt from around the snow fences and forcibly arrest a protestor."[155] In the crowd, "emotional states were fragile and shifting" as some "laughed and were enjoying themselves," some looked on, some were "visibly drunk," and "many appeared to be afraid."[156] The protestors repeatedly surged against the police lines, threatening the spearers and further escalating tensions. The *Milwaukee Sentinel* reported at least three injuries and more than one hundred arrests after "officers swung riot sticks and several protestors fell to the ground as a wave of demonstrators broke through police lines and pandemonium broke loose."[157] The events at Trout Lake seemed to confirm the fears on all sides that someone would be killed at one of the landings.

The spearers and their supporters remember that night vividly. Maulson recalls, "They could have killed us all, what they was saying that that is what they wanted to do."[158] He had brought an M-1 rifle with him that night, took the clips, but left the rifle in his truck. Gibby Chapman echoed Maulson's sentiment: "We thought they were going to kill us."[159] He recalls, "I was apprehensive when they broke through the police line," explaining that he and his fellow spearers "grabbed things to protect ourselves and walked up toward them with the lake to our backs and they stopped."[160] Perhaps emblematic of the seriousness of the situation, a man from Lac du Flambeau stayed in his truck with a loaded rifle behind the seat, believing they were going to be killed, and fully prepared to fire on the threatening crowd.[161] Nesper reports the man never picked up the weapon because a gust wind off the lake forced the protestors to the ground. As Chapman recalled, protestors "went down, they didn't sit down, but they went down. It was a spirit came through there.'"[162]

More than one hundred protestors were arrested, mostly for acts of civil disobedience. The protestors never succeeded in overrunning the landing as police repeatedly drove them back, prodding them with nightsticks.[163] That night, fourteen spearers harvested 175 walleyes and 27 muskies, 42 percent of the tribal quota.[164] Ultimately, the unseasonably cool weather kept the crowd sizes at the boat landings lower than projected. James Klauser, an aide to Thompson, remarked, "fortunately, Mother Nature cooperated better than Mother Crabb," suggesting the administration continued to view the court as an adversary.[165]

As the state fishing season opened for anglers on May 6, 1989, Wa-Swa-Gon, AIM, and the Lac du Flambeau tribal government held what they described as a "rally and feast to welcome non-Indian anglers to Wisconsin for the opening of the fishing season" at the Lac du Flambeau Community Center.[166] Allen spoke of the event as emblematic of "traditional Ojibwe generosity" and as "an opportunity for people of goodwill, Indian and non-Indian alike, to gather in solidarity against the outpouring of racial hatred that has been directed against us."[167] In order to ensure safety, tribal police stopped vehicles entering the reservation, searching for weapons.[168] Eddie Benton-Banai, a spiritual leader from Lac Courte Oreilles and one of the founding members of AIM, opened with a prayer ceremony. Speakers at the rally included important cultural and political leaders from Ojibwe communities as well as key Native and non-Native allies representing various organizations. Despite a delay due to a bomb threat, nearly fifteen hundred people attended the rally, feast, and powwow that evening.[169]

After the rally, a caravan of two hundred to three hundred cars left Lac du Flambeau for Butternut Lake, carrying an estimated fifteen hundred people. Treaty rights supporters overheard protestors saying to each other via CB radio, "Oh my God, the whole Ojibwe Nation is on the move."[170] A videotape shot by Lac du Flambeau tribal members shows a crowded boat landing where Ojibwe people and their allies well outnumbered the estimated six hundred protestors standing behind a snow fence erected by police, who had a force of 250 officers on hand.[171] The lake itself was crowded as well, with thirty protestor boats, twenty-nine DNR boats on patrol, and eight boats used by the spearers themselves.[172] Protestors taunted, "Go back to where you fucking came from!" and "Go back to your fucking reservation." Some chanted, "Equal rights! Equal rights!" as supporters chanted back, "Treaty rights! Treaty rights!" Slowly the men with the AIM drum began to move onto the small hill near the water, singing as they moved through the crowd, eventually displacing the protestors who had been standing there. That night, twenty-four spearers had harvested sixty-three walleye by the time they finished at 11 p.m.[173]

At a press conference the following day, Mike Allen declared a temporary end to the spearing season. The rally "showed the State that there is strong support for us against racism and in support of the treaties," he said, adding, "we can, if pressed, outnumber the racists at the landings."[174] Allen argued the Ojibwe people had demonstrated they would not yield to "empty promises from state politicians," noting that the federal court "will not be intimidated either" and "racial violence can't bully us into surrendering the right."[175] He asserted that the decision to end the spearfishing season was made in, by, and for Lac du Flambeau. He concluded by stating that it represented "a gesture of good will that neither the state officials nor the people of northern Wisconsin deserve, but that we are freely offering them anyway."[176] Nesper writes, "In 1989, STA and PARR were defeated in their home territories and largely on Indian terms, with Indians deploying both spiritual and material resources to gain an unforgettable victory."[177] Wisconsin's most violent spearfishing season was now officially over.

The Thompson administration turned its attention to other avenues for addressing the controversy. On May 9, 1989, Thompson met with the state's congressional delegation and the US secretary of the interior to request federal assistance.[178] He found federal officials to be "adamantly opposed to any attempt to abrogate, or unilaterally modify the government treaties."[179] The congressional delegation urged Thompson to seek an "agreement in which the tribes would agree to curtail spearing in exchange for money or social-economic programs."[180] The administration spent much of the remainder of the year negotiating with the tribal government for Lac du Flambeau, the band most actively engaged in spearfishing. Despite pressing economic needs on the reservation and divided political allegiances between the tribal council and Wa-Swa-Gon, the tribal membership at Lac du Flambeau, like at Mole Lake, defeated the agreement when it came to referendum.[181] The defeat left Thompson, Attorney General Hanaway, and DNR Secretary Carroll D. "Buzz" Besadny "stunned, dispirited, at a loss, if not for words, then for ideas of optimism" as they explained to the editors and publishers of the *Wisconsin State Journal* that the treaty rights controversy remained the state's most pressing problem.[182] Following the vote to reject the agreement, the state no longer had the upper hand.

Looking back on the 1989 season, authors Rick Whaley and Walter Bresette write, "Witnesses and numerous members of the press broke the taboo on the vile words and violence of the protests."[183] Members of Wa-Swa-Gon and Witness for Non-Violence stood together, and as member Anita Koser noted, they "showed us not all non-Indians hate us and want to harm us."[184] An editorial in the *Milwaukee Sentinel* declared that the

"terribly ugly side" to the treaty rights controversy "shames the state."[185]
The editorial described "insults that can only be defined as racist," including "spear a pregnant squaw, save a walleye," from a Vilas County boat
landing, and noted how "children in grade school were drawing pictures of
Indians being shot or speared."[186] Such rhetoric was "a sign that for every
spearfishing protestor who has valid concerns about the impact of spearing on the northland's economy, livelihoods and resource conservation,
there is pure hate in the hearts of others."[187] The *Wisconsin State Journal*
warned that another spring like 1989 "threatens the peace and potential
prosperity of Wisconsin's North Woods. The conflict also threatens to
tarnish Wisconsin's national image as a progressive state and undercuts
the apparent popularity of Thompson, a first term Republican preparing
for a re-election campaign."[188]

1990–1991: THE TIDE TURNS

After the 1989 spearing season, the dynamics changed. The media came to
view the matter as "a conflict of cultures, not a battle over resources," and
network and cable news footage from Wisconsin boat landings increasingly
appalled state residents and would-be tourists. One report included an
interview with a Chicago family who said they would stop vacationing
in northern Wisconsin, "not because of spearfishing, but because of the
racist displays surrounding it."[189] Eleven northern chambers of commerce
came out against the protestors in early 1990, stating that "continued
interference with the exercise of treaty rights threatens the social and
economic balance of northern Wisconsin," a move that so incensed the
town of Arbor Vitae that citizens threatened to withhold ten thousand
dollars from the Vilas County Chamber of Commerce.[190] The Wisconsin
Council of Churches held a press conference declaring its support for
Ojibwe treaty rights.[191] Leadership from the business community and a
growing effort from churches helped to turn the tide against previously
popular and politically safe anti–treaty rights positions.

Within sportsmen's and natural resources circles, many advocates
experienced a change of heart and pursued new, cooperative strategies.
Robert Herbst, national president of Trout Unlimited, Inc., had been
actively engaged in opposing treaty rights in Washington, Minnesota, and

Alaska but commented in 1990 that "there are now global environmental concerns, which demand our united attention. The magnitude of problems we jointly face make it imperative that we act as partners for the good of the resource itself, and not for the selfishness in each of us." This line of thinking led both Herbst and Trout Unlimited to end their opposition to treaty rights and advocate for comanagement.[192]

Racist and violent incidents continued to occur after the 1989 season, but as Witness for Non-Violence noted in its 1990 report, racism "was more hidden from the media and tended to be coupled with threats of physical and sexual violence."[193] The Witness report noted progress insofar as openly racist behavior had become "less publicly acceptable," at least in part due to condemnations from the chambers of commerce and churches.[194] Importantly, Witness for Non-Violence noted, "The Wisconsin State Legislature contributed to a long-term solution to institutional racism in the public schools by passing the American Indian Studies Committee Education Bill."[195] This attempt to craft an educational policy solution was already reported as having public policy effects, and Witness members further hoped to engage DPI staff in providing training on "Native American culture in the State of Wisconsin."[196]

In 1991, the federal courts vindicated spearers' and their supporters' sense that racism motivated the actions taken by STA, its leaders, and members, dating back to the late 1980s. The Lac du Flambeau Band and Wa-Swa-Gon, with assistance from the American Civil Liberties Union, successfully sued Dean Crist and other individuals associated with STA, as well as the organization itself.[197] Judge Crabb issued an injunction against STA members' activities, including assaults on tribal members, swamping their boats, and all other actions that were part of "a racially motivated campaign of violence and intimidation . . . to make it difficult or impossible for them to spear fish."[198] The court noted, "The stench of racism is unmistakable in this case."[199] Should they violate the injunction, the court warned, they would face prosecution under federal civil rights laws instead of the local justice system.[200] As lead attorney Brian Pierson explained, "the fig leaf was off" because "all of this pretense about equal rights or protecting the resource that Crist had featured in his public statements and that had been picked up by politicians and the newspapers just sort of fell away when you got a federal court calling it what it was."[201]

With Judge Crabb's ruling, the most virulently racist of the anti-treaty organizations was all but shut down by the time the *Voigt* litigation was complete, and as the numbers of protestors dwindled, so did the media presence.[202]

—||—

From the time the federal courts handed down the *Voigt* decision in 1983 until the early 1990s, tensions escalated, the number of violent incidents increased, and the possibility that someone would be killed as a result of those incidents became increasingly real.[203] The widespread public ignorance that guided and sustained anti-treaty organizations' efforts to disrupt the lawful exercise of newly affirmed treaty rights fueled a divisive public controversy and prompted dramatic, sensationalized coverage from local, state, and national media. The high-profile nature of these protests led to significant pressure by the State of Wisconsin on the Ojibwe bands to lease their usufructuary rights, restrict their harvest, or otherwise discontinue the exercise of their rights "all because a small group, often acting illegally, create[d] disturbances in opposition to the Chippewas' federally recognized legal rights."[204]

The state was hardly a neutral party itself. There was widespread belief among the Ojibwe and their allies that the DNR had manipulated bag limits in order to blame Ojibwe spearing for the reduction. Thompson and other administration officials were sympathetic to the anti–treaty rights protestors; critics alleged the governor had attended PARR and STA meetings while refusing invitations to attend meetings of the Wa-Swa-Gon Treaty Association.[205] The controversy tore apart communities, involved millions of dollars of public expense in law enforcement and courts costs, harmed businesses, and damaged Wisconsin's reputation, ultimately leading many formerly disparate segments of society to collaborate to find a solution.

It is no surprise that Act 31 emerged in 1989. Escalating tensions that year created a critical interest convergence among business leaders, community members, clergy, elected officials on both sides of the aisle, and the Ojibwe people and their allies, which led to the decision to look to the public schools as the basis for a solution. Graduates of Wisconsin schools had little knowledge and awareness of historical or contemporary American Indian issues, and advocates viewed this ignorance as a major contributing factor to racism and violence. They hoped an educational policy solution would restore the social fabric, heal existing wounds, and re-establish a positive reputation and business climate. In this respect, the violence and controversy surrounding the affirmation of treaty rights was one of the tangled roots of Act 31.

CHAPTER 5

COMMISSIONING
A SOLUTION

In the mid-1980s, in the wake of the *Voigt* decision, actions were taking place on several fronts. Leaders of the six Ojibwe bands in Wisconsin, along with their attorneys, pursued legal strategies for asserting, defining, and regulating treaty rights. Throughout the 1980s, Ojibwe tribal members in Wisconsin became increasingly active in exercising treaty rights, resuming practices from time immemorial. Their contemporaries also included those who recognized the public's limited understanding of these issues and foresaw the violent controversy that would ensue. They began to organize within months of the *Voigt* decision as negotiations for the first off-reservation deer hunt and spearfishing seasons were underway. These boards and commissions would come to play key roles in developing a legislative response to the Walleye War and the underlying ignorance, racism, and prejudice that fueled it.

Ronald N. Satz was in his second year as the dean of Graduate Studies and University Research at the University of Wisconsin–Eau Claire in 1984 when Veda Stone asked him to serve with her on the Ad Hoc Commission on Racism in Northern Wisconsin. Satz, a historian who specialized in American Indian history and the history of federal Indian policy, would bring an important perspective to the commission, and Veda Stone was not someone who easily took no for an answer. It was Stone's persistence as a staunch ally of American Indian peoples that led the governing board of the Lac Courte Oreilles Band of Lake Superior Chippewa to ask her to chair the commission.

Stone was an educator and social worker, and her life's work included nearly four decades of service to tribal communities. She was particularly close to the people of Bad River, who adopted her and recognized her with the name Beneshiohgezhegokway, "Thunderbird Sky Woman." In 1984, Stone was nearing the end of her professional career, serving as the director of Arts and Sciences Outreach at UW–Eau Claire. She had begun her work with tribal communities as a community service consultant in northwestern Wisconsin in the late 1950s. During the 1970s, Stone founded programs for American Indians at the University of Wisconsin–River Falls, Mount Senario College, and the University of Wisconsin–Eau Claire, where she also served as the first director of the American Indian Studies program.[1] She remained active in the lives of American Indian university students until the end of her life, and "Veda stories" provided a common bond among students from multiple generations and campuses.

CONTROVERSY OVER *VOIGT*

The 1983 *Voigt* decision, which affirmed "the sanctity of the treaties and the right of the Indians to hunt, fish, and gather on and off their reservations on public lands in ceded territory," was met with immediate controversy.[2] The public's negative reaction was the product of educational experiences broadly shared by generations of Wisconsin students, schooling that left them largely unaware of the history, culture, tribal sovereignty, and reserved treaty rights of their Ojibwe neighbors. Wisconsin citizens were effectively left, to paraphrase Bishop William Wantland, ignorant of their own ignorance, a situation that fueled misperceptions, including ideas about "special rights" and other purported social advantages enjoyed by American Indian people.[3] Sociologist George Lipsitz locates this violent backlash within "a broader racial project, one that had been sustained, honed and refined throughout the nation in populist white supremacist campaigns against school desegregation, affirmative action and social services for immigrants."[4] Media observers linked the violent protests to "the divisive class and racial animosities prevalent in the Reagan-Bush era" and to a lack of accurate information about Native people.[5] The protests themselves changed the way outsiders viewed Wisconsin, in turn forcing Wisconsin residents to reconsider how they viewed themselves.

AD HOC COMMISSION ON RACISM IN NORTHERN WISCONSIN

The first concrete recommendations for a curriculum policy solution to address racism and public ignorance related to tribal sovereignty and treaty rights came from the Ad Hoc Commission on Racism in Northern Wisconsin. The tribal governing board of the Lac Courte Oreilles Band of Lake Superior Chippewa, whose members launched the resurgence of the exercise of usufructuary rights, convened the commission on September 5, 1984. Its directive was to "study the incidence, prevalence, and impact of alleged racism, prejudice, and discrimination" on the tribe and its members by holding a hearing and issuing a report with its findings and recommendations.[6]

The commission's membership was comprised of volunteers invited to participate based on their roles in churches, educational institutions, and civil rights organizations, with Veda Stone as chair.[7] The Office of the Governor, the Wisconsin Indian Resource Council, and the Lac Courte Oreilles Ojibwa Community College, which provided administrative support, signed on as sponsors shortly after the commission was established. To guide their inquiry, commissioners developed a specific definition of racism: "an ideologically indefensible belief in the inherent superiority of a particular segment of the population" that denies the "basic equality of humankind and correlates ability and virtue with physical or cultural traits and characteristics."[8] Commissioners would use this definition as a rubric for analyzing the overall racial climate as well as individual incidents. For the commission, the roots of racism included "misinformation (stereotyping), fear (of people and behavior which is different), and hatred (a frequent manifestation of suppressed fear or anger)."[9] The commission viewed racism as harmful to all, both oppressor and oppressed, because it "feeds on and fosters ignorance, fear, and hurt" and thus "saps the creativity, rationality and the health of mind and spirit of both the victims of racism and the racist group or individual."[10] With this definition in mind, the commission began its investigation.

The commission held a public hearing on October 29–30, 1984, at Telemark Lodge in Cable, Wisconsin. Local newspapers had published hearing notices, and people wishing to testify were asked to make arrangements in advance through Lac Courte Oreilles Ojibwa Community

College. Its members heard testimony from forty-two witnesses whose sworn statements were recorded verbatim by a certified court reporter and videotaped by a commercial firm. Witnesses had also submitted twenty-three artifacts, including photographs, print documents, audio recordings, signs, and articles of clothing.[11] The commission allowed an additional seven days for written statements or documents to be added to the official record before it began to apply its definition of racism to evaluate the material provided.[12]

In its report, issued on November 30, 1984, the Ad Hoc Commission on Racism concluded that there was a significant level of anti-Indian racism in northern Wisconsin and that these sentiments were pervasive in many social institutions, including schools, churches, and the media. The report identified several themes: education, economic effects, government, mass media, social and psychological aspects, and religion.[13] Commissioners made specific recommendations relative to each category, frequently identifying and calling on other entities and organizations, including schools, churches, businesses, civic organizations, and the media itself to become active partners in taking positive steps to address latent and active racial animosity against Native people. Each recommendation involved addressing the root causes of racism—misinformation, fear, and hatred—by enlisting partners in existing social institutions to correct misconceptions and misinformation. This strategy offered the added benefit of providing opportunities for positive interaction between Native and non-Native communities.

The education section of the report opened with this statement: "Running like a thread through the testimony at the hearing was the school, the church and the home as the sources of racism. Also running like a thread between the lines was the desperate need for education and dialogue."[14] The commission's recommendations based on this "desperate need" proved to be the start of a policy dialogue that would culminate in the passage of new curricular requirements related to Wisconsin Indian history, culture, and tribal sovereignty—Act 31.

"Recognizing that while the Indian world has been under constant siege for generations," the report continued, "it never the less is very much alive and here to stay." Because large segments of the general public have come to view Native people as "aliens in their own land," the commission urged K-12 schools and university teacher education programs to develop "well taught courses on tribal sovereignty, the treaties, Indian culture and history" in order to "stem the current racism that exists in Wisconsin." The commission noted that too many K-12 teachers were ill-prepared to teach such a course and were even fearful of doing so. University faculty too often shared these fears, saying "they do not know them, do not understand them and therefore, do not wish to be bothered with them." Of the schools themselves, the commission argued that public school policies and practices had failed to incorporate concepts related to Native peoples.[15] The report identified the lack of learning opportunities as both a cause and an effect of racism.

The commission made a number of official recommendations. It addressed its first recommendation to the American Indian Language and Culture Education Board, which it described as "appointed by the governor, and responsible to Indian people." The report called upon the board to urge all schools in Wisconsin "to begin without delay to develop and implement courses that teach the meaning of tribal sovereignty, Wisconsin Indian Treaties [sic] and Wisconsin Indian culture and history." In doing so, the commission recommended that the board highlight "the problems [sic] emergency nature" and emphasize that assistance is available for schools to address it.[16] It also recognized the essential role of the Department of Public Instruction (DPI) and urged the board to "be firm" in dealing with the agency so that it would "take immediate steps to put whatever pressure is possible on schools to develop and strengthen their Wisconsin Indian programs."[17] The report reflects faith in DPI's power to drive change, but also cast doubt on its willingness to do so.

Next, the commission called on the Great Lakes Inter-Tribal Council (GLITC), a consortium of federally recognized tribal governments in the state plus one tribe in Michigan, to "reactivate its Education Committee under such structure that will ensure its continuance." It asked GLITC to make combating racism its top priority and "to develop a well thought out plan with all deliberate speed." The commission recommended that the re-established education committee "become active and visible in the state," perhaps anticipating a need for ongoing involvement.[18] (The reconstituted Great Lakes Inter-Tribal Council Education Committee would become the Wisconsin Indian Education Association in 1985.)

The commission's next recommendation advised the University of Wisconsin System to ensure that state universities be made aware of the problem and prepare to "positively respond to this urgent need." Again, perhaps reflecting more belief in the institution's ability to respond than its willingness to do so, the commission stated, "A time limit should be placed on the response." The commission colorfully called on the teacher training programs in the system to "take a look with a 'hydrochloric' eye at what they are teaching their prospective teachers." The report asked, "Where are these prospective teachers taught facts on tribal sovereignty, and treaties affecting Wisconsin Indians, Indian culture, history and current Indian concerns? What can be done NOW and in the coming years?"[19] The commission recognized the lack of understanding of these key concerns as a systemic issue, and it viewed meaningful involvement by teacher training institutions as a means to broaden the scope of the policy response and contribute an intergenerational quality to the effort.

In a similar vein, the commission recommended the involvement of private and parochial institutions. It recommended that the Wisconsin Association of Independent Colleges and Universities "be questioned also as to what they are doing" to provide their graduates with instruction on "tribal sovereignty, and treaties affecting Wisconsin Indians, Indian culture, history and current Indian concerns." The commission asked, "How are you training your teachers? How are you informing students if situations arise concerning racism? What can you do now and in the coming years?" The Ad Hoc Commission on Racism also recommended the involvement of the "Wisconsin Diocesan, Lutheran, and other private grade and high schools concerning education on Wisconsin Indian treaties, sovereignty, etc."[20] These recommendations indicate a concern for a comprehensive solution that provided opportunities to learn about these key concerns in all K-12 schools and teacher education programs in the state, whether public, private, or parochial.

For those already in the profession, the commission recommended a series of "in-service training programs" for K-12 teachers and "sensitivity sessions" for college and university professors. The report referenced testimony to a "Wisconsin brand of racism" that was "as virulent as the early stages of Hitlerism," and stated, "We need to attack it on all fronts." This section concluded by noting, "The higher educational institutions are not immune from racists."[21] The commission recognized educational institutions as part of the same social fabric and as affected by the same social ills as the broader society. Therefore, it recommended that any significant policy solution would need to address ongoing professional development opportunities at all levels.

A comprehensive policy solution, the commission noted, would also need to provide expanded learning opportunities for the general public. It first called on schools, colleges, and universities to publicize their efforts. The commission recognized the importance of the media in raising public awareness and understanding. It recommended developing contacts with the media "on all levels," feeding "factual information" to the media and actively encouraging media involvement. Unlike previous recommendations, this section does not name specific targets, perhaps because the commission sought to engage a broader range of allies.

Beyond making recommendations, the report also identified a number of "specific problem areas which . . . act as contributing factors toward creating a racist climate in Wisconsin schools." This section defined problems and offered suggestions related to a wide range of ongoing educational concerns across Wisconsin, including absenteeism and dropout rates in K-12 schools and in higher education, "learning disabilities and education handicapping conditions," poor-quality instruction, irrelevant and inappropriate curriculum materials, lack of opportunities for meaningful parental and community involvement in decision making, "emotional and behavioral problems which inhibit [students'] capacity to learn in the public school setting," and, specific to tribal members, issues related to the "deterioration of the traditional Indian family structure."[22] Many of these concerns reflect broad social issues that impact schooling, and most look to use schools to address them in a positive way. Whether the commission's concerns were directly linked to school-related concerns, its report showed great faith in the ability of educational institutions to serve as engines of social change.

Some of the "contributing factors" the commission referred to clearly fostered the widespread public ignorance of Wisconsin Indian history, culture, treaties, and tribal sovereignty.[23] The commission's report asserted that "over the last three years, evidence of both overt and covert racism has increased," saying it is "often couched in the guise of some form of socio-intellectual elitism." The report stated,

"Minority students, and staff, are kept effectively within certain defined 'caste' barriers." It charged that the resulting lack of opportunities arose because "university administrators and senior faculty verbalize 'equal opportunity' and 'acceptance' of minorities" yet "their actions far too often do not match their words."[24] To remedy these situations, the commission sought to reform both public and private colleges, universities, and teacher education institutions, and referred back to their specific recommendations regarding treaty rights.

The report recognized the failure of K-12 schools, colleges, and universities "to incorporate within their curricula and within school-related activities aspects of the rich heritage and many contributions of the American Indian cultures" as another factor contributing to "a racist climate in Wisconsin schools." The commission offered further recommendations to remedy this situation. First, it called on schools to "develop educational units for classroom presentation which incorporate the cultures and history of the American Indian nations, particularly those having reservations within Wisconsin." It recommended "occasional programs illustrating or based upon Indian traditions," including "talks by Indian leaders, 'pow-wow' dance demonstrations, display of handicraft, selected movies, etc." The commission suggested that "classroom material ... including both textbooks and references should be screened" and asked schools to withdraw "materials demonstrating either overt or implied racism." Furthermore, it called on schools to "make effective use of Indian parent committees in the development of curricula and programs."[25] This deceptively simple set of recommendations would require schools to reconsider how they answer implicit questions about whose knowledge counts and how it is made legitimate in schools.

The commission noted that its recommendations to schools "are meant to be on-going activities on the various levels as suggested." It acknowledged that "while great effort must be made on all levels to develop programs for immediate use, the importance is of long-range consistent efforts so that this situation does not arise again." A lasting solution would require "money and personnel," and it "means never forgetting that the human condition being what it is[,] that 'it can happen here' and that we must build strong programs in the 'school' and the 'church' so that the 'home' can be the source of understanding and compassion for those who are different."[26] The efforts of the Ad Hoc Commission on Racism, which began as a local effort by a tribal government asserting its sovereignty to study the impact of racism against Native people, soon took on broader impact as regional and statewide institutions joined the effort. The political legitimacy afforded to the commission lent credence to its recommendations and ultimately informed the development of statutory changes reshaping state-level curriculum policy.

These efforts, which occurred early in the post-*Voigt* era, provide insights into the racism that already existed in the state and yield a sort of baseline against which later anti-treaty attitudes and actions can be compared. Many of the commission's recommendations were ultimately implemented to some degree, and its ideas on education strongly informed the development of an educational policy solution through Act 31. The pace of implementation did not match the commission's sense of urgency, however. Commissioner Bishop William Wantland testified to the Wisconsin Advisory Committee to the United States Commission on Civil Rights in 1989, before Act 31 was passed, that the body's recommendations had been ignored.[27]

United States Commission on Civil Rights, 1984

On December 4, 1984, not long after the Ad Hoc Commission on Racism in Northern Wisconsin convened, the Wisconsin Advisory Committee to the United States Commission on Civil Rights conducted a community forum in Superior, Wisconsin, to investigate "problems between Indians and non-Indians in northern Wisconsin." The committee learned that "non-Indians' lack of information about treaty rights and their legal implications was a major problem," and it offered five recommendations targeting tribal members, the justice system, educational policy makers, and federal officials.

The first of the committee's recommendations was to distribute the commission's *American Indian Civil Rights Handbook* so that those affected might become better informed about their basic rights. They also called for "improvement in the quality and responsiveness of the State and local criminal justice systems" in addressing violations of the civil rights of Native people. Third, the committee sought new "material and exercises" to train law enforcement officers on the rights of Native people and improve their skills "in dealing with explosive situations." Fourth, it called upon the Wisconsin Department of Public Instruction to "promote improvement in the ability of local educational systems to provide accurate historical treatment of Indian rights issues." Last, in order to "clarify the unique status of Native Americans and encourage the use of appropriate enforcement and conciliation mechanisms," the committee called on the United States Commission on Civil Rights to "reaffirm" and distribute copies of its earlier report, *Indian Tribes: A Continuing Quest for Survival*.[28]

Like the Ad Hoc Commission on Racism, the Wisconsin Advisory Committee to the United States Commission on Civil Rights recommended a multifaceted approach to raising awareness and diffusing conflict. Instead, history would show that tensions escalated, rather than diffused, throughout the 1980s.

United States Commission on Civil Rights, 1989

Five years after its first report, while the 1989 spearing season was under way, the Wisconsin Advisory Committee to the United States Commission on Civil Rights reconvened in Wausau. At a community forum on April 29, the committee sought to "obtain information on discrimination against Chippewa Indians in northern Wisconsin" and to determine "the extent to which discrimination against Chippewa Indian people occurs due to resentment of their treaty rights."[29]

The committee received testimony from state officials Don Hanaway, the attorney general; Buck Martin, the governor's liaison for Indian affairs; and George E. Meyer, the enforcement administrator for the DNR.[30] Ojibwe representatives included James Schlender, executive director of GLIFWC; Tom Maulson, representing the Voigt Intertribal Task Force; and Michael Allen Jr., chairman of the Lac du Flambeau band.[31] Also testifying were Dean Crist, representing Stop Treaty Abuse; Rev. William Wantland, Episcopal bishop of the diocese of Eau Claire; Nick Van Der Puy, representing Citizens for Treaty Rights; Sarah Bacchus, from the Madison Treaty Rights Support Group; and Thomas Stricker, president of the St. Germain Chamber of Commerce and a resort owner.[32] In general, their testimony reflected the well-established positions of their respective organizations.

The committee's report, issued in December 1989, stated that "racism had intensified as tribes have gained legal victories and have pursued educational and commercial developments."[33] While the level of anti-Indian racism was already high in 1984, the exercise of off-reservation treaty rights in the coming years would exacerbate the situation significantly. The report highlights steps that state and local authorities took to protect the exercise of treaty rights, to address discrimination, and to raise public awareness.[34] The committee also provided additional recommendations intended to "encourage ongoing and constructive dialogue on the issues and provide an ameliorating effect on existing problems regarding this matter."[35] In most respects, these recommendations are substantially similar to or are anticipated by its 1984 report.

—||—

The actions of both the Ad Hoc Commission on Racism in Northern Wisconsin and the Wisconsin Advisory Committee to the United States Commission on Civil Rights highlight the extent to which the treaty rights controversy resulted in governmental responses at various levels. The formation of the Ad Hoc Commission was an exercise of sovereignty for the Lac Courte Oreilles Band of Chippewa. The involvement of the governor's office highlights the early and often contradictory role that the State of Wisconsin would play throughout the controversy. The federal government also had a role in addressing the situation through the United States Commission on Civil Rights.

Clearly, both commissions recognized the important role that education would play, both in terms of public information and more directly in terms of educational reforms addressing curriculum, teacher education, and professional development. While they were looking to schools, colleges, and universities to address a broad social problem, their responses suggested that shortcomings in the public educational system contributed to ignorance and fueled outrage. The multifaceted responses envisioned by these organizations closely resemble the policy framework enacted through the biennial budget act, 1989 Act 31.

PART 3

SOCIAL STUDIES
ON THE NATIONAL STAGE

CHAPTER 6

CURRICULUM POLICY AND AMERICAN INDIANS, 1916–1967

R ed Cliff Ojibwe author, activist, and educator Walt Bresette observed
that when the Seventh Circuit issued the *Voigt* decision, "No one in
the state was prepared—academically, intellectually—for the court ruling.
Everyone acted as though the judges in Chicago *gave* to the Chippewa, out
of thin air, special rights when in fact the Chippewa court was consistent
with a long series of court decisions." He explained, "The state educational
system and the media simply didn't know American law much less Indian
law . . . so in the vacuum which was created by misinformation emerged
the ugly head of racism."[1]

For Bresette, the central issue was always what the general public knew
from schools and the mass media. This was not a new issue. Historian
David W. Saxe similarly observed that social studies educators' "deficit
of historical orientation" has "crippled the field" by limiting their ability
to respond to societal concerns.[2] Curricular requirements related to the
history, culture, and tribal sovereignty of the federally recognized tribes
and bands in Wisconsin as part of the social studies curriculum suggest
that those involved with developing Act 31 in response to social conflict
saw gaps in the social studies field.

A historical analysis of social studies education examines the merits of
those assertions in several ways. First, it considers the shifting relationship
between the locus of decision making and relative attention to national,
state, and local concerns in curriculum content. Second, it examines the
field's fickle relationship with sociopolitical concerns external to schools

and curriculum content. These two dynamics highlight how curriculum policy served to legitimate certain ideas as "official knowledge" and illustrates the implications of these decisions for what students attending public schools had the opportunity to learn about American Indians.[3]

According to education policy analyst Michael W. Apple, Americans have long sought to use schools "as mechanisms for improving society," intending to "accomplish with its children" those things the nation is "unable or unwilling to undertake with its adults."[4] Because the focus of social change is on the adults these students will become, Apple contends we must evaluate our instructional programs in social studies "by the behavior of our alumni."[5] During the 1980s in Wisconsin, some of those alumni were engaging in violent, racist protests on boat landings, and some were organizing opposition to those views and working in support of treaty rights. Most, however, stayed disengaged. While Act 31 is consistent with the national trend to use curriculum policy to respond to broad societal concerns, its level of specificity regarding curriculum content was unprecedented. In order to understand this policy shift and consider the effectiveness of instruction to bring about social change, it is necessary to examine several decades of contested curriculum policy by asking what and whose knowledge decision makers deemed worthy of inclusion in the curriculum. This baseline of recognized knowledge represents what those who were adults in the 1980s would have had an opportunity to learn in social studies classes.

OFFICIAL KNOWLEDGE

Educational policy makers at the national, state, and local levels are responsible for making decisions about what students learn in public schools. Dynamic relationships between policy initiatives at each level profoundly affect teaching and learning, yet throughout most of the twentieth century, information about American Indians was typically outside the boundaries of what policy makers legitimated as "official knowledge."[6] National organizations of interest include the National Education Association (NEA), the National Council for Social Studies (NCSS), and the Association for Supervision and Curriculum Development (ASCD), each of which played important agenda-setting roles in policy discussions, as did, to a lesser extent, their state-level counterparts. This chapter traces the major curriculum policy developments in the social studies field, identifying trends resulting from decisions made by national, state, and local policy makers that often reflected broad sociopolitical concerns only indirectly related to schooling. Curriculum policy priorities served to constrain opportunities to learn even the most basic information about American Indian history, culture, and tribal sovereignty.

"Official knowledge" consists of the ideas and concepts that the state chooses to adopt and transmit through its institutions, particularly but not exclusively public schools. Through statutes, administrative rules, instructional materials and practices, and official and unofficial institutional customs, schools promote a "selective tradition" that represents "some group's vision of legitimate knowledge."[7] In this view, curriculum is "never simply a neutral assemblage of knowledge" but a product of dynamic power relations through which various social, cultural, and political groups are continually renegotiating curriculum policy.[8] Key questions used in analyzing the "politics of knowledge" and in determining what is legitimated as official knowledge include "what knowledge is of most worth?" and more importantly, "whose knowledge is of most worth?"[9] In social studies, this prompts the question, "Who gets to define what the United States (as well as the rest of the world) has been, is, and should be?"[10] For purposes of this chapter, the questions amount to knowledge about whom, whose knowledge, and whose perspectives on that knowledge are institutionally legitimated.

Before *Voigt*, only rarely did policy makers at any level consider American Indians worthy of inclusion in the curriculum, and even more rarely did curriculum content reflect an American Indian perspective. The resulting representations are characterized by absences and problematic presences such that American Indians are largely invisible and stereotypically portrayed when they are included.

NATIONAL, STATE, AND LOCAL POLICY DYNAMICS

Local control is a cherished ideal in Wisconsin, and it reflects the widely held principle that major curricular decisions should be made as locally as possible. Nonetheless, even in a local control state like Wisconsin, "educational practice has always been a product of the interplay of local, state, and national forces."[11] National curriculum policy conversations shape those at the state and local level, and ultimately shape instruction. As a result, "in some fundamental sense, curriculum is always simultaneously 'national,' 'state,' and 'local' in focus" because "state departments of education, state legislatures, national commissions and committees, and nationally marketed textbooks" all influence local curriculum decisions.[12] Textbooks themselves have functioned as one of the nationalizing forces affecting curriculum policy, due in large part to the market share of textbook adoption states, and, where local instructional objectives are poorly defined, they serve as a de facto national curriculum.[13]

National organizations have long shaped public schools, even as governance and funding mechanisms have remained local. The key ideas that have shaped policy decisions related to school governance and curriculum often emerged from national organizations such as the National Council for Social Studies, the Association for Supervision and Curriculum Development, and other professional associations. [14] The influence that the "federal government, educational foundations, publishers, professional associations, and education reformers" had on curriculum policy conversations increased in the wake of the Elementary and Secondary Education Act of 1965. As an essential part of President Johnson's War on Poverty, the Elementary and Secondary Education Act of 1965 dramatically expanded the federal role in public education, emphasizing high standards, equal opportunity, and accountability measures, while appropriating funds to carry out these new responsibilities.[15] Each of these entities continues to have strong influence on curriculum policy and other matters.[16]

State governments also play a key role in informing policy for local curriculum planning. District and school-based curriculum committees must be mindful of state laws requiring instruction in specific topics, typically the study of the home state and other topics in American history that may be of interest or importance at the state or local level.[17] As state legislatures "generated volumes of statutes related to education" in the 1970s and 1980s, shaping everything from school funding and special education, to student performance and academic standards, to teacher education and professional development, professional organizations stepped in to help schools make sense of the myriad requirements and ensure sound curriculum planning.[18] When key issues emerged affecting multiple states, professional organizations commonly formed national committees. In terms of curriculum policy, this shift risked placing key curriculum under the direction of those who generally lacked the interest and capacity to respond adequately to state-level requirements or were concerned solely with issues common to several states. A historical analysis of social studies curriculum policy highlights the interplay between those who shaped the field at various levels and shows how the multiplicity of influences established the context for the work of curriculum committees in Wisconsin.

Given all of these external influences and requirements, by the 1960s, local curriculum committees in Wisconsin and elsewhere were already heavily reliant on distant "experts" who were removed from and unfamiliar with state and local contexts.[19] Nonetheless, local curriculum committees remained responsible for developing curricula for their own students and communities.[20] Reformers at the national level called for a "modern social studies program" that was "cosmopolitan in character and global in scope," rather than dominated by assumptions regarding "an idyllic rural way of life" because, they assumed, most students would live in cities.[21] They advised local educators to recognize that social studies "touches the sensitivities of many" and to identify and address "potential sources of conflict" so they do not "develop into major areas of contention."[22] Curriculum committees were admonished to evaluate their efforts in terms of whether they led to "improved opportunities for pupils to learn."[23] Insofar as these concerns reflect interest in preparing students for life in a world that may be more cosmopolitan than their home community, they anticipate the 1989 Act 31 requirement that schools select instructional materials that reflect the cultural diversity and pluralistic nature of American society. Historical analysis of these considerations highlights intriguing links between past formulations of policy problems and more contemporary attempts to address them.

Curriculum Policy History

Education reformers have struggled to define the parameters of official knowledge for generations, and analyzing the history of curriculum policy can provide useful insights for understanding how decision makers' views of and responses to various issues and events affecting the nation came to define the field. Broadly speaking, "the historiography of social studies is one of contested curricular territory—territory that leaders define, constituents must vie for, and some people denounce."[24] This territory is the curriculum content that policy makers choose to legitimate as official knowledge, and its fluidity generally reflects changing relationships to and levels of engagement with sociopolitical concerns outside of schools. Demands for equality, along with changing immigration patterns, demographic shifts, and economic anxieties have contributed to shifting "demands for a curriculum of ethnic and cultural inclusion."[25] Overall, the twentieth-century history of social studies is perhaps best understood as an ongoing struggle to define the nature and purpose of the field, both in terms of its disciplinarity and its relationship to various crises and social movements.[26]

Throughout its existence, there has been a significant ongoing debate about the nature and purpose of social studies. At various points, the field has been defined as (1) "a merger of history, geography, civics, economics, sociology, and all other social sciences," (2) "a mishmash of courses such as career education, ethnic studies, gender studies, consumer education, environmental studies, peace education, character education, and drug education," and (3) "a field that defines its goals in terms of cultivating skills like decision making, interpersonal relations, and critical thinking, as well as the development of 'critical' attitudes like global awareness, environmental consciousness, multiculturalism, and gender equity."[27] An analysis of actual and missed opportunities to learn accurate and authentic information about American Indians illustrates the underlying arguments about the scope and purpose of social studies, how the field has been repeatedly redefined to address broad sociopolitical needs, and how a historical lack of connection between these themes led to absences and problematic presences in Wisconsin's social studies curriculum.

OFFICIAL KNOWLEDGE AND THE NATURE OF SOCIAL STUDIES

The emergence of *social studies* as an educational term dates only as far back as the early twentieth century, and many of its ongoing tensions are as old as the field itself. A close look at its origins and early decades shows how the parameters established by its founders continue to define what counts as official knowledge today. The National Education Association's Committee on Social Studies report, issued in 1916, established a scope and sequence for the new field, which merged history, civics, geography, and economics such that history was the central discipline, based in part on its place within both classical and modern courses of study.[28] This approach to social studies education was "basically conservative, narrative, expository," and it emphasized transmission of "selected aspects of the cultural heritage, which support the views of the dominant group at the time and which takes nationalistic loyalties."[29] From its inception, leaders in the field based this cultural transmission-oriented view of social studies on the need to assimilate an influx of recent immigrants. This concern, and the relative weakness and invisibility of American Indian nations at the turn of the century, effectively excluded curriculum content about tribal nationhood from the frame of official knowledge. Curriculum intended to emphasize the singularity of American culture and nationhood could hardly afford to place much value on politically and culturally distinct nations within the nation.

The origins of the term itself also suggest an inherently conservative, nationalistic purpose that deliberately selected and legitimated as official knowledge only those ideas that promoted the interest of dominant groups. Thomas Jesse Jones, chair of the National Education Association's Curriculum on Social Studies in 1916, was widely credited with coining the term "social studies." Jones was a former teacher of African American and American Indian students at Hampton Institute, and he had developed curriculum that prepared them solely for "vocational work and sought to keep them in the lower strata of society."[30] His curriculum "met the hegemonic political and social mandates of the time," exemplifying what many would later deem a social reproduction model.[31] In 1918, NEA's Cardinal Principles of Secondary Education further defined the goal of social studies education as "good citizenship" and declared "historical studies that did not contribute to social change had no value."[32] These progressive-era sentiments about the nature and purpose of public education rose and fell from favor over the next several decades, and social studies education continued to reflect ongoing debates about its scope, nature, and purpose.

An important event in the history of the social studies occurred in 1921 when leading educators in the field founded the National Council for Social Studies (NCSS). Since its founding, the organization has shaped teaching and learning through its conferences, publications, and efforts to set standards and develop and disseminate exemplary lessons. Throughout much of the early twentieth century, NCSS, like most social studies curriculum reformers, was generally aloof to contemporary sociopolitical concerns, preferring to focus on technical, instructional issues rather than those outside the classroom.[33] NCSS sometimes remained "silent on matters of great moment and squandered opportunities to lead," while at other times, the organization "staked out and vigorously supported prominent and right-minded positions."[34] Throughout its history, NCSS has been an important national influence in setting the curriculum policy agenda, a role it retains to this day.

SOCIAL STUDIES AND SOCIAL CRISES

Society often looks to social studies to address social issues and crises external to schooling itself. While the field was generally silent during the Great Depression, a scandal regarding "disgraceful" results of an American history test administered to college freshmen in the early 1940s sparked another round of controversy regarding the allegedly neglected role of history in social studies education.[35] As World War II unfolded, the nation began to view social studies quite differently, as exemplified by NCSS's 1943 pamphlet "The Social Studies Mobilize for Victory." In it, the NCSS's Committee on War and Education declared social studies to be "essential to the war effort" and called on the field to focus on "democracy, American traditions, world issues, and human diversity."[36] An October 1945 article titled "The Social Studies Look Beyond the War" and published in the NCSS journal *Social Education* staked a claim for contemporary relevance with an argument for educating world citizens and for "waging peace" by building "both the informational base and superstructure of understanding and attitudes" that are necessary to establish an informed citizenry.[37] Once again, American society expected schools to respond to broader contemporary concerns by adhering to a cultural transmission model of instruction.

The 1950s saw ferocious attacks on the perceived failures of public education, and in many respects, the curriculum policies of the 1950s were education-focused responses to broader societal issues. By the end of 1955, the United States was facing "a full-scale critique of public education" related to perceived neglect of the traditional academic disciplines, unfavorable comparisons to schools in the Soviet Union and Western Europe, the stalemate in the Korean War, and an ideological conflict about the purpose of schooling and core beliefs about human nature.

The biggest blow to American education in the 1950s came on October 4, 1957, when the Soviet Union launched Sputnik, because it "placed the United States in second place among those nations vying for world status" and "seemed to confirm the sorry state of American schooling to its critics."[38] The American media began to blame public education for what was widely viewed as the nation's inability to compete with the Soviet Union while political leaders lamented the state of American education and sought to refocus public education on scientific and technical fields.[39] The uproar over Sputnik, along with associated anxieties about the Cold War and America's place in the world, prompted major curricular reform in a number of disciplines, including social studies.

THE WAKE OF SPUTNIK: CURRICULUM REFORM AND OFFICIAL KNOWLEDGE

After Sputnik, an anxious nation came to associate education reform with the concerns of the Cold War and quickly transformed public schooling into a broad national concern. In 1958, Congress passed the National Defense Education Act (NDEA), connecting national security concerns to "the fullest development of the mental resources and technical skills of its young men and women." The act called for "additional and more adequate educational opportunities" because national defense "depends upon the mastery of modern techniques developed from complex scientific principles."[40] Its provisions focused initially on curricular revision in mathematics, science, and foreign languages, and only later in the social sciences and humanities.[41] Policy makers privileged fields that could be militarized, selectively transforming certain fields into official knowledge while neglecting others. Under NDEA, there was a significant shift in curriculum leadership away from schools, state departments of education, and teacher education programs and toward university faculty in academic disciplines, research and development organizations, and national agencies and foundations.[42] Because national entities are less likely to recognize, respond to, or possess the expertise and capacity to address specific issues at the state and community level, the locus of authority shifted professional and curricular attention away from American Indians except in the most general sense.

A 1960 publication from NCSS, *The Problems Approach to the Social Studies*, used sample lessons to illustrate its disciplinary-focused recommendations, some of which included content about American Indians. In the chapter titled "Problem Solving in the Elementary School," Charlotte Crabtree invites students to consider why the Great Basin is a desert region. In doing so, the authors are asking students to identify solely with the "hardships" of the "pioneers" moving westward from the Mississippi River to the Great Basin.[43] Students are never encouraged to consider the way of life of the people who lived in the Great Basin, nor even that the region was anything but empty and unpopulated.

Crabtree also contributes some ideas for teachers, including a dramatic play activity in which students act out "Westward Movement of the Pioneers" en route to Oregon as part of a lesson in human relations. The model lesson provides no scripts and simply asks students to identify roles, including "traders, trappers, wagon master, scouts, pioneer settlers, and Indians."[44] While the functions within the wagon train define the other roles, Crabtree indicates some students might choose to be "Indians." This generality seemingly provides ample opportunity to create and reinforce stereotypes. Students are again encouraged to identify with the "hard trek" of the pioneers and to circle the wagons when the "Indians" attack the wagon train. The example also provides a scenario in which the attack generates conflict among the students, but it relates to students choosing not to heed the wagon master's call to "Circle wagons!"[45] Crabtree's "Westward Movement" role-play activity encourages the teacher to challenge students by determining that "a wagon breaks down, because it is overloaded, while the train is moving through a narrow pass, and is endangered by Indians or by a snow storm."[46] It becomes clear that the "human" in human relations does not include Native people, because the authors position them merely as one of many "hardships" faced by brave "pioneers." This activity exemplifies problematic presences in the curriculum, where American Indians are marginal figures incidental to the larger point of the lesson, and as such, it represents the dominant view in the field that Act 31 was enacted to address.

In the early 1960s, despite the rise of discipline-centered social studies in the wake of NDEA, other approaches to social studies education, which might have provided opportunities for authentic learning about American Indians, remained prominent. Some proponents viewed social studies as an integrated field that drew on "the social sciences, humanities, and other areas of study for the purpose of examining all human relations among citizens."[47] Others linked it more specifically to citizenship and civic responsibility, calling on schools to prepare today's students to "learn how to come to grips with the realities of social and civic affairs in thoughtful, intelligent, and rational ways" so that they could become "adult citizens of their communities, holding offices, voting, serving on school boards, advising their elected officials, and making decisions individually and collectively on social and civic affairs."[48] These educators continued to see education, and social studies in particular, in terms of decisions students would make and actions they would take as citizens in a democratic society. Act 31 proponents would later use a similar rationale for teaching American Indian history, culture, and tribal sovereignty.

Other citizenship-focused social studies educators advocated for the "unreflective inculcation or imposition of certain content and values," an approach that focuses on "content (including myths as well as fact) by which budding young citizens may be indoctrinated with the 'right' beliefs and attitudes believed to be necessary for the unity of the nation and the loyalty of her citizens."[49] Its adherents based this authoritarian approach on assumptions about what knowledge and values are essential and without regard for building skills needed for effective decision making by citizens.[50] Even within a citizenship-oriented view of social studies, a focus on rote memorization of a cultural transmission curriculum limits opportunities to learn critical thinking and problem solving as well as to learn about non-dominant people groups or perspectives.

After 1965, as Cold War concerns shifted attention to federal priority areas such as math, science, and foreign languages, social studies curriculum reformers focused on elementary education.[51] Two important volumes published in 1967, *Guidelines for Elementary Social Studies*, published by ASCD, and *Social Studies Education: The Elementary School*, published by NCSS, both edited by John Jarolimek, were intended to help educators make sense of the new circumstances. These publications recommended an inquiry-based approach intended to provide "a body of informational content that is necessary for ordinary civic and social literacy."[52] Specific content was important only because "to think, one must be informed or have something substantive to think about," but Jarolimek argued, the specific body of knowledge was itself of no particular importance.[53] His remarks suggest that, at the elementary level, curriculum policy was moving away from both discipline-focused and cultural transmission models in ways that might have redefined official knowledge to include new content and perspectives.

Contributors to *Social Studies Education: The Elementary School* represented a variety of voices and perspectives. One recommended approach, which emphasized reasoning over accumulation of facts, left room for expanded content and multiple perspectives. Facts themselves were "only the beginning" of sound curriculum because "children must be guided in the utilization of facts to reach mediated conclusions or generalizations."[54] For example, "If a class studies early Indians or pioneer life, the teacher can aid them in seeing the viewpoint of the Indian to learn why he fought the white man. One might even broach the problem of the status of the Indian in our society today."[55] Thus, if schools defined curriculum content primarily in terms of skills to be learned rather than narrow, prescriptive content to be transmitted, it could present opportunities for new ideas in the classroom.

Another contributor, Nancy Bauer, offered a comprehensive vision of relevant, citizenship-focused social studies education that seems to be a missed opportunity for including instruction about American Indians. She was acutely aware of the danger of curriculum policy leadership disconnected from the realities of schooling and the sociopolitical pressures that schools face, noting, "to be a rational human being requires not only a life study of changing academic knowledge but a life-long commitment to an internally consistent and rationally based value system."[56] To this end, geography, for example, must include "not only where places are and how to locate them but why we care about the people who live there" so that academic skills may be learned "in the context of solving real problems."[57] While contemporary scholars might interpret these outcome-oriented statements as an opportunity to include instruction about American Indian history, culture, and tribal sovereignty, there is no evidence to suggest that those shaping both curriculum policy and classroom instruction in the late 1960s did so. Indeed, even as scholars sought to identify social studies' enduring questions, and a few explored its role in shaping future "social and civic affairs," leaders in the field were silent on questions surrounding the essential purpose of social studies within a pluralistic society despite the various social movements occurring around them.[58]

The field remained contested as issues of pluralism and curriculum politics persisted throughout the 1960s. Critics claimed that public education was too slow to recognize "the concerns of its clients, the problems faced by the society which supports it, and the moral/ethical dilemmas interwoven in all the human social situations it selects for curricular content."[59] Too many of the reforms of the era ignored "events and attitudes in the culture and society of which the institution of education is a part."[60] Because the dominant approach in the 1960s viewed social studies in terms of selecting, organizing, and teaching narrowly defined content, education policy makers were unlikely to redefine official knowledge to include American Indian history, culture, or tribal sovereignty because they did not recognize the sociopolitical issues that merited doing so.[61]

Historians have noted that the conflict in the social studies field was itself a product of cultural politics resulting from "the pluralism of the American culture."[62] A focus on academic disciplines and on structures of knowledge led to relative neglect of important pedagogical considerations and left questions of facts and values unsettled. Those who viewed curriculum design as a simple, mechanical process of selecting what knowledge is of most worth were ill equipped to respond to political developments in schools and society. One frustrated critic argued that "acceptance of diversity and pluralism is a must if we are to live successfully with emerging peoples within our country and without."[63] This early voice of dissent urged his colleagues to recognize that while disciplinary concerns were important, teachers and students alike "need to be made alive to crucial issues of our times," without requiring them to think alike nor "even interpret alike the criteria for thoughtful citizenship."[64] Overall, the failure of leaders in the field to develop appropriate strategies for addressing social issues and policy alternatives later "became nightmares for project leaders and staffs as civil rights, student activism, and Vietnam exploded across the nation."[65] Similarly, as violent protests rose up on Wisconsin boat landings in the 1980s, curriculum policy makers were sorely unprepared to respond to social crises or consider viable policy alternatives, particularly those that challenged decades of official knowledge.

Despite the best efforts of reformers, social studies remained highly resistant to change through the 1960s. Critics of the status quo charged that schools still functioned as "emporiums of popular small-town mythologies" in which "school history is pretty history" and "social studies instruction perpetuates sentimentalities about agrarian, rural, entrepreneurial America."[66] They lamented that "social studies goals and curricula will continue to be fashioned of a combination of national tradition, suggestive state programs, locally prescribed curricula, the considerable influence of textbooks, universities, and professional organizations, and the final distillation of these and other influences by the classroom teacher."[67] Teachers, too, one critic charged, "have an emotional stake in maintaining averted eyes, in schooling children while looking the other way" because "it is painful and threatening to face the hard evidence of conflict, strife, and racism that is importantly a part of the history of this country."[68] The significant "discrepancy between the conflictual history that is known and the pretty history we concoct for children" in order to "shelter them" is "simply to project onto children the wishes and fears of their elders."[69] Proponents of Act 31 made similar arguments as they sought new curricular reforms.

Within such an environment, the field largely ignored racial or ethnic minorities or included them in problematic, often stereotypical ways.[70] One particularly astute observer commented, "Only after Negroes have yanked our heads around to look directly at their social circumstances have we been able to consider even timid text revisions."[71] American Indians were invisible outside the mythical past depicted in films and television Westerns.[72] The disconnect between what was happening in the country and what was taught in schools was striking, but, as with Act 31, sociopolitical concerns led to curriculum policy change only after the associated crises became acute.

—ıⱼ—

From the founding of the social studies in the early twentieth century through its development in the 1960s, curriculum policy makers struggled to define it. Their efforts touched on the need to define official knowledge, select traditions to embrace, and decide whose knowledge and perspective to legitimize and prioritize. The inherently contested nature of these issues is as characteristic of social studies as any field.

In its earliest inception as conceived by Thomas Jesse Jones, social studies was a field adapted from a rudimentary curriculum intended to prepare African Americans and American Indians for subordinate roles in the broader society. The choices made regarding official knowledge were deliberate and strategic, purposefully made to respond to sociopolitical concerns external to schools. Over time, curriculum reformers struggled over when and how to adapt social studies curriculum for new generations of students, especially as sociopolitical concerns arose including immigration, World War II and the Cold War, social movements concerned with civil rights and other issues, and concerns about American economic and technological competition. Simultaneously, other reformers held different commitments and struggled to define social studies primarily as an intellectual activity, either as a discipline or a collection of disciplines. These struggles led to fluidity in purpose, scope, emphasis, and instructional methodology, each of which held implications for official knowledge. One of the few constants was the exclusion of American Indian nations from social studies curricula and classroom instruction. At best, Indian nations were included only at the margins, and then only as caricatures that perpetuated false, damaging stereotypes. This was especially acute when leadership of curriculum policy conversations shifted away from the particular concerns of any individual state and to the national level.

Wisconsin Act 31, when framed as a response to the treaty rights controversy, is consistent with policies and practices of this era. As an attempt to use social studies curriculum to respond to a social crisis external to the schools, it resembles the field's national reactions to World War II, the Cold War, and the civil rights movement. By the 1970s, education reformers sought to be more proactive, and curriculum policy moved in a more inclusive direction. A decade later, a competing series of reforms reflected renewed economic concerns about American competitiveness.

When Wisconsin created new statutory requirements for instruction in the history, culture, and tribal sovereignty of the federally recognized American Indian tribes and bands in the state, it did so in an era when policy talk in this dynamic field moved through a more inclusive phase and began cycling back in a more conservative direction. The next chapter examines these shifting policy trends in the 1970s and 1980s.

CHAPTER 7

SOCIAL STUDIES EDUCATION AND CONTEMPORARY ISSUES: THE 1970S AND 1980S

The reforms of the 1970s, as well as the counter-reforms of the 1980s, have their roots in the political events of the late 1960s, an era when in a "society torn by civil rights, women's rights, and antiwar protests, it was difficult to maintain the illusion that a unified history of progress and consensus was possible."[1] As attention turned to social issues, leading social studies educators and curriculum policy makers began to recognize the importance of factors such as race, class, and gender, as well as long-term trends and enduring structures evident from quantitative analysis.[2] Many educators in the field had experienced "the awakening of a heightened social consciousness . . . in response to the war in Vietnam and to the violence and racism at home."[3] They began to raise critical questions about the roles of values in social studies education in response to war and civil rights protests as well as "generational conflicts over lifestyles."[4] Growing concerns and attention to issues of race and racism, cultural pluralism, racial and ethnic studies, and individuals' emotions and values began to receive significant attention.[5] This chapter focuses primarily on the late 1960s through the 1980s, a period of significant controversy and reform in social studies that marks a notable departure from previous views of the field, and an era that shaped the worldviews of many of those both fighting for, and fighting against, treaty rights in northern Wisconsin after the *Voigt* decision—and, of course, their children.[6]

Several distinct positions emerged regarding the role of contemporary social issues in the classroom. Some educators engaged in what they called "guerrilla history," arguing that scholarship should lead to "personal/social commitment and action" on behalf of oppressed peoples.[7] Those holding a more centrist position sought to "ensure that knowledge and skills are applied to constructive rather than destructive ends and to familiarize the pupil with the role expectations society has for him as a citizen."[8] Within this deeply contested field, others stressed only "academic dialogue" and the development of sound academic conclusions.[9] The central issue implicit in the debate was whether schools should engage contemporary sociopolitical issues, and if so, whether the purpose was to prepare students to address those concerns or whether they simply served as the content for abstract academic exercises.

The National Council for Social Studies itself was slow to engage on matters of race. Between 1950 and 1965, only three editorials published in *Social Education* mentioned race or racism.[10] Only Supreme Court Justice William J. Brennan Jr.'s 1963 article "Teaching the Bill of Rights" directly addressed the contemporary civil rights movement.[11] Despite a stated concern for values and personal engagement, it was only in 1969, a full five years after the Civil Rights Act was passed, that *Social Education* published two special issues on African Americans and urban areas and that NCSS took an active stand against racism.[12] In October 1969, the organization formally adopted a policy ordering that all its actions and positions "be tested in respect to whether or not these actions in any way perpetuate racism and social injustice," which it referred to as "America's central social issue."[13] As a national leader in curriculum policy, NCSS was finally engaging with key sociopolitical concerns and encouraging those in the field to do likewise. No longer was the occasional article enough. Now, the organization was embarking on a new policy direction, one more relevant to contemporary issues.

The Turn to Ethnic Studies: Curriculum Reform in the 1970s

In the early 1970s, many scholars turned their attention to textbooks, offering a critique of "the three D's—distortion, denial, and deletion."[14] Rupert Costo and Jeannette Henry, writing in 1970 for *The Indian*

Historian, found that "not one book is free from error as to the role of the Indian in state and national history" and concluded that textbooks "lie, hide the truth, or insult and malign a whole race of people."[15] A 1970 study conducted for the Anti-Defamation League concluded that textbooks still portrayed a "principally white, Anglo-Saxon, Protestant account of the nation's past and present while largely neglecting the accomplishments and problems of minority groups" to the degree that no single volume "presented a reasonably complete, relatively undistorted picture of the pluralistic reality of America."[16]

Another textbook study documented examples of omission, which the author termed the "great lie of silence," and commission "in the form of stereotyping, ethnocentrism, Eurocentrism, and use of prejudicial statements or caricatures that demean minorities."[17] A follow-up study found that "references to the American Indian of today were almost non-existent," although the portrayal of the relationship between American Indians, the federal government, and white settlers "seemed to be more objectively presented."[18] These and other studies found that "despite a few isolated references—a Crispus Attucks here, a Geronimo there," textbooks "reflected the values, norms, and myths of the dominant, mainstream society" while neglecting the concerns and contributions of less powerful social groups unless "they became a problem to the majority and obstructed what was perceived as forward progress."[19] It was only through sociopolitical crises or broad social movements that historically marginalized people drew attention sufficient to warrant inclusion in curriculum policy and instructional materials.

As race began to become a meaningful area of inquiry among researchers in social studies education, James Banks and others were developing an inquiry-based approach that he termed "ethnic studies." In this model, teachers would guide student inquiry into the "problems of racial discrimination, institutional racism, the meaning and social functions of race, and the struggle that ensues when one race dominates others in a society."[20] Banks initially focused on African Americans, and he and others further developed this concept more fully from "a single group study to an examination of a variety of groups based on the intellectual concept of cultural diversity" that developed into and is now widely recognized as multicultural education.[21]

In its 1971 publication, *NCSS Curriculum Guidelines*, the National Council for Social Studies included "contemporary focus, cultural, racial and/or ethnic focus, value conflicts, flexibility, variety of media, variety of learning activities, active involvement of students, and active involvement of teachers."[22] Perhaps reflective of internal conflict or to mollify critics, the organization explained that they did not intend the guide to serve as a "statement of standards that will be appropriate for all time, nor even appropriate for all schools at this time."[23] Its emphasis on "current developments in the larger society" reflected particular concern for socio-political issues external to schooling narrowly defined.[24] The *Guidelines* also represent the organization's attempt to exert influence at the local level and to move social studies education toward a more explicit focus on ethnic studies and what later scholars might term social justice. As an organization, the National Council for Social Studies was embracing ethnic studies and cultural pluralism as official knowledge for purposes of curriculum content and was advocating for a view of the field that would prepare students to be agents of social transformation.

The *Guidelines* authors were cognizant of biases present in the traditional curriculum, making frequent mention of human dignity and human diversity and stressing relevance to the concerns of students such that "all students are entitled to expect that they, their concerns, and their social origins have a place in the social studies curriculum."[25] Social studies curriculum, they argued, should "deal with the real social world" in ways that allow students to analyze and confront key social issues, including "economic injustice, conflict, racism, social disorder, and environmental imbalance" and avoid "ethnocentric bias" by accepting the "legitimacy of their own cultural group identity as well as the ways of others."[26] The *Guidelines* noted that "'school history' is often repetitive, bland, merely narrative, and inattentive to the non-Western world; it is distorted by ignoring the experiences of Blacks, Chicanos, native [sic] American Indians, Puerto Ricans, and Oriental Americans."[27] It is unclear what local curriculum committees would do with these statements or how classroom teachers would use them, but groundwork was being laid to support authentic student understanding of peoples historically marginalized and excluded from the realm of official knowledge.

By the early 1970s, NCSS was beginning to use its influence to redefine official knowledge to include previously excluded people of color. Ethnic studies came to dominate its bulletins, curriculum series, and yearbooks, including one titled *Teaching Ethnic Studies: Concepts and Strategies*.[28] Other organizations followed suit as highlighted by an annotated list of materials addressing race and ethnicity, developed by ASCD and the Commission on the Social Studies.[29] Their mere existence shows how ethnic studies advocates had effectively redefined the field of social studies.

Congressional actions also bolstered the turn toward ethnic studies. In 1972, Congress passed the Ethnic Studies Heritage Program Act, authorized through Title IX of the Elementary and Secondary Education Act, which declared that "all students in elementary and secondary schools of the Nation should have an opportunity to learn about the differing and unique contributions to the national heritage made by each ethnic group." Congress intended to "assist schools and school systems in affording each of their students an opportunity to learn about the nature of his own cultural heritage, and those in which he has an interest, and to study the contributions of these forebears to the Nation."[30] The new law recognized the United States as a "multiethnic society" in which "an understanding of the contributions of one's own heritage and those of fellow citizens" could help to "contribute to a more harmonious patriotic and committed populace."[31] Although the act did not appropriate any new funding until 1974, it called for currently funded programs to "cooperate with persons and organizations with a special interest in the ethnic group or groups with which the program is concerned" in order to advance "activities which related to the history, culture, or traditions of that ethnic group or groups."[32]

In 1975, Congress followed up by enacting Title VII of the Elementary and Secondary School Assistance Act and Ethnic Heritage Act to fund the development of new curriculum, instructional methods, and professional development activities that would provide all children in districts under court-ordered desegregation plans with opportunities to learn about "the language and heritage of all groups."[33] These sentiments would echo in the passage of Act 31, with attention to "Black Americans, American Indians, and Hispanics," but increased attention to race and ethnicity would not prepare students to understand tribal nationhood, sovereignty, and treaty-based relationships because Title VII conflated American Indians and racial minorities.[34]

By 1975, the efforts of a broad coalition of national organizations, including the National Education Association, United Federation of Teachers, and the American Association of Colleges of Teacher Education culminated in the establishment of the Ethnic Heritage Center for Teacher Education, which was intended to "provide a national focus for multicultural and ethnic studies research."[35] This was a significant shift from the late 1960s when newly developed ethnic studies programs were typically set apart from the regular curriculum, "as though to isolate those who dared question the prevailing mythology." Many such programs were "ideological in nature, feeling-oriented, non-intellectual, and expressive of not unwarranted hostility toward rigid, racist systems."[36] The nation was beginning to confront its past and to complicate the standard narrative of American exceptionalism that had long characterized social studies education. Previously marginalized views had become legitimate school knowledge.

Scholars connected these curricular concerns to the social costs of racism and other forms of prejudice, and critiques of traditional social studies curriculum began to receive significant national attention. Critical issues of justice and inequality, once hidden by consensus-focused curriculum, had become mainstream topics of study in social studies, and NCSS called on both teachers and students to "confront their own racial feelings and perceptions of the other" before studying ethnic content so as not to have its impact reduced and "its integrity seriously violated."[37] No longer satisfied with incorporating knowledge about historically marginalized peoples, these critics sought to legitimize the voices and perspectives of the peoples themselves.

NCSS Curriculum Guidelines for Multicultural Education

In 1974, the National Council for Social Studies received an Ethnic Studies Heritage Program grant from the federal government, which it used to develop *Curriculum Guidelines for Multiethnic Education*, published in 1976.[38] The NCSS Task Force on Ethnic Studies Curriculum, chaired by James A. Banks, developed the document to provide "sound guidelines for designing and implementing ethnic studies programs and for integrating their curricula with ethnic content."[39] The committee members sought broad changes in public education and called for transformed school climates that were cognizant of and respectful to ethnic diversity because "reforming the course of study is necessary but clearly insufficient."[40] Act 31 proponents would later echo its comprehensive, transformative vision of ethnic studies.

Banks and his colleagues sought to redefine the mainstream of social studies by promoting "ethnic pluralism," an approach intended to address the "contributions of ethnic groups and the problems resulting from ethnic discrimination in American society." Committee members saw ethnic studies as the purview and responsibility of all curricular areas and grade levels, and they argued that it was "needed by all students regardless of their ethnic, social class, or racial background" and not simply as a compensatory program.[41] This recommendation recognized ethnic studies as a key part of a redefined mainstream official knowledge, as proponents of Act 31 would later argue.

In developing their rationale for ethnic studies, Banks and his fellow committee members noted several sociopolitical factors that made ethnic studies necessary. They noted that ethnic pluralism is a "societal reality" that affects young people's lives and that "in one way or another, individuals do acquire knowledge or beliefs sometimes invalid, about ethnic groups and ethnicity." These "beliefs and knowledge about ethnic groups limit the perspectives of many and make a difference, often a negative difference, in the opportunities and options of members of ethnic groups." The task force described the result of taking these factors into account as "ethnic literacy," which it defined as "a solidly based understanding of ethnicity and ethnic groups."[42] Implicit in this definition were dispositions, outlooks, and attitudes salient for professional practice, which favor and respect ethnic pluralism, yet despite this, the understanding of what constituted plural ethnicities was weak.[43] The guide includes "Native Americans" among the definitions provided, but as simply another ethnic group, without acknowledgment of tribal nationhood or linguistic and cultural diversity among Native peoples.[44] In this respect, NCSS's effort to promote awareness actually furthered an incomplete understanding of Native people, one that promoted the kinds of views held by those who sought to terminate government-to-government relationships and abrogate treaties. Nonetheless, the guide represents an attempt by a national educational professional association to define diversity as constitutive of the shared characteristic of ethnicity and offers an expressly justice-oriented view of what a reconstructed American society might look like.

The authors of the *Curriculum Guidelines for Multiethnic Education* recognized that if these lofty goals were to be realized, professional development on these topics must "begin at the preservice level and continue as inservice when educators are employed by schools."[45] Such efforts must focus on helping staff members to recognize and understand their attitudes toward their own ethnic group and those of others, provide content knowledge related to historical experiences and social characteristics, increase instructional skills suited to multiethnic settings, improve skills related to multiethnic curriculum development, and increase knowledge and skills related to "creating, selecting, evaluating, and revising instructional materials."[46] The knowledge, skills, and dispositions identified as important for implementing ethnic studies were also those embedded in Act 31. It was a vision of societal reform through education reform, of addressing historic inequalities by including populations historically invisible or problematically presented in the curriculum as part of what counts as official knowledge.

As a result of socialization and problematic curriculum policies and instructional practices, the *Curriculum Guidelines* authors argue that too many Americans know only the "values, behavioral patterns, and beliefs of their own ethnic groups, cultural groups, and our communities" and therefore view others as "abnormal" or "deviant."[47] Traditional approaches to social studies have omitted both content about and perspectives of many groups, particularly "Afro-Americans and American Indians," and when such content is included, the lessons often serve to reinforce stereotypes by failing to incorporate the group's own perspectives.[48] Similarly, traditional instructional methods have focused on "the social problems which ethnic group members experience" in ways that conflate them with their "cultural characteristics," leaving students with little more than "stereotypes about ethnic groups other than their own."[49]

The authors argue that as a product of prevalent stereotyping, Native Americans and Chinese Americans in particular "are often judged not as individuals but on the basis of the racial and or ethnic group to which they belong" and therefore need to "be helped to understand how they are perceived and identified by the larger society."[50] To remedy these issues, the task force argued, schools must adopt curricula that reflects the "totality of the experiences of American ethnic groups" by including the "present culture, historical experiences, sociopolitical realities, contributions to American development, problems faced in everyday living, and conditions of existence in society."[51] This vision of social change looked to empower students to reconstruct a more racially just American society by teaching about ethnic groups in ways that actively challenge stereotypes and by teaching ethnic groups themselves about the stereotypes the broader society has about them.

The guide also framed ethnic studies in terms of citizenship education to foster the development of students' "decision-making abilities, social participation skills, and sense of political efficacy as necessary bases for effective citizenship in an ethnically pluralistic nation."[52] Schools could also show "strength in diversity" and teach students that "social cooperation among ethnic groups is not necessarily predicated upon their having identical beliefs, behaviors, and values."[53] In aggregate, multiethnic education could also transform society's thinking about conflict by teaching students to recognize that it "does not have to be destructive or divisive" and as an inherent factor in a pluralistic society, it might serve as a "catalyst for social progress."[54] By articulating their proposal in terms of timely educational concerns, student knowledge and skills, and more social reconstructionist-oriented goals, the NCSS Task Force on Ethnic Studies Curriculum, together with the guidelines it published, sought to broaden their base of support at the state and local levels. This level of attention to implementation concerns was notably absent from prior national projects and signaled a turn in the approach to developing curricula that would address national, state, and local concerns.

MULTIETHNIC EDUCATION IN THE 1970S

During the 1970s, the social studies field began to respond to issues of pluralism, racism, and sexism in significant and positive ways, leading one scholar to remark, "No one is quite sure when the 'Melting Pot' fell apart, but one thing is certain: the jagged pieces fell abruptly into the confines of the social studies curriculum and gained increasing legitimacy in the 1970s."[55] New multiethnic programs in schools and teacher training programs in universities arose in response to the court-ordered desegregation plans, the "often violent pressures of the Black community," and "parallel drives for inclusion by other ethnic groups."[56] Banks's research confirms this view, concluding, "ethnic studies programs are strongest where there are widespread ethnic protest and revitalization movements."[57] This suggests that sociopolitical issues external to education were driving curriculum reform toward ethnic studies.

As various education organizations involved in curriculum reform issued position papers throughout the 1970s, a number of points of convergence emerged. Organizations called for multiethnic education in all grades to provide students with a "sense of control over their lives" and "decision-making and practical and social action skills" that would empower them to "change society for the better."[58] Most multiethnic education programs sought to promote a level of respect that "would lead to the elimination of discriminatory practices and prejudices and eventually to a society unified in diversity." However, they often failed to instill the requisite "thorough understanding of how and why these practices developed, how and why they were maintained, who benefited from these practices, and why they continue to exist."[59] It is from these understandings, "fundamental of any attempt to relieve racial and social tension," that "harmonious relations between various groups will ensue as a natural consequence of a just and humane society."[60] As the decade came to a close, the NCSS's 1979 "Revision of the NCSS Social Studies Curriculum Guidelines" stated: "The basic goal of social studies education is to prepare young people to be humane, participating citizens."[61] At least at the level of national curriculum policy leadership and agenda setting, social studies education remained a key tool for promoting social transformation, yet more traditional approaches were still commonplace.

Research on curriculum policy in the late 1970s indicates that actual instructional time devoted to social studies was decreasing at a time when the scope of curriculum content legitimated as official knowledge was expanding. The period is characterized by concern for a decline in instructional opportunities in history and other traditional courses, renewed attention to citizenship education, and an ongoing controversy over the continuing influence of past reforms.[62] Despite its acknowledgment of "human relations" and citizenship education, social studies curriculum policy research does not reflect the sort of consensus that might have created learning opportunities about American Indians as either a cultural or a political group.[63]

THE 1980S: CONTINUITY AND CONSERVATIVE RESTORATION

The policy trend characterized by ethnic studies and social justice continued in 1980, when the National Council for Social Studies published a booklet entitled *Racism and Sexism: Responding to the Challenge*. Beryle Banfield, in a chapter titled "Biting the Bullet: Racism and Sexism and the Challenge for Social Studies," argues, "Most Americans have indeed been programmed in that they have been effectively socialized to accept racist and sexist practices that have created an economic, political, and social underclass of minorities and women."[64] Instead, she advocates for a transformative approach, writing, "logic demands that education be the means by which individuals are equipped with information to challenge values that could result in a more just and humane society."[65] As an example, she notes that "Native Americans are charging a 'Red Backlash' in Congressional actions, which they claim is tantamount to genocide."[66] Banfield urges authors and publishers to include regular, appropriate references to "Native Americans" so that their history texts do not, for example, "negat[e] the history of Native American women" by focusing their discussions of women's history on white colonial women.[67] Banfield is exceptional among social studies curriculum researchers of the era in that she includes perspectives of as well as information about historically marginalized groups.

When James Banks assumed the presidency of NCSS in 1982, he called for educators to "strive to attain a delicate balance between educating students to be bearers of a continuous cultural tradition and educating them to be social critics interested in social change."[68] That delicate balance is reflected in the organization's 1982 NCSS bulletin, *Teaching American History: New Directions*, in which the organization renewed its call for a more inclusive history and provided bibliographic and other resources to support such an approach.[69] The "new directions" featured included women's history, social history, labor history, public history, family history, and, represented by a single article, Native American history.

The 1980s also marked the beginning of a shift away from attention to pluralism and a rearticulation of a common "American identity" as part of a broader conservative agenda. These dynamics also shifted power relations among policy makers as state-level leaders came to eclipse federal officials and other national leaders.[70] Federal withdrawal of "leadership in educational policymaking" and strong state economies allowed state governments, which often included chief state school officers and boards of education as checks on gubernatorial power, to devote resources to education and reshape education policy.[71] This devolution was part of an overall rightward shift in education and in the broader society. Curriculum policy gradually came to reflect these shifts.

Earlier curriculum policy trends had problematized key social studies concepts such as historical knowledge and historical truth, to the point that "the history of racial and ethnic groups, labor and class history, and gender history fundamentally alter[ed] the traditional curriculum."[72] However, social institutions are essentially resistant to change except where there is support among educators themselves and where the reforms sought are "within the limits of existing cultural and institutional arrangements."[73] As a result, a conservative restoration movement articulated in terms of "back to basics" and "community norms" was beginning to emerge, particularly in the wake of 1983's *A Nation at Risk* report.

In the 1980s, conservative scholars, many of whom were affiliated with the Reagan administration, came to dominate curriculum policy discussions at the national level. They had long been concerned history was being diluted by women's studies and ethnic studies courses. They advocated for a cultural transmission–oriented, disciplinary view of history in terms of "cultural literacy," which they viewed as "necessary for cultural survival."[74] Through national conservative political organizations, including the Educational Excellence Network and the Bradley Commission on History in the Schools as well as more mainstream education organizations such as the National Geographic Society, they collaborated to recenter traditional subjects and disciplinary-focused social studies. They sought to "expose the breadth of historical ignorance among high school juniors and seniors," and their work further spurred the back-to-basics movement.[75] By the late 1980s, the curriculum policy trends that had stressed race, ethnicity, gender, class, and multiple perspectives had been replaced by more traditional, disciplinary-oriented approaches that did not threaten, or necessarily connect to, existing social, political, and economic relationships.

In an attempt to develop a shared vision of social studies, several key professional organizations, including NCSS, the American Historical Association, the Organization of American Historians, the National Geographic Society, and the Carnegie Foundation for the Advancement of Teaching, jointly sponsored the National Commission on Social Studies in the Schools to collaborate on a compromise document. This effort yielded policy recommendations published in 1989 as *Charting a Course*, which sought to retain the field of social studies while emphasizing history and geography as essential disciplines.[76] The commission intended the guide to define a "balanced and comprehensive curriculum program adapted to the needs of present day society and suggests direction for the future," and it offered essays from discrete social science disciplines including anthropology, economics, US history, world history, political science, psychology, and sociology. The authors argued that instruction in the field should involve a rich mix of media and involve methods that "help students become both independent and cooperative learners who develop skills of problem solving, decision making, negotiation, and conflict resolution."[77]

This compromise document, jointly written by several major stakeholder organizations, was attempting to address purpose, scope, emphasis, and instructional approach, all the key issues that had divided the field and made it so difficult to define social studies. Some scholars viewed *Charting a Course* as "a reaffirmation of the argument for progressive education," while others saw it as "the 1905 Committee of Eight recommendation brought up to 1980s standards" because it retained history as its core and regarded the social sciences as separate subjects.[78] As such, it represents a reassertion of leadership by key national organizations, and it marks the late 1980s, the era in which Act 31 was signed into law, as an era of attempted compromises over the nature of official knowledge.

—⊣⊢—

When Wisconsin created new statutory requirements for instruction in the history, culture, and tribal sovereignty of the federally recognized American Indian tribes and bands in the state, it did so in an era when policy rhetoric in this dynamic field was cycling back in a more conservative direction. When framed as a response to the treaty rights controversy, these concerns were consistent with past attempts to use social studies curriculum to respond to societal needs external to the schools, as with World War II, Korea, Sputnik, the civil rights and anti-war movements, and economic crises. Viewed solely as an attempt to redefine official knowledge in ways that reflected a more broadly inclusive human family, the shifts in social studies curriculum policy are consistent with the curriculum policy trends of the 1970s. By 1989, however, state-level policy was counter to the broader, more conservative national trends in the field as a whole, and its commitments to connecting social studies to particular sociopolitical concerns, to expanding the domain of official knowledge to include broad understandings of human relations and cultural pluralism, and to instilling an understanding of tribal nationhood as well as history and culture, mark Act 31 as decidedly outside the era's mainstream of curriculum policy concerns.

When it was enacted, Act 31 was already an anachronism in a time of conservative restoration in curriculum policy because its focus was outside the selective tradition that reflected broadly conservative political and cultural trends nationally. Given the interplay between national, state, and local curriculum policy forces, each sector does not move at the same speed nor in the same direction, so by the time curriculum policy leaders in Wisconsin finally began to respond to sociopolitical concerns related to American Indians, their views were decidedly outside the mainstream of national curriculum policy. It is clear that although the effort to redefine official knowledge in Wisconsin to include American Indian history, culture, and tribal sovereignty was a significant struggle, it was, in that respect, consistent with the broad historical trends in the field.

PART 4

OFFICIAL KNOWLEDGE AND THE STATE OF WISCONSIN

CHAPTER 8

WISCONSIN
CURRICULUM POLICY

Previous chapters addressed how curriculum policy discourse and trends in the field of social studies resulted from the interplay between national, state, and local factors and how, as a result, certain forms of content knowledge became legitimated as official knowledge. That analysis demonstrated that American Indians were largely invisible and stereotypically portrayed when included in curriculum guides and other policy documents due to broader national concerns in the field. This chapter shows how sociopolitical dynamics within social studies helped to shape curriculum policy at the state level.

As with the nation as a whole, state education agencies and local school districts embrace a "selective tradition" that includes or excludes knowledge about certain groups, privileges some groups' knowledge, and honors only specific perspectives on those topics. Through state statutes, administrative rules, district policies on textbooks and other sanctioned instructional materials, as well as instructional practices and related aspects of the hidden curriculum, curriculum policy is being continually renegotiated in state and local contexts.[1] In order to examine these dynamics, this chapter focuses on the study of Wisconsin history, typically offered at the fourth-grade level, as a notable exception to the problem of invisibility.

Fourth-grade social studies is more insulated from broader national concerns and more attuned to the unique features of the state's policy landscape and state and local sociopolitical concerns that the field as a

133

whole historically has failed to address. It is the only grade with a significant focus on Native people in Wisconsin, as opposed to the occasional lessons students might encounter about other culturally and linguistically distinct peoples elsewhere in North America within the scope of US history or other courses. This allows consideration of the nature of American Indian presences and locally defined domains of official knowledge and how those domains reflect the state's unique character.

This chapter establishes the policy landscape for Wisconsin. It explores the relationship between the Wisconsin Department of Public Instruction (DPI) and more than four hundred public school districts, illustrating how these entities together shape curriculum policy in the state. Relying on curriculum guides and policy bulletins published by DPI, the following discussion documents the myriad ways that the state shaped curriculum policy and how it attempted to respond to various sociopolitical realities.

EDUCATION POLICY IN WISCONSIN:
THE WISCONSIN DEPARTMENT OF PUBLIC INSTRUCTION

The Wisconsin Constitution vests responsibility for "supervision of public instruction" in an elected state superintendent that an individual state law recognizes as the head of the state education agency, the Wisconsin Department of Public Instruction.[2] This elected official is required to "ascertain the condition of the public schools, stimulate interest in education and spread as widely as possible a knowledge of the means and methods which may be employed to improve the schools," signifying a lead role in a process of perpetual school reform. To that end, DPI is the primary source of curriculum policy guidance at the state level, and the agency regularly publishes curriculum guides and other bulletins for public schools. These documents are the product of various incarnations of the Social Studies Curriculum Study Committee consisting of the DPI staff member responsible for social studies and selected administrators, teachers, and university professors from across the state. They reflect the interplay between state and local influences and can be recognized as the arbiter of state-level official knowledge. These curriculum policy documents serve as a means to assess what local school districts recognized as official knowledge before the passage of Act 31 and what opportunities to learn accurate, authentic information about American Indians followed from those decisions.

Unlike many other states, Wisconsin has no state school board, and it vests the proper authority for local oversight of schools in locally elected school boards. State law defines the duties of the school board as providing "curriculum, course requirements, and instruction" that reflect concern for student development in four main areas: academic skills and knowledge, vocational skills, citizenship, and personal development.[3] Local officials are also responsible for determining a course of study consistent with state standards, which includes providing "regular instruction" in social studies for grade spans K–4 and 5–8, and "access" to social studies in grades 9–12 through course offerings, independent study, and cooperative arrangements with other school districts or postsecondary institutions.[4] These are the key elements in local control of curriculum, and while school districts may defer to state recommendations, curriculum guides and other policy bulletins are largely nonregulatory.

WORLD WAR I AND WORLD WAR II: PATRIOTISM AND "PURE HISTORY"

The first critical issue facing Wisconsin schools in the social studies era reflected ongoing concerns over US involvement in World War I, factional rivalries in the state Republican Party, and ethnic politics. In the 1920s, history dominated the new field of social studies, and Wisconsin, as elsewhere, was concerned with the instruction students were receiving in its public schools. State politics and state-level political responses to US involvement in World War I touched off a textbook censorship law that lasted more than half a century. Sen. John E. Cashman, a progressive Wisconsin Republican, viewed American entry into the war as a product of British propaganda, and he sought to end what he viewed as "anti-patriotic bias" in American history textbooks.[5] Cashman argued that "so-called American history is written from the British viewpoint" such that schools were "used to teach treason and defame the nation's founders and defenders," thereby risking their transformation into "agencies of propaganda to undermine the Republic."[6]

As enacted by the state legislature and signed by Governor John Blaine on April 5, 1923, the new law stated, "No history or other textbook may be adopted for use or be used in any public school which falsifies the facts regarding the war of independence or the war of 1812, which defames our nation's founders or misrepresents the ideals and causes for which they struggled and sacrificed or which contains propaganda favorable to any foreign government."[7] The law established a complaint procedure through which a complaint signed by five or more citizens would require the state superintendent to hold a hearing on the book. If the superintendent found the book in violation of the law, DPI would then remove it from the list of approved instructional materials, and all superintendents in city and county schools would be required to discontinue its use.[8] Despite a national outcry against Wisconsin's "Pure History Law," a name mockingly bestowed by J. Franklin Jameson of the *American Historical Review*, the legislature amended it in 1927 to increase its scope to include all books used in schools.[9]

Despite the vigorous debate surrounding its passage, DPI never received a formal citizen complaint, never held a hearing, and never acknowledged the new law nor its responsibility for enforcement in any of its biennial reports or its correspondence with school districts.[10] Nevertheless, the legislature amended the law several times. During the Cold War, a 1953 amendment replaced language regarding the Revolution and War of 1812 with "facts regarding the history of our nation."[11] Another amendment in 1967 repealed the implementation provisions because the state superintendent no longer compiled the list of approved texts referenced in the statute. By 1984, the Wisconsin legislature repealed the policy itself.[12] The historian A. Clark Hagensick observes, "That its cumbersome implementation procedures were never formally invoked provides mute testimony that the enactment of a law is only the first, and certainly not a conclusive, step in the process of altering public conduct."[13] The "Pure History Law" shows how sociopolitical factors external to the schools shaped state laws regarding education. It also highlights the inadequacy of legislative changes without additional changes to the overall educational policy structure.

Patriotism also influenced social studies policy in the Second World War. During World War II, NCSS defined the field as "essential to the war effort," and Wisconsin quickly followed suit. DPI published two bulletins in cooperation with the Wisconsin Wartime Study Committee, "A Challenge to Every Wisconsin Teacher" in 1942 and "The Social Studies in Wisconsin Schools" in 1943. Both documents urged public schools to develop curriculum more suited to the needs of a nation at war and described the need to instill patriotic feelings and the values of democratic citizenship in students.[14] In this respect, the state government was expressly linking curriculum policy considerations to sociopolitical issues otherwise external to education, and in this example, it moved toward a cultural transmission, citizenship-oriented curriculum policy.

State Curriculum Policy in the 1960s

Curriculum policy in Wisconsin mirrored general national trends in the early 1960s, reflecting the influence of national concerns such as the Soviets' launch of Sputnik and the National Defense Education Act (NDEA), which rapidly redefined American educational priorities. The field was less responsive to other contemporary social issues, largely ignoring the emerging civil rights movement. Struggles within the field between a citizenship-oriented view of social studies and a disciplinary-based approach rooted in the methods of inquiry were also at play.

Wisconsin's response to these sociopolitical factors is evident in *A Conceptual Framework for the Social Studies in Wisconsin Schools*, the first of the post-NDEA curriculum policy documents published by DPI. The Wisconsin Social Studies Curriculum Study Committee began its work on the guide in 1962 and released the first edition two years later. The guide focuses solely on content knowledge and identifies history, anthropology-sociology, political science, economics, and geography as components of the field. It offers what it terms "developmental variants" on content knowledge in each domain. After receiving significant national recognition for "giving direction to the new social studies," the department issued a second, substantially similar edition of the guide in 1967.[15] By 1977, it had become recognized nationally as an important conceptual frame of "germane concepts and generalizations that might constitute a structure of the several social sciences, history and geography consistent with the body of theory that composes the cognitive knowledge for the social studies."[16] On a practical level, the guides provided critical policy guidance to local school districts, but importantly, they could set forth no requirements not otherwise established in state law because curriculum development remained a matter of local control.

The recommended scope and sequence suggested that students learn Wisconsin history in fourth grade, focus on US history to 1896 in tenth grade, and study US history post-1896 in eleventh grade.[17] "Developmental variants" for fourth graders include several statements that serve implicitly to define such key concepts as periphery and core, normalcy and deviance, and us and them. In an apparent reference to colonization and immigration, the content guidelines for Wisconsin history state that "early settlers came here from many parts of the world and brought many changes in the area that became Wisconsin," implicitly promoting the notion of unsettled wilderness and effectively erasing Native presences.[18] Another guideline states, "Citizens of Wisconsin usually have demonstrated a concern for the rights of minorities," minimizing or erasing actual historical conflicts while implicitly drawing a contrast between "citizens of Wisconsin" and "minorities."[19] The history guidelines subtly center the European experience as normative for Wisconsin.

The guidelines for anthropology-sociology for fourth grade note, "Although they looked somewhat different, the Indians lived in families and communities and carried on many activities similar to those of the white settlers." This statement, which addresses "the Indians" in aggregate, creates and reinforces a singular category, "Indian," which blurs significant linguistic and cultural distinctiveness among Native peoples in Wisconsin. The guide also seems to validate Native cultural practices only insofar as they resembled those of "the white settlers," and seemingly casts cultural differences as deviant.[20]

The other variants offer few opportunities to learn about American Indians. The political science strand is silent with regard to Native peoples or cultural differences more broadly.[21] It does not mention tribal sovereignty, tribal governance, or relationships with the federal or state governments. The economics strand includes a statement indicating that "lack of specialization in pioneer Wisconsin forced its early settlers to spend most of their time securing a minimum of food, clothing, and shelter for survival," which, combined with the anthropology strand's explicit characterization of the settlers as white, necessarily narrows curricular focus. Geography offers an opportunity to address critical issues, noting the existence of "'cultural' landscapes" that result from people "appraising and using the different natural elements of Wisconsin," but offers no further substance to guide or inform instruction.[22]

STATE AND LOCAL CURRICULUM POLICY IN THE 1970S

As social dynamics changed in the late 1960s, the Wisconsin Social Studies Curriculum Study Committee began work on another curriculum guide to help local school districts adjust to a changing landscape. Because of increasing national attention, the civil rights movement, the war in Vietnam, the women's movement, and other social issues were forcing their way onto the curriculum policy agenda. The disconnect between contemporary issues and social studies instruction threatened the fragile consensus in the field about citizenship education and exposed the limitations of isolated exercises in contemporary issues, no matter how rigorous or well designed. Curriculum policy leaders in Wisconsin, along with the field as a whole, had to move to prepare students to deal with the sociopolitical crises facing the nation. Once again, external concerns prompted changes to curriculum policy in the state.

Knowledge, Processes, and Values in the New Social Studies, published by DPI and based on work conducted by the Wisconsin Social Studies Curriculum Study Committee between 1968 and 1970, draws on such giants of curriculum theory as Ralph Tyler and Benjamin Bloom to articulate the need for "any effective social studies program" to include attention to "knowledge," "skills and processes," and "values."[23] This is in marked contrast to the 1964/1967 document, which focused solely on content knowledge. For its part, the newer bulletin makes explicit the role of all three components in attempting to "give social studies educators greater insight into both the ends and means of social studies education."[24]

The DPI guide defines knowledge in the discipline through such examples as "the nature of man, the nature of the world, the heritage of the past, and the totality of contemporary social life."[25] Consistent with the New Social Studies goal of engaging students in developmentally appropriate methods of inquiry in the component disciplines of the social studies, the guide defines "skills and processes" as "those skills employed by social scientists."[26] The guide also reflects the era's concern for values, defining "valuing" as developing the ability to "recognize the social values of our society," to "clarify their own structure of values," and, again reflecting the state of the field circa 1968, to "reconcile value conflicts."[27] Even as DPI issued subsequent bulletins, *Knowledge, Processes, and Values in the Social Studies* remained recognized as an important addendum to the *Conceptual Framework*.

It is clear that the newer guide is a compromise document, a fitting result reflecting the ideological commitments in the previous publication. First, the committee notes that because social studies curriculum content is fluid, it "requires continuing professional growth" yet provides the possibility that classes "can take on 'life-like' characteristics because life too is constantly changing."[28] The authors do not seem to draw a causal relationship between fluidity in life and fluidity in course content, seemingly denying a connection between schooling and broader social issues. Second, the guide identifies social and cultural transmission, "the tendency to perpetuate the status quo," as reflective of "the aspiration of all societies toward self-preservation," yet it observes that, in the "progress oriented" United States, schools are also tasked with the contradictory role of being "expected to assist in the change and improvement of the culture."[29] Such a responsibility would require engagement with contemporary social issues. Third, the authors recognize a tension between socializing students to "function effectively as a member of both primary and secondary groups" and supporting their ability to "attain personal autonomy."[30] The guide explains that students "must see a democratic society as a reconciliation between 'socializing' and 'individualizing,'" and its authors argue that this tension can ensure that the course is "reality oriented."[31] The authors walk a fine line between individual and group interests, and the apparent tension among curriculum policy leaders in the state reflects those in the field as a whole.

The authors of *Knowledge, Processes, and Values in the New Social Studies* clearly connect the field to social developments, noting that "steadfast faith in progress" has meant that "educators have never been satisfied and have continually sought greater improvements." The "ferment of the social studies" reflected an unprecedented "demand for improvements" in the 1960s, and the authors project a continuing trend into the 1970s. They note how "rising expectations of different groups within our society for or against change have also encouraged searching re-assessment of traditional social studies programs" such that "prodding" comes from both liberal critics who "have unlimited faith in education as the solution to any and all social problems" and their conservative counterparts who "decry the changes in traditional curriculum and seek preservation of the familiar." The authors observe the critical influence of the mass media's ability to instantaneously transmit information, the "abundance of stimuli" that it provides, the resulting "greater numbers of options in pleasure, education, and work," and the resulting pressures from critics for "curriculum workers and teachers to update social studies overnight."[32] The media itself brought sociopolitical crises such as the Vietnam War into American living rooms, increasing the average citizen's degree of connection with and engagement to these issues while calling attention to their limited exposure to and ability to participate in public debates. Overall, the guide calls for curriculum committees to connect social studies instruction to contemporary issues more clearly.

THE MID-1970S: CURRICULUM POLICY BULLETINS FOR THE DISCIPLINES

In the mid-1970s, amidst the ongoing national debates among curriculum policy makers and the general turn to curricular relevance and ethnic studies in the field as a whole, DPI began to issue a new series of policy bulletins. Over a ten-year period, the agency convened Social Studies Curriculum Study Committee subcommittees to assist local curriculum committees seeking to improve student knowledge in individual disciplines within the field of social studies at all grade levels. These brief guides, which range from six to forty-three pages, circulated unbound to Wisconsin schools.

The first bulletin in this new series, *Descriptors for Political Understanding: A Guide to Asking Questions About Learning Related to Political Literacy in Wisconsin Schools, K-12*, was intended to assist local curriculum committees seeking to improve student understanding of topics related to civics and government. It reflects an inquiry-driven approach characteristic of the Second Wave New Social Studies. "Through inquiry" the guide lists several items that students are to learn, including "how local, state, national, and planetary agencies can provide different yet important services to the communities of the world."[33] The guide repeats this statement under the subheadings "Political Knowledge" and "Larger Community."[34] In explaining basic concepts, it defines "interdependence" in terms of the "division of responsibility at all levels of government; local, state, national, and international."[35]

The guide is silent, however, about tribal government, excluding federally recognized tribes in each of several listings of levels of government, though it refers several times to international or "planetary" government without defining those terms.[36] It is silent once again on tribal government as it suggests "Major Political Science Concepts" for grade bands K–3, 4–6, and 7–12.[37] This exclusion takes on an ironic quality given the statement, "Knowledge about the political process should be accurate. It should focus on the ways in which politics works and not only upon formal or ideal models."[38]

Looking back on an era marked by multiple social movements, the Kent State University shooting of unarmed students, and the Watergate scandal, the need for responsive political science guidelines is apparent. Yet by excluding tribal sovereignty or any discussion of government-to-government relationships in this curriculum planning tool, state officials effectively denied students the opportunity to learn about treaty rights and related themes. Those curriculum policy decisions would have serious consequences in the coming decades.

PROGRAM IMPROVEMENT FOR SOCIAL STUDIES EDUCATION, 1977

Amidst differing views in a field dominated by an NCSS-led turn toward ethnic studies, DPI again stepped in to provide clarity for local curriculum committees by publishing *Program Improvement for Social Studies Education in Wisconsin* in 1977.[39] Appropriate to a local control state, it is a self-assessment guide written by the State Social Studies Curriculum Study

Committee, once again composed of teachers and administrators from school districts across the state. It articulates a series of "new challenges" related to the implementation of the "new social studies," which brought both "renewed vigor" and "new problems" to the field.[40] In many ways, it is a repudiation of 1970's *Knowledge, Processes, and Values*, because the new bulletin strongly critiques the kinds of lessons recommended in that document, although the authors are careful to recognize its role to "expand and clarify the structure for the social studies in Wisconsin schools."[41]

The authors of *Program Improvement for Social Studies Education in Wisconsin* lament that attention to "cognitive (inquiry) skills and affective" domains, as recommended by the earlier guide, meant that "some educators ignored a balanced approach."[42] Reflecting a concern raised by critics of the New Social Studies' focus on disciplinary skills, the State Social Studies Curriculum Study Committee regretted that "students were led down a bewildering trail of inquiry exercises that sharpened the data gathering and processing skills, but had no substantive destination."[43] The curriculum policy pendulum was swinging rightward again, favoring transmission of factual knowledge over personal decision making and engagement with contemporary social and political issues.

The authors addressed many longstanding concerns with values clarification and similar instructional trends, lamenting how "misguided 'humanization' of the schools made a mockery of previously heralded rational decision making" and "embroidered" new content into the familiar scope and sequence.[44] The guide welcomed and praised the emergence of new courses in social sciences as "undoubtedly healthy," but characterized these trends as contributing to "a serious lack of program coherence at the secondary level."[45] In a time when ethnic studies was rising to dominate social studies as a whole, the authors dismissively lump together those who sought to include "'multi-ethnic texts' that accurately portrayed the status of minorities," those who sought innovative ways to incorporate media in classroom instruction, and those who sought to advance role-playing as an instructional method.[46] In describing the ideal social studies curriculum, *Program Improvement for Social Studies Education in Wisconsin* states, "Certainly, social studies education must put the student in touch with his or her cultural heritage," which it defines as "that body of facts, concepts, generalizations and theories that constitute the organized disciplines of the human family."[47] It does not explain how these various members of the human family are to learn about cultural heritages other than their own. This use of "cultural," as opposed to NCSS's choice of "ethnic," is perhaps a repurposing of that language in ways that reflect more conservative approaches detrimental to ethnic studies.

Appendix A of *Program Improvement for Social Studies Education* describes the eleven goals for elementary and secondary public education and connects them to the economic and sociopolitical concerns of a "highly technological, rapidly and dramatically changing society."[48] Many of these goals reflect the desire to provide opportunities for students to learn about their own cultures and those of others so they would develop a positive cultural identity, understand and respect cultural differences, and "manage conflicts in values."[49] The goals also address learning outcomes related to lifelong learning in an "ever-changing social, economic, and political environment" and the ability to think critically about "personal problems and societal conflicts."[50] A social studies program that fostered these understandings and attitudes might have helped the state to avoid the violent controversy that followed from *Voigt*, yet the learning goals related to "citizenship and political understanding" focus narrowly on the "locality, state, nation, and world" and exclude concepts of Native nationhood from the domain of official knowledge.[51]

Although NCSS had largely moved away from a narrow, discipline-focused approach to social studies, disciplinary integrity remained a concern in the late 1970s, particularly at the high school level. DPI responded to this trend by publishing *Descriptors for Anthropology: A Guide to Asking Questions About Learning Anthropology Facts and Concepts in Wisconsin Schools, K-12*, in 1978, continuing the efforts it began two years earlier with *Descriptors for Political Science*. This very brief policy bulletin provides an outline of the field overall with very few references to any particular people or culture area other than Mesopotamia. The team of university faculty members who authored the publication strongly imply that classroom teachers are incapable of making appropriate choices of instructional materials, again harking back to the "teacher-proof" ideals of the previous decade.[52]

State and Local Curriculum Policy in the 1980s

During the 1980s, national curriculum policy was moving away from practices associated with perceived fragmentation in the field to a view that focused on commonalities between peoples and cultures and stressed cultural transmission rather than critical thinking. Despite these national trends, some of the initiatives of the 1970s still had momentum, illustrating that the interplay among national, state, and local influences on curriculum policy meant that the pace and direction of policy change was far from uniform. Tensions between various political and philosophical views of the field are evident in several DPI publications issued in the 1980s. These documents reflect the potentially confusing and contradictory messages about official knowledge issued by the state as to how local school districts should define that domain.

In 1985, DPI published another very brief bulletin in the series addressing individual social studies disciplines across the grade levels. *Descriptors for Sociology: A Guide to Asking Questions About Learning Sociology Facts and Concepts in Wisconsin Schools, K-12*, provides a series of statements defining "sociology education goals." These include "to gain a greater sensitivity to the differences and similarities in groups, societies, and cultures" and "to gain a greater tolerance of differences between people and cultures, through a diminishing of the student's ethnocentrism." These ideas reflect the philosophy and instructional goals set forth by James Banks and others a decade earlier, showing that, at least in some disciplines, there was a lasting impact. Under the heading "Descriptors: Knowledge and Skills Students Should Gain," the guide lists "an understanding of and tolerance for various cultural and social institutions and systems," "an awareness of the influence of one's biases and prejudices on one's perceptions," and "an understanding of the nature of social problems, their causes, and alternative approaches to their resolution."[53] These goals are more in line with mid- to late-1970s concerns for ethnic studies and curricular inclusivity than Ronald Reagan's "Morning in America," which suggests that these approaches persisted, at least within disciplinary enclaves.

The next bulletin in the discipline-focused series for social studies was in the highly contested field of American history. *Descriptors for*

Understanding United States History: A Guide to Asking Questions About Learning Related to History in Wisconsin Schools, K-12, published in 1986, is much more reflective of the conservative mood of the nation during Reagan's presidency. The overall tone of the guide reflects concern for relevance to contemporary youth and critical thinking, noting that too often "what sense of past and future that does exist is often distorted by the fantastic lens of 'Dungeons and Dragons' at one end of the time line and that of 'Star Wars' at the other."[54] It differentiates between concepts, "those basic ideas which are the stuff of the social studies," and themes, which it defines as "particularly important and widely applicable concepts."[55] The authors stress the importance of content knowledge, outlining a cultural transmission–oriented rationale for the study of American history wherein "the stuff" is rather narrowly defined.

The five themes, described as "particularly important and widely applicable concepts," are those ideas that the committee deemed "knowledge . . . so basic and fundamental that it [is] everyone's business."[56] These themes represent a clear articulation of official knowledge from state curriculum policy leaders. The Wisconsin Social Studies Curriculum Study Committee describes these themes in terms of common sense, "so basic" and "fundamental" as to be "everyone's business" to master the selective traditions represented in this curriculum content. How and indeed whether to implement these guidelines in a particular school district is at the discretion of local curriculum committees acting on behalf of elected school boards. Political considerations would likely make it very difficult to resist an appeal to common sense.

Under the heading "Environmental Factors," the guide asserts, "The interplay between people and the land" has been a major theme in American history.[57] "A recognition that the United States has always been a pluralistic society and that this pluralism has been one of our most powerful social dynamics" suggests an inclusivity not otherwise reflected in the guide as a whole.[58] In these descriptors of the geographic factors that shaped the nation and its history, the authors note the importance of cash crops, river networks, and so forth, concluding that "any understanding of the whole westward movement is dependent upon an understanding of our environmental and geographic realities."[59] Students might be forgiven if repeated exclusionary references to "we" and "our," as well as references to such dynamics as "the settling of the continent," lead them to fail to realize that American Indian peoples inhabited all of these lands.[60]

"American pluralisms" is another key theme, and the guide notes that "the United States is now, has always been, and apparently will always be a multi-racial, multi-lingual, and multi-ethnic society."[61] The authors call on teachers to "confront the history of various racial, ethnic, and age groups which comprise our population" as well as "the process by which these groups have interrelated with each other and by which they all have affected public issues and policies."[62] In noting how "geographic and technological factors" have affected the nation's pluralistic character, the guide notes "the nature of English relationships with the American Indian was shaped by the technological sophistication of the Europeans."[63] The descriptors related to this theme call on students to "recognize the unique historical experiences of Blacks, Hispanics, Asians, and American Indians in U.S. history."[64] Such views serve to normalize Eurocentrism and Eurocentric perspectives while including the historical experiences, perspectives, and voices of American Indians and people of color only at the margins as exceptions to the primary narrative of progress. This approach also reinforces the idea that American Indians are simply another minority group rather than nations within a nation who have a unique relationship with the federal government of the United States. Such a limited description is itself intensely political.

The guide's discussion of the "American political system" focuses on the experiences and traditions of "the settlers who established colonies along the eastern seaboard of North America."[65] The text attributes such key features as the separation of powers and checks and balances to European innovation as part of the legacy of such documents as the Mayflower Compact and "the interplay of beliefs and experiences."[66] The authors write, "If any factor permeates America's political history, it is that our political institutions were born and reached fruition on a vast rich continent, far removed from the disruptive and corrupting influences of Europe."[67] The guide also stresses the unique character of American political institutions without mentioning even the scholarly debate about the role of the Iroquois Confederacy on American political systems. Nowhere does the guide acknowledge tribal sovereignty, nationhood, or government-to-government relations with the federal government as expressly defined in the Constitution.

The theme of "international and global affairs" reminds students that "the westward expansion of the United States was an international event that brought us in contact, and in conflict, with England, France, Spain, Mexico, and Russia."[68] The descriptors note that students "should be comfortable in discussing concepts such as imperialism, nationalism, Manifest Destiny, and isolationism within the context of American history."[69] There is no mention of American Indians in this context, nor in any other related to this theme, despite the fact that the United States recognized tribal nations as the holders of legal title to these lands and with whom the federal government signed 367 ratified treaties between 1778 and 1871.[70] It would appear that students are to learn that land title was simply acquired through negotiations between the United States and various European powers, and that land title simply passed from one European colonial power to another before coming into the possession of the United States.

Overall, *Descriptors for Understanding United States History* incorporates some of the lessons of the previous decade of social studies curriculum reform in terms of content about American Indians and people of color, yet it does so in a selective, problematic manner that seemingly encourages local curriculum committees to ignore the perspectives of these groups. In this respect, it is absolutely contrary to the work that James Banks and others had been doing with curriculum policy through NCSS to trouble the master narrative and create a more complex, decentered historical narrative of the United States. It is more in line with the moderate to conservative trend that dominated Wisconsin curriculum policy for decades. This shows that the curriculum policy pendulum did not swing as far nor as fast in Wisconsin as it did at the national level.

The next major DPI publication addressing social studies was *A Guide to Curriculum Planning in Social Studies*, published in 1986. In many ways, the book serves as a compilation of the discipline-based descriptors that the agency had been issuing since the mid-1970s, but the checklists and similar documents suggest how it might really serve to guide the work of local curriculum committees. The Social Studies Curriculum Development Task Force, chaired by DPI Social Studies Education Supervisor H. Michael Hartoonian, comprised K-12 educators and university education faculty, both active and retired, in nearly equal numbers, which reflects a balance between attention to preservice and in-service teacher education and professional development.[71] Because it attempts to serve multiple audiences, its attention to the field is broadly comprehensive.

Several pieces in the guide provide key policy statements on social studies education, which can be read as a state-level description of the parameters of official knowledge in the field. In a section titled "Equity and the Curriculum," the authors explain how stereotypical views and biased actions based on gender, race, color, ethnicity, and physical and mental ability limit opportunities and experiences. The department "recommends the inclusion of all groups in the curriculum and in teaching materials" and calls for the elimination of "invisibility, stereotyping, imbalance and selectivity, unreality, fragmentation and isolation, and linguistic bias."[72] As an alternative, it calls on school districts to "actively value all persons by including the contributions, representations, and experiences of all groups in curricular objectives and classroom activities."[73] The introduction locates the guide in terms of the ongoing debate in the field about the nature, scope, and purpose of social studies. This section explains that the primary purpose of social studies is essentially "to ensure our survival as a free nation through the development of enlightened citizens."[74] Thus, the authors have expressly linked concerns for equity to the citizenship-related goals of the field. DPI legitimated diversity, broadly defined, as a key characteristic of official knowledge.

A Guide to Curriculum Planning in Social Studies offers five educational goals of social studies education that served to define official knowledge in the field: "enlightened democratic citizenship in order to participate effectively in local, state, national, and international affairs"; "appreciation and understanding of our cultural heritage and its role in contemporary society"; "acquisition of knowledge and skills related to the several subjects that study the motives, actions, and consequences of human beings as they live individually as well as in groups and societies in a variety of places and time settings"; "the joy of learning about self, others and human history"; and "'learning how to learn'—how to understand complex ideas and how to create new ideas."[75] These can be understood as state-level definitions of official knowledge in the field as a whole. The guide also reprints the "Statement of Ethical Principles" developed in 1980 by the National

Council for the Social Studies, giving it a place of prominence.[76] Given that most school districts convened committees to examine and revise their curriculum and instructional practices every five to seven years, the guide likely had significant influence on their work during the late 1980s.

The guide locates the work of local curriculum committees within a broader context characterized by past curriculum experiences, contemporary public concern for school reform, and the coming "Information Age."[77] It calls on teachers to "be sensitive to the insights from their history" of curriculum development, to recognize that "curriculum revision is often a reaction to social change," and to differentiate between information, knowledge, and wisdom in planning for the future.[78] The authors discuss the nature of anticipated changes in curriculum content, including additional information and points of view, the rise of interdisciplinary studies, the "increased rate of obsolescence," and a shift in the role of the teacher from a "source of information" to a "broker of information."[79] This framing of official knowledge de-emphasizes the importance of curriculum content in favor of general principles.

The authors devote significant attention to textbook selection guidelines and processes, recognizing the often-problematic process of establishing official knowledge at the local level.[80] They wryly note that "when textbooks wear out or administrators seek school accreditation, the 'infamous' curriculum committee is appointed."[81] They suggest that as the evaluation process begins, committees too often simply consider "which book or series seems most teachable to the kinds of students who show up in classes every day" instead of asking about educational purposes, strategies for attaining those purposes, methods of organizing content and experiences, and means for determining whether instructional goals are being met.[82] They acknowledge that these concerns are admittedly "removed from the classroom teacher's concern of lesson plans for the next class," which can mean that "the books chosen imply the answers," such that "the tail appears to wag the dog."[83] In a sense, the authors are asking local curriculum committees to become more deliberate as they work to select materials that will embody official knowledge at the local level.

The authors note the tensions between "knowledgeable and skillful" textbook authors, who often have thought deeply about curriculum questions, and publishers, who "are in a business to sell books, so they insist on publications that can be used in a variety of ways—some justifiable and others not." As a result, they argue, most student editions are merely content readers, while most teachers' editions "are full of suggestions for participatory classes." "The former," they write, "prepare the students for Trivial Pursuit" whereas "the latter, if executed skillfully, can lead to informed citizenship." Ultimately, the guide "endorses the use of a textbook if it is exercised responsibly so that students actually learn something worthwhile." The committee expressly links these matters to school budgets, instructional resources, professional development, and "a salary worthy of a professional."[84] In a sharp departure from past decades' attempts to "teacher-proof" the curriculum, the authors appeal to teachers' professionalism to improve the processes used to define official knowledge at the district level.

It is important to examine the guidance that the State Social Studies Curriculum Development Task Force provides for teaching Wisconsin history. In the recommended scope and sequence, this instruction is entrusted to fourth-grade teachers, and the task force notes that they have "a unique opportunity" to provide "interdisciplinary studies of our culture, environment, people, challenges, and successes." The study of the state provides opportunities to learn about "our state heritage" by exploring "interrelationships in a unique and exciting local laboratory." The guide identifies four key themes for the study of Wisconsin history, noting that curriculum committees can weave them into many different organizational structures. The themes include the "exploration of different geographic regions," with attention to Wisconsin, the Great Lakes, and the Midwest; the "unique land system of Wisconsin which provides a laboratory for studying the earth, and the environmental and life systems we create"; the "institutions and special heritage" of the state; and the "social, economic, and governmental institutions" of the state.[85] The ten "illustrative examples" include the statement, "Explain how Wisconsin Native Americans, explorers, immigrants, and community builders influenced the state's development and that of the Great Lakes region," clearly signaling to local school districts that the study of Native people should be within the scope of official knowledge at the local level.

The guide features American Indians prominently in several of the topics and their corresponding lists of concepts and key ideas. Under "Where is

Wisconsin?" one of the sample questions provided to guide curriculum planning includes the statement, "Where are Wisconsin's Native Americans located? How do they contribute to our state?" While the "we"/"they" language is problematic, these questions nonetheless are likely to spark important local conversations that could lead to meaningful curricular inclusion. One of the concepts that corresponds with this topic is "Indian nation," which shows that from a state perspective, tribal nationhood is important and worthy of being legitimated as official knowledge at the local level. There are several references to Native Americans associated with the sample question "How has the culture of Wisconsin developed?," each of which implies a relationship between American Indians and other peoples.[86] One asks how "Native Americans, explorers, immigrants, and settlers use and adapt habitats," suggesting a relationship between peoples and place. Another asks how "Native Americans and immigrants" have influenced the state's history, suggesting an ongoing legacy.[87]

Further curriculum development questions related to the state's culture ask, "How did Native Americans and settlers cooperate?" and "How were they in conflict?," suggesting multiple perspectives on these interaction patterns. The last of the planning questions that explicitly reference Native Americans asks "What heritage, customs, and traditions did we adopt from the Native Americans in our state?," which suggests a lasting cultural influence even as Native Americans are implicitly excluded from the "we" and "our." Another exclusionary planning prompt suggests the questions "Who are our ancestors?" and "Where did they come from?" The questions imply that "we" share an experience as the descendants of immigrants. The list of key terms in this segment includes "reservation treaty," "land ethic," "prejudice," "heritage," "endangered resources," "culture," and "stereotypes," all of which could be used to shape curriculum in interesting and useful ways that foster nuanced understanding of American Indian issues.[88] The guide also reflects the task force's value of curriculum content about American Indians in other places, particularly for those grade levels where the United States is the focus.

—II—

The study of instructional opportunities in Wisconsin history shows how the interaction between state and local curriculum policy makers shaped official knowledge in the state over time and how these educational leaders responded to implicit questions about whose knowledge and perspectives should be included. State curriculum guides and related policy bulletins published by DPI, the state agency charged with providing educational leadership and oversight to public schools, exemplify official knowledge as determined by the state.

By the mid-1980s, state curriculum policy makers had come to recognize the importance of engaging with broader sociopolitical concerns. The 1986 edition of *A Guide to Curriculum Planning* explicitly connects with this mission such that when advocates for expanded curricular attention to American Indians began to pursue legislation to that end, their ideas were not as outside mainstream curriculum policy at the state level as they were out of step with broader national trends in the field. Nonetheless, given the interplay between national, state, and local curriculum policy forces, it is clear that the effort to redefine official knowledge to include American Indian history, culture, and tribal sovereignty would be a significant struggle.

Less than three years after the publication of *A Guide to Curriculum Planning in Social Studies*, on August 8, 1989, the State of Wisconsin broke precedent with decades of curriculum policy when it created new statutes requiring instruction in the history, culture, and tribal sovereignty of the federally recognized tribes and bands in Wisconsin. In addition to the biennial budget bill through which it enacted these requirements, the legislature passed only thirty-four education-related bills during that session.[89] Only one of these bills, Act 203, dealt with instructional matters, and most of its provisions requiring instruction on AIDS and HIV did not survive the governor's veto pen. Instructional requirements on American Indian history, culture, tribal sovereignty, and related issues remained unique in the degree to which they were contrary to cherished traditions of local control.

CHAPTER 9

OFFICIAL KNOWLEDGE AND THE STATE HISTORICAL SOCIETY OF WISCONSIN, 1923–1964

In order to understand the nature and intent of Act 31 in terms of both local curriculum policy and instructional materials, it is necessary to consider the range of options available to local school boards and to analyze the materials widely used in Wisconsin classrooms before Act 31 was passed. Their choices demonstrate how local curriculum policy makers in Wisconsin responded to broader trends in the field and how and when they considered American Indians worthy of inclusion in the curriculum. In this respect, textbooks and other classroom materials serve as the local embodiment of official knowledge, and curriculum research in social studies has repeatedly established the centrality of the textbook as an instructional tool.[1] Because the adoption process involves decision making at many levels—author, publisher, school administration, and teachers—it is reasonable to conclude that the contents were "approved and accepted as solid historical fact at the time it was published."[2]

There is perhaps no more "official" knowledge about Wisconsin's history than that which has been selected and promoted by the State Historical Society of Wisconsin. As both a state agency within the executive branch of state government and a membership organization, the Society has long functioned as a key arbiter of official knowledge about the state's history and culture. As the oldest publisher in the state, it has published materials on Wisconsin's history for more than 150 years, with Society staff and lay and professional historians contributing articles to the *Wisconsin Magazine of History* and writing books and pamphlets on various topics related to the state's history. It is no surprise that some of the earliest materials suitable for a social studies classroom were produced by the agency.

In the first half of the twentieth century, the Society published two major resources for students of the state's history that take a strikingly different approach to promoting broad understanding of Native peoples. The first was Charles E. Brown's pamphlet, "Wisconsin Indian Tribes," which appeared in multiple editions in the 1920s and 1930s and was more appropriate for college classrooms than for young readers. The other was *It Happened Here: Stories of Wisconsin*, a textbook written by Margaret G. Henderson, Ethel Dewey Speerschneider, and Helen L. Ferslev and published by the State Historical Society of Wisconsin in 1949. As the first textbook published by the Society to address state-level social studies curriculum needs, it is notable in its exclusion of Native stories and history and a clear departure from Brown's earlier work.

Beginning in 1947, the society began to publish what would be its greatest pre–Act 31 effort to introduce young students to Wisconsin history, a journal for elementary-age children titled *Badger History*. Under various editors, its approach to and coverage of Native topics shifted in both subtle and not-so-subtle ways over many decades. Although it included stories and special issues on American Indians in Wisconsin, and even included pieces written by authors who were themselves Native, it often overlooked Native perspectives and reinforced an "us and them" dynamic. Though it was not a formal textbook, because new material was published regularly over a span of decades, *Badger History* provides a fascinating and informative look at the social studies curriculum and materials used in the decades before Act 31. It also shows evidence of what was taught and learned in Wisconsin classrooms through its inclusion of exemplary student-generated material.

This chapter assesses the early efforts of the State Historical Society to meet the needs of younger students and scholars in the changing field of social studies, with particular focus on the inclusion and exclusion of Indian topics such as sovereignty, treaty rights, Native culture and history, and Native perspectives.

CHARLES E. BROWN'S "WISCONSIN INDIAN TRIBES,"
1923, 1927, 1931

In 1923, Charles E. Brown, chief of the State Historical Museum in Madison, authored the first of several editions of "Wisconsin Indian Tribes," an eight-page booklet "Prepared for the use of Students."[3] Brown, an archaeologist, was himself a formative figure in the "History of Wisconsin Civilization, from the Indian settlements on down."[4] In addition to his role at the museum, he was a founding member and secretary of the Wisconsin Archaeology Society from 1903 to 1941 and its president from 1941 until his retirement in 1944. He also served as the editor of its journal, *The Wisconsin Archaeologist*, from 1903 to 1941. Brown's scholarship focused on "Wisconsin archaeologists, Indians, folklore, archaeological technique, collections, exhibits, museums, meetings and conventions, mound types, frauds, and airplane photographs," and included thirty publications on archaeological surveys, primarily mounds, and at least thirty-nine articles on "Indian implements."[5] Notably, his work was instrumental in passing laws for the protection and preservation of effigy and burial mounds and other historically significant sites in Wisconsin. Upon his retirement as museum director, the journal Brown had edited for nearly forty years devoted an entire issue to celebrating his scholarly accomplishments. Colleagues and friends, including such notable figures as August Derleth and Chief Yellow Thunder, lauded Brown's scholarly accomplishments.[6] At the time of publication, perhaps no scholar of Wisconsin history was as widely esteemed as Charles E. Brown.

Brown divides his discussion in "Wisconsin Indian Tribes" into five sections: three by linguistic family ("Siouan tribes," "Algonkian tribes," and "Iroquoian tribes"); one on "Indian Remains"; and a seven-item bibliographic section titled "Literature." In nearly every case, the author uses the people's traditional names for themselves and provides a definition. Overall, Brown does not distinguish between peoples with an ongoing, contemporary presence and those whose presence or relationship with the region is primarily historical. He includes some contemporary information on reservations, populations, and the locations of schools and Indian agencies, but students would have to read quite closely to understand who the Native peoples living in the state were in 1923.

The booklet is scholarly in both language and tone, so while the content is valuable, its actual suitability for a young audience is questionable.

The Winnebago (present-day Ho-Chunk), who Brown notes "have been known to white men since 1634," themselves arrived in the region "in prehistoric time during the westward migration of a group of Siouan tribes from their primitive home on the Atlantic seaboard."[7] Based on archaeological remains, they have "been long, possibly for centuries, in undisturbed possession of Wisconsin soil," from Lake Michigan to the Mississippi River, and from present-day central Wisconsin to northern Illinois.[8] Brown's capsule history has a strong military history focus, noting alliances with the Menominee, conflict with the Illinois, support for Tecumseh, and "opposition to American occupation" leading to support for the British during the War of 1812. Alluding to the Ho-Chunk leader Red Bird, he argues, "In 1827, only the presence of a number of troops at several frontier forts in Wisconsin prevented serious Winnebago troubles."[9]

Brown discusses Winnebago treaties signed in 1825, 1832, and 1837, as well as the series of removals to Iowa, Minnesota, South Dakota, and Nebraska that followed. He provides population figures for 1820, 1881, and 1910. Addressing their contemporary status, Brown notes the presence of an Indian agency in Tomah, schools in Tomah and Wittenberg, and a current population of 1,283.[10] He concludes the section with brief discussions of the Dakota and Ioway peoples, the latter of whom he notes have a tradition that they were once part of the Winnebago people.

Brown opens his discussion of the Algonkian peoples by describing the Chippewa, noting they are also known as "Ojibway, 'to roast till puckered up.'"[11] He notes that this group of almost thirty-two thousand people in the United States and Canada migrated to present-day Wisconsin "from some point to the northeast shortly before the beginning of white history," perhaps 1640 or even a century earlier according to their own traditions.[12] He describes historic alliances with the Potawatomi and Ottawa peoples as the Three Fires Confederacy and explains the tribe's conflict with the Dakota over wild rice beds. Brown notes the existence of reservations and schools at Red Cliff, La Pointe (Bad River), Lac du Flambeau, and Lac Courte Oreilles, and a current population of approximately thirty-eight hundred.[13] Brown is correct to omit the present-day reservations at St. Croix and Mole Lake, as both did not secure reservation lands until the 1930s.

Brown explains that the Potawatomi first encountered the French near Green Bay in 1670 and thereafter spread along Lake Michigan's shores as far south as present-day Milwaukee and Chicago. He notes their military alliance with the French through the end of the French and Indian War, involvement with Pontiac, and alliance with the British during the War of 1812. Brown notes treaties signed in 1829 and 1835 led to removals to Iowa and Kansas. Of their contemporary status, he states only that "a portion of the Prairie band resides in Forest and other northeastern counties" and an agency exists at Laona serving a population of approximately four hundred.[14]

Brown writes that the "Menomini" people are commonly known by a name derived from the Chippewa word for "wild rice."[15] They are close relatives of the Sauk and Fox and "probably came from some point south of Mackinac" to the mouth of the Menominee River where they were circa 1634. "They have generally been at peace with the whites," Brown reports.[16] Of their contemporary status, Brown states that the government "ceded to them their present-day reservation in Shawano County" in 1854, and that their "present number is 1,788."[17]

The Stockbridge are "Massachusetts Indians, their original home being in the Housatonic Valley."[18] Brown reports that they moved to Oneida in 1785, then to Wisconsin with the Oneidas in 1822, and lived first near Kaukauna, then moved to Calumet County in 1834, and then to their present reservation in 1856, which is home to a population of 606.[19] He notes that the Munsee "became incorporated with them" at Kaukauna.[20]

Brown describes the Brothertown as "individuals of Connecticut, Rhode Island and Long Island, Algonkian tribes," who lived among the Oneida by 1788. "Before 1830," he writes, they came to Wisconsin, eventually settling in Calumet County. Of their population figures, he states simply, "Their population is small."[21]

He devotes several full paragraphs to the Fox, whom he describes as a "restless and warlike tribe," and to the Sauk, for whom an 1804 land cession and "disagreement over this transaction" led to the Black Hawk War.[22] Of the Kickapoo, Mascouten, and Miami tribes, Brown explains they are of "small importance" in Wisconsin history but had villages near Berlin circa 1665.[23]

The section titled "Iroquoian Tribes" is the shortest. Brown explains that the Oneida tribe is "originally from central New York" but "purchased lands on the Fox River in Wisconsin in 1821 with the Stockbridge and Brotherton."[24] He reports a contemporary population of 2,657. This section also briefly mentions the Wyandot people who "fled to Washington Island, Wisconsin, to escape destruction from their relatives the New York Iroquois."[25]

Brown's section "Indian Remains" is lengthy, perhaps reflecting his assessment that "the recorded Indian history of Wisconsin has been supplemented and extended by a study of its very numerous aboriginal remains," which can be found "on and near the shores of nearly every lake and stream."[26] He describes the work of archaeologists, including Increase Lapham and the Wisconsin Archaeological Society, in surveying and exploring these sites. He notes the presence of more than ten thousand mounds, stating the "effigy or animal shaped earthworks are the most singular aboriginal structures in the United States."[27] He acknowledges several notable mounds in parks in southern Wisconsin, including Man Mound and Aztalan, and he contrasts the efforts to preserve these earthworks with the threatened status of over one hundred mounds in the Madison area. Brown writes, "In view of their present rapid destruction through various causes and their great historical and scenic interest, it is desirable that many more should be permanently preserved."[28] He concludes this section by reporting on collections of artifacts "assembled for the use of students of the rich field of Wisconsin Indian history."[29]

The final section, "Literature," provides citations for seven pieces, including scholarly articles and ethnographic reports in *The Wisconsin Archaeologist*, from the Bureau of Ethnology, or in the Wisconsin Historical Collections.[30]

The State Historical Museum published the second edition of Brown's "Wisconsin Indian Tribes" in 1927. It was "Prepared for Students" attending summer session at the University of Wisconsin.[31] The document is substantially similar to the previous edition such that even the "present day" population estimates are the same as in 1923. The "Third Issue," published in 1931, is also identical down to the population figures, but the "Literature" section has expanded to include eleven entries.

According to the State Historical Society of the 1920s and 1930s, American Indians were worthy of study, albeit largely as a sort of relic or curiosity. American Indian men's high rates of enlistment and military service in World War I led to favorable public opinion and was a major factor in the passage of the American Indian Citizenship Act in 1924. Brown's pamphlet reflects these attitudes, and the multiple editions suggest sustained interest. However, that interest was not maintained, as the next example shows.

It Happened Here: Stories of Wisconsin, 1949

In 1949, the State Historical Society published *It Happened Here: Stories of Wisconsin*, a book intended to "have some small part in building an appreciation of our democratic ideals as they developed in Wisconsin."[32] In their introduction, the authors pose a number of key questions about Wisconsin history, sending some subtle messages about "our way of life" and later becoming more explicit about the nature of that "we."[33] The briefest section of the book, the first chapter, titled "How It Started," sends a clear message about official knowledge and the sociopolitical relationships that it reflects. After the retreat of the glaciers, the authors explain, "people came here to live. It is thought that they came from Asia, but we cannot be sure. They left no written records telling their story. Later the woodland Indians came, perhaps from Canada. Many legends have been told about them. You can read these stories in other books. This book is about the white people who came to our state."[34] This book, which expressly touts the study of the state's history as a key to developing democratic ideals, specifically excludes knowledge about American Indians, and symbolically, people of color more broadly, from Wisconsin democracy.

American Indians are first misrepresented and then dismissed from the narrative only to be relegated to the role of extras in stories of brave explorers, Jesuit priests, fur traders, and agency families. A section titled "Folklore Tells History" is an example of how the few American Indian stories included have been appropriated and repurposed in a new context to be mere "legends and folk stories," presented as akin to Paul Bunyan tales rather than stories of or belonging to an Indigenous people.[35] This example provides a clear link between questions of what knowledge is of most worth, in terms of knowledge about whom, whose knowledge counts, and who counts in society.

In this respect, the book is an extension of nineteenth-century textbook narratives that cast descendants of European immigrants as the "American Race." Historian Joseph Moreau writes, "In narratives dominated by themes of territorial growth and social progress, which were dependent to varying degrees on White racial strengths, people of color receded to the periphery of the national community" where they "remained outside the direct address of the writers 'we' or 'us' and often became obstacles on the path of national development."[36] American Indians in the mid- and late nineteenth century served as a "picturesque element of the country's past" that "counterbalanced the story of a new, practical-minded young republic" thereby "affirming its unique national identity."[37] Except as features in the landscape and as cameos in a story of European settlement, the authors of official Wisconsin history relegated American Indians to mere "legends" that students could seek elsewhere. In so doing, the Wisconsin State Historical Society effectively excluded content about American Indians from the domain of official knowledge of the state's history.

After World War II and decades after Brown's seminal publication, public attitudes toward American Indians changed again. The federal government promoted policies that unilaterally severed the nation-to-nation relationship with Native peoples and encouraged individual tribal members to relocate to urban areas far from their communities. *It Happened Here* reflects the attitudes of that era. This relationship between instructional materials and the sociopolitical climate of the era in which they were published shows a link between schooling and external matters even in the absence of a clear agenda.

TEACHING AND LEARNING OFFICIAL KNOWLEDGE: *BADGER HISTORY*, 1947–1964

From 1947 until 1980, the State Historical Society of Wisconsin published *Badger History*, a journal for elementary students studying the state's history. For nearly the first half of its existence, the journal came out monthly, nine issues per year during the school year. Starting in the mid-1960s, *Badger History* instead came out quarterly, four issues per academic year. The content was a mix of articles written by professional historians, often staff of the State Historical Society or members of local historical societies, and student-generated content, including both classroom assignments and reports from school-based history clubs. The material authored by adults for students represents official knowledge in that it demonstrates what the state selected to convey about its history. For many years, *Badger History* also served as a sort of newsletter for co-curricular clubs of Junior Historians around the state, the largest such network in the nation.[38] The student-authored material represents official knowledge at both the state and local levels. Student work typically originated as a classroom assignment and was then selected as exemplary by the teacher and ratified by *Badger History* editors. In this latter respect, *Badger History* goes beyond highlighting what knowledge was legitimated by the state to provide a window into what was actually taught and learned in Wisconsin classrooms.

Over the years, the journal frequently included content about Native people in its pages, sometimes as an article's primary subject and sometimes secondary to a focus on explorers, pioneers, or other figures. In both cases, however, these depictions were often problematic, positioning "the Indians" as a largely undifferentiated group that existed primarily as marginal figures in a narrative about European exploration, white settlement, and economic development. At several points in its existence, often annually, *Badger History* published entire issues that were primarily about Native peoples. Although the contents often showed great favor to European explorers, immigrants, and their descendants, these issues are particularly valuable for understanding the material offered about American Indians at both the state and local levels.

THE RYAN ERA, 1947–1955

The first editor of the new *Badger History* journal was Mary Tuohy Ryan, a former assistant librarian at DPI who in 1947 became the first supervisor of school services at the State Historical Society of Wisconsin.[39] Under Ryan's leadership, the society published nine issues each school year. The main section, *Badger History*, focused on students in grades seven through nine, and a second section, *Junior Badger History*, fourth through sixth grade. She opened each issue with a letter to students, always signed "Your Wisconsin Friend, Mrs. Ryan," which previewed the contents of each issue for both age groups of students, and included announcements, comments on the work of history clubs across the state, and acknowledgments of correspondence with teachers, students, and local historical societies.

In addition to being an instructional resource for teachers and a means to engage students in the study of the state's history, *Badger History* was also a vehicle for showcasing student work about Wisconsin. Ryan encouraged her readers to submit "stories, pictures you draw, bits of poems, geography tours and maps, the field trips you make, stories of industries in your own community—and OH! almost a hundred things that lively boys and girls see and do as a learning history activity in school."[40] Students responded well to this invitation, and the journal frequently published their reports, essays, poetry, and plays. One imagines that this work was first favorably evaluated by the classroom teacher, then sent to Madison for further evaluation by "Mrs. Ryan" and perhaps others at the State Historical Society of Wisconsin before being published in *Badger History*.

From its inception, *Badger History* was also a vehicle for a network of clubs of Junior Historians at elementary and secondary schools across the state, and by 1955, there were nearly twelve hundred chapters of Junior Historians serving almost twenty thousand students.[41] These clubs took field trips to historical sites, studied their local history, wrote and produced pageants and plays, and held annual conventions for more than a decade. Although she stepped down shortly before the Junior Historians held their first convention in Green Bay, the five thousand students in attendance presented "Mrs. Ryan," the founder of the program, with a resolution and a plaque naming her "honorary president for life."[42]

In the early years under Mary Tuohy Ryan, *Badger History* frequently included content related to the study of Native peoples, but these pieces varied greatly in quality and tone, perhaps because many were written by students in elementary, middle, and high schools. The inaugural issue included a piece titled "Lake of the Short Ears," written by fifteen-year-old Donna Duehr, in which the young author shares the story of traveling with her family to the Hayward area and learning from Chief Johnny Frog how Lac Courte Oreilles got its name.[43] In a later issue, John Jenkins of the Wisconsin Historical Museum challenged this account, stating, "It is a very interesting legend, but it is not wholly true." Jenkins argued that the story must have changed through multiple retellings, citing "a man here at the University" whose research found that it means "the lake where the short eared Indians live." He wrote, "Possibly the story behind this is not as interesting as the legend Donna Duehr reported, and again it might be much more interesting."[44] Whether or not it is the intended lesson, the message seems to be that students should value the knowledge of university-based "experts" over the cultural knowledge of Native people themselves.

The first issue also included a piece on the Indian Agency House at Portage, a topic the journal would frequently cover during its run.[45] The first issue, which highlights treaties signed with the Winnebago (Ho-Chunk) in 1826, the Treaty of Chicago in 1833, a treaty with the Menominee in 1836, the Sioux treaty of 1837, and the death of Black Hawk in 1838, begins the practice of including such events in its calendar of prominent historical events.[46] The first *Junior Badger History* is similar in that it includes a piece written by a Lake Mills fifth grader on Aztalan and an essay about Milwaukee by a sixth grader from Madison's Randall School.[47] Perhaps reflecting the intent to engage students individually and in groups in the study of history, Jenkins provided the first of many columns addressing state history and encouraging students to make it their hobby.

The first issue of *Badger History* included the first of many direct references or allusions to Black Hawk or the Black Hawk War. In "A Friendly Hello!," her letter opening the *Junior Badger History* section, "Mrs. Ryan" writes of "a noble Indian named Black Hawk" who said, "Rock River was a beautiful country. I liked my town, my cornfields, and the home of my people. I fought for them." She asks her readers, "Do we all love beautiful Wisconsin as Black Hawk did?" She encouraged students to learn as much about their state and to love it as much as Black Hawk did.[48] In most contexts and in most later issues, Black Hawk would not be depicted as favorably and certainly not as a role model. Indeed, *Badger History* often depicts him as a tragic figure whose ultimate and inevitable defeat opened the way to settlement and statehood.

The Ebenezer Williams Junior Historians from Portage submitted "Badger ABC" to the May 1948 issue. The students wrote a series of four-line poems about the state, each beginning with a different letter of the alphabet. Several contained references to Native peoples. For example, "C is for corn, / the Indians sold, / for the shining money, / that looked like gold." Another was "H is for hardships / the settlers had. / They shot Indians (many) / who were cruel and bad." The letter Q stood for "quickness the Indians had. / They killed the settlers / and made them feel sad." Lastly, T stood for "tom tom, the Indian drum. / They used it for dances / and it sounded quite dumb." Printed below the poem is a brief response from Ryan, stating simply, "Boys and girls, reread 'B.' What do you think of it? —M. T. R." She chose to direct students' attention back to the section reading "B is for Badger, / so big and great, / who helped make Wisconsin / A 'Badger State,'" while implicitly validating the overt bigotry of the other entries.[49]

At several points in its existence, *Badger History* published entire issues about Native peoples, the first of which was in November 1948. In her opening letter, Ryan explained that the issue focused on American Indians because "they are so much a part of our history," and she noted that "Dr. Hill of Oneida," the "outstanding Indian of 1947," had become an honorary member of a Junior Historian club in Green Bay.[50] She encouraged students to continue their learning by asking, "Just how do we treat our Indians, a minority people, in Wisconsin? Let's see." The main section of the issue included several essays, reports, and pieces of creative writing from students, an essay called "Things to Do: Studying the Prehistoric Indian" by John Jenkins, traditional stories relayed by folklorist Dorothy M. Brown, a policy statement from the Governor's Task Force on Human Rights, and a piece titled "Indian Boys and Girls Today." The *Junior Badger History* section similarly is filled with a mix of student work, a review of Stand Rock Indian Ceremonial, and recommended books that might be in school libraries. In many of the articles, especially those authored by students, "our Indians" are a people of the past, an exotic other who is "a different race than ours," phrasing which establishes a dichotomy between Wisconsin students and "the Indians."[51] In contrast, those written by professional staff emphasize contemporary Indian life, cultural continuities, and similarities with mainstream values and practices, especially where those represent assimilation.

A high school student from Appleton, writing from the perspective of the Fox River, offered a piece titled "I Saw the Last of the Fox." The river, which is the narrator in this account, "loved to carry those gay and gallant Frenchmen" who sang beautiful songs as they traveled, whereas the Fox "never sang on the water nor did they change one trifle in all the years I carried them."[52] The river notes that it "had no objection to toting them around" until the Fox began to "stop my favorite French traders to exact tribute from them" as they passed through Fox territory.[53] The piece describes several military actions taken by the French and their Menominee, Huron, and Ottawa allies against the "tricky Fox" and how the hill at Butte de Morts "once ran red with human blood" as a result. The river "softened" in its views of the Fox, allowing some to escape, but those who it did not were to serve as a "warning to all other treacherous tribes." The piece concludes by noting that "the last of a famous Indian tribe—the Foxes" died in that spot.[54] In addition to being historically incorrect, this student-authored essay excusing genocide was published by the State Historical Society of Wisconsin at a time when the horrors of the Holocaust were still fresh. The irony is further heightened by its inclusion in the same issue as an article about the Governor's Task Force on Human Rights, a policy statement that begins by stating that "the world tragedy from which we have just emerged was rooted in race prejudice, excessive nationalism, religious persecution and inhumanity to man."[55]

The article "Indian Boys and Girls Today" counters the tendency to portray Native Americans as people of the past, reminding its readers that "the American Indian is not vanishing, as many people think."[56] Readers, whom the editor seemingly presumes are non-Native, learn about the "12 or 1300 Indian boys or girls in the public schools of Wisconsin during the school year 1948-49." They learn that although there are "influential Indian schools" elsewhere in the United States, the federal government closed the Indian schools and converted those at Lac du Flambeau, Neopit, and Stockbridge-Munsee to public schools.[57] The article indicates that there are "a number of areas called Indian reservations" in the state, listing those at Red Cliff, Bad River, Lac Courte Oreilles, Lac du Flambeau, and "Menomini," which is a "closed reservation where all activities on the Reservation are under the Indian Council."[58] It also notes there are other "nontaxable lands on which many Indian families live."[59]

Many of the examples in the piece are about the Menominee Reservation. The article praises their "profitable cooperative sawmill" and "wise conservation practices."[60] It highlights the development of a public school district on the reservation after the July 1, 1948, transition to public education, noting that "there is no color line of any kind" in the state's schools.[61] For the first time in the United States, the Menominees took over "governmental activity" on "exactly the same basis that a white community would take it over."[62] The discussion of the "Indian education fund" and the transfer of state funding to school districts serving Indian students seems more suited to the curiosity of teachers and administrators than students themselves. Of perhaps more interest is the discussion about "Mr. Bert F. Johnson," the state school supervisor "in charge of the education of Indian boys and girls" who is "their friend" and "tries to give all a square deal."[63] The piece again seeks to engage students in supporting the goals of the state, concluding that "Wisconsin is taking good care of Indian boys and girls in school" and pointing out readers could help by "being fair and neighborly to them every day."[64] The article is an early example of the journal's practice of making students aware of contemporary historical developments.

Each November, *Badger History* devoted significant attention to American Indian topics. In November 1949, Ryan's opening letter framed the articles about "our Indians" in terms of the celebration of the spirit of the new United Nations. She concludes by sharing some correspondence with the Potawatomi Council Chapter at Lake Beulah in which the students tell of digging up "a skeleton of an Indian buried upward and the whole collection of arrowheads with him." The letter validated this gruesome act as "very definite evidence of early *Badger History* in the Stewart School District" and commended the "fine teacher."[65]

As with past issues, the November 1949 issue of *Badger History* included submissions from both students and professional historians. Two students wrote about Black Hawk, one focusing on Madison, the other on Vernon County.[66] Another student submitted an article examining "when rustic Wisconsin was host only to the red man," the "many scattered tribes of Indians."[67]

Among the professionally written pieces was an epic poem, "Legend of Monona." The poem tells the story of the many "braves," "squaws," and "papooses" who had made their homes along the Madison-area lakes before the "White Destroyer cometh" with his "stick which belches thunder" and "heart full of murder" to "debauch our daughters, kill our warriors, burn our wigwams, steal our forests, lakes and cornfields."[68] An update to "Indian Boys and Girls of Today" celebrates desegregation of schools, with special attention to Lac du Flambeau, Neopit, Shawano, Bowler, New Post, and Black River Falls, and it notes that hot lunches and transportation for all students "helps all of us to have opportunities to learn."[69] "A Man of Peace Beloved by All" tells the story of Oshkosh's 1926 disinterment and reburial "when the citizens of Oshkosh decided to bring to their city the remains of this warrior from his unmarked burial place on the Keshena Reservation near the upper waters of the Wolf River."[70]

Overall, in its earliest years, despite a tone that is often mildly condescending toward Native Americans and other racially and ethnically diverse peoples, *Badger History* tended to exemplify an early form of human relations education. The articles frequently stress the contributions of various groups and describe how "our Indians" and others each helped to make the state into a homeland in which students could rightly take great pride. The inclusion of articles about Native people in issues other than those with a special focus helps to highlight connections between key themes and events in Wisconsin history.

By the mid-1950s, amidst the ubiquitous articles on missionaries, fur traders, Black Hawk, Nicolet, and mounds, *Badger History* devoted a considerable amount of its professionally written content to the Menominee's pending "independence from federal supervision."[71] The discussions of the Laird Bill, which terminated the Menominee Nation's government-to-government relationship with the federal government, essentially ending their legal status as Indians (until they secured restoration in 1973), were detailed and highly optimistic. According to a piece called "Q and A about Wisconsin History," the Menominee people would "get full title to their sawmill" and "manage their reservation or other tribal property themselves."[72] One of the questions prophetically asked, "What are some of the problems ahead for the Menominee?" The answer was "Payment of taxes, sales of the timber lands, business management, exploitation by greedy men, treaty rights, abiding by state game laws, buying hunting and fishing licenses, improvement program for health, youth and family conditions on the reservation."[73] A photograph of the ceremony at which President Eisenhower signed the Laird Bill, surrounded by Menominee representatives, carries the caption, "We in Wisconsin would not ever wish to exploit our Indians. Our Menominee Indian reservation is a place of extraordinary beauty. Well-informed junior historians can discuss helping to prepare the Indian for his freedom. Is he ready for it?"[74] While it is certainly condescending and patronizing in tone, it also again represents an attempt to connect history to current events and to enlist Junior Historians in shaping, or at least debating, these developments.

Students at Lac du Flambeau Public School, "a junior historian chapter since 1948," submitted a March 1955 article titled, "Lac du Flambeau Centennial Year, 1854–1954," excerpts drawn from a book of that name, written by "the students, faculty and interested people of our community."[75] Students learned that "the story of the Chippewa Indians in Wisconsin has not for the most part been a happy one," and "how he has managed to survive through the years is indeed a sign of great stamina and courage on his part."[76] Indeed, much of the article focuses on land cessions, the Removal Order, and the treaty securing the reservation. In its discussion of the Treaty of 1837, the article explicitly states, "Even though this land was ceded to the government, the Chippewa still had the privilege of hunting, fishing, and gathering wild rice on it as long as the President should feel that the Indian needed it."[77] Of the Treaty of 1842, it says little more than "the Indians were permitted to remain upon these lands until required to move by the President."[78] The authors describe the 1850 Removal Order as the product of "pressure that was put upon the President by the white man as he invaded the area," which meant the "Indian no longer had the right to remain on the lands."[79] Although the removal order meant "the Chippewa moved north and west away from the land of his people," the United States later agreed to set aside land within the 1837 and 1842 cessions for their use. The segment concludes by stating, "the Chippewa looks forward to the next hundred years."[80]

The next section of "Lac du Flambeau Centennial Year, 1854–1954," titled "Lac du Flambeau Before the Coming of the White Man," describes the geographic features of the area and notes how they served "as a means of protection not from wild animals alone but from other savage Indian tribes."[81] It discusses warfare with the Sioux and the early fur trade era.

Finally, it appears that this last article of the issue was appended by *Badger History* editors. This brief passage describes and praises the school's facilities, teachers, staff, and students. It lists "Indian dances" among the more typical list of extracurricular activities. The book on which the article is based apparently sold out of its initial print run, but the principal indicated that another print run could be ordered if they received five hundred requests.[82] The piece again exemplifies *Badger History's* practice of drawing students' attention to history-making events in their own lifetimes, connecting past and present, and subtly reinforcing the idea that American Indians still exist in the state despite what an overall fascination with digging up mounds and writing romanticized accounts of the Fox Wars and Black Hawk might lead them to conclude. This article is also an early example of the journal's publication of pieces written by Native authors. It is particularly noteworthy for including information about usufructuary rights, the only such mention in *Badger History*, and for the pointed language about removal. These concepts became highly contested decades later because there had been very limited opportunity to learn about them. Interestingly, the immediate area around Lac du Flambeau saw some of the worst of the violent controversy in the 1980s.

THE PLATT ERA, 1955–1961

Doris Platt assumed the editorship of *Badger History* beginning with the October 1955 issue.[83] Under her leadership, the journal tended to concentrate its American Indian content in a November special issue. There were still occasional student-submitted pieces describing travel to a historic site, or something similar, and occasional references to such standard topics of Wisconsin history as Black Hawk and Jean Nicolet. The dearth of articles referencing Native people aside from the special issues is a relative retreat from the connections that *Badger History* had emphasized under Mary Tuohy Ryan.

Platt's first special issue focusing on Native people, in November 1955, was less exclusive than that of her predecessor, and it included several articles unrelated to the theme. The editor made several references to Native people—historical, mythical, and real—in her letter to students. She wrote of Iowa's Fort Atkinson, "the only fort ever built to protect the Indians," and its brief existence in protecting the newly removed Winnebago (Ho-Chunk) from the Sioux and Sac and Fox. In reference to the mythical Indian, Platt writes, "Isn't the name of our famous baseball team appropriate—the Braves? Wisconsin was the home of three of the greatest Indian tribes—the Sioux, the Iroquois and the Algonquins. We also had Hurons, Kickapoos, Mascoutens, Miamis, Fox, Sauk, Dakotas and Ottowas. So Milwaukee, a city with an Indian name, rightly has its Braves."[84] Her celebration of Milwaukee baseball obscures the fact that Alqonquins are a language group that includes most of the nations in her next sentence and misses that Dakota and Sioux are names for the same people. In response to a student who wrote in about the plaster Indians in the "Indian life" exhibits at Milwaukee Public Museum, she promised some "real Indians" at the upcoming convention.[85] Based on the overall contents of the journal, students might well have expected to meet living fossils.

In the November 1955 issue, Warren Wittry, curator of anthropology at the State Historical Society of Wisconsin, told of an Old Copper Culture site that had been uncovered by a thirteen-year-old boy from Oconto. Overall, the article follows the journal's general trend of discussing archaeological sites in terms of artifacts to be protected rather than as evidence of human cultures. It concludes by providing student readers with important connections to world history, noting that "men lived in Wisconsin so many years ago, long before the Egyptian pyramids were in the planning state or the building of King Solomon's temple."[86] Because so much of the state's history is taught as if it began with Nicolet in 1634, this line, emphasizing the ancient history of Native peoples, is in stark contrast to the standard narrative.

Student work, which provides some insight into classroom instruction, remains problematic. The November 1955 issue of *Badger History* includes an excerpt from a serialized play, "It Did Happen Here," put on by fifth graders from Roosevelt School in Eau Claire. Act IV of the play focuses on Indians and features the line, "I suppose with all this talk of Indians that we will be minus a scalp in the morning."[87] The "Indian" characters demonstrate a "powwow," which student readers learn "was performed whenever a group of Indians got together."[88] As described, the dances bear little resemblance to the actual Snake Dance or Buffalo Dance. The dance that ends with an eagle feather in the dancer's teeth and the tomahawk dance, which involves a duel to the death, exemplify the worst kinds of stereotypes of Native people.[89]

The strong presence of negative stereotypes in student work relative to submissions from professional historians suggests a difference in perspective between classroom teachers and the State Historical Society itself. For example, "The Kidnapping of Two Young Wisconsin Pioneers," written by a sixth grader from Antigo, portrays "the Indians" as a sort of monster to be feared. A shabbily dressed Indian who arrived at a pioneer cabin to sell baskets "was horrible looking" because his "nose had been frozen off" and he had "high cheek bones and many wrinkles on his face."[90] The man takes his revenge on the pioneer family by kidnapping two of their children, who are never seen again.

The contents of the special issues of *Badger History* published in the 1950s do not focus solely on Native Americans, instead mixing in pieces on places or events that had varying degree of Native involvement.[91] One highlight, from November 1956, was "A Trip to Lac du Flambeau," a piece authored by a Milwaukee seventh grader. The young man reports a wonderful experience on the reservation, and he explains, incorrectly, "The Menominee Indians have a reservation there." In describing the Indian Bowl, the author states, "Here the Menominees performed a wide variety of Indian dances and other ceremonies." While it is clear the students had a positive experience, neither they nor their teacher nor *Badger History* staff correctly noted that Lac du Flambeau is an Ojibwe reservation.[92]

The November 1957 special issue featured a historical mystery authored by a young woman in eighth grade. "The Lost Partridge Child" tells the story of a young white boy who disappeared from his family's farm in 1850. White settlers' suspicions that a young Menominee woman's child was the missing boy led to an extended legal battle that received significant coverage in the *Milwaukee Sentinel*. Despite multiple legal victories for the Menominees, the Partridges kidnapped the young boy and fled to Kansas. Some years later, the author notes, the remains of a young boy of the appropriate age were found in a marshy area near where the Partridges' son had disappeared. Still, she suggests that the fate of both boys remains a mystery. It is a fascinating story that exemplifies extraordinary scholarship for a junior historian.[93]

This issue also included articles written by professional historians, such as "The Stockbridge Indians" by Nelta Oviate Friend, "a curator of the State Historical Society and editor of *Creative Wisconsin*." It is a highly sympathetic account that focuses on the Revolutionary War through the 1850s, an era characterized by "cheating, crowding, and shouting," leading to multiple removals. Friend uses dialogue and other elements of historical fiction to humanize key figures, establish a sense of connection, and create a sense of drama. The piece misidentifies Red Springs, the final destination in a history of several removals, as being "beyond the Mississippi" rather than the current reservation in Shawano County, Wisconsin.[94] Overall, however, "The Stockbridge Indians" is remarkable in that it portrays the people as historical actors making strategic decisions to advocate for themselves and ensure their survival. In this respect, it is quite different from the "inevitable victim of historical circumstance" approach that marks most *Badger History* content in this era.

The State Historical Society was certainly not alone in portraying Native peoples problematically. An excerpt reprinted from "The Indian Room," a bulletin published by the Oshkosh Public Museum, exclusively used the past tense, referred to "chanting the strange rhythms on the gourds and drums," and challenged the origins of the Big Drum, before commenting on contemporary life. The piece closed with the statement, "Indian life was primitive, but it was probably happier than the Indian life today on a reservation where the Redman has had a difficult time adjusting to the Whiteman's way."[95] This is yet another example of how *Badger History* naturalizes and excuses historical injustices as simply inevitable.

Two pieces in this issue, the article "A Famous Wisconsin Indian—Red Bird" and an excerpt from Col. Thomas L. McKenney's account, focus primarily on Red Bird's arrest and execution. Instead of exploring the full historical and cultural context of Red Bird's actions, which might provide insight into his motives, the journal instead leaves students to wonder about this "mysterious" figure who would "murder and scalp for the honor of his race, and then sacrifice himself for the same reason."[96] Together, they exemplify the romantic, subtly triumphalist view *Badger History* takes of the "inevitability" of such events.

Consistent with many publications of the era, *Badger History* refers to Menominee "independence" rather than termination, noting that "in 1958, over 3,000 of them became free citizens." The article lists only five reservations in the state, omitting Forest County Potawatomi, Stockbridge-Munsee, St. Croix, and Mole Lake, and perhaps causing confusion over the slightly different legal status of Winnebago (Ho-Chunk) people's lands. Students learn instead that "the Winnebago who welcomed

Nicolet at Green Bay in 1634 have almost disappeared. A few give nightly entertainment at the Wisconsin Dells amphitheater in the summer."[97] The piece concludes, "Although the redmen were driven from Wisconsin in the same way they have been from other states, at the present time through the Governor's commission on Human Rights, relations between Indians and whites in Wisconsin are without serious problems"—misrepresenting both history and contemporary conditions.[98]

Another special issue appeared in November 1959, and as with other issues published while Platt served as editor, this one devotes varying degrees of attention to Native Americans. As before, the contents include pieces written by professional educators and historians as well as those offered up as exemplary student work in Wisconsin history. It is the first to list Doris H. Platt, editor, Donald N. Anderson, assistant editor, and Thurman O. Fox, consultant, whereas it had been common practice to list only the editor. This was the first of the special Indian issues not to include a separate section for younger students, reflecting overall changes in the journal itself. It would also be the last of the annual "Indian issue."

Assistant editor Donald N. Anderson, of the State Historical Society's school department, contributed a piece titled "Our Seventy-Second County—Menominee." As with other articles on termination, the piece stresses "liberty," noting that the Menominee and Klamath peoples are "the only tribes congress selected for acts leading to independence."[99] The article praises the Menominees as a "wealthy tribe" due to sustained-yield logging but attributes that to federal policy rather than cultural traditions. In discussing the transition to county government, Anderson notes that while it "won't be an easy job," the Menominees are "progressive, intelligent people, anxious to show what they can do on their own."[100] With assistance from the state government and the university, the Menominee people "proudly look forward to their equal role in the state" and "Wisconsin is glad that at last, in a small way, it can return something worth-while to the Indians."[101] This article represents one of the strengths of the *Badger History* journal, conveying to students the historical importance of contemporary events.

Thurman O. Fox, chief of school services, contributed an article titled "For Your Wisconsin Notebook," the first of a two-part series that would conclude in the next issue. The piece opens by observing, "It is difficult to realize that the white man was not always in Wisconsin."[102] Fox discusses prehistoric Wisconsin, arguing that although the lack of written records made understanding of that era dependent on archaeology, it was clear that Indians had lived in the state for more than ten thousand years. He retells the mythologized story of Nicolet, complete with pistols and Chinese robe, and in doing so, claims that the Winnebago "were a part of the great Sioux nation, a warlike people who would allow only one foreign tribe—the Menominee—to occupy the Wisconsin region with them."[103] Much of what Fox shares is about everyday life, homes, food preparation ("only one indication of the primitive status of Indians when their region was explored for the first time"), and the education of young people, all topics of likely interest to student readers.[104]

THE ANDERSON ERA, 1961–1964

Donald N. Anderson, who had previously served as assistant editor, became editor of *Badger History* in 1961. The staff also included Howard Kanetzke, Special Features, and Thurman O. Fox, Consultant. The journal continued its tendency to publish content on Native Americans more irregularly than in the early years. Under Anderson, these articles were often written by professionals, and student-authored pieces on Native Americans appeared less frequently. It is unclear whether this represents a shift in classroom instruction or if it is a product of what seems to be diminished attention to the Junior Historians on the part of the journal.

   Badger History frequently provided students with the opportunity to understand historical events happening in their own time. The article "From Reservation to What?" submitted by Menominee students from St. Anthony School in Neopit and published in the May 1963 issue, was an important contribution to that effort. The article explains that Menominee County had been the Menominee Indian Reservation until April 30, 1961, when it became "the first all-Indian County in the United States and also the smallest county in northeastern Wisconsin."[105] It notes that the community is largely Catholic, with other churches in three of four communities. The students also comment that "some of the backwoods Indians prefer remaining isolated from those who have adopted modern ways" and continue to "follow the ancient burial rites of the early American Indians," which they exotify.[106] The article describes how their reservation had been under federal supervision since 1854, noting that "legally they were a separate 'nation,' but at the same time they were American citizens."[107] Land had been held in common, which allowed "any self-respecting Menominee to 'squat' on any piece of land and build himself a house," and even the termination agreement included "safeguards" limiting the amount of land non-Indians could own.[108] Much of the article focuses on the history of logging on the reservation and the recent establishment of Menominee Enterprises, Inc., which was owned by Menominee shareholders. The authors close by sharing a joke going around in their community, "humor the white man seldom hears," with, "Now maybe white man go to the moon, and give Indian reservation back."[109] The inclusion of this article written by their Menominee peers provides readers an important opportunity to encounter a contemporary Native voice on a current issue.

In the December 1963 issue, local historian Dorothy G. McCarthy of Portage contributed a lengthy biography titled "Chief Yellow Thunder . . . Man of Honor." McCarthy notes his "story of trouble" in the history of the nation, but argues "the true cause of the trouble probably came from the white man at the very beginning" and details "black marks on the pages of our history."[110] Yellow Thunder, she explains, was to become the namesake for a state trail in Sauk and Colombia Counties because even though he was "a victim of the white man's greed and dishonesty, he stood out as a man of honor."[111] The article discusses his role as a delegate to Washington, a reluctant signer of the Treaty of 1837, an opponent of removal, and a Wisconsin homesteader. The reverent tone of the article on this "man of dignity and honor" is exceptional for this journal and for most scholarship of the era.[112] While it retains a heroes-and-villains approach to history, this issue of *Badger History* offers students an important new perspective by using Yellow Thunder as a case study.

—II—

As a publication that spanned many decades, this issue of *Badger History* provides a valuable window into the study of Wisconsin history at both the state and local levels. In this respect, it shows what the State Historical Society of Wisconsin and local schools validated as official knowledge about the state's past. Under Mary Tuohy Ryan, *Badger History* was particularly effective in generating involvement and interest in state history, as evidenced by reports of chapters of Junior Historians from across the state and exemplars of student work. Student work provides valuable insight because it illustrates not just what was taught as official knowledge, but what was actually learned by students, praised by classroom teachers, and selected by the experts at *Badger History* for publication. Often these examples demonstrate factual errors and show tremendous bias, particularly racism and sexism, toward their subjects.

Under Doris Platt's leadership, *Badger History* concentrated most of its Indian content in a November special issue. Many of these issues included articles on contemporary historical events, particularly Menominee termination. There are several examples of Native people authoring pieces that offer an important perspective on Wisconsin's past and present.

Badger History published less on Native people during Donald Anderson's brief tenure as editor, but "From Reservation to What?," written by Menominee students attending St. Joseph's School, represents a critically important learning opportunity for young readers. These opportunities to learn about American Indians would increase under the next editor, Howard Kanetzke, who led the publication in a more professional direction, thereby reducing opportunities for students to publish their own work on Wisconsin history.

CHAPTER 10

New Directions in *Badger History*, 1964–1980

Howard Kanetzke, who first joined *Badger History* in 1961 to write special features, became editor in 1964. The journal's staff had grown to include Kathryn Schneider, managing editor, and consultants Doris Platt and Joan Morgan. Perhaps in recognition of the relative decline in content related to American Indians, the first issue published under Kanetzke's editorship was the "Indian issue." In his letter to "Wisconsin Juniors" that opens the issue, the new editor acknowledges student interest in "Indian legends" to be used "in programs, poems, and articles" as well as "fine murals and sketches."[1] Two of the student-authored submissions, "The Old Man of the Dalles" and "The Making of Man Mound," were pieces of historical fiction that had won the Nelta O. Friend Award for "place name legends."[2] Both stories offer faux "Indian lore" to explain natural or man-made features of the landscape. The editor drew most of the rest of the journal's content from the Bureau of American Ethnology, including "Menomoni Tales of Manabush" and "Menomoni Folktales," from the 1892–1893 Annual Report, and "Chippewa Indian Legends," drawn from Frances Densmore's 1929 book *Chippewa Customs*. Another, the story of the siege of a "Sauk and Outagamie" fort by the "Chippewas, Potawatomis, Ottawas and way more," titled "The Legend of Red Banks," had been told to Charles Robinson by a woman identified only as "O-kee-wah."[3] *Badger History* portrays these stories quite simplistically and implies by association that the people are as well.

Kanetzke made two significant changes beginning with the 1965 volume. He shifted to a quarterly publication schedule and focused each issue on a single theme. On occasion, issues made reference to Native people in the context of the chosen theme. The first issue in the new thematic format, September 1965, focused on "Wisconsin Indians," and it included several articles authored either by Kanetzke or assistant editor Lorraine Nelson. For the first time, the issue did not begin with a letter to readers nor did it contain any student-authored articles.

The first article of the September 1965 issue, "A Word About Indians," provided a brief sketch of the history of Native Americans in the state. It explained that the Indians who lived in Wisconsin "hundreds of years ago" would be unable to recognize "*our* Wisconsin if they could come back for a look, nor do we know *their* Wisconsin" due to changes in the landscape.[4] It is attentive to linguistic and cultural differences, noting that Native peoples "spoke different dialects," some "raised crops, while others hunted or fished," and, dubiously, "a few were cannibals!"[5] Students learn "Indians did not write history books" so "the story of their lives is in some ways a puzzle" to be pieced together based on archaeological evidence and the written accounts of European explorers.

The brief passage on the Black Hawk War is all but incomprehensible. The article states, "After the Black Hawk War in 1832, most Indians left Wisconsin. Settlers moved in. The remaining Indians and the settlers did not understand each other. The settlers wanted to cut the forests and plow the prairies. The Indians wanted these left for hunting."[6] As with previous issues, the Black Hawk War is often referenced as a key turning point in the state's history, but, as here, it is not fully discussed. Of contemporary Native peoples, students learn "Indians live in only a few places in Wisconsin— some on reservations and in our newest county, Menominee."[7] This statement includes a rather cryptic reference to Menominee termination and omits the era's significant and growing population in Milwaukee and other urban areas.

Much of the issue addresses archaeology. Nelson contributed a lengthy article on the Old Copper Culture, and Kanetzke contributed articles on effigy mounds and Aztalan.[8] Cathy May's "The Woodland Indians" is remarkably detailed but its narrow focus on material culture in the precontact era without reference to a specific time period is problematic.

It sets up an implicit comparison between ancient Indians and more recent Europeans, and it contributes to a tendency to overgeneralize and ignore salient cultural differences between peoples.[9]

Another contribution from Nelson, "Black Hawk: A Play," provides a remarkably thorough and critical, though age-appropriate, account of the Black Hawk War. It is clear that the conflict centers on a disputed land cession and that Black Hawk's initial intent was to grow corn, not go to war. In referencing the Battle of Bad Axe, Nelson's narrator explains that despite the white flag, "the soldiers mercilessly shot the Indians who were trying to cross the river on rafts or were swimming" and states plainly, "The Indians were massacred."[10] The play concludes with Black Hawk explaining, "I did not fight because I hated the American people. Rock River was a beautiful country. I liked my town, my cornfields, and the homes of my people. I fought for them."[11] Presenting the story of the Black Hawk War as a play is a particularly effective instructional strategy because it conveys emotion extremely well.

Niki Smith's "Menominee County—A Modern Experiment" represents *Badger History*'s ongoing efforts to provide students with the opportunity to develop an understanding of a particularly important historical issue happening in their own lifetime. The author, a staff member at the Wisconsin Legislative Council, begins the piece by addressing media-driven stereotypes about "red men" and tepees. Smith asks, "Can you believe that young Indians dress, talk, and live in houses like you do?" She explains that "young Indians have adopted many of the white man's customs" but "their parents try to help them remember some of the old Indian ways."[12] Much of the article focuses on the struggle to adapt to the "modern 'non-Indian' world," including the "responsibilities and problems of county government" after the "federal government turned over its care of the Menominee Indian reservation to the state of Wisconsin."[13] Notably, the article does not note that termination stripped the Menominees of their legal status as Indians under federal law.

A significant portion of the article focuses on education. Smith describes low levels of academic achievement and high dropout rates despite the presence of two parochial and two public schools on the reservation and a public high school in Shawano. She explains to her readers that if you were a Menominee child, "[m]ost likely, your parents do not push you to continue school, because if you do get an education, you must leave the county to find steady work" because the only local jobs are at the sawmill.[14] She also mentions that many "do not want their children to adopt all of the non-Indians habits," including the "'dog-eat-dog' business world ideas" if they leave home. Smith writes that "as with any group of people, there are those families who just don't care what happens to their children," so some "wouldn't continue school no matter how many opportunities were offered to them."[15] She also argues that Menominee students "may be slower in learning" because of deficiencies in their preparation and lack of parental support, but "that a child is Indian does not, therefore, make him slower in learning."[16] Although this section seems intended to engage and perhaps refute a negative view of the readers' Menominee peers, it is unclear what students might have gathered from it based on the overall tone. The focus on poverty and pathology continues in a section titled "Other Problems," which notes the lack of entertainment options, the presence of tuberculosis, and a new VISTA program to address educational and social issues.[17]

In discussing the transition to county government, Smith explains, the Menominee people are "learning the proper ways to run their county government" and to understand the new relationships it entails.[18] This transition was necessary because "it was decided" that the Menominees "could take care of themselves apart from federal government supervision."[19] The Bureau of Indian Affairs's role was to help "plan the termination, or end, of this federal control." Smith warns, "If the Menominees fail to support themselves and go back to being a reservation, many other Indian tribes (there are five in Wisconsin alone) will be very cautious about breaking away from federal supervision and the reservation program." Smith cites this as proof of the important roles to be played by young Menominees, which she explains "are very different from those shown in movies and books or on television" because the "Indian of today is quite different from those in history books!"[20]

Smith explains that the "Indians' problems are new, and their old customs sometimes prevent them from progressing rapidly."[21] She argues that "the Indian child wants many of the same necessities, privileges, and products that other children do" but "faces a bigger challenge in getting them." As "member[s] of a minority group," Smith explains,

Indian children "may suffer mistreatment." The "segregated" nature of reservation life limits economic opportunity such that it is "easier to have the government give them help than to leave their homes and find new work." All of these things are "obstacles" that young people must overcome as part of the "fight for survival."[22] The article explains but stigmatizes cultural differences as contrary to "progress." The overall tone of the piece reflects how scholars of the era wrote about poverty and communities of color, so in this respect, *Badger History*'s approach to historical events happening during readers' lifetimes is quite solid.

Two years later, in 1967, *Badger History* published "Wisconsin Indians II." Overall, the contents focus heavily on Winnebago history, with pieces on the Decorah family, Red Bird, and Yellow Thunder. The opening article, "Wisconsin Indians," contrasts the fundamental values of "Indians" and "Europeans." Indians, "Wisconsin's first residents," were people who "accepted Wisconsin's landscape" and "were happy to live here and take a living from the land."[23] Europeans "were not content to leave this landscape as they found it," and "lawmakers and pioneers generally felt that Indians stood in the way of progress."[24] As a result, "Wisconsin's first citizens were moved from place to place" to "new lands" that were "poorer and smaller," which meant "the Indians could no longer live in the old ways."[25] The article explained, "Some well-meaning people talked of 'civilizing' the Indians" but they "did not realize that the Indians had their own culture and did not want to change."[26] In an attempt to provide a contemporary perspective, it stated, "Today Indians live only in a few places in Wisconsin— on reservations, in our newest county, Menominee, and in some cities," and they "have the difficult task of solving problems which are rooted in history."[27] Stressing Indians' own efforts to do so, the piece concludes with a brief discussion of the Great Lakes Inter-Tribal Council, a contemporary organization that exists "to preserve Indian heritage and promote economic welfare" so that Indians "will be better able to move into the mainstream of American life—and at the same time, preserve their Indian identity."[28] This short piece glosses over historical realities and omits critical context about the distant past, but importantly acknowledges contemporary tribal actions for addressing current concerns.

The issue includes an article on the Decorah family, descendants of the French trader Sabrevoir Decorah and Glory of the Morning, whom *Badger History* calls "the largest and most powerful Winnebago family" in the early 1800s.[29] The article explains, "The chief gave the Frenchman Decorah his daughter to open the roads between the Indian and the European."[30] Students learn that after her husband's death in the French and Indian War, Glory of the Morning "became chieftess of her tribe," leading a village of "fifty houses and two hundred warriors" among one thousand people.[31] The accounts of the lives of her sons and grandsons are quite colorful, and each is portrayed sympathetically as an honorable leader who lived in times of conflict.[32] Included among the biographical accounts of Decorah men is the life story of Angel Decorah, an art teacher at Carlisle Indian School who "ranks among the best American Indian artists."[33] The article also notes that thirty-five Decorahs served in the United States Army during World War I, and "only one of the men in that family came back from the war."[34] The piece concludes by praising the family as "wise and brave," noting that they "never forgot that they were part European as well as Indian" and "can be proud of its heritage."[35] These biographies highlight those who led their people in times of immense crisis, and overall, it praises them for their accommodationist strategies.

In contrast to the *Badger History*'s normal practice for realistic illustrations, "Words to Learn and Use" in the same issue includes ridiculous caricatures of Native people. One such example is an Indian holding a bowler hat and looking quizzically at a nearby white man to illustrate "Imitate" as "to copy or follow as a guide." In another, the definition of *portage* is supplemented by a drawing of a loincloth-clad Indian, bent over with his tongue out, and incorrectly carrying a canoe cross-ways on his back.[36]

Howard Kanetzke's "Red Bird: Winnebago Chieftain" opens with a quote from Red Bird, offering that there are many examples of those who start wars, but "seldom . . . have these people given their lives to stop the war that they started."[37] Red Bird and his Winnebago people lived along the Wisconsin River until the actions of settlers who mined lead, cut trees, and diminished game left them "upset and angry" from "being crowded off of their land."[38] Kanetzke's account positions rumors of the death and dismemberment of two Winnebago prisoners at the hands of US soldiers, actions that would have precluded their entry into the spirit world, as the tipping point in this conflict. Students learn that "revenge was a sacred duty" and that although he attempted to avoid conflict, Red Bird ultimately killed members of the Gagnier family. In order to save his people from a prolonged war, Red Bird chose to surrender in dramatic fashion. His party entered the army camp carrying three flags, the American flag in the front and rear and the white flag of surrender in the center. Red Bird wore "eye catching" clothing and sang his death song as he approached.[39] Overall, he is portrayed as a tragic figure, a man of honor who died at Fort Crawford in 1828 because "he refused to eat."[40] Of Red Bird's demise, readers learned that "by sacrificing his life, the noble Winnebago was able to stop a war and save many of his people from death." Although the article is quite reverential, it also contains an air of inevitability.

Kanetzke also authored an article focusing on Joseph Street in "Agent for the Winnebago." He portrays Street as a longtime friend and defender of the Winnebago people, serving as agent from 1827 until 1839. Known as Meah, or "Trail," in the Winnebago language, Street was a key figure advocating for Red Bird, attending to Black Hawk, adjudicating disputes between families, and defending the people from unscrupulous traders. The article discusses Street's role in opening and operating a school reflecting his beliefs that "Indians must be educated as children—starting always with simple rules" and that "their hands should be educated" as farmers and blacksmiths.[41] By the time Street left for his next post in 1839, seventy-nine students attended the school.

Elsie Patterson's "Yellow Thunder" portrays the Winnebago chief as "a wise leader, who wanted peace between Indians and settlers," but whose "brothers in Washington" had "betrayed his trust."[42] A significant portion of the article is about Mrs. Yellow Thunder, known also as the "Washington Woman" because she often accompanied her husband when he was on official business. As part of one of the delegations to Washington, Yellow Thunder signed the 1837 treaty after much coercion and fraud. As a result of this treaty, students learn, the Winnebago people were removed from lands east of the Mississippi and "went first to Iowa and then to Minnesota and Nebraska."[43] Some returned and "hid in the swamps and lived deep in the woods."[44] Yellow Thunder himself avoided removal by having a white friend help him buy land so that "as a landowner, he could not be sent to the reservation."[45] He lived the rest of his days on "his 'forty' like an ordinary citizen," paying taxes and holding large annual celebrations where Indians "played tom-toms and flutes and shook hollow shells filled with beads."[46] Yellow Thunder lived to be approximately one hundred years old and was buried on his land next to his wife, until 1909, when "the Sauk County Historical Society moved the Thunders to a different place."[47] Patterson describes Yellow Thunder as a "war chief who wanted peace" and an Indian who "bought land and lived with the settlers," but who "never forgot his Indian traditions and ceremonies."[48] She closes by declaring him to be "a fine Indian and a good Wisconsin citizen."[49] He serves as an example of an individual celebrated for what he represents, in this case "the good Indian," and the hope of racial harmony.

A second piece on Yellow Thunder, Lydia Flanders's "Recollections of Yellow Thunder," tells of "a friendship that lasted until his death." Flanders wrote admiringly of her friend, noting that "everyone respected this man with the deep voice and quiet manner" who "firmly believed that as a leader he should set a good example for his people."[50] In her account, Yellow Thunder was "well-known to many settlers," was welcome in their homes, and they in his.[51] Again, this piece seems to serve as an example of the possibility of racial harmony during the civil rights movement.

One of the things *Badger History* often did very well was to make students aware of the key historical developments happening in their state in their own lifetimes. "Government and Indians," an adaptation of a speech delivered by Commissioner of Indian Affairs Robert L. Bennett at the State Historical Society of Wisconsin on January 28, 1967, is yet another example of this practice. Although he is not identified as such in the article, Commissioner Bennett was an Oneida from Wisconsin and the first Indian to serve in his role for nearly a century. His speech stresses independence, explaining that in contrast to past practices, "What we want to do is advise—not supervise."[52] Commissioner Bennett explains that "Indian administration" in Wisconsin is similar to other states in that "a few tribes live on part of their original land," some "have moved and resettled several times," and others "were forced to shift from one spot to another before they found a place to call their own."[53] At times in his speech, Bennett was highly critical of federal Indian policy, citing the government's "poor planning" involved with the Potawatomi's move to Forest County and the failure of the allotment policy. He spoke of wanting to "divide this job" to be "partners with Indians to help them enjoy the same social and economic rights as other Americans."[54] He closed with the statement, at a time when the Menominee, Klamath, and many other tribes had already been terminated, "They are ready to come into full partnership in their America."[55] Although *Badger History* did not help students to make this connection, the speech nonetheless represents an important learning opportunity for student readers. It is the last major piece in this issue.

The 1970 issue of *Badger History*, with the theme "Wisconsin Historical Sites," uses concepts related to Native people to exemplify key vocabulary concepts. "Preserving Landmarks," written by Donald N. Anderson, assistant director of the Historic Sites Division, explains that "a *structure* is any work made by man, like an Indian mound," and gives Aztalan as its example of a *site*. Spirit Rock is used as an example of "an *object* of reverence to Indians."[56] In actuality, Spirit Rock is of cultural significance to the Menominee Nation, not Native peoples in general. This issue also includes references to "the Indians" in its discussion of Villa Louis ("Indians built a huge mound of dirt on an island in the Mississippi River") and casts "Indians" as extras in stories of European settlers at Madeline Island, a site of immense spiritual and historical significance to Ojibwe people.

Also in this issue, Marguerite Van Hulst's section, "The Grignon Home," focuses on Augustin and Nancy Grignon, who had "inherited the land she has been living on from her Indian mother."[57] Readers learn that Augustin and Nancy's son, Charles, could sit on his porch and "look across and see the wigwams of an Indian camp" that "supplied the family with fish and game in exchange for fresh bread."[58] Eventually, as more white settlers arrived in the Fox Valley, Van Hulst remarks, "Indians left the territory as the government acquired more of their land."[59] There is no further explanation and no suggestion of a relationship between these events.

The January 1972 issue focused on archaeology and anthropology, and many of the examples and illustrations provide opportunities to learn about Native peoples. In a featured article titled "About Archaeologists and Anthropologists," students learn their primary concern is culture, which it defines as "the set of ideas, beliefs and customs that people in any group share."[60] One of the examples of cultural change notes that "once only Indians lived in Wisconsin," but then "traders, missionaries, and settlers arrived" with a different culture. Their steel tools and other trade goods meant "Indians no longer needed stone implements and lost the skills for making them."[61] Cautioning students against judging cultures, the article warns, "Anthropologists, however, never judge one culture as being better or poorer than their own or another one," before concluding that they "work to *understand* people—not to change them."[62] This stated message stands in contrast to the overall tone of many of the other articles in this issue.

In contrast to the strict focus on artifacts and material culture that characterized earlier issues of *Badger History*, in this one Peggy Moore's "Indian Rockshelters" describes in detail the way of life of the "early Indians" and the clues archaeologists study to draw those conclusions.[63] "Manners and Social Customs of the Indians" features the observations of Jonathan Carver, a British surveyor and mapmaker who traveled in the region in the late 1760s. Carver shares what he learned about hunting, clothing, hairstyles, shelter, social customs, dances, games, religion, death, and time in a tone that conveys both curiosity and admiration.[64] Another article, "Wild Rice, Then and Now," also draws upon Jonathan Carver's observations of the harvesting, processing, and eating wild rice. A section on "Wild Rice Today" provides a contemporary perspective, asserting that "all the wild rice growing in Wisconsin lakes belongs to the state," and that while it might cost "almost $8.00 a pound," it is "interesting to know that the Indians who harvest this rice get almost $3.25 a pound."[65] These sections are important because they would have helped student readers recognize cultural continuities dating back thousands of years.

Badger History devoted a great deal of attention to the Fox people, and this issue continues the trend with "The Fox Indians in Wisconsin: A Discovery Unit." Students learn that they called themselves Mesquakie, "the Red-Earth People," but were known to others as Outagamie, "Those Who Live on the Opposite Shore," and to the French as Les Rennards, or "The Fox."[66] The unit covers observations from European explorers, the migration of the Fox from the Wolf River to the region west of Lake Winnebago, the conflicts with the French that nearly led to their destruction, and the archaeological evidence of their presence at the Bell site on the south shore of Lake Butte des Morts. It highlights the connections between historical understanding and the kinds of physical evidence studied by archaeologists.

The November 1972 issue of *Badger History* focused on medicine. In an article titled "Indian Medicine," student readers are first reminded, "The first Europeans came to Wisconsin in 1634." At that time, "the science of medicine in Europe was not advanced," and "in many ways the skills of Indian healers were as helpful as those of European doctors." Much of the article is excerpted from Jonathan Carver's writings in the 1760s. Other sections feature illustrations of various plants and their uses, described as "a few cures used by Wisconsin Indians that are recognized by the United States government."[67]

In September 1973, the Wisconsin Territorial Days issue featured an article titled "William Hamilton, Wisconsin Mining Pioneer and Indian Fighter," about Alexander Hamilton's son, a central figure in conflicts with the Winnebago and the Sauk and Fox. The section focusing on the Black Hawk War closes with the deaths of Sauk people shot under a white flag of surrender two different times, noting in the first instance "twenty-three were killed," and in the second, "many women and children died."[68] The article's reference to "hundreds of warriors" is not supported by historical evidence and the journal provides no opportunity for students to question why, if Black Hawk was leading a war party, there were women and children present at all. In any case, there is little to connect Hamilton to these massacres. Students learn that Hamilton later died in California during a cholera epidemic while seeking gold.

The September 1974 issue of *Badger History* focused on "prehistoric Indians." Many earlier issues of the journal had included information on the lives of Native peoples in the precontact era, but this issue, much like the 1972 issue on archaeology and anthropology, was as much about daily life as about artifacts of material culture. Students learn that "not all the Indians in Wisconsin's past were alike" because "at different times, Indians lived in different ways" and had different "food, tools, and languages."[69] Much of the contents focused on teaching students about four cultural eras, Paleo-Indian, Archaic, Woodland, and Mississippian, and several articles discuss the major characteristics and lifeways associated with each.[70] Other articles explore specific cultural aspects of one or more eras, including Copper Culture, effigy mounds, quillwork, and the use of birch bark for making containers and canoes.[71] There are also in-depth pieces on Aztalan and Hopewell Indians.[72]

Student readers would have learned a great deal about the weapons, tools, ornaments, diets, and burial practices of ancient peoples. There is a great deal of speculation, particularly about the meaning of the effigy mounds and their contents and particularly those that contain human remains. Some of the information might seem contradictory. In one section, students learn that "although these Indians built unusual mounds, their life was simple," based on hunting, fishing, and gathering wild plants.[73] In another article, students learn of extensive trade networks that allowed effigy mounds in Wisconsin to have "shells from the Gulf of Mexico, grizzly bear teeth from the Rocky Mountains and copper from northern Wisconsin" among their contents.[74] Ultimately, as stated in "Aztalan," "there is no way for us to discover the beliefs of these people by digging in the ground."[75] This article also highlights actions that Wisconsin citizens took to preserve Aztalan as a historical site and later a state park, suggesting again that there are important actions that students can do to commemorate historical events and sites.

In the March 1975 issue of *Badger History*, "Westward to Wisconsin," an article titled "Three Wisconsin Maps" purports to show how the state "grew between 1832 and 1850." It features maps from 1832, 1841, and 1850. Both the 1832 and 1841 maps were originally produced to be given to people in New York, so the "unsettled part of Wisconsin" is obscured by a map of Albany, New York. The 1832 map included only the eastern half of the state, but astute readers will spot the lands of the "Mennomonies," "Chippeways," and "Winnebagoes." The 1841 map has a similar map of Albany covering the western portion of the state, but includes lands of the "Chippeways," "Menomonies" and the "New York Inds.," a reference to the Oneida, Stockbridge-Munsee, and Brothertown peoples. The most complete map, 1850, was produced from a German map and does not include any tribal lands. The opening line in the article repeats an erroneous statement that appeared often in the journal's pages: "Most Indians left Wisconsin after the Black Hawk War."[76] While the Black Hawk War did indeed escalate pressure in the 1830s for land cessions and, ultimately, for removal, the Ojibwe and Menominee peoples never removed, and the Stockbridge-Munsee, Oneida, and Brothertown peoples had been removed to Wisconsin a decade earlier.

The opening article, "Changes in Indian Life After 1634," signals the theme of the March 1976 issue, "Wisconsin Indians Since 1634." Students learn that traders, missionaries, and settlers "changed the Indian ways of life," which had been based on hunting, fishing, growing vegetables, and gathering wild plants.[77] Traders made barter "an important part of the Indian way of life," missionaries "came to tell Indians about Christianity" and start schools, and explorers' accounts led settlers to move to Wisconsin.[78] The first settlers, students learned, were lead miners, and "Indians were not happy to see more of these men arrive each year."[79] These settlers cut down trees, plowed prairies, and killed game. Eventually, "Indians were asked to sign away their lands," and by 1848 most of those lands had been lost.[80]

Much of this issue seems to have been repurposed from earlier issues of the journal. For example, "The Decorah Family" is substantially similar to an article published in *Badger History* in 1967. This version of the article shifts its attention to the "sons and grandsons of Glory of the Morning" who were "Winnebago chiefs."[81] The piece concludes similarly to the first, however, praising the family as "wise and brave" and noting that the family "never forgot that they were part European as well as Indian" and was "proud of its heritage."[82] These biographies praise them for their accommodationist strategies.

"Red Bird and Winnebago Lead and Land" is substantially similar to Kanetzke's "Red Bird: Winnebago Chieftain," from 1967, with some minor differences. The article provides students with important historical context, such as the influx of settlers from a population of two hundred in 1825 to six thousand only two years later.[83] The article portrays Red Bird himself as a man of integrity who was a "friend of the 'men with hats'" who "had obeyed the laws of his people" but "had broken the laws of the United States."[84] It frames his surrender and death at Fort Crawford in 1828 as a tragedy because despite his sacrifice, "the Indians were forced to move again and again" until "the Winnebago left Wisconsin." The article closes with a resigned tone, stating, "Red Bird had saved the lives of some of his people. But he could not save their way of life or their lands."[85] This is a romanticized account that seemingly reinforces the sense of inevitability of Native succession by settlers.

Kanetzke also authored an article focusing on Joseph Street in "Agent for the Winnebago," a piece that is substantially similar to his earlier one on Street. This article has a slightly different discussion of Street's school, stating that "Indians should become the same as whites, and were to be educated in the same way."[86] Any potential controversy is shrouded by the statement, "Not all Indians agreed with him. Many of them wanted to keep their own ways. They knew, however, that Joseph Street was trying to help them."[87] The article denies students of Wisconsin history the opportunity to learn about these concerns or efforts of the Winnebago people, known today as the Ho-Chunk Nation, to resist assimilation and to explore issues of cultural conflict, seemingly in the interest of providing a positive example of a white man and government official.

Black Hawk had been a common subject throughout the years *Badger History* was in print, most often as the personification of a turning point in the state's history. This issue's "Whose Land? A Story of Black Hawk," a play by Anne Jordan, continues that trend by providing a sympathetic story that explores the events that led up to the Black Hawk War, Black Hawk's motivations, and those of his supporters and opponents among the Sauk people. This slightly surreal version of the story incorporates dreams and experiences that an elderly Black Hawk shares with his biographer, Antoine Le Clair. Black Hawk describes an idyllic way of life at Saukenuk, a village that was more than one hundred years old, and a place where he himself had lived for sixty-four years.[88] Students experience the central conflict, a dispute over the validity of the 1804 treaty, in a dramatic scene involving General Gaines, Black Hawk, and Keokuk that leads to a split among the Sauk people. Black Hawk explains that the promises of aid from other tribes and from the British were false, and he sought to surrender. When his envoys were killed under a white flag, he explains, "My little band of forty warriors charged the soldiers to avenge these deaths," clarifying that this first battle resulted from an attempted surrender.[89] After the narrator describes the circumstances through which "most of the Indians were killed," Black Hawk laments that he fears "that in a few years, the Americans will begin to drive our people away."[90] The closing line of the play has the narrator stating, "The Sauks moved just ahead of the settlers as Black Hawk had feared they would."[91] Jordan's play about the senselessness of the Black Hawk War very effectively exposed students to the underlying fear and misunderstanding, thereby reaching both the head and the heart. Its publication date also suggests that it may be intended as an allegory for the Vietnam War.

Other articles in this issue demonstrate the inconsistent way *Badger History* depicted Native people. The two maps featured in "Indians Lose Lands in Wisconsin" are the antithesis of the Black Hawk play. The description simply states "Between 1815 and 1848, Wisconsin Indians signed away rights to almost all of their lands," and lists the treaties through which each parcel depicted in Map 1 was ceded. The description makes no mention of terms, payments, or other obligations the federal government took on in these agreements. The second map erroneously uses verbs like "given" and "granted" to describe the basis for current landholdings, framing it in terms of federal largesse rather than obligation.[92] By contrast, "The Picture Gallery" powerfully highlights cultural change by providing drawings, etchings, and photographs of various locations and subjects, including several from as recently as the 1950s.[93]

"Oshkosh and Menominee Lands" opens with a brief description of termination, a topic that had been of great interest in *Badger History*, and acknowledges, even more briefly, restoration. The article reminds students that "government officials offered to end control of the reservation" in the 1950s, so "the reservation became a Wisconsin county" in 1961. After this decision, "Many Indians were unhappy" because they "saw that they were losing tribal unity and lands." In response, "some of the Menominee went to Washington" and "in 1973, Congress passed a new law" so that "lands owned by the Menominee once again became a reservation."[94] The article portrays this contemporary event as similar to nineteenth-century efforts to seize Menominee lands. As with many other issues of *Badger History* in the 1970s, it valorizes Oshkosh. The most striking aspect is that it is the first mention of Menominee Restoration. Termination of tribal status and the transition to county government had received a great deal of attention in *Badger History*, which provided students with an important opportunity to understand historical events happening in their own time. The efforts of DRUMS, Determination of Rights and Unity for Menominee Shareholders, to repeal termination were also contemporary historical events, but they were ignored until March 1976 when they received passing mention.

The closing article, "Wa Kun Cha Koo Kah, Yellow Thunder," is substantially similar to Elsie Patterson's article from 1967.[95] The article describes Yellow Thunder as a "war leader who wanted peace."[96] As before, readers learn of his role as part of a delegation coerced into signing a fraudulent treaty, his successful attempt to avoid removal by purchasing land, and his long life among a growing population of settlers. *Badger History* casts Yellow Thunder as the "good Indian" and uses his life story to highlight historical concepts and celebrate personal qualities.

For the bicentennial, *Badger History* published "The Revolutionary Era, 1750–1815." Kanetzke's article, "Soldiers of the Revolution," profiles some of the veterans buried in Wisconsin, noting that among the farmers, doctors, and ministers, "one soldier was an Indian chief."[97] The article profiles Aupaumut, who first enlisted at age eighteen, perhaps serving at Bunker Hill, and continued to serve in the army until 1782, rising to the rank of captain. His work for the new government included serving as an emissary, which "helped the government to win new friends among the Indians."[98] The Stockbridge-Munsee people's removal experience, while not the focus of the article, is reduced to one line: "In 1821 the Stockbridge Indians decided to move to Wisconsin."[99] When they "bought land from the Menominees," Aupaumut moved west, where he died and is buried near Kaukauna in the Stockbridge Indian Cemetery.[100] However incomplete this account may otherwise be, Kanetzke's story of Aupaumut connects the history of Wisconsin Indians to the Revolutionary War, thereby providing students with new context and an opportunity for new insights.

Badger History's 1977 geography issue also incorporated Native content in an article titled "Place Names in Wisconsin History." Amidst explanations of French names, names of forts, and places named for people, students learn that "the Indians probably also had area names which were never written down" and that "some Indian languages are no longer spoken."[101] For example, to translate Koshkonong, which the journal explains is "Ojibwa," a "University professor" searched "early word lists which do not always copy the exact Indian sounds" and "wrote letters to experts," to determine that it held one of several possible meanings describing a foggy place.[102] None of the "experts" were Ojibwe people, and apparently only one was familiar with the language.

In 1978, *Badger History* published an issue with the theme "Wisconsin Pioneers." In an article titled "Pioneers Come to Wisconsin," students learn that prior to the 1830s most of the state was "Indian land" until "lawmakers made agreements with the Indians." Subsequently, "Many Indians moved westward. Wisconsin waited for settlers."[103] This description denies students an opportunity to understand treatymaking and Indian removal and portrays successionary "settlement" as natural or inevitable. This idea is reinforced in another piece, Gail Van Every's "Pioneering," which explains that "in 1831 things began to change" because "the government had land surveyed or measured" and "[m]ost Indians left Wisconsin."[104] A segment of this article, "Some Indians Remain," explains that Indians and pioneers traded metal tools for furs, and "Indians sometimes stopped at farm homes" seeking food, tobacco, or cloth.[105] Student readers likely would have concluded that most Indians inexplicably went elsewhere and those who remained often begged at farmhouses.

One of the final issues of *Badger History*, 1979's "Wisconsin Women," prominently includes a drawing of Ada Deer and includes her name among those of other prominent women in Wisconsin history in a collage-style illustration centering on an outline map of the state. In "Modern Wisconsin Women," students learn that Ada Deer is a Menominee woman who has "earned degrees in social work and law," but is "perhaps best known for her work in helping to restore tribal status to Wisconsin's Menominee Indians." The caption also notes that she teaches at the University of Wisconsin in social work and Native American studies.[106] *Badger History* had devoted a great deal of attention to Menominee termination and the transition to county government, but there was no attention to the efforts of the Menominee people, including Ada Deer, to overturn that decision and no attention to their success in doing so. This brief mention, and a brief March 1976 reference accompanying an article on Oshkosh, are the extent of the journal's discussion about restoration. This is a critical oversight, particularly because, in several previous issues, *Badger History* had very effectively provided students with an opportunity to understand termination as an important historical event happening in their own lifetimes.

—ıl—

In 1980, after thirty-three years and through four distinct eras, *Badger History* ceased publication as a Wisconsin history journal for young people. As a tool for teaching students in Wisconsin's schools about the history of their state published by the State Historical Society of Wisconsin, it was the epitome of official knowledge. Howard Kanetzke transformed *Badger History*, shifting from nine monthly issues to four themed issues per school year, and increasing the content provided by himself and other professional historians. Under Kanetzke, *Badger History* published several issues with Native themes and provided students with additional opportunities to learn about Native peoples and to make connections with other content.

Throughout its publication, *Badger History* was an important resource for promoting interest in and understanding of Wisconsin history, including the history of Native people in the state. Student readers would have become steeped in a narrative filled with heroes and villains, an account in which ancient mound builders were succeeded by Nicolet. Red Bird and Black Hawk surrendered, which, according to the master narrative transmitted through the journal, began both an Indian exodus and an inevitable tide of white settlers who transformed the landscape, building farms and creating industry. Those few Indians who remained struggled to adapt to the "white man's ways" but were both watched over and granted independence. Such an account leaves little opportunity for students to have learned about the treaties that ceded land to create the new state, the obligations incurred by the federal government, or the rights reserved by Native peoples.

Badger History is not the only example of a classroom text aimed at the social studies curriculum in Wisconsin. The next chapter explores another textbook, penned not by experts sanctioned by the state government through the State Historical Society but published by a Chicago educational publisher, Follette Publishing. Published in several editions from 1957 to 1977, *Exploring Wisconsin* serves as a fascinating counterpoint to the *Badger History* series and another test case for how curriculum policy was implemented at the state and local levels. As one of the most popular Wisconsin-focused textbooks of its era, it also had great influence across the state. Perhaps most significant, the children who learned their state's history from the pages of these books would become the adults embroiled in the treaty rights controversy of the 1970s and '80s, whose understanding of sovereignty, rights, and Native culture and history was directly informed—and more often misinformed—by what they had learned in social studies.

CHAPTER 11

EXPLORING WISCONSIN, EXPLORING WISCONSIN CURRICULUM POLICY

Social studies is a textbook-driven field.[1] In Wisconsin, where local control of education is both a legal matter and a prized cultural tradition, responsibility for selecting textbooks and other instructional materials rests with school district officials.[2] Until 1967, the state superintendent maintained a list of recommended instructional resources from which local districts could make their selections.[3] Although textbook adoptions are handled locally, the choices available to curriculum committees are largely determined by textbook publishers responding to national market forces dominated by states with statewide textbook adoption policies. As a result, the content of most textbooks "is national in character and largely beyond the influence of any single school or district," with the likely exception of those on the history of an individual state.[4] An analysis of these texts yields important clues about the era in which they were published and adopted because it highlights contemporary concerns and suggests influences by the "current social, political, economic, and cultural events taking place in what they considered the 'present.'"[5] Given that social studies instruction is required by statute, history and social studies textbooks with a Wisconsin focus serve as a means to assess what local school districts recognized as official knowledge and what opportunities to learn accurate, authentic information about American Indians ensued from these choices.

Before Act 31, the leading social studies textbook with a focus on Wisconsin had long been *Exploring Wisconsin,* by Louis G. Romano and Nicholas P. Georgiady, published in six editions spanning 1957 to 1977.

A staple of fourth-grade classrooms in Wisconsin for more than two decades, it was supplemented by the State Historical Society's *Badger History* journal.[6] This chapter takes a close look at three editions of *Exploring Wisconsin* and the 1977 edition, *Exploring Our State, Wisconsin*, to assess the content and approach to Native topics, particularly in relation to the inclusion and exclusion of Native history and culture, sovereignty, and treaty rights. These editions would have been familiar to those who, decades later, were witnesses and participants in the spearfishing and treaty rights protests. The knowledge gleaned by the students of the 1950s, '60s, and '70s shaped the attitudes of those who gathered at the boat landings, whether to stand with the spearfishers, to rail against them, or to exercise their rights as tribal members.

EXPLORING WISCONSIN, 1957

In 1957, Chicago-based Follette Publishing Company published *Exploring Wisconsin*, by Louis G. Romano and Nicholas P. Georgiady, the first of six editions, three of which included substantial revisions. The authors worked with education professors Theodore J. Jenson, from the Ohio State University, and Edward A. Krug, from the University of Wisconsin–Madison; several staff members from the Wisconsin Department of Public Instruction; and representatives from the Wisconsin State Historical Society, the Wisconsin Conservation Department, the dairy industry, leading manufacturers, and the Milwaukee Municipal Port director.[7] Later editions of this landmark text were still very likely in use in Wisconsin schools into the early 1980s.

The text uses the frame story of Jean and Jerry Jenson, students who are new residents of Wisconsin learning about the state for the first time. Jean and Jerry learn about their new home in school as well as from Father, an authoritative figure with intimate knowledge of Wisconsin who travels with them around the state. The book's eight units provide several opportunities for students to learn about "the Indians," typically portrayed as a homogeneous people of the past, as opposed to the French, English, Germans, and others who are introduced as specific groups and who remain an ongoing part of the story. It includes American Indians within the domain of official knowledge only in very limited ways.

In the introduction, "We Look at Wisconsin's Map," Father unfolds a map of the United States to show his children where Wisconsin is located. After pointing out several of the state's distinctive features, including the "thumb on a mitten," Father explains that they can explore their new state and learn about its "early days." He remarks, "We can find out what our state was like long ago, before anyone lived here. Indians lived in Wisconsin for many years before white men came here. We can learn more about the Indians' life, and about the many changes that have taken place since those early days."[8] Father's comments appropriately foreshadow the text's linear, celebratory story of uninterrupted progress, and the undifferentiated reference to "the Indians" would become a familiar motif that signals a distinctly non-American Indian view of Wisconsin history.

The first unit, "Early Days in Wisconsin," reinforces this perspective with the teacher's remark, "Many, many years ago, before the white man and even before the Indians lived here, most of Wisconsin was covered with a great sheet of ice."[9] She promises Jean and Jerry, "We will read about the Indians who lived here long ago. We will also learn about the brave French explorers who came in search of gold but found instead a new and rich land."[10] A series of "I Wonder" statements includes, "I wonder what it would have been like to have been an Indian boy in Wisconsin long ago," "I wonder what the first white man was looking for when he explored Wisconsin," and "I wonder what the Indians thought when they saw the first white man come into their land."[11] The abrupt transition from "the Indians," who merely "lived here," stands in contrast to the more active description of "brave French explorers," foreshadowing the text's relative positioning of American Indians and Europeans.

The next section, a four-page spread titled "Wisconsin's Early People," uses the story of "Little Hawk," an "Indian boy about your age" who was a "member of a tribe of Woodland Indians called the Menominees," to explore everyday life. Students reading this section learn about Little Hawk's mother and father, as well as everyday chores and activities of the family, including making maple sugar (which the book fails to note is a seasonal rather than year-round activity).[12] The maps and illustrations in this section show shirtless men hunting with bows and arrows, a village scene showing reed mat and birch-bark-covered wigwams, where women in long, fringed buckskin dresses scrape a stretched hide while another woman smokes skewers of meat over an open fire and a man dressed only in a loincloth makes a snowshoe. All of the people depicted in these illustrations have long black hair and reddish brown skin. The illustration carries the historically unlikely caption, "These boys are playing while the grownups work," which does not reflect the fact that children would have had age-appropriate tasks that contributed to the life of the village.[13] The description of Little Hawk's father and mother, and his interactions with them and no other people, serves to map a nuclear family model onto the precontact Menominees instead of a tribal, extended family kinship network. This segment also reinforces the category of "Woodland Indians" over specific tribal identity, again privileging non-Indian perspectives.

A caption on a map labeled "Indians in Wisconsin—1650" acknowledges, "Many different Indian tribes have lived in Wisconsin," and it names "the chief Wisconsin tribes." According to the authors, the "chief Wisconsin tribes" include the Menominee, incorrectly located near the present-day Lac du Flambeau Ojibwe reservation; the Sauk, Winnebago, and Fox along Lake Winnebago; the Kickapoo and Potawatomi in southern and southwestern Wisconsin; and the Dakota along the western border with Minnesota. The map represents Chippewa people as living outside the state, in northeastern Minnesota and in the eastern part of Michigan's Upper Peninsula.[14] While the authors recognize the importance of including American Indians in Wisconsin history, they do not appear to attach similar value to doing so in a historically or geographically accurate manner. There is no explanation here or elsewhere of why or how the list and locations of tribes changed over time. Similarly, the characterization of some as "chief tribes" remains unexplained.

Several paragraphs begin with questions in bold print prompting students to think about housing, transportation, and food. Students learn that Little Hawk's people "lived in small huts" that "were made of strong poles covered with birch bark," and moved with the seasons to catch fish in the summer and hunt in the winter.[15] For transportation, the Menominees "moved about from place to place on foot" because "there were no horses in America until white men brought them from across the sea," and they "used birch bark or dugout canoes to travel on waterways."[16] Even before contact, "white men" appear in the narrative as bringers of progress.

For food, the book states that the Menominees grew corn, squash, and beans in small gardens tended by children, and gathered "wild rice, fruits, nuts, and certain roots." Little Hawk's father "and the other braves" hunted animals for food and clothing, and the boy and his friends would sometimes hunt small game, including rabbits and squirrels. Students learn that "the Menominees were good fishermen," that fishing was one of the first things that young men like Little Hawk learned to do, and they all enjoyed "eating the delicious fish dinners that his mother cooked for the family."[17] While these aspects are essentially accurate, the failure to mention any adults other than Little Hawk's father and mother suggests a nuclear rather than extended family model. The use of the terms "braves" and "squaws" effectively exclude the Menominees from the more typical human categories of men and women.

In response to the question, "What was the Menominees' most important food?," the authors explain, "The Menominees were known as 'rice eaters.'"[18] Students learn that wild rice grew in shallow lakes in "that part of Wisconsin," which according to the map was well northwest of their actual homelands, and that "the Indians liked rice because it was easy to cook and could be stored without spoiling during the winter."[19] A section titled "Getting Ready for the Rice Harvest" describes in great detail the process of harvesting and processing wild rice, beginning with Little Hawk building a birch bark canoe because "the squaws will need a strong canoe."[20] Little Hawk and his father harvest the bark and build the frame while his mother sews the bark together, laces it to the frame, and waterproofs the craft with pine pitch. Illustrations in this section show a boy and a woman waterproofing the canoe and another shows a man wearing two braids, clad only in a loincloth, and wearing feathers in his hair, who is paddling in a stream. The caption asks what the "Indian boy" is doing and explains, "the white men adopted the Indian canoe as the best lightweight river craft they had seen."[21] As for the rice harvest itself, the book explains, "The women were given the job of harvesting the rice, while the men went hunting for deer and other animals."[22] Students learn about the roles women played in harvesting the wild rice, how the boys unloaded the wild rice–filled canoes onto drying frames, and how the women threshed and winnowed the rice. The authors describe how wild rice was stored for winter and how the Menominees could use potential surpluses to share with other tribes.[23] This section shows interdependence and cooperation relative to an activity that many contemporary Native and non-Native people practice.

The next section, titled "The White Man Comes to Wisconsin," focuses on the story of Jean Nicolet and begins the process of relegating American Indians to the background of Wisconsin history. The book explains, "After Columbus opened up the New World, many countries sent men to explore parts of it," including the French, who sought a route to China.[24] Instead, "they found a rich and beautiful land and many animals whose furs were valuable," so they "began building trading posts where the Indians could bring their furs."[25]

Samuel de Champlain, an early governor of New France, was concerned that "the Indian tribes in the country west of Quebec were fighting among themselves," which meant that "as long as the Indians spent their time fighting, they could not trap animals and bring their furs to the French trading posts."[26] Champlain sent Nicolet as his envoy to "make peace among the Indians" and to "look for the western ocean and the way to China."[27] The narrative suggests that the tribes in the region would likely have been consumed by warfare without benevolent French intervention. Eventually, Nicolet and "seven Indians from the Huron tribe traveled to a town called *Michigonong*" explaining that "Lake Michigan gets its name from the Indian name for it."[28] Later they landed near Green Bay "in a land the Indians called *Meskonsing*," whose "name was changed several times until it finally became Wisconsin."[29] Students do not learn what languages these words are in nor who changed the names, which serves to further reinforce the homogeneous category of "the Indians."

Nicolet had heard that people called "Men of the Sea" who lived in the region spoke a different language, and he concluded that he was near China. When canoes carrying Nicolet and his men arrived near Red Bank, he "put on a brightly colored silk robe that he had brought along to wear when he met the Chinese."[30] When Nicolet fired his pistols into the air, "some people half hidden behind bushes and trees" quickly "turned and ran away through the forest, afraid" before eventually coming out to meet him.[31] When they revealed themselves, he realized that they "were not richly dressed Chinese," but "wore clothing made of animal hides" and their "skins were red, not yellow."[32] Indeed, the illustration shows shirtless men dressed in leggings and loincloths, wearing two braids and feathers in their hair, staring at Nicolet, clad in a colorful robe and plumed hat, and shooting pistols into the air, as women and some men run into the distance. The caption reads, "When Nicolet fired his pistols, the Winnebago Indians were frightened. They had never seen guns."[33]

Nicolet, although disappointed not to have found China, was "friendly" to the "Men of the Sea," who were actually "members of the Winnebago tribe."[34] "The Indians were afraid of the brightly dressed stranger," and although they "could not forget the thunder that seemed to come from his hands," they welcomed him and "several thousand Indians" for a feast in his honor.[35] While among the Winnebagos, the people known today as Ho-Chunk, the book explains, Nicolet made a peace treaty with them, and they in turn agreed to "make peace with other Indian tribes" and to "bring furs to trade for French goods at the trading posts."[36] This begins another recurring theme, that of the fearful, superstitious Indian, contrasted with the technological wonders brought by Europeans. Further, it frames the relationship between the Ho-Chunk and the French as one of tacitly approved Native deference. It also tells a familiar mythologized account of Nicolet, popularized by the history of the time but not based in historic fact.[37]

The next section, titled "Marquette and Joliet," describes how Louis Joliet, along with Father Marquette, "a priest who had come to teach the Indians about Christianity," accompanied Joliet intending to "teach his religion to the Indians they would meet."[38] This section reinforces the theme of the fearful Indian and brave Europeans, portraying "the Indians" as being afraid of the Mississippi River, believing that it was dangerous, "full of monsters who ate men and canoes." In the south, "the heat was so great it burned any man who went there," but "the Indians' stories did not frighten Marquette and Joliet."[39] The authors repeat this theme several times, wherein "the Indians" tell stories of "dangers and hardships," but each time the French explorers are "not afraid."[40] On their journey, they met "a village of friendly Illinois Indians" who "held a feast for the white men and smoked the pipe of peace with them" before giving them a calumet to take with them to signal to other tribes that they were friendly.[41] Again, the authors seem to imply a duty for American Indians to be deferential toward Europeans. After an arduous journey back to

Quebec, Marquette and Joliet claimed for France all the lands they had passed through, thereby naturalizing European colonization.[42]

The book reinforces this idea later in a segment in Unit 3, "Three Flags over Wisconsin," which acknowledges the French as the first rulers of Wisconsin.[43] Under the heading "Wisconsin's First Towns," in Unit 3, "Wisconsin Becomes a State," the authors briefly discuss the fur trade with "the Indians" and the network of French forts that made that practice more convenient. The book explains that small farms surrounded the forts, and "in case of trouble with the Indians," families "could quickly get inside the stockade or walls of the fort."[44] The text leads students to identify with the French, and there is no suggestion as to what "the Indians" might do in case of "trouble" with the Europeans. A segment titled "The British Flag over Wisconsin" states simply, "In 1763, a war between the British and the French ended," seemingly legitimizing the transfer of power from one European colonizer to another, while "The Stars and Stripes at Last" makes no mention at all of American Indians.[45] The succession of European powers to the United States was now complete.

A two-page spread with the title "The Black Hawk War" states, "Southwestern Wisconsin was the home of the Sauk Indian tribe" and "when lead was discovered, many whites came into this part of the state."[46] It then explains, "The Indians had signed a treaty or agreement giving all of their land east of the Mississippi River to the United States," and "the government sold some of this land to miners who were looking for lead" as well as "settlers who wanted to live here and farm."[47] However, "a Sauk chief named Black Hawk said that the tribe should not have to give up all its best lands" and instead "should be allowed to live on a small part of it."[48] Black Hawk led "a large group of Indians" back to "part of their old land." Although "they did not want to bother the settlers," the "settlers became frightened and there was fighting."[49] As "wild stories about Indian massacres spread rapidly, even though they were not true," soldiers and volunteers "set out after the Indians."[50] In the fighting that ensued, "The Indians suffered great losses when they tried to protect themselves," as "most of their braves were killed," and "Indian women and children were killed, too."[51] During the Black Hawk War, "The whites followed the Indians for many weeks" until "the end of this sad story came when Black Hawk and the few Sauks who were left surrendered."[52] This account implies a war party rather than a village of people seeking to return to their homes. The use of passive voice and the description of this as a "sad story" portrays the war as an inevitable clash of civilizations, continuing the narrative of progress that began with Nicolet and his pistols.

Back in the narrative of *Exploring Wisconsin*, Jean and Jerry Jenson see a Smokey Bear commercial while watching television, prompting a discussion about forests with their father. Jerry notes how in an "Indian story" he was reading, he learned that the forests were "the favorite place for the Indians to live and hunt." Father explains, "In Indian days, our state was covered by forests," adding that "the Indians" did not "destroy the trees" because they "needed the wildlife in the forests."[53] In this description, "Indian days" are clearly part of the past, once again reinforcing the narrative of progress and European succession.

In Unit 6, "Manufacturing in Wisconsin," the theme of the superstitious Indian re-emerges. On a factory tour led by Mr. Blake, the guide tells Jean and Jerry a story "about an old Indian chief who went to New York City for the first time." When asked what he had liked best about the city, "he surprised everyone with his answer" because he "did not choose the subways or the Empire State Building" but "instead, he chose the bubbler [water] fountains that were on all the floors of the buildings he had been in." Mr. Blake explained, "To the Indian chief, the bubblers were almost magic. When you stop to think of all the wonderful machines we have today, they are almost like magic."[54] The "Indian chief" is clearly a figure of the past who serves as a foil to reinforce the theme of progress and modernity, and his wonderment seemingly justifies European succession.

Unit 7, "Cities of Wisconsin," tells the story of Jean, Jerry, and Father traveling the state to learn about its cities. Father suggests, "Let us drive north to *Mahnawaukee-Seepe*."[55] When Jean questions the "funny name," Father explains, "It is an Indian name which means 'gathering place by the rivers,'" adding that Father Marquette found three rivers emptying into Lake Michigan in the area and "the Indians who lived here found wild rice and game, and grew corn, beans, and squash."[56] Father explains to Jean and Jerry that the city of Milwaukee contains many Indian mounds, "the burial grounds of the Indians," many of which "were destroyed as the city grew."[57] He tells them of Solomon Juneau, an early settler who was a "great friend of the Indians," who was "not only a handsome man, but one of the strongest."[58] He was a generous trader, but "if an Indian became troublesome, Solomon would simply pick him up and toss the Indian right over his head."[59] The black-and-white illustration of Juneau portrays him dressed in fringed buckskin throwing a shirtless Indian over his head while another group of six Indians dressed in fringed buckskin and feathers points and laughs.[60] The caption reads, "Big Solomon Juneau had his own way of handling quarrelsome Indians who came to his trading post. He got along well with most of the Indians."[61]

The narrative again quickly relegates American Indians to the status of historical background figures who are either dead in "burial grounds" destroyed by an expanding city or tossed by a famous trader. Two notable exceptions include County Stadium, the "Home of the Braves," and an Indian exhibit at the Library and Museum the text describes as "the finest in the world."[62] The text makes no mention of a significant contemporary American Indian presence in the city, an influx due in large part to the federal relocation program that was at its height in the 1950s. The Jenson family also visits several other cities, including La Crosse, where they learn that "in the early days, a trading post was built in this Indian territory."[63] A drawing of a lacrosse game carries the caption, "Several hundred Indians at once sometimes took part in a fast, hard game of lacrosse."[64] Again, *Exploring Wisconsin* privileges a narrative that leaves American Indians in the past.

Unit 8, "America's Vacation Land," focuses on tourism and carries illustrations of white people camping, fishing, and enjoying other outdoor activities. The text portrays the state's people, who are "as interesting as the state," as part of the draw for tourists, noting that "you can meet people of many different nationalities in Wisconsin." Each of these peoples "have their special holidays, when many of them dress in their national costumes," and "sing the songs and dance to the music of the countries they came from." The Jensons learn that "all of them have helped our state to become great."[65] The text explains, "Many people have left Europe to come to America" to "seek freedom of religion and government, or to start a new life in this new country."[66] The people of Wisconsin include those from Iceland, Poland, Italy, Germany, Norway, Switzerland, Holland, Belgium, Ireland, Sweden, and Luxembourg, and the text acknowledges their distinctiveness.[67] By contrast, the text erases both the cultural distinctiveness and contemporary existence of American Indian people.

Jean and Jerry learn several lessons about American Indians while traveling the state. They learn that Lizard Mound Park is an "ancient Indian burial grounds."[68] A colorfully illustrated map labeled "Wisconsin Vacation Map" has crude illustrations representing cabins, baseball fields, lumberjacks (including Paul Bunyan), waterfalls, deer, fish, geese, and bears, and various scenes of outdoor recreation.[69] The map also features shirtless Indian men wearing fringed pants and feathers in their hair in several locations around the state. Based on the rock formations, one is likely Wisconsin Dells, another is near the Menominee or Stockbridge-Munsee reservations, a third is approximately at Lac du Flambeau, a fourth is near Lac Courte Oreilles, and a fifth is near Bad River.[70] Even when portrayed in association with contemporary tourism, American Indian representations still carry strong connotations of the past, as living relics akin to Milwaukee's "finest in the world" museum collection.

Jean and Jerry Jenson learn how important tourism is to Wisconsin when their family rents a cabin "in the Wisconsin woods" and meets people from several other states who are there as well.[71] In a small subsection titled "Hunting and Fishing," Father explains to the children that "Wisconsin is a wonderful place for fishing," adding "what a thrill it is to catch a muskellunge."[72] Jerry asks Father, "How many different kinds of fish are there in Wisconsin?," leading the ever knowledgeable Father to reply that there are "174 types of fish in 8,800 lakes and 10,000 miles of streams."[73] In response, Jerry remarks, "So many people go fishing that you would think all the fish would be caught."[74] This idea would echo in the 1980s, applied exclusively to Ojibwe spearers rather than to anglers of any background. Clearly, hunting, fishing, camping, and other outdoor activities were important economic activities, and the textbook effectively markets this idea to children.

The 1957 edition of *Exploring Wisconsin* incorporates American Indians in the domain of official knowledge, but only as primitive, superstitious people of the past who were naturally or inevitably succeeded by Europeans, albeit under sometimes regrettable circumstances. Often American Indians are passive, secondary characters in a narrative explaining how the state passed from the French, to the British, and eventually to the Americans. Overall, it provides very few opportunities to learn accurate or authentic information about American Indian people in Wisconsin. These themes remain in varying degrees in subsequent editions of this widely adopted text, showing that knowledge about American Indians was not highly prized at the local level.

EXPLORING WISCONSIN, 1967

A new, expanded edition of *Exploring Wisconsin*, by Romano and Georgiady, arrived in 1967. As before, the authors worked with representatives from the State Historical Society, the Conservation Department, representatives of the dairy industry, leading manufacturers, UW–Madison professor of education Edward A. Krug, and a school principal. The text again uses the frame story of Jean and Jerry Jenson, students who are new residents learning about the state for the first time. There are several changes between earlier versions and the expanded 1967 edition, including thirty-two pages of additional text, and changes in the illustrations from black-and-white, cartoon-like line drawings to many rich watercolors painted in a more realistic style and significantly more color photographs.[75]

As with previous editions, the text contains many references to American Indians, most of which deal with the period before statehood and reinforce a narrative of progress and inevitable European succession. A significant portion of the new content is in a new unit, "Reading Maps and Globes," which is an expansion of the "Maps Tell a Story of Wisconsin" segment that introduced previous editions. In the new edition, Father still explains that "Indians lived in Wisconsin for many years before white men came here," but none of the new maps, which show precipitation, soil, growing seasons, population, and manufacturing areas, suggest that presence in the past or present.[76] There is no political map, although the population and manufacturing maps show the locations of several major cities, and none shows reservations or other tribal lands in the state.[77] These maps do not include any of the tribes of the state in the contemporary story they tell, and the section suggests *It Happened Here* for further reading, a book that specifically excludes American Indians from the domain of official knowledge.

A significant portion of the expanded content addresses French exploration and interaction with American Indians. A brief passage tells the story of Dulhut, who "was kept busy trying to keep peace among the many Indians of Wisconsin," and trying to "protect other French explorers and missionaries who were captured by unfriendly Indians" while he himself sought to learn the source of salt that he was given by "the Indians."[78] Reading this section, students learn that, as with Nicolet, "the Indians" depended on the French to keep peace among them. There is also a new section on Nicolas Perrot, a man from a "poor French family" who traveled to Canada "to seek his fortune" as a fur trader. Near Green Bay, Perrot encountered a Potawatomi Indian village where he "made friends with the Indians" who "thought he was a god because he had a gun which made a great noise like thunder."[79] This again reinforces the image of the fearful, superstitious Indian. He traded iron tools and other goods in exchange for furs, and "soon became the most well-known trader and Indian agent in Wisconsin."[80] Students read about how Perrot would be "greeted as a friend" by "the Indians," who would "sit on the ground in a circle" with him and "smoke the peace pipe."[81] As they smoked, "the Indians would blow smoke in Perrot's face," which he recognized as a "great honor" and a "good sign."[82]

The trader is portrayed as quite generous since "even the Indian children were not forgotten," as he gave them "bright glass beads of many colors to use for ornaments."[83] As part of his travels, Perrot "even went as far as present-day Dubuque, Iowa, where he showed the Indians how to get lead out of the rich mines located there," a practice "the Indians" continued.[84] The section concludes by stating, "While Perrot had worked among the Indians of Wisconsin, he had helped keep peace among them. The Indians feared and respected their friend. When he left, the Indians began fighting among themselves again."[85] Again, only through fear could the exotic, smoke-blowing, superstitious Indians remain at peace, which left them dependent on seemingly benevolent French colonial rule.

American Indians next appear in the book in the context of the French and Indian War, as troops led by French trader Charles de Langlade, the "Father of Wisconsin."[86] Langlade is described as having "lived with the Ottawa Indians as a boy," and it is said "their chief was his uncle."[87] Although he had defeated the British troops, the French lost the war, and the French possessions became British. Langlade stayed and served as Indian agent.[88] This is a significant expansion of the single sentence that described the French and Indian War in previous editions, and it further reinforces the idea of European succession as power is transferred from one European nation to another.

There are few significant differences in how Romano and Georgiady describe the Black Hawk War in this edition. They describe the Sauk as "an Indian tribe that had earlier moved from Michigan into eastern Wisconsin" who were living in the southwestern part of the state by the early 1800s.[89] It is unclear that students would recognize that in 1832 Wisconsin was still part of Michigan Territory, yet the text implicitly ascribes recent immigrant status to the Sauk. Romano and Georgiady explain, "The Indians had signed a treaty giving all their land east of the Mississippi River to the United States," who then sold it to settlers seeking lead.[90] When Black Hawk led his people back across the river, the settlers "did not trust the Indians" and "became frightened and there was fighting."[91] This account describes the settlers rather than American Indians as "frightened" and mistrustful, suggesting that misunderstood stories of massacres led soldiers and volunteers to "set out after the Indians."[92] This "sad story" is otherwise substantially similar to the 1957 edition in its attention to the apparent inevitability of the war, and Black Hawk's inevitable defeat.

Unit 7, "Wisconsin Cities," includes information about historic and contemporary American Indians. In Milwaukee, Solomon Juneau still tosses quarrelsome Indians, but the references to the Braves, who left the state in 1965, and the "finest in the world" exhibit on American Indians are all absent in 1967.[93] Romano and Georgiady describe how during the fur trade, "blanketed Indians and frontiersmen in buckskin" traveled to Prairie du Chien to trade and that La Crosse got its name from the French "for a game they saw the Indians play."[94] As the Jensons drove from Superior to Ashland and Rhinelander, "They drove through Indian reservations, too," although readers are left to infer that they drove through Bad River, Lac du Flambeau, and perhaps Red Cliff.[95] A photo of a Native male traditional dancer standing on a rock formation overlooking the river is captioned, "Every year thousands of visitors enjoy Indian ceremonials at the Dells. Many take hikes along the banks of the Wisconsin River to see the marvelous rock formations."[96] The text includes contemporary American Indians merely as a source of entertainment for tourists, who presumably are white like Jean and Jerry's family, on par with natural features of the land.

In Unit 8, as Jean and Jerry are on vacation with their father, Romano and Georgiady provide additional dialogue about hunting and fishing that teaches students that "laws protect our animals" and that hunting seasons and conservation laws mean that "they are allowed to kill only a small number of animals."[97] Father explains the important role of the Conservation Department in stocking lakes and rivers through the use of hatcheries and "trying to keep our streams clean."[98] When considered with the information stressing the economic importance of tourism in "America's Vacation Land" that carries over from previous editions, the text clearly connects hunting, fishing, and legal protections of fish and game to statewide financial concerns. Some of the economic anxieties of anti-treaty protestors and resort owners may have a basis in the social studies lessons they received as children.

Other sections on tourism address American Indians as contemporary or historical peoples. The paragraph on the Apostle Islands notes, "On Madeline Island are Indian burial grounds and a historical museum."[99] The text observes, "Indian Ceremonials at Lac du Flambeau are colorful Indian dances which may be seen during the summer months."[100] Because it reflects a publication date during a period when the federal government had terminated the tribal status of the Menominee Nation, the text explains simply, "The Menominee Indian Reservation was part of Shawano and Oconto Counties before 1961. Today it is the 72nd county in Wisconsin. Indians live and work in Menominee County."[101] There is no discussion of federal termination policy, which withdrew federal recognition of Menominee sovereignty and their government-to-government relationship with the federal government. Examples of past presences are also visible as "Indian Mounds" near Endeavor, Montello, and Packwaukee, where "good examples of Indian earthworks can still be seen," and at Pictograph Rock, near Friendship, which "shows pictures that Indians of long ago cut into the rock with stone implements."[102] Overall, these references reinforce the idea that American Indians are people of the past.

In the segment "Wisconsin's People," the text again discusses peoples of various European ancestries as well as "Negroes" and "Indians."[103] Reading the paragraph on Indians, students learn, "Most of Wisconsin's Indians live on reservations. Menominee County, northwest of Green Bay, is entirely owned by Menominee Indians. Lumbering is the main industry. The tourist business is an important source of income. People come to see the colorful Indian ceremonials in the summer and to visit the restored Indian village and logging camp."[104] A photograph showing students in a classroom carries the caption "Fourth-grade children at school in Menominee County. Do you know what people live and work in this county?" The caption provides no answer, although an earlier section of the unit indicated that Menominee County was formerly the Menominee Reservation. Overall, much of the new information about American Indians in this unit is a mixture of historic and contemporary references, and it is unclear what students might conclude.

As with the 1957 edition, the text excludes American Indians from the unit on Wisconsin government. There is no acknowledgment of the tribal nations within the state's boundaries, nor of principles of tribal sovereignty and governance. The glossary includes definitions for two related terms. Students learn that a reservation is "a tract of land which the government has set aside for Indians," and that a treaty is "an agreement made between two or more countries or groups of people."[105] The text makes no connection between these two key concepts, which makes the definition of reservation seem like the simple largesse of a benevolent government.

Official knowledge of American Indians in 1967 reinforces connections to the state's earliest history and includes very little about contemporary Native people. The historical references depict Europeans as successors to primitive, superstitious people who warred among themselves without European intervention. The few contemporary references are quite vague and confusing, offering no clear connection between past and present. The scope and tone of the text suggest that there is little of importance that students should know about American Indians aside from their relationship to European exploration and settlement. Those local curriculum committees and school boards who chose to adopt this text for use in their schools sanctioned this information and these views as official knowledge.

EXPLORING WISCONSIN, 1970

The fifth edition of Romano and Georgiady's *Exploring Wisconsin*, published in 1970, is substantially similar to the 1967 edition. Jean and Jerry Jenson are still learning their way around the state, and indeed, the text of the two volumes is nearly identical.[106] One striking change is that the illustration of "Big Solomon Juneau" dressed in fringed buckskin throwing a shirtless Indian over his head has been replaced with another black-and-white illustration showing Juneau measuring out generous lengths of cloth as three shirtless men with feathers in their long hair watch. It carries the caption, "Unlike some fur traders, Big Solomon Juneau was fair to the Indians. His odd method of measuring gave them extra cloth in trade."[107] The shifting perspective on Juneau, along with the addition of a few African Americans in photographs and illustrations, suggests that the authors or publishers attempted to make some minor revisions to reflect the civil rights movement, but that they were not so committed to the task to reconsider their overall approach to the state's history. The narrative of progress and the inevitable succession from American Indian to European control of Wisconsin remained official knowledge in Wisconsin schools despite growing sensitivity to race relations.

Exploring Our State, Wisconsin, 1977

In their final, expanded edition of *Exploring Wisconsin*, published in 1977 as *Exploring Our State, Wisconsin*, Romano and Georgiady have abandoned the frame story of Jean and Jerry Jenson and their knowledgeable, authoritative father, as part of an overall update of the book's appearance. As might be expected of this era, the text devotes greater attention to racial and ethnic diversity and gender, as well as more nuanced descriptions of people and events. While in many ways this edition of *Exploring Wisconsin* retains its narrative of progress, and perhaps even inevitability, the tone is more balanced and less celebratory than previous editions.

The 1977 edition dramatically enlarges the first unit, "Expanding Maps and Globes," adding an additional ten pages of geography content that places Wisconsin more clearly in the context of United States and world geography, including a new glossary of geographic terms.[108] The maps are colorful, interesting, and likely to engage student interest. As in previous editions, there is no political map in this section, and the relief map that shows the locations of Wisconsin cities and waterways does not include tribal lands. As before, the unit includes "Maps Tell a Story of Wisconsin," but that tale does not include American Indians.[109] Twenty years after its initial publication, *Exploring Wisconsin*, a textbook repeatedly adopted as the embodiment of official knowledge about the state, consistently excludes American Indians from certain domains that might meaningfully portray a contemporary presence in the state.

The second unit, which carried the title "Early Days in Wisconsin" in previous editions, carries the new title "Before It Was Wisconsin" in the new edition.[110] It provides greater attention to glaciers and glaciation than previous editions, consistent with the increased attention to geography. Students still learn about "Wisconsin's Early People" through a story of Little Hawk who is now described as "an Indian boy about nine or ten years old." Reflecting new attention to gender, Little Hawk now has a sister, Singing Bird, who is "nearly twelve," and like her brother, she is "a part of the Menominee tribe."[111] The book retains the inaccurate map depicting the Menominee well northwest of their actual homeland.[112] The scope of the narrative has changed little, except to incorporate Singing Bird into various activities, including moving the village, building the canoe, and harvesting wild rice, thereby highlighting the importance of women rather than implying they were drudges, as in previous editions.[113] Four full-color photographs of contemporary American Indians harvesting and processing wild rice show how "these Chippewas are harvesting wild rice the same way the Menominees did hundreds of years ago."[114] This is an important addition to the book because it shows the continuing presence of American Indian people, demonstrates cultural continuity into the present day, and provides another example of how "the Woodland Indians" often had shared many cultural practices. Unfortunately, the text itself leaves students to infer these points.

Claude Allouez is the first of many newly added historical figures the authors chose to highlight in half-page profiles. This format allows them to incorporate a number of individuals, including women and people of color, without having to alter their overall narrative of the state's history. The authors claim that the Miami Indians, upon meeting Allouez, called out, "Let the earth give us corn, and the rivers yield us fish. Let not disease kill us anymore, or famine treat us any longer so harshly." As a missionary, the text explains, "his job was to visit Indian tribes in the area, teaching them about Christianity," but "not all the tribes greeted Allouez with cries of help" as the Miamis had. This passage sets up the persistent Allouez in contrast to those Indians who "refused to help him in his travels," who "laughed at his weak arms as he carried heavy loads," and who "stole from him" as he strived to baptize "10,000 new Christians." Implicitly, students are encouraged to identify with the resilient Allouez rather than Indians who "did not want to learn a new religion" and "chose to keep their own beliefs and ways of worshipping."[115] Again, the text shows European figures as more deserving of sympathy and admiration.

The story of Nicolet has undergone some minor revision in the 1977 edition. He remains Champlain's envoy in search of the western ocean, but he no longer believes he is en route to China. The text uses the same illustration as previous editions, but explains the robe and pistols by stating, "Nicolet wanted to be sure he looked important."[116] Consistent with the illustration, students learn, "At first the Indians were afraid of the brightly dressed stranger," but after a feast in his honor, "the friendships Nicolet made with the Winnebago Indians were very important" because "when other French people came to Wisconsin to trade or to live, they knew the Indians were their friends."[117] This section maintains the relative positioning of the two groups, making the Ho-Chunk people secondary characters in the story of French acquisition of Wisconsin. Their fear of Nicolet, who "asked the Indians not to fight with other Indian tribes," distorts and seemingly justifies French motives and actions by disconnecting his efforts from colonial and commercial efforts. The text repeats the theme of the fearful Indians in the tale of Marquette and Joliet, but acknowledges that Joliet's mission was "to claim all the new lands he saw for New France."[118] The account is substantially similar to previous editions in other ways.

Unit 3, "Wisconsin Becomes a State," focuses on early French settlement, the presence of the English, including Langlade's leadership during the French and Indian War, the Black Hawk War, and a segment titled "Wisconsin: A State at Last," which addresses statehood and the Civil War.[119] The description of the Black Hawk War presents a very different narrative than previous editions. It discusses how as "more and more people came to Wisconsin to mine the lead deposits," the Indians "were pushed further and further west."[120] The Sauk, who "had already left their homes in Michigan to live in eastern Wisconsin," had "signed a treaty to give up their lands in Wisconsin for some lands west of the Mississippi."[121]

Although it repeats much of the information from previous editions, this version of the story is detailed and sympathetic to Black Hawk.

The 1977 edition explains that the Sauk returned to Wisconsin "after seeing the tribe's new lands," concluding "they could not make a good life" there. Once the army sent troops "to make sure the settlers were safe," Black Hawk could see that "his small group of Indians could not win against the army." The text describes how Black Hawk attempted to notify the army of his peaceful intentions, but soldiers killed the runners he sent. After being forced to fight, Black Hawk defeated nearly three hundred soldiers with only forty men before they "began to suffer great losses" as the fighting spread. The text notes that he sent most of the women and children ahead, hoping they could escape west, but "they were killed when Indians of another tribe discovered his plan." The authors explain that "even though Black Hawk was a great leader in war, the soldiers were able to defeat him," and he was taken prisoner after only 150 of his people made it back across the river.[122]

Following the war, students learn that Black Hawk "later became a hero," and "even some soldiers who fought against him thought he had been right," including Abraham Lincoln, who "thought that the Indians had been treated unfairly." The segment concludes that the government continued to make treaties with tribes in the area, and by the 1830s, the Potawatomi, Chippewa, and Ottawa had all signed treaties with the United States. A photograph accompanying this segment shows "a Winnebago family" circa 1900, "seventy years after they gave up their Wisconsin lands."[123] The choice of another tribe from another era still functions to relegate American Indians to the role of outsiders in their own homeland and makes them minor characters in those stories.

This narrative of the Black Hawk War provided in the 1977 edition of *Exploring Wisconsin* is more sympathetic to Black Hawk and his people than previous editions had been. It stresses the valor of a fallen foe and the tragedy of war, likely legacies of the United States' recent experiences in Southeast Asia, yet it reinforces a sense of inevitable American victory. The text portrays the Sauk as tragic casualties of American expansion who "were pushed further and further west."[124] The use of passive voice is an indicator of the narrative of progress and suggests that the Black Hawk War was a necessity, however regrettable it may have been.

The text assigns no responsibility for pushing the Sauk west; it simply reinforces common tropes of Indians necessarily fading off into the West as America grows.

Unit 4, "Wisconsin's People: Our Rich Heritage," exemplifies the field of social studies' turn toward ethnic studies.[125] The section "The First People in Wisconsin" opens with Nicolet's arrival in the region, noting that prior to his travels, "there were no white people in the state," thereby defining the earliest days of the state in terms of the absence of Europeans and defining American Indians as peripheral characters in the story of European exploration and settlement.[126] Settlers who followed Nicolet initially came to trade for furs, but others "wanted to make Wisconsin their new home," and they "began taking up the Indians' land" as they "built their homes and farms."[127] Students learn, "Our country's government also moved several eastern Indian tribes to Wisconsin," including the Oneida and Munsee tribes from New York who "were moved to Green Bay," and the Stockbridge and Brothertown Indians who "were moved to the eastern shores of Lake Winnebago."[128] This expanded section, new to the 1977 edition, is an incomplete and inaccurate representation of Native experiences that ignores the strategic choices reflected in these alliances and voluntary removals that these nations sought as a means of self-preservation.[129] As with earlier maps showing the incorrect locations of many tribes, the account presented in *Exploring Wisconsin* is simply incorrect.

The narrative of inevitability continues as the text states that, "to make room for the many white settlers coming to Wisconsin, the government began to buy Indian lands," and "one by one, the Wisconsin Indians gave up their lands." In another historically inaccurate gloss, the authors explain that "often they did not want to, but they could not fight the government," so "many Indian tribes gave up their land in Wisconsin this way." The text presents American Indians unquestioningly as barriers to white settlement who necessarily needed to be removed "to make room" instead of depicting them as sovereign nations with whom the federal government negotiated treaties.[130] The conclusion that "they could not fight the government" seemingly limits the agency and options of the tribes in responding to incursions into their homelands, framing the matter in terms of perceived tribal incapability rather than as strategic responses to European incursions.

Unlike the previous edition, which made only a brief mention of contemporary American Indians and focused primarily on Menominee County, the 1977 edition of *Exploring Wisconsin* is more explicitly contemporary and detailed. Students learn, "Today, Wisconsin has nearly 20,000 Indians," many of whom "live on reservations and are poor."[131] Reinforcing a narrative of dependency, the text states, "the money from the tribes' businesses is not enough to pay for their needs," so "the government runs the schools and may help the Indians get good health care."[132] This deficit-focused description ignores the fact that educational and health care services stem from treaty provisions and federal trust responsibility, thereby promoting a key misconception about "free" services. These themes often appeared later in the rhetoric of anti-treaty protestors.

"The First People in Wisconsin" continues with very brief descriptions of each tribe. Students learn that "the Chippewa tribe is one of the largest in the state" and that "their reservations include Mole Lake, Red Cliff, Bad River, Lac du Flambeau, and Lac Courte Oreilles." The only additional information about them is that their "businesses include harvesting and selling cranberries and wild rice." The authors provide no explanation for why they chose to focus on this particular point nor as to why they excluded or simply omitted St. Croix from the list of reservations. In any case, the text does not explain that each band is independent of the others and has its own tribal government.[133] To do so would require a discussion of tribal sovereignty, tribal government, and treaty making.

Previous editions mentioned the Menominees as residents of Menominee County and made no mention of the termination policy, just as the 1977 edition makes no mention of the historic restoration of their tribal status. The text states simply, "The Menominees live in the same land that has always been their home," and notes they have more than three thousand members. The description continues by noting, "The tribe's sawmill is probably the largest Indian business in the state."[134] Given that the Menominees were one of a few large tribes to experience termination, and by 1977, the only one to have successfully pursued restoration of tribal status, this is a significant omission of contemporary Wisconsin history.

Contemporary information about other tribes merits even less space in the book. Of the Stockbridge-Munsee, students learn, "The Stockbridge Indians live south of the Menominees" and some "live on reservations with the Munsee and Brotherton Indians along the eastern shore of Lake Winnebago."[135] This brief passage includes several factual errors. The Stockbridge-Munsee, who by the late nineteenth century were politically one people, have held reservation lands adjacent to the Menominee reservation since 1857. The Munsee have not been an independent polity since the mid-nineteenth century. A treaty signed in 1839 allotted and dissolved the Brothertown reservation. The federal government maintains that this treaty, the first of its kind, also dissolved the tribe as a federally recognized, self-governing nation. While it is important to include more current information about American Indians, the brief mentions in these examples seemingly contribute to misunderstandings.

Of the remaining Native peoples in the state, the book states, "Oneidas live in Brown and Outagamie counties. Winnebagos live around Black River Falls, Neillsville, and Tomah. Potawatomis live in Forest County."[136] Of all that the text might have included about these peoples, the authors, and by extension the curriculum committees who adopted *Exploring Wisconsin*, determined that this vague, minimal information represented the only ideas worthy of inclusion in the domain of official knowledge. It serves as a stark reminder that official knowledge represents a selective tradition that is a product of policy makers' choices.

The book notes that there are a number of historical markers related to American Indians around the state. In an attempt to bridge past and present, the text states that "at some reservations, visitors can watch Indian ceremonies that are hundreds and hundreds of years old," and "the Indians are also a part of today's world."[137] The authors explain that "nearly 4,000 Indians live in the Milwaukee area," and, "like many other groups of people" they are "working together to make their lives better."[138] A color photograph that accompanies this section depicts two Native men wearing fancy dance outfits, and it carries the caption, "Once a year, Indians of many tribes come to Black River Falls for a powwow. They often wear special clothes and do special dances."[139] It is important that the authors chose to recognize the continued existence of American Indians in Milwaukee and elsewhere, but it is unclear what students might conclude from these vague and exoticized depictions of contemporary life.

A half-page section profiles Yellow Thunder, "a chief of the Winnebago tribe" who "liked his Wisconsin home" and "did not leave it without a fight." The text explains that "settlers wanted the land and fought with the Indians for it," but that "the Indians lost the fight." This impossibly vague statement makes it very difficult to determine what "fight" the authors are referring to here. Students learn that Chief Yellow Thunder traveled to Washington in 1837 to talk with "government leaders" who persuaded him to sign a treaty that led to his people's forcible removal from Wisconsin. Yellow Thunder, the passage explains, "refused to stay" on their new lands in Iowa and returned to Wisconsin where he claimed a forty-acre parcel and "lived peacefully on his homestead until he died." The section concludes by explaining that although "Yellow Thunder could not win a victory for his tribe," his people "still respected his personal victory" and "remember him as a man who returned to the land he knew was his home."[140] This section reinforces misconceptions about the loss of the tribal land base in Wisconsin and does not tell the story of the Winnebago people's return to the state, nor political reorganization as the Wisconsin Winnebago Tribe in 1968, nor their adoption of a new form of government and return to their traditional name, the Ho-Chunk Nation. Like previous discussions of the Black Hawk War, it seemingly laments what it portrays as an inevitable defeat of American Indian peoples by the United States as part of a narrative of progress toward the contemporary state of Wisconsin.

Reflective of the turn toward ethnic studies in the field as a whole, this unit also highlights various groups of European immigrants. "Europeans in Wisconsin" focuses on the Germans, Swiss, Polish, Norwegians and "other Scandinavian people," Italians, Dutch, and Belgians.[141] While each European ethnic group has its own section, other populations receive much less attention. A segment titled "Blacks, Latin Americans, and Other People" provides very brief historical vignettes that center on the implied white heroes who ran the Underground Railroad, helped Joshua Glover to remain free, and currently seek to eradicate poverty among Latinos. While there is some attention to contemporary issues, as with the statement "Wisconsin, like other states, works hard to enforce laws that make equal opportunities for all of its people," *Exploring Wisconsin* creates a false sense of social harmony based on a selective history that stresses cooperation, all but eliminates conflict, and misrepresents the contemporary struggle for civil rights in heavily segregated Wisconsin cities.[142] One brief paragraph discusses "people from China, Japan, and the Philippine Islands," noting significant population increase between 1960 and 1970, apparently reflecting the decision that only the barest demographic information about Asian Americans was legitimate curriculum content.[143]

Unit 8, "Cities of Wisconsin," includes some minimal attention to an American Indian presence. Solomon Juneau, upon whom previous editions had lavished attention and depicted in illustrations as either throwing Indians over his head or measuring generous amounts of cloth to trade, now occupies only one brief paragraph where students learn that "Indians in the region liked him. He was always fair when they traded goods."[144] Only in the discussion of Milwaukee neighborhoods does the text revisit the discussion of various, almost exclusively European, ethnic groups.[145]

Unit 9, "America's Vacation Land," highlights tourist destinations around the state.[146] The text devotes attention to state parks and forests, and describes a number of historical sites including Aztalan, "a very early Indian village."[147] The revised "Wisconsin Vacation Map" no longer has the problematic depictions of American Indians that had seemingly indicated the location of tribal lands, yet they are otherwise completely absent from the map despite earlier references to "colorful Indian ceremonials" on reservations. The text again highlights outdoor activities, including swimming, camping, hunting, fishing, boating, hiking, biking, and winter sports.

In Unit 10, "Wisconsin's Government," American Indians are background characters on the narrative of inevitable progress rather than distinct sovereign nations with their own governments and treaty-based relationships with the federal government. This section discusses Governor Dodge's negotiations for lands in the state, noting that "he was very fair in dealing with the tribes and fighting did not break out."[148] The unit covers county, city, town, and village government in Wisconsin, and even discuss the state's role in the national government, yet it makes no mention of tribal governments in the state. As events of the 1980s suggest, this may have been a costly omission.

The 1977 edition of *Exploring Wisconsin* is the first to include significant content about non-European racial and ethnic communities, and in this respect, it clearly suggests a connection between national trends in the field, state policies affecting curriculum issues, and what is legitimated as official knowledge at the local school district level through textbook adoption. The authors' and publisher's attempts to incorporate this new content into a dramatically revised and expanded edition of their text likely reflects an attempt to remain current with trends in the field.

In their attempts to provide an account of Wisconsin history that reflects the racial and ethnic diversity in the state as well as a degree of gender balance, the authors portray a scene of racial harmony, with communities of various European ethnic groups around the state, and discrete communities of American Indians on reservations, blacks in Milwaukee, and Latin Americans employed as migrant workers and living in Racine. The segregation in the text's content implicitly suggests yet ignores the very real racial segregation of the 1970s.

The only hints of the struggles for civil rights the authors included in *Exploring Wisconsin* are in the story of Joshua Glover, wherein whites helped an escaped slave to remain a free man, thereby reinforcing the narrative of racial harmony, and the statement about equal opportunity, which serves a similar purpose. Although this edition perhaps reflects an increase in attention to race and ethnicity and women in history, both the information selected for this purpose and the perspective privileged in the narrative is still not that of any of these groups. The "gaze" is the same as earlier editions, and the actual incorporation of racial-, ethnic-, and gender-focused content is mostly cosmetic. Romano and Georgiady's approach exemplifies the potential dangers of a turn toward an ethnic studies approach without appropriate knowledge of the various groups to be included in revised social studies curriculum.

—||—

An examination of widely adopted elementary Wisconsin history textbooks highlights how local textbook selection committees translated and operationalized state-level guidance to make their own choices about legitimate school knowledge. The largely incremental changes in the contents of these texts also shows both enduring and dynamic attitudes about gender, race, and indigeneity between the late 1950s and the late 1970s. The staying power of Romano and Georgiady's text thereby exemplifies the local education policy history context in which the state enacted Act 31 in

1989 and suggests potential problems with implementation. Because Act 31 represented unprecedented specific directives to local school districts about curriculum content, it was contrary to traditions of incremental change and local control.

PART 5

PASSING ACT 31

CHAPTER 12

TALKING BACK TO
THE CURRICULUM

A merican Indian people have long sought to transform education policy to make it more responsive to individual and tribal needs and to ensure that others develop a more accurate understanding of Native realities.[1] This chapter begins with a discussion of some of the earliest efforts by American Indians, those led by the Society of American Indians and the Grand Council Fire of American Indians in the 1910s and 1920s, to challenge misconceptions about Native history and identity that were accepted as official knowledge in American schools. It traces similar efforts at the state and national levels from the 1960s to the 1980s as tribal leaders and academics called for reforms that would transform local curriculum as well as the textbooks and other materials that served as primary tools of instruction. These efforts to talk back to the curriculum are part of a long tradition of Native people pressing for educational change.

AN INDIAN SOLUTION TO "THE INDIAN PROBLEM":
THE SOCIETY OF AMERICAN INDIANS

American Indians have been working to reform education nearly as long as they have experienced schooling. Several members of the first generation to experience off-reservation boarding schools, particularly the Hampton Institute in Virginia and Carlisle Indian Industrial School in Pennsylvania, organized in the early twentieth century as the Society of American Indians (SAI). Their reform agenda gave education policy a prominent place as they worked to create a new future for American Indian people, one characterized by formal education and American citizenship. Its leaders sought to challenge the dominant view of their peoples as members of a "vanishing race" by asserting a new identity that was simultaneously assimilationist, nationalist, and Pan-Indian in nature.

Those gathered in Columbus, Ohio, at the first meeting of the SAI chose October 12, 1911, Columbus Day, to signal a new beginning for Native people. Most of those who gathered from October 12 to 17 were graduates of off-reservation boarding schools, but several had attended public schools alongside white students. Many of the founding members had completed their higher education at prestigious universities, such as Dartmouth, Yale, Barnard, and Boston University, and entered the professions, including two members who served as staff at Carlisle. In addition to the assimilationist messages they received at school, they also developed a distinct Pan-Indian racial identity, were proud to be "Indian," and consciously promoted the idea of "the Indian race," despite tenuous ties to their own tribal communities. For most, this sense of distinct racial identity was more important than tribal membership, and indeed for some, the tribe was important only in that it was what made one an Indian.[2]

The SAI advocated for curricular reforms in the federal Indian schools, particularly the off-reservation boarding schools. They argued that when students left these schools their "knowledge of most things was of little use to [their] kinsmen" and they lacked the necessary skills to make a living or contribute to the larger society.[3] Most SAI members were themselves highly educated physicians, attorneys, teachers, and other professionals, and they critiqued the "retarding influences of the present system" that effectively denied most students the opportunities to acquire advanced knowledge and skills.[4] One member argued, "The Indian should be taught the history of this country more, and of his own race, and of his rights as a citizen—civil government is what he needs in his education more than anything else" if Indians were to be effective advocates for themselves and for their people.[5] Overall, members of the SAI advanced a sophisticated critique of their educational experiences and the policies that shaped them. Despite frequent disagreements about policy solutions, they sought to use schooling as a means to empower their people.

Laura Cornelius, a Wisconsin Oneida woman and founding member of SAI, was among the first Native people in Wisconsin to advocate for reforms in education policy at the national, state, and local levels. She had attended public schools, including Grafton Hall in Fond du Lac, Wisconsin, graduating in 1898, and she called them "the white man's greatest institution in this country."[6] She denounced the "greatest fallacy" in the federal Indian schools as "tak[ing] away the traditions of the youth on which all other nations build their hopes and then expect[ing] to make him a great man." She viewed this practice as detrimental to students' pride and argued, "There is no race on the face of the earth that is so rich in pride as the Indian race."[7] Many SAI members proudly proclaimed themselves to be "new Indians," but she argued that "the idea of being a new Indian is fake," itself a product of boarding school education. She called upon SAI members to declare, "I am not the new Indian, I am the old Indian adjusted to new conditions."[8] Those in attendance applauded her comments, suggesting broad agreement with the concept of curriculum reform as a means to foster student pride and "adjustment to new conditions."[9]

The founders of SAI were sensitive to white opinion and strove to shape the public view of Indians. They spoke of core values shared among tribes, stressing the similarities between these values and those of the white middle class. Their rhetoric was rife with talk of "improvement" through self-help and self-reliance. Much of the sought-after improvement was to come through schooling, including higher education. The fact that many were professionals and at least eleven were current or former employees of the Bureau of Indian Affairs reflects this belief in higher education and self-improvement.[10]

The ideas espoused by the organization, and even sometimes by individuals within the organization, were complex and contradictory. Present-day scholars seem to regard the organization with ambivalence about its assimilationist politics or view it as simply a precursor to later national Indian organizations, including the American Indian Movement.[11] Understood in its proper context, however, the Society of American Indians is actually quite radical for a group that came of age in an era characterized by boarding schools, the allotment of remaining reservation lands, dissolution of tribal governments, the suppression of traditional cultural and spiritual traditions, and the tragic massacre at

Wounded Knee. For them to struggle for a uniquely Indian voice, and to use that voice to advocate for educational change, was a mark of great courage. Regardless of what their collective voice was actually saying, the SAI set forth a path that other Native advocates for education reform would soon follow.

Challenging the Textbooks:
Grand Council Fire of American Indians

In the 1920s, American Indians entered into a textbook controversy in Chicago and expressed concern over the depiction of Native people in instructional materials. Chicago Mayor William "Big Bill" Thompson had vowed that he would "never rest until the histories in use" in the city's schools had been "purged of their pro-British propaganda," and he initiated hearings on textbooks then in use.[12] Thompson's efforts reflected disillusionment with the World War and involved an attempt to appeal to the city's growing Irish, Polish, and other ethnic populations. He proclaimed "all nationalities are entitled to a place in the sun," and "our national heroes are the stars in the firmament of our patriotism."[13] Thompson's vision of an American history textbook that reflected a multi-ethnic pantheon of American heroes did not include non-Europeans, but American Indians and African Americans joined the fray to ensure their people were included along with Italians, Norwegians, Poles, Lithuanians, and Germans.[14]

Amidst the textbook controversy, the Grand Council Fire of American Indians sought to appeal to Thompson's sense of *"real 100%* Americanism."[15] "Indians and interested friends" founded the organization in 1923 "to provide legislative, educational, and social services" to urban and reservation Indians. Its president, the "Chief of Chiefs," was always a Native person, as were most other officers, but the secretary, or "Chief Story Teller," was a non-Native, Marion Gridley.[16] Compared to the Society of American Indians, the organization was staunchly anti-assimilationist. Through the 1930s, the Grand Council Fire was "the only significant association" in Chicago's Native community.[17] The group, which the New York Times characterized as "a committee of Indians in war-paint and eagle feathers," presented Mayor Thompson with a resolution "asking that the Red Man's point of view be incorporated in the school texts."[18] Its organization's message, "Memorial and Recommendations of the Grand Council Fire of American Indians," submitted on December 1, 1927, suggested that "while you are teaching school children about America First, teach them the truth about the First Americans."[19] The organization wrote that "school histories" were "unjust to the life of our people" and repeatedly pointed out the double standards that portrayed Native people as "murderers," "treacherous," "thieves," and "savages," while celebrating white heroism, patriotism, and civility.[20] They asserted Indian accomplishments in the arts, oratory, music, and athletics and asked that schools teach about those aspects of American Indian history and culture.[21] They urged Thompson to "tell your children of the friendly acts of Indians to the white people who first settled here" and to teach about Indian involvement in World War I. They wrote, "Tell how the Indian fought for a country of which he was not a citizen, for a flag to which he had no claim, and for a people that have treated him unjustly."[22] The Grand Council argued, "The Indian has long been hurt by these unfair books" and "[we] ask only that our story be told in fairness" because "a true program of America First will give a generous place to the culture and history of the American Indian." President Scott H. Peters and seven delegates signed on behalf of the organization.[23]

Their evidence provided example after example of historical events and understandings that traditional school histories had distorted or omitted, including the Black Hawk War. In contrast with *Exploring Wisconsin's* account, the Grand Council Fire of American Indians noted that the Black Hawk War arose "because of the forcible removal of Black Hawk and his people from their lands and of the attack upon him and a small party of white soldiers when they were going peacefully to their homes."[24] They also note the role that Shabonna played when he "rode throughout the State of Illinois warning settlers of the approach of Black Hawk and thus saving thousands of lives." Scholars Rupert Costo and Jeannette Henry identify this as the "first official action of the Indian people protesting the distortions and inaccuracies of the school books," an early effort that would serve as a direct inspiration to coming generations.[25] Nearly a half-century later, Costo and Henry reprinted the statement in its entirety in the first publication by the Indian Historian Press.

"Let the People In": The Indian Historian Press

The Grand Council Fire of American Indians provided inspiration for a new generation of American Indian scholars seeking to challenge and correct historical understandings about Native people. Rupert Costo, Cahuilla, and Jeannette Henry, Cherokee, founded the American Indian Historical Society in the mid-1960s as an "All-Indian organization of scholars and Native historians," and they began publishing a quarterly journal, *The Indian Historian*, in December 1964.[26] On August 19, 1965, representatives of the American Indian Historical Society testified before the California State Curriculum Commission that they had studied the textbooks currently in use and others under consideration and determined that "not one book is free from error as to the role of the Indian in state and national history."[27] They argued that while "a person has the right to be wrong," textbooks have "no right to be wrong, or to lie, hide the truth, or falsify history, or insult and malign a whole race of people," but "that is what these textbooks do." The American Indian Historical Society proclaimed the books to be "extremely superficial in their treatment of the American Indian, oversimplifying and generalizing the explanation of our culture and history, to the extent where the physical outlines of the Indian as a human being are lost." Instead, the textbooks contain "misinformation, misinterpretation, and misconception," such that a "true picture of the American Indian is entirely lacking."[28] The organization found that its challenge to traditional depictions of the state's history and the alternative criteria they submitted for reviewing and adopting textbooks caused "an outcry" that led to their recommendations being largely ignored.[29] Nonetheless, their efforts caused a "new movement" that inspired similar efforts in other states, as "falsification of Indian history by textbooks" became a nationwide concern.[30]

The American Indian Historical Society attempted to address the issue of biases and stereotypes in textbooks in other ways as well. Representatives testified before the Senate Committee on Indian Education on January 4, 1969, proclaiming, "There is not one Indian in this country who does not cringe in anguish and frustration because of these textbooks. There is not one Indian child who has not come home in shame and tears after one of those sessions in which he is taught that his people were dirty, animal-like, something less than human beings. We

Indians are not just one more complaining minority. We are the proud and only true Natives of this land."[31]

After testifying before state and federal policy makers, the American Indian Historical Society chose to take on the textbook publishers directly, founding the Indian Historian Press, Inc., as "an independent Indian publishing house" in 1969. In their words, it was started as a "direct result of the failure of the publishers, educational writers, and school administrators to provide accurate classroom instructional materials."[32] The Indian Historian Press, Inc., released its first publication, *Textbooks and the American Indian*, in 1970. The book was the culmination of the efforts of thirty-two Native scholars and historians to review textbooks and other instructional materials published between 1950 and 1970 that were in use in elementary or secondary schools. Their analysis relied on the criteria they had originally presented to the California State Curriculum Commission. They concluded that none of the materials evaluated "could be approved as a dependable source of knowledge about the history and culture of the Indian people of America" because most were "derogatory to the Native American" and "contained misinformation, distortions, or omissions of important history."[33] The reviewers made an important distinction between books for a general audience, where individuals can choose what they read, and textbooks, because students are "compelled to study from an approved book." Because of the compulsory nature of textbooks, the authors defended their "right to insist upon truth, accuracy, and objectivity."[34] Their efforts, including *The Indian Historian*, the *Wassaja* newspaper, the regional and national gatherings they hosted, and other publications, initiated a line of scholarly inquiry and inspired subsequent efforts to transform curriculum policy in Wisconsin and other states.[35]

Lawanna Trout was among those later scholars who focused specifically on teaching and learning about Native people. For over twenty years, Trout led National Endowment for the Humanities–funded seminars for teachers through the Newberry Library in Chicago.[36] In "Native American History," a chapter in the 1982 NCSS bulletin *Teaching American History: New Directions*, Trout argues that approaches to the field must include a focus on inter- and intratribal issues instead of just Indian-white relations, must be "open to new interpretations," and must recognize the validity of oral and written sources on tribal history.[37] Regarding the widespread omission of curriculum content about American Indians, Trout observed, "Most high school teachers omit Native American tribal history and distort the history of Indian-White relations" because they are "simply unaware of its existence."[38] Trout laments that secondary-level textbooks are "equally unreliable" because "extraneous notes on Native Americans are tucked in with material about the landing of the Pilgrims and the winning of the West."[39] In these textbooks, "Pocahontas saves John Smith, Chief Joseph surrenders, and Geronimo goes to the Ft. Sill prison," but American Indians "do not speak from treaty proceedings or in tribal meetings."[40]

By the 1980s, Trout notes, textbooks include "photographs of Red Cloud and Sitting Bull along with quotes from Black Hawk and Crazy Horse, but the revisions are cosmetic." The use of George Catlin and Edward Curtis in lieu of American Indian artists "perpetuate[s] a cycle of cultural blindness."[41] To provide a different perspective, she recommends Robert Berkhofer's The White Man's Indian to understand how "whites created self-serving stereotypes which they used as ideological weapons in their subjugation of Native Americans."[42] She observes that "the effects of those stereotypes are still multiplying," a comment reflective of the state of the field approximately one year before the Voigt decision.[43]

—ıı—

Efforts by the Society of American Indians, the Grand Council Fire of American Indians, and Indian Historian Press represent a long tradition of Native people talking back to the curriculum and trying to reshape schooling to be more responsive to their needs. The first generation to experience off-reservation boarding schools sought to use the position and prestige afforded by their education and professional experiences to advocate for new approaches to schooling. Urban Indians first became actively involved in textbook controversies in the 1920s, and a new generation continued those efforts in the 1970s while publishing instructional materials of their own. A growing network of national organizations brought these organizations and individuals into contact with one another, allowing them to assist and inspire one another's efforts.[44] A similar level of coordination in Wisconsin would lead to the passage of Act 31, a true victory for Native people challenging curriculum policy.

CHAPTER 13

TRANSFORMING CURRICULUM POLICY, 1979–1989

By the mid-1980s, American Indian educators and their allies in Wisconsin were clearly echoing the words of Elmer L. Davids Sr., the Stockbridge-Munsee tribal member who spoke so memorably at the 1961 American Indian Chicago Conference. Of particular influence was his question, "Is it fair to the Indian to use the textbooks in our public schools that tend to justify the acts of early settlers and make the poor Indian, resisting in proud self-defense, a culprit and a savage?"[1] Their call for an education policy response to the acts of violence and racism plaguing the state in the 1980s drew clear connections between what was being taught in Wisconsin classrooms and the need for reform.

This chapter examines the efforts of American Indian educators and their allies to reform curriculum policy to ensure that all students receive accurate, authentic instruction about Indian history, culture, and tribal sovereignty in Wisconsin. As the backlash to the *Voigt* decision escalated, those seeking an educational reform solution looked to the American Indian Study Committee (AISC) and the American Indian Language and Culture Education Board (AILCEB) for guidance. They looked to the Indian Education Act as a potential model. The actions of these groups are best understood as a critical response to the backlash against the *Voigt* decision as well as the education policy decisions of the past that contributed directly to the widespread public ignorance. They were also part of American Indians' ongoing efforts nationwide to transform public education and to raise public awareness of historical and contemporary tribal issues and concerns. These highly coordinated efforts culminated in the passage of education-related amendments regarding American Indian history, culture, tribal sovereignty, and related issues in the state's 1989–1991 biennial budget, commonly known as Act 31.

WISCONSIN WOODLAND INDIANS SERIES

The development of the Wisconsin Woodland Indian Series, educational materials to be used in elementary classrooms, marks an important step toward Act 31. In a very real way, by the 1970s Native people had transitioned from historical objects of study to critics of curricular bias to producers of authentic curriculum materials. The series resulted from a new collaborative effort in the mid-1970s to produce curriculum materials about the history and cultures of the Native peoples in the state. The project was administered by the Rhinelander School District and funded through grants secured under Title IV-C of the Elementary and Secondary Education Act, additional support from the Wisconsin Department of Public Instruction (DPI), assistance from the Great Lakes Inter-Tribal Council, Inc., and the tribes themselves.

Through the three-year Wisconsin Woodland Indian Project, which operated from 1979 until 1982, Lac du Flambeau tribal members Ernie St. Germaine and Robin Carufel, along with non-Native Shelley Oxley, produced units suitable for use in elementary classrooms. The project focused on the "six major tribes" in the state, collaborating with tribal members from each community to produce *The Stockbridge-Munsee Tribe: A History of the Mahican and the Munsee Indians*, *The History of the Potawatomie Indians of Wisconsin: Keepers of the Fire*, *History of the Oneida Indians*, *The History of the Menominee Indians*, *The History of the Hochungra People (Winnebago Tribe) of Wisconsin*, and *The Anishinabe: An Overview Unit of the History and Background of the Wisconsin Ojibway Indian Tribe*. To accompany the overview of the Anishinabe, the project created individual units on each of the six Ojibwe bands. They also published a unit on a nation without federal recognition, *The History of the Brotherton Indians*.[2]

In addition to the tribe-specific publications, the Wisconsin Woodland Indians Project developed a series of units on various aspects of traditional culture: *American Indian Dance Costumes*, *Winnebago Applique*, *Corn:*

The Gift of the American Indian People, American Indian Foods, Porcupine Quillwork on Birchbark, Indian Dwellings, Music of the Woodland Indians, Methods of Travel and Migration Among the American Indians, Names and Maps Tell a Story of Wisconsin, Beadwork: Beadwork Design of American Indians, What Is An Indian?, The Web of the Creator: Basketry, The Uses of Birchbark, Eagles, The Moccasin Game, Bijpindjiganaong: The Bone Game, and *Harvesting Manomin.* DPI later republished many of these materials beginning in 1990 to meet the immediate demand for materials after Act 31's passage.[3]

THE WISCONSIN INDIAN EDUCATION ACT

Reflecting on the organization's origins, the AILCEB described the 1970s as "a long struggle by Wisconsin Indian tribes, communities, and individuals concerned with quality Indian education to establish a credible, visible Indian group to advise state agencies that impact their education and the education of their children."[4] Their efforts culminated with the passage of Assembly Bill 807, the Wisconsin Indian Education Act, which Governor Lee Sherman Dreyfus signed into law on May 7, 1980.[5] The law "recognizes special cultural and language needs of American Indian pupils and acknowledges the unique historical status of these pupils as both citizens of this state and of their respective tribal governments."[6] Reflecting concern for the educational achievement and attainment of American Indian students, the Wisconsin Indian Education Act established provisions for introducing language and culture education programs in public schools and provided a measure of state aid for such programs in alternative schools with at least 75 percent Indian enrollment.[7]

NEW ADVOCATES EMERGE

The establishment of the American Indian Language and Culture Education Board in 1980 may be the most important outcome of the Wisconsin Indian Education Act. AILCEB, a new entity explicitly charged with recommending changes to education policy, included "Indian parents, Indian teachers and school administrators, school board members, persons involved in programs for American Indian children and persons experienced in the training of the teachers of Indian language and culture programs." Members were appointed by the governor for staggered four-year terms based on "recommendations by various Indian tribes, bands, and organizations."[8] Their primary charge was to advise the state superintendent; the Higher Education Aids Board; the Board of Vocational, Technical, and Adult Education; and the Board of Regents of the University of Wisconsin System "on all matters relating to the education of American Indians."[9]

AILCEB, which was under the administration of the Wisconsin DPI, was responsible for establishing "standards of certification for teachers of Indian history, culture, and language" and "standards of certification for home/school coordinators, counselors, and aides." Each biennium, it was to submit a report to the governor and legislature "regarding the needs of American Indian communities, evaluation of American Indian language and culture programs established under the law, and make recommendations for legislation in the area of Indian language and culture education."[10] Over the course of the next decade, AILCEB emerged as a key advocate for curriculum policy reforms designed to create learning opportunities for all students related to Wisconsin Indian history, culture, and tribal sovereignty.

Another entity in Wisconsin state government, the Joint Legislative Council's American Indian Study Committee, played a critical role in enacting Act 31. Made up of elected members of the Wisconsin Assembly and Senate and public members representing tribal nations in Wisconsin, AISC was to study "issues relating to American Indians and the American Indian tribes and bands in this state and develop specific recommendations and legislative proposals relating to these issues."[11] They began to discuss implementation of the Indian Education Act less than a year after *Voigt*. At its December 13, 1983 meeting, Rep. Sharon Metz (D-Green Bay) identified the program as a means to provide intercultural education and expand learning opportunities for American Indian students. She expressed concern about the voluntary nature of American Indian Language and Culture Education programs and urged the committee "to consider a statutory change to *require* establishment of an Indian education program if the population in any specific school, rather than a district, exceeds a designated percentage" (emphasis in original).[12] She indicated that her proposal might affect approximately fifteen to twenty school districts. Public member Dorothy W. Davids, who was also a member of AILCEB, sought and received an assurance that the AISC would "seek input from the tribes" on the proposal.[13] As AISC continued to monitor both the Indian Education Act and events ensuing from *Voigt*, its members, including some of its public members who also served on AILCEB or the Great Lakes Inter-Tribal Council Education Committee, began to see the seeds of an educational solution in the 1980 Indian Education Act.

The AISC's first major discussion of the *Voigt* decision occurred at its July 20, 1984, meeting, held at the tribal office on the Lac Courte Oreilles Reservation. The timing coincided with the Honor the Earth Powwow, and as noted by one of the public tribal members in attendance, the location was "an important departure from the typical pattern of tribal people always having to go to Madison to conduct business."[14] An elected member of the committee explained, "Meetings such as these help to improve relations between state government and the tribes."[15] Elected members of AISC had greater opportunity than the general public to become aware of and develop a genuine understanding of controversial "Indian" issues. They recognized the importance of authentic learning opportunities as a component of sound public policymaking, which they brought to bear in advancing curriculum policy recommendations about American Indians.

At Lac Courte Oreilles, committee members heard testimony from several key figures involved with implementing the *Voigt* decision. The panelists included Henry M. Buffalo Jr., Red Cliff Ojibwe tribal member and executive administrator of the Great Lakes Indian Fish and Wildlife Commission (GLIFWC); George Meyer, representing the Wisconsin Department of Natural Resources; Paul DeMain, Oneida, representing the Wisconsin Governor's Office; and William Wildcat Sr., representing the Lac du Flambeau Tribal Council. The first speaker, Henry Buffalo, explained the treaties, the concept of reserved rights, ongoing negotiations with the state regarding the exercise of treaty rights, and GLIFWC's role in biological services, law enforcement, and public information. Buffalo identified GLIFWC's core functions as providing information to the public on treaty-based hunting and fishing rights and facilitating "discussion of tribal treaty rights between the various Chippewa bands and the state and to serve as a forum for inter-tribal discussions of natural resource issues," adding that "this issue is such an emotional one for the general public."[16] He also noted the organization's efforts "to counter the emotional arguments against the exercise of tribal hunting and fishing rights put forth by such groups as ERFE [Equal Rights for Everyone]."[17] Tribal leaders and leaders of intertribal organizations had identified and acted on the need to educate and inform the public even before the treaty harvests had started.

In addition to his testimony on negotiations with tribes on natural resource management, fire protection, environmental protection, and law enforcement activities, George Meyer discussed the DNR's efforts to educate the general public about issues related to tribal sovereignty and treaty rights. Meyer noted that treaty rights disputes in other states "caused great damage both to the natural resources and to human relations and that serious racial problems have resulted."[18] He explained that the DNR was "on a tightrope" because its efforts to negotiate were "being second-guessed by state hunters and fishers" whom he described as "quite savvy about the limitations of various resources." Meyer also minimized anti–treaty rights groups such as ERFE, which he described as "fairly localized in their impact," but noted that the DNR stood ready to "address all interested groups concerning the treaty rights issues."[19] In response to Meyer's presentation, Rep. Sheehan Donoghue (R-Merrill) noted that due to the "terrible and inaccurate rumors about the large number of deer that will be killed during the Chippewa hunting season," there was "a great need to get accurate information about the treaty rights out to the general public."[20]

In response to a question from Rep. Metz about other organizations the DNR had met with concerning treaty rights, Meyer indicated that the agency had "spent a great deal of time discussing tribal treaty rights issues with the Wisconsin Conservation Congress and the Wisconsin Wildlife Federation."[21] Particularly with regard to conservation organizations, Buffalo explained, "it is important to educate the public to the fact that a reasonable exercise of treaty rights can actually help protect the resources involved."[22] Rep. Metz acknowledged that groups in her district and that of Rep. Cathy Zeuske (R-Shawano) "want to go straight to Congress and have treaty rights abrogated." DeMain explained that ERFE had made abrogation one of its central issues, noting that "the caliber of people in these groups is not the greatest and that not all are law-abiding citizens."

He urged the DNR to "continue to talk to the reasonable citizenry on this issue."[23] Even before the first treaty-based harvest had occurred, tribal leaders and state policy makers already recognized the existing information vacuum and the social costs associated with the resulting lack of public awareness.

The first report of AILCEB, delayed until 1984 due to staff turnover, contained the requisite recommendations for each relevant state agency and highlighted the need to address ignorance of treaty rights. AILCEB recommended that DPI use the biennial budget process to request $250,000 for new programs "to address the educational and cultural needs of American Indian students," specifically for those districts with "an Indian student population large enough to provide valid statistical information concerning the merits of bilingualism."[24] They also called on DPI to create an "Indian Teacher Training Institute" and "strengthen the human relations component of teacher certification by requiring a course or courses in Wisconsin Indian history (multicultural approach)."[25] As they explained, "Future teachers need accurate knowledge about Wisconsin American Indians and the unique characteristics of each tribe."[26] The report also noted that AILCEB had succeeded in its efforts to develop licensing rules for educators working in an American Indian Language and Culture Education program, acknowledging that DPI adopted the necessary administrative rules on January 27, 1982.[27]

In an appendix to the report, AILCEB provided "Informational Packets for Establishing AILCE Programs in Public or Alternative Schools," which described the purpose of such programs as making the curriculum more relevant for Indian students, "reinforc[ing] self image," and "develop[ing] intercultural awareness among pupils, parents, and staff."[28] The program could encompass a broad range of activities, including language, literature, history, and culture instruction; in-services "in regard to methods of teaching American Indian pupils"; vocational education and counseling; "modification of curriculum, instructional methods and administrative procedures to meet the needs of American Indian pupils enrolled"; identification of Indian students; and "classification of American Indian pupils enrolled by grade, level of education, age, and achievement."[29] With the exception of eligible alternative schools, there was no funding available to support the founding or operation of such programs, but even with this limitation, many advocates viewed the Wisconsin Indian Education Act as a template for future reforms.

A Model Emerges

The first concrete recommendations for a curriculum policy solution to address racism and public ignorance related to tribal sovereignty and treaty rights came from the Ad Hoc Commission on Racism in Northern Wisconsin (AHCR), convened in 1984. Because AHCR recognized educational institutions as part of the same social fabric and affected by the same social ills as the broader society, it called for expanded learning opportunities for the general public through educational institutions and the mass media. Its 1984 report shows great faith in the ability of educational institutions to serve as engines of social change.

In the report, AHCR concluded that the lack of opportunities for students to experience "well taught courses on tribal sovereignty, the treaties, Indian culture and history" were themselves both cause and effect of racism. As a remedy, they called upon AILCEB to develop courses where public grade school and high school students would learn "the meaning of tribal sovereignty, Wisconsin Indian Treaties and Wisconsin Indian culture and history."[30] They also sought to ensure that students enrolled in private and parochial schools received similar instruction. This indicates interest in a comprehensive solution that provides opportunities to learn about these issues in all K-12 schools and teacher education programs in the state.

AHCR noted that teachers similarly experienced limited opportunities to learn about these issues such that many were left "woefully ignorant of Indian culture and history."[31] They recognized a distinct lack of opportunity to learn about tribal sovereignty, treaties, tribal cultures, history, and contemporary issues as a key issue in teacher education and saw that any meaningful solution must include teacher training institutions. As a remedy, they called on public and private colleges and universities to ensure their graduates received instruction on "tribal sovereignty, and treaties affecting Wisconsin Indians, Indian culture, history and current Indian concerns."[32] AHCR recommended a series of in-service trainings for those currently in the profession.[33]

The report recognized the failure of K-12 schools, colleges, and universities to offer opportunities to learn about "the rich heritage and many contributions of the American Indian cultures" as a key factor contributing to "a racist climate in Wisconsin schools." AHCR offered four recommendations to remedy this situation. First, it called on schools to "develop educational units for classroom presentation which incorporate the cultures and history of the American Indian nations, particularly those having reservations within Wisconsin." It recommended "occasional programs illustrating or based upon Indian traditions," including "talks by Indian leaders, 'pow-wow' dance demonstrations, display of handicraft, selected movies, etc." The report suggested that "classroom material . . . including both textbooks and references should be screened" and that schools withdraw "materials demonstrating either overt or implied racism." Furthermore, it called upon schools to "make effective use of Indian parent committees in the development of curricula and programs."[34] This deceptively simple set of recommendations would require schools to reconsider how they answer implicit questions about whose knowledge counts and how it is legitimated in schools.

AHCR recommended strong programs in the school and the church so that the home might be the source of understanding and compassion, noting that this would require ongoing work and significant investments in programs and personnel.[35] As part of that ongoing work, the group called on the Great Lakes Inter-Tribal Council to revive its education committee and become an active part of a permanent, statewide solution.[36] One year later, the education committee became the Wisconsin Indian Education Association. The efforts of the Ad Hoc Commission on Racism, which began as a local effort by a tribal government asserting its sovereignty to study the impact of racism against Native people, soon broadened its goals as regional and statewide institutions joined the effort.

Advocacy for Curriculum Policy Reform

The American Indian Language and Culture Education Board became the first entity to take up the recommendations of the AHCR. On October 5, 1985, AILCEB submitted an interim report in follow-up to its 1984 biennial report. In this document, AILCEB described its role in terms of "increasing opportunities for Indian and non-Indian students to become knowledgeable about American Indian history, language, and culture."[37] AILCEB explained that its "priority goals pursued during the past year" related to AHCR's findings that "overt racism, which surfaced in northern Wisconsin after the *Voigt* decision in January of 1983, was the result of general ignorance of the relationship between Indian tribes and the federal government."[38] AILCEB acknowledged AHCR's charge to "urge all Wisconsin grade and high schools to begin without delay to develop and implement courses that teach the meaning of tribal sovereignty, Wisconsin Indian Treaties and Wisconsin Indian history" and to "use language expressing the problem's emergency nature, emphasizing that assistance is available to schools."[39] The report acknowledged AHCR's request that AILCEB "be firm" with DPI, and it reports several actions taken to support school-based efforts to establish appropriate programs.

In response to requests from AHCR, AILCEB offered a workshop at Nicolet College on April 26, 1985, titled "Methods and Activities for Including Wisconsin Indian Histories and Governments in Your Junior High Curriculum," which was funded in part by DPI, the first effort of its kind endorsed at the state level. The report noted that AILCEB and DPI "are currently seeking similar cooperative funding to enable a second workshop to be offered in the southern and central parts of the state" but to date "no funding has been located for this purpose." Although it was administratively attached to DPI, AILCEB had separate funding and position authority, which often left it unable to sponsor its own events. The board identified this dependence on DPI for funding to conduct workshops as "an ongoing problem."[40]

AILCEB also reported on its efforts to develop and disseminate appropriate resources for teaching about Wisconsin Indians. AILCEB notes that Dr. Michael Hartoonian, DPI social studies consultant, and Dr. Ronald N. Satz, dean of professional studies and professor of history at the University of Wisconsin–Eau Claire and member of the Ad Hoc Commission on Racism, attended the September meeting to discuss "ideas for the inclusion of Wisconsin Indian history in the elementary and secondary curricula."[41] The report indicated that AILCEB allocated funds to distribute to requesting schools copies of the Wisconsin Woodland Indian Series, "a 37 unit culture and tribal history packet developed by the Rhinelander School District, and copies of *American Indian Tribal Governments*, developed by the Madison Metropolitan School District."[42] It was seeking additional funding to "print and disseminate Wisconsin Indian history and government materials to all school districts in the state in the 1985–1986 school year" but had not yet received a response.[43] This was yet another example of the limitations of its complicated relationship with DPI.

Other events were clearly reinforcing the perception that changes to curriculum policy were needed to address prejudice and discrimination. In response to DPI's *Crandon Report*, "dated December 1980 and April 1984, outlining its investigations and recommendations for correcting discriminatory practices in the Crandon School District," and indications from "local Indian communities" that "little real progress has been made toward that end," AILCEB passed a resolution on June 10, 1985, seeking cooperation from "key people statewide" to help "establish an atmosphere conducive to learning for all students." The board also sent a letter to the Crandon School Board president, urging the district to incorporate "Wisconsin Indian history curricula at all grade levels and to promote increased understanding among students and teachers" and offering to "provide assistance in the form of curriculum materials and workshops for their effective use." Although the board describes its role as acting in a "neutral advisory capacity," it clearly took its advocacy role quite seriously.[44]

By 1985, the American Indian Language and Culture Education Board had identified the voluntary and unfunded nature of the AILCE programs as a barrier to implementation in public schools. The board noted a "continuing concern" related to the "lack of set-aside funds to support language and culture programs in the public school districts."[45] Describing discussions at a recent meeting with district administrators, AILCEB members lamented that when districts realized no additional funds were available, they received "no further consideration."[46] Because there was a growing sense that the programs could meaningfully address growing incidence of discrimination, the board called on the Wisconsin legislature to "take this matter under study to ensure that language and culture programs will be available in the public schools of Wisconsin" in order to address the low adoption rate of programs it viewed as sorely needed to address achievement issues and provide opportunities for intercultural learning.[47]

In its 1987 biennial report, which covered its activities during the 1985–1987 biennium, AILCEB again connected its efforts to those of the Ad Hoc Commission on Racism, affirming the commission's view that "overt racism" was a product of "general ignorance of the relationship between the federal government and Indian tribes." The board acknowledged its charge to "urge all Wisconsin school districts to develop and implement courses that would teach the history of all Wisconsin tribes and the concepts of tribal sovereignty and treaties." It noted several successful efforts to "make Wisconsin Indian curriculum materials available to teachers throughout the state" and acknowledged DPI's ongoing cooperation in making "Wisconsin tribal histories and a unit on tribal government" available for sale through the agency's publications sales unit.

AILCEB also reported its efforts to provide professional development opportunities related to "the effective use of culture-based curriculum materials," to disseminate these materials and provide additional learning opportunities for educators at statewide conventions, including those sponsored by the Wisconsin Education Association and the Wisconsin Indian Education Association. The report stated, "The board believes it is imperative that Indian history be incorporated in the public school curricula throughout the state," and acknowledged its ongoing concern about the "lack of set-aside funds to support Indian education programs in the public schools." The board reiterated its conclusion that local interest wanes when school districts learn that no additional funds are available to operate the programs.[48]

AILCEB clearly identified the AILCE programs as viable models for curricular intervention. Nevertheless, it found the existing policy framework of unfunded, voluntary programs for incorporating lessons on Wisconsin Indian history, culture, and tribal sovereignty to be inadequate as "an effort to establish peace and harmony in the State of Wisconsin."[49]

AILCEB had articulated a solution in its recommendations to DPI, but without funding, implementation was uneven. In order to address the barrier to implementation posed by lack of earmarked funding, the board recommended that DPI "actively support legislation that would provide set-aside monies to public school districts for American Indian history and/or culture programs." Again expressing its view that opportunities to learn accurate, authentic information about American Indians provided the best means to address racism, the board called on DPI to "require coursework in Wisconsin Indian history in the public schools as recommended in a resolution passed by the board on September 14, 1987." Other recommendations were that DPI "require Wisconsin Indian history as part of its teacher training human relations component" and "require a course in Wisconsin Indian history for renewal of teacher licenses."[50] The board's Resolution 1-87 best captures the rationale for the specifics of these recommendations.

AILCEB Resolution 1-87 begins by acknowledging the board's statutory role to make "recommendations for legislation in the area of American Indian language and culture education." Consecutive "Whereas" statements noted that "rampant racism due to American Indian treaty stipulations has become a critical educational issue in the State of Wisconsin," much of which "can be directly attributed to misinformation on the treaty rights issues." The resolution asserted that AILCEB "believes that all citizens of Wisconsin have the right to proper education on issues that affect peace and harmony in the schools and the state in general" and that "it is the duty and responsibility of schools to promote peace and harmony among ethnic groups." Reasoning that "all school districts in the State of Wisconsin teach social sciences including history," and that "the American Indian Peoples of Wisconsin and their treaties are an important segment of Wisconsin history," the board stated that "accurate historical and contemporary perspectives of American Indians will promote peace and harmony while benefiting all citizens through knowledge and understanding of native cultures." The board recommended that DPI, the AISC, and tribal governments collaborate to "develop and implement curriculum units at the fourth grade, middle school, and high school levels which accurately describe the history of the tribes of Wisconsin and their government to government relationship with the United States and the State of Wisconsin" and to be taught in all Wisconsin school districts.[51] The organization continued to criticize the voluntary, unfunded nature of the AILCE programs, and with the passage of Resolution 1-87, it signaled that it was directing its efforts toward advancing a statewide curriculum policy proposal.

COMING TO CONSENSUS

American Indian educators' efforts began to coalesce around the broad principles outlined in AILCEB's resolution. Alan J. Caldwell, a Menominee tribal member and education consultant in the DPI Bureau for Equal Educational Opportunity, addressed the American Indian Study Committee at the Wisconsin State Capitol on February 1, 1988. He noted, "There have been a number of calls by Indian tribes, gubernatorial-appointed education advisory boards, Indian education associations, educators, both Indian and non-Indian, and ad hoc commissions on racism for the development and inclusion of education curriculum on American Indians in all Wisconsin public schools." As the 1988 spearing season approached, he said, "This concern is genuine and the need may be great in light of recent developments."[52] Caldwell acknowledged that many schools had already developed and incorporated appropriate curriculum materials that "reflect the history, culture, and lifestyles of Wisconsin Indian people."[53]

As part of its efforts to provide quality instructional materials to local school districts, for instance, DPI and AILCEB had distributed copies of curriculum materials originally developed by local school districts. The agency sent complete sets of the thirteen-unit Wisconsin Woodland Indian Series, initially developed by the Rhinelander School District, and "a copy of an excellent tribal government unit developed by the Madison School District," to all 432 school districts.[54] Caldwell noted that DPI had been conducting workshops and presenting at conferences on "curricular development and incorporation" and working with teachers to "include the history, culture, and lifestyles of American Indians in their classes throughout the school year and not just at Thanksgiving."[55] "The problem for inclusion," Caldwell explained, "is not lack of materials or information, but is the situation of local districts to determine the content of their curriculum."[56] Caldwell viewed local control of curriculum policy, a cherished tradition and legally protected right in Wisconsin, as a barrier that in many cases all but precluded local use of these instructional materials.

Caldwell's testimony shows that Native educators' thinking connected education and amelioration of racism more broadly than curriculum policy alone. He also addressed other recommendations that he described as coming from "the Department of Public Instruction, in conjunction with the cooperation of the American Indian Language and Culture Education Board, the Wisconsin Indian Education Association and Indian educators" as part of their efforts to "seek solutions to and provide for an equal educational opportunity for all students in Wisconsin public schools."[57] He stated that he had presented "workshops for school administrators, classroom teachers, community-based organizations, parent and student groups (including the Wisconsin Indian Education Association Conference and the Wisconsin Indian Youth Conference)" on Wisconsin's Pupil Non-Discrimination Act, "which prohibits discriminatory actions in public education" and requires districts to develop and disseminate appropriate policies and procedures to students, parents, and community members.[58]

Caldwell, who was also a member of AILCEB, explained that the board's request for an increase in funds for alternative schools reflected that the total appropriation and per pupil funding level had not changed since the program began in 1980. As a former administrator at the Lac Courte Oreilles Ojibwe schools, Caldwell explained that AILCE programs are "an important part of the development of self-esteem and cultural pride of our student body."[59] He also discussed the need "for teachers and potential teachers of Indian children to know and understand the culture, the history and learning styles of Indian children," and he noted the efforts that he and others were engaged in to that end. Caldwell's testimony indicates that advocates for instruction on history, culture, and tribal sovereignty viewed those issues as part of broader efforts related to ending discrimination and increasing student achievement.

BUILDING THE COALITION

Later that month, the American Indian Study Committee again addressed education at its February 29, 1988, meeting held in Oneida, Wisconsin. The committee heard from Rose Mary Korbisch, a resident of Birnamwood, Wisconsin, who "commented that she believes that some school districts are not in compliance with" the Wisconsin Indian Education Act and the 1985 Pupil Non-Discrimination Act.[60] Korbisch "noted that public schools do not have classes on tribal government and Indian culture and that public schools could help erase prejudice by providing these opportunities to their students."[61] She argued that the "integration of Indian culture, history and government into the school curriculum will serve the dual purpose of having non-Indian students learn to respect and appreciate Indian culture and allowing Indian students to gain pride in and credibility for their heritage."[62] Her testimony shows how the views expressed by the Ad Hoc Commission on Racism, American Indian Language and Culture Education Board, and others were gaining broad support beyond these organizations.

In response to Korbisch's testimony, Rep. Tom Loftus (D-Sun Prairie), committee chair, indicated future plans to invite State Superintendent Dr. Herbert Grover to speak to these matters. He called on Caldwell, who represented DPI as a technical advisor to AHCR, to address the matters raised in Korbisch's testimony. Caldwell noted that the Pupil Non-Discrimination Act was passed in 1985 and protects students in public schools from discrimination based on sex, race, national origin, and other factors. Regarding instruction about tribal government, he explained that "he encourages districts to include the study of tribal government as a local government," and that "all districts are provided with information on tribal government," but there is "no state requirement to include the study of tribal government in the social studies curriculum."[63] Public member Gordon L. Thunder, representing the Wisconsin Winnebago Tribe (now Ho-Chunk), responded to the discussion by stating that Winnebago children did "not have a lot of connection to the schools" but "if Indian subjects were included in the curriculum, it might help to alleviate stereotypes regarding Indians."[64] Just as Caldwell's testimony reflects a growing link between instructional requirements and formal instruction about American Indians, Thunder's comments reflect a growing optimism about the improved relationships between Native and non-Native communities in Wisconsin that might follow from them.

Jo Deen B. Lowe, Great Lakes Inter-Tribal Council's state-tribal liaison, summarized recent political developments related to Indian education in a June 12, 1989, memo to the "GLITC Board of Directors and Other Interested Parties." She noted, "Recently, several high ranking officials in State government have been echoing comments from Indian Country concerning the education of children," recognizing that "there is a lack of knowledge and understanding about American Indians."[65] Lowe discussed a proposal presented by Wisconsin State Rep. Frank Boyle (D-Superior) to the Democratic Party Caucus in May 1989 that acknowledged the importance of ongoing professional development for teachers and expanded learning opportunities for students.

She notes that although the "issue of mandatory education concerning the history and culture of Wisconsin's Tribal people has been raised previously," the current iteration originated at the request of the Democratic Party Caucus. Representative Boyle's proposal was the subject of a meeting he held on June 1, 1989, with AILCEB representatives, Legislative Reference Bureau staff members, legislative aides, DPI staff, and "other interested persons."[66] Lowe reports, "Those present agreed that it was time for the educational system to assume a role in mitigating the pervasive ignorance about Wisconsin Indians." Two potential plans emerged from the meeting, both of which identified a need for permanent positions at DPI to staff a "Wisconsin Indian Education Program" that would "educate the educators and develop appropriate curriculum and training materials to be used in the local school districts." The memo explains that the first steps involve piloting the program in identified school districts before expanding the initiative to all school districts.[67] "Secondly," Lowe notes, "the proposal would mandate curriculum inclusion of American Indian studies."[68] Lowe's memo suggests that those present focused more on building instructional capacity in Wisconsin schools and less on creating new curriculum requirements.

Lowe also reported that Boyle and AILCEB members met on June 6, 1989, to discuss two policy proposals for achieving these goals. One option called for "twelve (12) permanent, full-time training specialists which would cost $354,600 annually," while the alternative involved contracting with individual educators in lieu of permanent staff. Those present clearly preferred the first option, but recognized the alternative as a fiscally sound means to address the issue. They noted that both Minnesota and Michigan had long had requirements similar to those contained in the proposal and that Wisconsin was unique in that it had a relatively large American Indian population but no program for Indian education at the state level. Lowe concluded this section of the memo by encouraging "all interested Tribal persons [to] attend" the mid-June Democratic Caucus to demonstrate their support for the measure."[69] This memo is critical for understanding the roles that Indian Country played in the legislative process.

THE BOYLE AMENDMENT

Based on his consultation with AILCEB members and others, Rep. Boyle introduced an amendment to enact a version of their recommendations. His amendment to the biennial budget bill, Assembly Amendment 1 to SB 31, proposed to "increase the dollar amounts for fiscal year 1989–1990 by $200,000 and for fiscal year 1990–1991 by $400,000 for the purpose of providing funds for the American Indian education program and increasing the authorized FTE [full-time employee] positions for the department of public instruction by 6.0 GPR [general program revenue] positions for the American Indian education program."[70] Assembly Democrats supported the measure to increase funding from the $50,000 included in the Senate bill to $600,000 and to authorize the hiring of a director of Indian education, three research and training specialists, and two program assistants. They explained their support was "a door-opener to further minority education programs" and a "direct outgrowth of protests in the spring over Chippewa spearfishing."[71] In an interview with the *Milwaukee Journal*, Boyle described his proposal as part of "the groundwork for a series of minority education requirements in Wisconsin schools" and "the beginning of what should have existed in this state already." The newspaper noted the proposal's requirements for students and teachers on Wisconsin Indian history, culture, and tribal sovereignty and described it as creating "a new mini-bureaucracy within the State Department of Public Instruction."[72]

The *Milwaukee Journal* acknowledged the connection between the proposal and protests at Wisconsin boat landings, "which Boyle has labeled as racist," noting that the incidents "underscored the need for better education about Indians and their contributions to Wisconsin." Boyle explained that he sought to "eliminate the [negative] stereotypes my children are bringing home from school" by requiring instruction in "Wisconsin Indian studies" and by providing school districts with state-sponsored professional development opportunities and instructional materials. Although his amendment dramatically increased the "$50,000 Indian culture program" included in Senate Bill 31, he indicated that "he was optimistic the Senate would go along with his version."[73] Unfortunately, the article's focus on Boyle neglected the efforts of American Indian educators and allies to establish such a program.

While Boyle and the Assembly Democrats might have defined the problem in such a way as to merit a significant allocation of state resources for funding and position authority, Boyle's colleagues in the Senate supported the concept but not the full appropriation. On Friday, June 30, 1989, the Conference Committee offered Conference Amendment 1 to Assembly Amendment 1 to 1989 Senate Bill 31, which cut the authorized funding and staffing levels in half and added the provision, "No more than one of these positions shall be housed in the city of Madison."[74] On August 8, 1989, Governor Tommy Thompson signed Senate Bill 31, the 1989–1991 Biennial Budget Act, which included these new statutes related to instruction in the "history, culture, and tribal sovereignty of the federally recognized tribes and bands in the state" and related issues. The bill became known as 1989 Act 31, or in common parlance Act 31, upon publication on August 20, 1989. In Indian education circles, it lent its name to the instructional requirements themselves.

Legislative Victory

Act 31 represented a significant victory for Indian educators and their allies. Its statutory requirements represented the kind of comprehensive approach recommended by the Ad Hoc Commission on Racism and supported by subsequent individuals and organizations. One provision redefined the general duties of the state superintendent: "In coordination with the American Indian language and culture education board, develop a curriculum for grades 4 to 12 on the Chippewa Indians' treaty-based, off reservation rights to hunt, fish and gather," thereby addressing the immediate impetus for enacting new instructional requirements.[75] Other provisions addressed broader issues related to race and human relations apparent at the boat landings, requiring "each school board" to "provide an instructional program designed to give pupils" an "appreciation and understanding of different value systems and cultures" and "at all grade levels, an understanding of human relations, particularly with regard to American Indians, Black Americans and Hispanics."[76]

Issues related to teacher education were a recurring theme, and the biennial budget addressed this by prohibiting the state superintendent from granting a teaching license to anyone who has not "received instruction in the study of minority group relations, including instruction in the history, culture and tribal sovereignty of the federally recognized American Indian tribes and bands located in this state."[77] In practice, this made the requirements applicable to teacher education programs in Wisconsin and to any individual who completed a teacher education program outside the state but planned to teach in Wisconsin. Advocates for curriculum policy reform often identified textbooks and other instructional materials as contributing to ignorance and racism, and the biennial budget enacted a provision that required school districts to provide "adequate instructional materials, texts and library services which reflect the cultural diversity and pluralistic nature of American society."[78]

Given the crucial role that social studies education historically has played relative to citizenship education and socialization, the new law required schools to "include instruction in the history, culture and tribal sovereignty of the federally recognized American Indian tribes and bands located in this state at least twice in the elementary grades and at least once in the high school grades" within the scope of their social studies curriculum beginning the first school day of the next biennium, September 1, 1991.[79] With the passage of Act 31, advocates for curriculum policy reform, both American Indians and their allies, had succeeded on multiple levels, securing a comprehensive approach to address a complex set of social and educational concerns.

—ıı—

Elmer L. Davids Sr.'s 1961 speech at the American Indian Chicago Conference, given on a national stage, called for greater non-Indian awareness and understanding of Indian issues as a prerequisite for social harmony. His role represents the connection between national efforts to reform curriculum and those in Wisconsin. His words were echoed in the report of the Ad Hoc Commission on Racism. The commission's efforts, initiated by the Lac Courte Oreilles Band of Lake Superior Chippewa, led to recommendations to various bodies within state government. These entities—the Department of Public Instruction, the American Indian Language and Culture Education Board, and the Joint Legislative Council's American Indian Study Committee—all afforded a Native voice at the table. In many cases, the same tribes, families, and individuals were involved, and additional advocates worked through the Wisconsin Indian Education Association.

Indeed, the movement to change curriculum policy in Wisconsin to require instruction in the history, culture, and tribal sovereignty of the federally recognized tribes and bands in the state represents a broad-based effort on the part of advocates working inside and outside of governmental and educational sectors. As Alan Caldwell, DPI education consultant from 1984 to 1991, explained in 2009, "I was credited for being the one who drafted some of the legislation that we commonly refer to now as Act 31." Yet, as he noted, it was not an effort by a single person that led to the passage of Act 31. Caldwell concluded, "Being that I was the Indian education consultant at the Department of Public Instruction at the time the legislation was developed and enacted, I get some of the credit for that although there were others who had a hand in it."[80]

CHAPTER 14

ACT 31 AFTER PASSAGE

G reat hope and serious concerns related to implementation became apparent almost immediately after the passage of Act 31. There were multiple stakeholders, and they needed to work together for implementation to succeed. In the months after the legislation was passed, questions from stakeholders about what the new law meant and how it was to be implemented continued to surface. These included concerns about instructional materials, professional development, enforceability, and the adequacy of the new program's funding and staffing levels. Because the specificity of the new requirements represented an unprecedented state directive to school districts, many of these questions hinged on state versus local control. While the state's Department of Public Instruction (DPI) would produce materials and curriculum on Wisconsin Indian tribal sovereignty, culture, and history, it could not force local school districts to adopt it. The role of the organizations that strove to implement Act 31 was to provide instructional support, not law enforcement. These issues would continue to follow Act 31 in the years and decades that followed.

CONCERNS FROM THE COALITION

On August 18, 1989, less than two weeks after the legislation passed, the American Indian Study Committee (AISC) made the new law a significant part of its agenda. At the meeting, Menominee tribal member Alan Caldwell spoke in his official role as a DPI education consultant. Caldwell acknowledged the ongoing partnership between the Wisconsin DPI and American Indian Language and Culture Education Board (AILCEB) to disseminate instructional materials to every school district in the state. As part of their efforts to promote appropriate professional development, both organizations would also be instrumental in the upcoming Wisconsin Indian Education Association Conference.[1]

Oneida tribal member William Gollnick, vice chancellor at the University of Wisconsin–Green Bay, spoke in his role as AILCEB chair. Gollnick acknowledged the important role that AISC committee chair Rep. Frank Boyle had played and reminded the members of the efforts of Indian educators and their allies in securing the new requirements. He also noted the law established their ongoing role in implementing them. He explained that the statutory language recognized the importance of AILCEB's involvement by requiring DPI to collaborate with the organization to develop instructional materials on Chippewa treaty rights. To support efforts related to teaching and learning about Wisconsin Indian history, culture, and tribal sovereignty, the budget act authorized three new positions at DPI and appropriated three hundred thousand dollars to implement the initiatives, plus an additional fifty thousand dollars per year to fund professional development on tribal sovereignty and treaty rights.[2] For the first time, Native educators representing DPI and AILCEB appeared before AISC to report success in changing state-level curriculum policy and to thank the legislators for their role in creating these new requirements.

Several members of AISC, however, did not share the enthusiasm for the new requirements. Nick Hockings, a public member representing Lac du Flambeau and an active member of the Wa-Swa-Gon Treaty Association, supported an educational solution but questioned "why so little money [was] spent on Indian education in Wisconsin" as compared to law enforcement expenses at the boat landings.[3] Caldwell explained that prior to the passage of Act 31, DPI had "no specific budget for Indian education" and that the new initiatives represented the first appropriations for this purpose.[4] Gollnick reiterated his point that "education is needed to address current problems related to the treaty rights" and noted that the budget act was the "first pro-active effort to address the problem."[5] He compared it with similar efforts in Minnesota, where the state awarded five hundred thousand dollars in competitive grants to local school districts to support curriculum development efforts and has a "Director of Indian Education with adequate staff and a high level of responsibility." Hockings replied that even that was "a small amount to spend on Indian education."[6] Despite Caldwell's and Gollnick's efforts to portray Act 31's passage as a success for Indian education, it was apparent that concerns were already emerging.

Elected members of the committee addressed their own issues and concerns. Sen. Robert Jauch (D-Poplar) disputed the need for the new program, suggesting that existing DPI staff could address these issues and that the agency should rely on federal funds for curriculum development and dissemination.[7] In response to a question from Rep. Thomas Ourada (R-Antigo) about schools' use of DPI curriculum materials, Caldwell explained that "some school districts use the curriculum materials to good advantage, while others 'shelve' them," and added that both Madison and Milwaukee were using the materials and developing additional instructional materials.[8] Rep. James Holperin (D-Eagle River) acknowledged that "the effort to educate non-Indians about Indian culture and history was in response to the current crisis over Chippewa treaty rights," and that similarly, specific curriculum policy requirements on other matters might be needed in the future. He suggested that DPI focus the funding on reservation tours and presentations on treaty rights, and he reasoned that the larger portion of the funds needed to be spent in northern Wisconsin where the controversy was most acute.[9] Caldwell explained that tours were within the authorized scope of the program, and he expressed general support of Holperin's idea, noting that Madison-area teachers found that field trips provided the most meaningful learning experiences.[10]

Committee members expressed additional concerns about DPI's ability and willingness to implement the new provisions in the budget act. Rep. Boyle questioned "whether DPI will divert the Budget Act funds to other uses or whether the funds will really be available for the intended purposes." Alan Caldwell countered that "Superintendent Grover will rely on the AILCEB, the Wisconsin Indian Education Association and other Indian educators for guidance on the use of these funds and on Indian education issues generally." Caldwell's comments reinforced the role these entities had played in securing Act 31's passage and strongly suggested the need for their continued engagement. He added that AILCEB, which consisted of Indian educators appointed by the governor, supported the legislation, as did DPI, the University of Wisconsin System, and the Vocational, Technical, and Adult Education system.[11] Oversight was needed, however, if implementation was to be effective. Jauch added that "leadership from Superintendent Grover and the DPI will be needed to implement the program," and public member Lewis Taylor, representing St. Croix, said it would be necessary "to make Indian education a priority for Dr. Grover."[12] Many of these concerns would continue to emerge in later years.

Other attendees shared information on the new program relative to their organization's ongoing efforts. Terry Mac Taggart, the chancellor of University of Wisconsin–Superior, acknowledged the budget act's support for "a joint Indian studies program" to be operated as a partnership between his institution and Lac Courte Oreilles Community College during the second year of the biennium. He explained that the program would include workshops on "Indian culture, language, education, laws and other subjects," provide a "public forum in which to discuss areas of conflict between the Indian and non-Indian community," and coordinate with DPI-led initiatives on these issues.[13] Bob Goslin, Indian studies coordinator at UW–Superior, and Bill Arbuckle, representing St. Croix, explained that "it was a historic moment to have the UW–Superior Indian Studies Program funded in the Budget Act," and that it "could benefit both the Indian and non-Indian communities."[14] Their comments expressed great hope for the new program.

Several people provided testimony related to the new requirements during public testimony, a period in which citizens could address issues of their choice. Mary Rehwald, an instructor at both Wisconsin Indianhead Technical College–Ashland and Northland College, was skeptical that classroom teachers would use materials developed for use in schools. She based this assessment on her experience with materials that she had developed for teaching about Wisconsin Indian history, culture, and tribal sovereignty and on what she viewed as widespread opposition to the new requirements among school administrators in northern Wisconsin.[15] Rehwald called on DPI to "consult with educators who have experience in the development and implementation of these curricula before implementing the Indian Education Program created in the 1989–91 state Budget Act" and to earmark funds for "field trips, speakers bureaus and other special programs that will stand out as memorable educational experiences in the minds of the students."[16] Her comments suggest the public may not have been fully aware of the nature or scope of DPI's existing efforts. Public member Bob Powless, representing Bad River, assured those present that tribal communities possessed the capacity to provide training and support to campuses and local schools.

Others expressed concerns about the direction of the new efforts. Ken DeFoe, representing the Bayfield-based First American Prevention Center (FAPC), argued that "curricula for and about Indians" needed to be based on oral traditional teachings from tribal elders and should include cultural lessons as well as history. He testified that "improperly designed Indian education programs tell Indian children who and what they should be, based on perceptions of their history, rather than allowing them to be who they are, based on their current culture."[17] DeFoe spoke about the FAPC's experience in developing and implementing curriculum materials and explained that "we definitely have concerns about the proposed Indian Education Office and its approach to introducing Indian culture and history into public schools."[18] DeFoe highlighted the importance of sound professional development, explaining, "Developing a textbook or some workbooks/pamphlets is not enough. Teachers cannot be expected to effectively teach a subject unless *they* fully understand it" (emphasis in original).[19] He explained that FAPC has "an inviolable policy that no school may receive any part" of their materials unless they participate in the accompanying teacher training efforts. Addressing the teachers themselves, DeFoe argued that "because of past education institutions' mistakes of omission and inaccuracy, Indian history and culture has become a sensitive topic," and many teachers "who may have friends and neighbors incensed over treaty or fishing issues, are reluctant to teach things that may add new perspective to these issues" while others "are sympathetic to the worthy-sounding cry of 'equal rights for everyone.'"[20] These teachers, he argued, "are victims of a deficient educational system that for years forbade, by law, teaching anything—true or not—that put the U.S. Government in a bad light." Despite the success of their materials and the expertise of their staff, he concluded, "It's difficult to see how or if it will fit into the state's plans," but "we must jealously guard against any inappropriate use of our material or concepts."[21] DeFoe's statement reflects concern that the parties involved needed to recognize the new legislation as the beginning of work to be done rather than as an accomplishment in itself.

Other speakers addressed the new requirements in the broader context of concerns about educational opportunities for Native people, suggesting that efforts to enact new curricular requirements had overshadowed the pressing need for quality education for Wisconsin Indian youths. Public member Rita Keshena, an attorney representing the Menominee Nation, noted that the issue came down to "education of non-Indians about Indians," but "the education of Indian youths" had been overlooked. She explained that third graders attending the Menominee Indian School District scored lowest on state reading exams, and she questioned DPI's engagement with that issue.[22] Mary Duffy, director of the Red Cliff Education Department, affirmed the importance of programs intended to "solv[e] recurrent problems relating to 19th Century treaties," but lamented the lack of funding to support opportunities for higher education. Keshena similarly characterized educational opportunities for American Indians as "very late in coming, noting that the Brown v. Board of Education court case was decided 30 years ago." The last speaker, Margaret Cooper, director of higher education for Lac Courte Oreilles, expressed her view that "quality education for Indians is necessary to break the cycle of poverty in which many Indian families are caught" and to "break the cycle of racism against Indians." She described the new program as "good steps in this direction."[23]

The testimony received just after Act 31's passage serves as a stark reminder that it was not the only issue needing attention in Indian education even though it had been the most visible for nearly a decade. The urgency of these issues and the need for state action, from DPI, AILCEB, and other members of the coalition that had advanced Act 31 posed immediate challenges for implementing the new policy.

A QUESTION OF LEADERSHIP

The next meeting of the American Indian Study Committee took place on December 12, 1989, with State Superintendent Herbert J. Grover in attendance at the committee's request. Committee Chair Rep.

Frank Boyle had asked Grover to address several issues, including DPI's plans for implementing the new Act 31 requirements, the achievement levels of American Indian students, and recommendations from AILCEB. Grover began by announcing that he had assigned Alan Caldwell, who had accompanied the superintendent to the meeting, to lead the American Indian history and culture program. He noted he was currently recruiting for a second position. A statewide conference was planned for the next year in northern Wisconsin instead of the series of smaller events throughout the state as envisioned by many elected officials and tribal communities.

Appearing alongside the state superintendent, Caldwell addressed the concerns of AISC members regarding instructional materials that DPI would develop and disseminate. He explained that many items were already available, others were being prepared for the statewide conference, and the agency was revisiting its policy on reprinting only school district– or CESA-developed materials as it considered requests to reprint GLIFWC materials.[24] Public member Luverne Plucinski encouraged the agency to disseminate GLIFWC materials, noting they were "well researched and reputable documents." Grover indicated that while DPI would "use material from these publications," there were "problems with portions of them, particularly with the way in which certain information is presented."[25] In the summary of the proceedings, neither party elaborates on this exchange.

In response to the ongoing concern that districts were not using materials made available to them, and Rep. Ourada's interest in requiring their use, Caldwell explained that school districts were "largely autonomous from the DPI" and that the agency could not "compel a school district to use certain materials in its curriculum." No matter what materials were used, however, Act 31 "created the Indian education program as a new standard which must be met by all school districts." Although DPI could not compel the use of materials it produces, he continued, "the districts are required to address those subjects in their curriculum."[26] In response to a question from Rep. Zeuske about sanctions for noncompliance, Grover explained that under existing law, DPI had the authority to "withhold up to 25% of general aid for a district which fails to meet state standards." Although the agency had "established deadlines for districts to come into compliance with these standards and ha[d] on one occasion directly threatened to withhold aid," he added that no district had been subject to this sanction.[27] Grover's response is reminiscent of past state superintendents' views of the Pure History Law's complaint process. The extreme nature of the noncompliance penalty made it politically impractical to enforce.

The instructional requirements included the history, culture, and tribal sovereignty of all of the federally recognized tribes and bands in the state, a point that representatives from other tribes continued to make. Public member Gordon Thunder, representing the Wisconsin Winnebago (Ho-Chunk) tribe, reminded the state superintendent that "the need for education regarding Indian culture, history, and sovereignty is not limited to the north woods area." His tribe, in fact, was "located in 14 counties and 17 school districts in the southern portion of the state."[28] Thunder also asked about procedures for reviewing materials developed by DPI, and Grover explained that while the agency would rely on AILCEB to review materials, they could share them more broadly. Thunder's comments serve as an important reminder that while Chippewa treaty rights may have been the immediate impetus for Act 31, the broader concerns that led to widespread ignorance of historical and contemporary legal and cultural issues affecting Native communities had considerably broader impact.

Thunder observed that the law was silent about the specific obligations of school districts to provide instruction on Wisconsin Indian history, culture, and tribal sovereignty. He asked the state superintendent whether schools would teach these topics for "one hour, one week, or some other length." The superintendent responded that DPI "would not expect a school district to devote an entire week to this subject, but that they would not accept superficial treatment of the subject." Grover did not define "superficial" and simply called for "judicious balancing." He again noted that "DPI does not control the details of local curricula."[29] Traditional deference to local control clearly colored how education policy leaders approached the implementation of these new statutory requirements and sent a message about how local officials might choose to respond to newly recognized official knowledge. Grover's suggestion that an "entire week" was excessive indicates that educational leaders did not similarly value all official knowledge.

The new curricular requirements arose again in the committee's discussions of discrimination against American Indian students.

In response to a series of questions posed by Boyle about DPI's efforts to "address hostility and racism in public schools," Caldwell explained that the agency offered a "list of workshops, in-service training sessions and other events addressing these and other issues," and was disseminating "information on the Chippewa treaties and related subjects to school districts." Caldwell also noted that existing state law prohibited discrimination on the basis of race, ancestry, and other traits.[30] Grover "stated his categorical intolerance of discriminatory practices" and explained that "he contacts school districts whenever he becomes aware of specific problems related to discrimination, to determine what must be done to correct the problem." In Grover's view, "racial discrimination is a broad societal problem, which is often reflected in the schools."[31] Grover was seemingly as reluctant to embrace his agency's authority and responsibility to address discrimination as he was to robustly enforce curriculum requirements related to treaty rights. His comments suggest that he did not recognize discrimination against American Indians as part of the impetus for new instructional requirements.

Grover concluded his presentation by addressing the 1989–1990 recommendations of AILCEB, expressing his support for increases in aid to alternative schools operating AILCE programs and for providing start-up money to public school districts seeking to establish similar programs. The state superintendent then thanked the committee and encouraged them "to continue following the American Indian education issues."[32] The overall tone of Grover's report highlights his ambivalent support for the new direction in curriculum policy, and it identifies his agency's limited range of enforcement options along with his apparent reluctance to use them.

IMPLEMENTING ACT 31

In its 1987–1989 Biennial Report, published in January 1990, the American Indian Language and Culture Education Board reported on the successful adoption of new statutes substantially similar to the curriculum policy solution advanced in AILCEB Resolution 1-87. The report reflects a new description of the board's role, describing its purpose as to "advise and comment on two key aspects of Indian education, viz., the education of

Indian students and education about Indian people, history, cultures, and languages," and notes "AILCEB has been very involved in both arenas."[34]

Board Chair William Gollnick wrote, "Of particular note is the overview of the Indian education-related amendments to the biennial budget," which he termed "a dramatic step forward for all of Wisconsin's students."[35] The report offers a brief history of its role in implementation that connects the passage of the amendments to the *Voigt* decision by describing AILCEB Resolution 1-87 as a direct response to the Ad Hoc Commission on Racism report, which itself emerged from a study of public reaction to *Voigt*. It notes, "Resolution 1-87 was widely disseminated and gained broad-based support" and represented the "culmination of efforts by Indian and non-Indian individuals, groups, and organizations [as] reflected in Indian education amendments to . . . Wisconsin Act 31."[36] While AILCEB clearly played a highly visible and well-documented role, the organization made a point to acknowledge the broad base of support for its efforts, framing the passage of Act 31 as a victory for Native educators and their allies rather than as the narrow legislative victory of a governor-appointed advisory body.

The report also discussed AILCEB's hopes for the new statutory requirements, stating that "through this new law, our schools will have the resources to accurately address the information gap which contributes to the strife and misunderstanding across our state and in our classrooms."[37] The board embraced its assigned role "to collaborate with DPI to develop curriculum for grades four through 12 on Chippewa Indians' treaty-based rights" along with the "state educational goal and expectation" for human relations education.[38] Through the new Indian education office, "factual material about Indian history and contemporary issues will be developed and disseminated to all Wisconsin schools, and training opportunities will be extended to our state's teachers."[39] It also applauded the appropriation of one hundred thousand dollars GPR and thirty thousand dollars in student fees in 1990–91 for UW–Superior to create "an Indian studies program for on-campus instruction and for outreach."[40] Advocates for a curriculum policy solution that would create opportunities for students to learn about American Indian history, culture, and tribal sovereignty had apparently achieved victory, but the recommendation to "provide first year start-up money for public school districts planning to establish American Indian language and culture programs" remained unaddressed.[41]

AILCEB continued to work to build instructional capacity in school districts across the state. The board was active in professional development and curriculum development activities through the Wisconsin Education Association Council, the Wisconsin Indian Education Association, and the Wisconsin Association of School Boards, as well as the "first statewide multicultural youth conference" and district-level in-services.[42] Because of the "need for readily available and reliable curriculum materials, AILCEB, in cooperation with the DPI, continued to edit and reprint existing instructional materials while working to develop new resources, including a section on tribal government for a new DPI publication, *Classroom Activities in State and Local Government*.[43] Despite progress on so many fronts, the board lamented the fact that "lack of funding discourages districts" such that the "Menominee Indian School District operates the only American Indian language and culture education program in the public schools," foreshadowing ongoing issues with funding.[44]

In its report for the 1989–1991 biennium, AILCEB noted the development of a new policy infrastructure. The report lauded the creation of the "American Indian Studies Program in the Equity and Multicultural Section of DPI, providing two Indian education consultants to review and develop curricula and to respond to requests for assistance from school districts and plan an annual Wisconsin Indian education conference for Wisconsin educators."[45] The board noted "assistance may be provided to teacher training institutions as they implement DPI's human relations requirement for teacher licensure to provide instruction by 1992 [sic;1991] in the history, culture, and tribal sovereignty of Wisconsin's federally recognized tribes."[46] In order to continue its curriculum development efforts, the board recommended that DPI "contract with Dr. Ronald Satz for the development of histories of the following federally recognized tribes in the State of Wisconsin: Menominee, Oneida, Potawatomi, Stockbridge-Munsee, and Winnebago to facilitate districts' compliance with s.121.02(1)(L) of Wisconsin statutes."[47] They recommended that the curriculum "be developed in cooperation with the tribes" and "be completed no later than two years from the date of the contract."[48] To ensure that the American Indian Studies Program budget was sufficient, the board recommended that DPI "review the budget implementation of Indian education provisions of Wisconsin Act 31 and, if funding level is found inadequate, request an increase."[49] The board recognized that funding remained an issue at the local level as well, as it again called for "first year start up money to schools which plan to establish American Indian language and culture education programs."[50]

The board provided additional insights into the development of the new program in its testimony to the Governor's Task Force on Schools for the 21st Century in July 1991. Gaiashkibos, chairman of the Lac Courte Oreilles Tribal Governing Board and a member of the Governor's Task Force on Schools for the 21st Century, convened a meeting to inform the work of the task force. In a July 8, 1991, letter written by William Gollnick, the board addressed both state-level and tribal/community-level considerations. The board explained:

> It is clear also that many schools (even those with good intentions) have no knowledge of Indian country and the issues which exist there. Most have few resources from which to teach and/or train teachers. Because Indian education has also come to mean education about Indians, I would hope that this assembly of educators would also therefore consider what should be taught in Wisconsin's public schools to accurately show the Indian condition. I feel that it is very important that thought be given to appropriate goals and elements for the state's curricular efforts.[51]

The board identified the current situation in terms of "school curricula which often involves little reference to the Indian reality—especially the contemporary reality" and sought to address it through "identification of appropriate materials, resources, and content for instruction in public schools."[52] They noted that if it is "to be received favorably by the teachers who will be expected to use this, it is important that it be factual, as free from bias as possible, and 'classroom ready.'"[53] As the American Indian Language and Culture Education Board noted, serious concerns remained even after securing long-sought legislation to change state-level curriculum policy.

—II—

Despite successful passage of new curriculum policy reforms that seemingly ensured that school districts would recognize issues related to Wisconsin Indian history, culture, and tribal sovereignty as official knowledge, serious questions remained. The new policy was unprecedented in the specificity of its directives to local school districts, raising important questions about the future of local control.[54] Local control also provided those opposed to the required content with non-content-based grounds to articulate their concerns. Deference to traditions of local control, rather than strict adherence to statutorily defined curriculum policy, affected how even the advocates for instruction on Wisconsin Indian history, culture, and tribal sovereignty framed the issues and discussed implementation.

Questions about the adequacy of funding and staffing levels had been a concern from the moment the advocates first discussed the new program. The legislature, governor's office, DPI, and AILCEB continued to debate the number, location, and classification of the authorized positions. A hiring freeze in the first biennium of its existence posed further challenges.[55]

The need for and nature of instructional materials to be developed or provided by the state, or to be used in local classrooms, was an ongoing, politically sensitive question.[56] The specific focus on "Chippewa treaty rights" seemingly contributed to ambivalence from other tribes who had themselves been the subjects of widespread ignorance and the targets of discrimination. In tribal communities across the state, where educational leaders had temporarily placed other important issues on hold until after the struggle for curriculum policy had concluded, and because these concerns now required urgent attention as well, much of the energy and enthusiasm shifted.

Public education is inherently a political matter, and it is always marked by considerable debate. In this respect, concerns about the direction of the new policy, actual and perceived conflicts with other policies and political traditions, and the adequacy of funding, staffing, and service levels are not unusual. Arguably Act 31, as written, has had multiple, contradictory outcomes. The policy change created an opening for those ready and willing to provide instruction in the history, culture, and tribal sovereignty of the federally recognized tribes and bands in the state. Proponents could rightfully point to state law to justify their actions. But the limited nature of Act 31 also hampered implementation. The state's inability to override traditions of local control, limited staffing and funding levels, and ambivalent leadership from the state superintendent constrained the law's potential transformative effects in the early years after its passage. Even today those ripples are felt across the state as implementation continues at an uneven pace, with some districts and schools embracing the challenge to offer Native curriculum wholeheartedly, while others are unaware of or choose to defy and ignore the mandate.[57] It is my hope that this study will inform the efforts of those seeking to reshape curriculum policy at the state and local levels. *The Story of Act 31* might also illuminate a path such that those seeking similar reforms in other states might learn from these experiences.

CONCLUSION

While discussing treaty rights on a radio call-in show during the summer of 1989, a caller asked historian Ronald N. Satz whether "the Chippewa treaties actually contained a provision designating any ten or more Indians leaving the reservation together as a war party that could be fired upon in self-defense by whites without criminal penalty."[1] This anecdote shows the level of dangerous ignorance and misinformation circulating in Wisconsin from the time the Seventh Circuit Court of Appeals handed down the *Voigt* decision in 1983. In the absence of authentic knowledge about American Indians, tensions escalated as violence increased, as did the fears that someone might be killed at a Wisconsin boat landing. The controversy tore apart communities, cost millions of dollars in law enforcement and court expenses, harmed businesses, and damaged Wisconsin's reputation, ultimately leading many formerly disparate segments of society to collaborate to find a solution. It is no surprise that Act 31 emerged in 1989, because escalating tensions in the years leading up to it encouraged cooperation among business leaders, community members, clergy, elected officials on both sides of the aisle, and the Ojibwe people and their allies. Together, they determined that public schools had to help resolve a number of challenging social problems. In the midst of this crisis, the voices of Native people, who had been challenging their depiction in curriculum materials and in popular culture, were finally heard.

Act 31 was the culmination of decades of work by American Indian educators and their allies, who sought to use schooling to address widespread discrimination that they believed was fueled in part by the omissions and inaccuracies in curriculum. The great hope for Act 31 was that as schools implemented the mandate to teach history, culture, and tribal sovereignty, knowledge would replace ignorance and understanding would be built between Indian and non-Indian communities. As Chickasaw sociologist Gary Sandefur asserted, "If more people in Wisconsin knew the history of Indians in the state, if more people knew how much Indians were forced to give up, and if more people knew about the historical symbolic significance of treaty rights, the misunderstanding over treaty rights and the resentment against Indians would quickly disappear."[2] This faith in education as an instrument of social change to transform the violence and controversy surrounding the court's affirmation of treaty rights was foundational to Act 31.

Despite what is rightfully viewed as a victory for American Indian educators and their allies, however, implementation has been an ongoing challenge. The new policy was unprecedented in the specificity of its directives to local school districts, raising important questions about local control even among Act 31's advocates. The law may have provided those eager to offer this instruction with the necessary political power to do so, but there was no viable mechanism to compel instruction where interest was not already present. Concerns about the adequacy of resources allocated to the Department of Public Instruction (DPI) to support the requirements arose early and remain a perennial concern. Reductions in staffing and budgets meant that services supporting instruction were eliminated, scaled back, or had to be provided in a different way, which has affected teacher education and licensing. The need for and nature of instructional materials to be used remains an ongoing, politically sensitive question, one that has not been fully addressed though there is buy-in from several state and public agencies to create new and engaging resources. In addition, policy changes from 1989 to the present—including the Model Academic Standards and No Child Left Behind—have impacted priorities for curriculum planning. Because of these continuing challenges, implementation of American Indian Studies–related provisions has proceeded unevenly.

By the time I arrived at DPI in fall of 1996, the American Indian Studies (AIS) program had undergone significant changes. The initial staffing allocation for two full-time education consultants, one education specialist, and one program assistant had dropped to one education consultant and a shared program assistant. Alan Caldwell, who was the first to hold the consultant position, left the agency in May 1991. Education specialist Paul Borowsky, who joined DPI in 1990 to organize the statewide conferences, had also left DPI by this time. Caldwell's successor in the Madison office, Ho-Chunk educator Francis Steindorf, started at DPI in May 1991. William Gollnick, who established the northern office at University of Wisconsin–Green Bay in June 1991 when he assumed the second education consultant position, left less than two years later. Steindorf staffed a new northern office at UW–Stout from 1993–1995. Cynde Yahola Wilson succeeded Gollnick and held the second position in Madison until budget cuts eliminated her position in July 1995. Budget cuts also forced the closure of the northern office and forced Steindorf to return to Madison. Steindorf himself left the agency in October 1995, leaving the program without an education consultant for nearly a year before I took the position in September 1996. Program Assistant Connie Ellingson had worked with the AIS program since it began, and stayed with the program until after I left it in 2011 (she now works elsewhere at DPI). By the time I joined AIS, the program had been fully staffed at the level appropriated by 1989 Act 31 for a total of less than three years.[3] My successor, David O'Connor, currently holds the only education consultant position.

Reductions in staff and budget resources allocated for the DPI American Indian Studies program directly impacted the agency's ability to implement the new policy. These changes affected the provision of direct services to schools, school districts, and university-based teacher education programs as well support for these constituencies' own efforts to carry out their new responsibilities. Each element of the Act 31 legislation was affected, from instructional resources and teacher education to social studies, human relations, and multicultural education.

During the early years, DPI published reprints of the Wisconsin Woodland Indians Series, originally published by the Rhinelander School District, as well as the *American Indian Resource Manual for Public Libraries*, which was published under a federal grant.[4] In 1991, it also published *Classroom Activities on Chippewa Treaty Rights*, fulfilling the statutory requirement to collaborate with the American Indian Language and Culture Education Board to publish "a curriculum for grades 4 to 12 on the Chippewa Indians' treaty based, off-reservation rights to hunt, fish, and gather."[5] In 1996, DPI published *Classroom Activities on Wisconsin Indian Treaties and Tribal Sovereignty*, authored by Ronald N. Satz and members of the UW–Eau Claire Wisconsin Indian History, Culture, and Tribal Sovereignty Project.[6] This comprehensive instructional resource contains lesson plans for elementary, middle, and high school students as well as the complete text of every treaty signed with a Native nation in Wisconsin. This guide won the Wisconsin Library Association's Distinguished Document Award. Due to budget cuts, it also marked the last of DPI's AIS publications.

The agency also identified and purchased collections of materials for each of the twelve regional Cooperative Educational Service Agencies in the state which they could then lend to districts in their regions, supplementing available print resources.[7] This was in support of the legislative directive to school districts to "provide adequate instructional materials, texts and library services which reflect the cultural diversity and pluralistic nature of American society."[8]

After 1996, in my role as the DPI American Indian Studies Consultant, I worked closely with staff at other state agencies, supporting their efforts to produce new instructional materials related to the history, culture, and tribal sovereignty of Native peoples in Wisconsin. These partnerships included the Wisconsin Historical Society Office of School Services, which published materials through the Wisconsin Historical Society Press, the Educational Communications Board (ECB), Wisconsin Public Television (WPT), and other entities. In each case, these agencies took the lead in producing high quality materials for classroom use. Examples include the video series "ENGAGE! State.Tribal.Local.Government" by WPT with the ECB and hosted by the Wisconsin Media Lab; the classroom reader and activity book, *Native People of Wisconsin*, by Patty Loew, in the Society Press's New Badger History series; and the fourth-grade textbook *Wisconsin: Our State, Our Story*, also published by the Society Press. *Native People* and *Wisconsin: Our State, Our Story* are now in their second editions, published in 2015 and 2016 respectively.[9]

Most recently, the Wisconsin Act 31 Coalition—consisting of DPI, WPT, the ECB, Wisconsin Media Lab, the Wisconsin Indian Education Association, the University of Wisconsin–Madison School of Education, the University of Wisconsin–Green Bay First Nations Studies program, the University of Wisconsin System, and the Wisconsin Historical Society—collaborated to create a new online resource to support Act 31 implementation.[10] The resource, WisconsinAct31.org, provides recommended resources, model lessons, video clips, and other tools to support accurate, authentic instruction about the Native nations in Wisconsin.

Budget cuts also limited the agency's ability to implement statutory provisions related to teacher education and licensing.[11] This affected the education of preservice teachers and preparation of teachers currently in the classroom by limiting professional development opportunities. After 1991, the earmarked funding that had allowed the agency to organize statewide conferences in 1990 and 1991 was gone, and the smaller budget limited the capacity to provide in-services for local school districts. DPI did, however, continue to support professional development in American Indian studies through the statewide Equity Convention. Arguably, this move better highlighted Act 31's provisions related to human relations education and presented a new context through which to understand the requirements.[12] The AIS program remained visible with key constituencies, including the Wisconsin Indian Education Association (WIEA), Wisconsin Council for Social Studies, Wisconsin Education Association Council, and the Wisconsin State Human Relations Association, with staff presenting at and participating in their statewide conferences. In my role as American Indian Studies consultant from 1996–2011, I regularly attended and presented at conferences and other events sponsored by these organizations.

The AIS program's signature event, the American Indian Studies Summer Institute, began in 1997 as an outgrowth of the workshops Ronald Satz and I did to roll out the publication, *Classroom Activities on Wisconsin Indian Treaties and Tribal Sovereignty*. Twenty years later, this event remains an intensive, week-long professional development opportunity for educators organized in partnership with one or more tribal communities. During my tenure at the agency, we worked with the Ho-Chunk Nation, Menominee Nation, Stockbridge-Munsee Band of Mohicans, and Oneida Nation.[13] More recently, the agency has partnered with the Stockbridge-Munsee, Lac du Flambeau, Sokaogon Chippewa Community, and Forest County Potawatomi to hold this event.

Aside from budget cuts, perhaps the most important factor influencing Act 31 implementation is the change in the policy context between 1989 and the present. In 1989, the new legislation transformed the "Twenty Standards," the "minimum expectations for every district's education program" that ensure uniform educational opportunity across the state.[14] These changes are specifically reflected in Standard (h), which addresses library media services, and Standard (L), which covers instructional requirements.[15]

The Twenty Standards effectively institutionalized the new requirements, and the agency's audit procedures provided an established mechanism for monitoring compliance. Audit teams from DPI conducted site visits to approximately 10 percent of the school districts in the state each year. By rule, the agency conducted onsite monitoring of each school district at intervals between six and ten years.[16] The relationship between the audits and the State Constitution's call for uniform opportunities among the public schools in the state may have blunted potential concerns about intrusions on local control. In 1995, the state budget, 1995 Act 27, specifically eliminated the DPI audit teams, leaving the state with no means for monitoring or enforcing Act 31 implementation.[17]

The adoption of the Model Academic Standards in August 1998 again legitimated the history, culture, and tribal sovereignty of the federally recognized tribes and bands as official knowledge. The standards were already in development when I arrived. Each draft circulated broadly, and I often added language related to Act 31 requirements to those that came across my desk. WIEA and other organizations that had been involved in Act 31's passage mobilized to provide public comments both in writing and at hearings, and the final product reflected these. The social studies standards included learning goals related to the "history, culture, tribal sovereignty, and current status of the federally recognized tribes and bands in the state" for each grade range.[18] Large-scale assessments known as the Wisconsin Knowledge and Concepts Exams tested students' mastery of the content covered in the Model Academic Standards. Beginning in 1998, Act 31–related content was in the statutes, the standards, and the tests. Attendees packed conference sectionals with titles such as "A Standards-Based Approach to American Indian Studies." Similar content offered prior to the adoption of the new standards had generated less interest. Educators in Wisconsin seemed to be recognizing these concepts as legitimate, official knowledge.

Less than three years later, new federal legislation reshaped the educational policy landscape once again, to Act 31's detriment. The No Child Left Behind Act of 2001 made reading and mathematics a high priority and both funding and accountability measures led schools to shift instructional time and effort to those areas. Curricular attention to social studies diminished overall, and evidence suggests that subfields like American Indian studies followed that trend.[19]

The most recent study of Act 31 implementation, conducted in 2014, suggests that Wisconsin's schools have yet to realize the vision of those who worked for its passage. In order to "determine how state and tribal agencies can help provide information, training, and technical assistance to school districts in teaching about Wisconsin American Indian sovereign nations," WIEA partnered with the Survey Research Center at the University of Wisconsin–River Falls. The study asked administrators and teachers about their existing curriculum, instructional practices and resources, and anticipated professional development needs.[20]

The results suggest that most schools include Wisconsin Indian history and culture as part of their social studies curriculum, and many incorporate these topics into English language arts, reading, and art. However, significantly fewer schools are addressing tribal sovereignty or contemporary issues in their social studies curriculum. Teachers reported that they provide, on average, eleven hours of instruction on these issues per year, either as a single unit, by integrating content throughout the year, or a combination of these approaches. They rely on textbooks as their primary resource, while principals noted the important role DVDs play as well. Both groups indicate an interest in and need for new instructional materials and more professional development opportunities. A majority of the teachers indicated that their teacher education programs did not adequately prepare them to provide this instruction or that they do not recall receiving it.[21]

—⊣⊢—

The enactment of specific instructional requirements related to the history, culture, and tribal sovereignty of the federally recognized tribes and bands in Wisconsin represents a significant victory for American Indian educators and allies. This is particularly apparent given the state's strong history of local control of education. Implementation remains a challenge, and the original vision of those who identified the need for curricular reform has been elusive, but it can be realized. The key is organizing and mobilizing, as advocates did in 1989 when the policy change was enacted, and as they did a decade later, when many of those same parties worked to ensure the inclusion of American Indian materials in the Model Academic Standards.

Montana's experience with a similar policy highlights the importance of clear goals and adequate resources at both the state and local level. The state first required instruction about Native peoples at its constitutional convention in 1972, leading to the creation of a provision called "Indian Education for All."[22] In 2005 in response to a lawsuit about the adequacy of school funding, the state government ensured that the Montana Office of Public Instruction and local schools had adequate resources to carry out that long-standing mandate.[23] The state developed clear learning outcomes for the program, published instructional resources tied to those outcomes, offered appropriate professional development opportunities for those tasked with providing instruction, and included the program in their statewide assessment regime.[24] Montana appropriated seven million dollars for use by local school districts to carry out this new mandate and three million dollars for the Office of Public Instruction to support their efforts.[25] Adequacy of resources is the key to implementation. By comparison, Wisconsin's approach has never been adequately resourced.

At the American Indian Studies Summer Institute, we used to say, "If you know why, you will figure out how." *The Story of Act 31* provides a historical analysis intended to highlight why we need such a policy, to suggest why it took the shape it did, and to call our attention to potential ways to realize the "why" in our own contexts. History is often a contest for power and authority, and schools and education have often been in the middle of that struggle. The important factors that shaped Act 31 are not point-in-time controversies, like spearfishing, gaming, or land into trust, but the deeper principles of a commitment to understanding a shared history, including historical and legal relationships embodied in nineteenth century treaties and a deeper recognition of our shared humanity. Curriculum policy decisions at the national, state, and local levels must provide opportunities to learn about human differences even as policy contexts and other cultural and political considerations change. It is hoped that this re-examination of Act 31 might prove useful to contemporary advocates for education reform by serving as a reminder of past successes and as a reminder of the broad principles that informed the efforts to secure them. The history of the origins of Act 31 is essential to improving upon it and to realizing the original vision set forth by those who transformed public education in Wisconsin.

NOTES

Introduction

1. Elmer L. Davids Sr., "Our People—Past, Present and Future: The Stockbridge-Munsee Band of Mohican Indians," address delivered at the American Indian Chicago Conference, June 1961, Arvid E. Miller Historical Library/Museum, Bowler, Wisconsin.

2. Davids, "Our People," 3.

3. Ibid.

4. See Jeannette Haynes Writer, "'No Matter How Bitter, Horrible, or Controversial': Exploring the Value of a Native American Education Course in a Teacher Education Program," *Action in Teacher Education* 24 (Summer 2002): 9–21.

5. Wis. Stat. § 115.28(17)(d) (1989).

6. Wis. Stat. § 118.01(c)7-8 (1989).

7. Wis. Stat. § 118.19(8) (1989).

8. Wis. Stat. § 121.02(1)(h) (1989).

9. Wis. Stat. § 121.02(1)(L)4 (1989).

10. Ronald N. Satz's *Chippewa Treaty Rights: The Reserved Rights of Wisconsin's Chippewa Indians in Historical Perspective* (Madison: Wisconsin Academy of Sciences, Arts and Letters, 1991) was the first book-length study of the legal and historical issues. Rick Whaley and Walt Bresette's *Walleye Warriors: An Effective Alliance Against Racism and for the Earth* (Philadelphia: New Society Publishers, 1994) focused on the efforts of individuals and organizations working to promote broader understanding and to support the Ojibwe people. Patty Loew's body of work on these issues includes television news segments; documentary films, including *The Spring of Discontent* (Madison: WKOW, 1990); and several scholarly articles in the *American Indian Quarterly* spanning almost fifteen years. Sandra Sunrising Osawa's documentary film, *Lighting the Seventh Fire* (Seattle: Upstream Productions, 1999), provides a powerful look at the events surrounding the 1989 spearfishing season. Larry Nesper's *The Walleye War: The Struggle for Ojibwe Spearfishing and Treaty Rights* (Lincoln: University of Nebraska Press, 2002) is an ethnohistorical study focused on the reassertion of treaty rights among the Lac du Flambeau Ojibwe. Lawrence Bobo and Mia Tuan's *Prejudice in Politics: Group Position, Public Opinion, and the Wisconsin Treaty Rights Dispute* (Cambridge: Harvard University Press, 2006) is a sociological analysis of public opinion and racial attitudes related to the exercise of treaty rights. Most recently, Erik M. Redix's *The Murder of Joe White: Ojibwe Leadership and Colonialism in Wisconsin* (East Lansing: Michigan State University Press, 2014) contributes valuable insights into the Ojibwe people's efforts to retain their way of life and exercise reserved rights under increasing state oppression.

11. Larry Cuban, "Review: Can Historians Help School Reformers?" *Curriculum Inquiry* 31, no. 4 (Winter 2001): 453.

12. William J. Reese, *America's Public Schools: From the Common School to "No Child Left Behind"* (Baltimore: Johns Hopkins University Press, 2011).

13. Michael W. Apple, *Official Knowledge: Democratic Education in a Conservative Age* (New York: Routledge, 2000).

14. Louis G. Romano and Nicholas P. Georgiady, *Exploring Wisconsin* (Chicago: Follett, 1970); Louis G. Romano and Nicholas P. Georgiady, *Exploring Our State, Wisconsin* (Chicago: Follett, 1977).

15. My approach to using these problematic terms interchangeably follows Writer, "'No Matter How Bitter, Horrible, or Controversial,'" 9–21.

Chapter 1

1. Verplanck Van Antwerp, *Proceedings of a Council Held by Governor Henry Dodge, with the Chiefs and Principal Men, of the Chippewa Nation of Indians, July 20–29, 1837,* Documents Relating to the Negotiation of Ratified and Unratified Treaties with Various Indian Tribes, 1801–1869, Microcopy Roll T494, Roll 3, Record Group 75, Washington, DC: National Archives and Records Service, 0558-0559, cited in Ronald N. Satz, *Chippewa Treaty Rights: The Reserved Rights of Wisconsin's Chippewa Indians in Historical Perspective* (Madison: Wisconsin Academy of Sciences, Arts and Letters, 1991), 18.

2. Van Antwerp, *1837,* 0558-559, cited in Satz, *Chippewa Treaty Rights,* 19.

3. Ibid.

4. Ibid.

5. Ibid.

6. Rennard Strickland, foreword to Satz, *Chippewa Treaty Rights,* xi.

7. The US Constitution specifically mentions "Indians" three times: in Article I, Section 3; in the Fourteenth Amendment, as "Indians not taxed," referencing noncitizens; and in the Commerce Clause, Article I, Section 8, which assigns Congress the duty to "regulate Commerce with foreign Nations, and among the several States, and with the Indian tribes." Federal authority stems specifically from the Commerce Clause and the Treaty Clause, Article II, Section 2, which authorizes the president to negotiate treaties "with the Advice and Consent of the Senate."

8. David R. Wrone, "Indian Treaties and the Democratic Ideal," *Wisconsin Magazine of History* 70, no. 2 (Winter 1986–1987): 88.

9. Francis Paul Prucha, *American Indian Treaties: The History of a Political Anomaly* (Berkeley: University of California Press, 1994), 1.

10. U.S. Const. art. I, § 4, cl. 2.

11. Wrone, "Indian Treaties and the Democratic Ideal," 88.

12. Ibid., 87.

13. Charles F. Wilkinson, "To Feel the Summer in the Spring: The Treaty Fishing Rights of the Wisconsin Chippewa," *Wisconsin Law Review,* no. 3 (1991): 385.

14. Wrone, "Indian Treaties and the Democratic Ideal," 87.

15. Steven E. Silvern, "State Centrism, the Equal-Footing Doctrine, and the Historical-Legal Geographies of American Indian Treaty Rights," *Historical Geography* 30 (2002): 36; Charles F. Wilkinson, *American Indians, Time, and the Law* (New Haven, CT: Yale University Press, 1987), 101.

16. Prucha, *American Indian Treaties,* xiv, 2.

17. Ibid., 2.

18. JeDon A. Emenhiser, "A Peculiar Covenant: American Indian Peoples and the U.S. Constitution," in *American Indians and U.S. Politics: A Companion Reader,* ed. John M. Meyer (Westport, CT: Praeger, 2002), 7; David Michael Ujke, "State Regulation of Lake Superior Chippewa Off-Reservation Usufructuary Rights: Lac Courte Oreilles Band of Chippewa Indians v. Wisconsin, 653 F. Supp. 1420 (W.D. Wis. 1987)," *Hamline Law Review* 11, no. 1 (Spring 1988): 153–181, 165.

19. Worcester v. Georgia, 31 U.S. 515, 557–558 (1832).

20. Johnson v. M'Intosh, 21 U.S. (8 Wheat) 543 (1823).

21. *Worcester,* 31 U.S. at 557–558.

22. Cherokee Nation v. Georgia, 30 U.S. (5 Peters) 559–560 (1831).

23. United States v. Wheeler, 435 U.S. 313 (1978).

24. Prucha, *American Indian Treaties,* 5; Emenhiser, "A Peculiar Covenant," 7; *Wheeler,* 435 U.S. 313.

25. United States v. Bouchard, 464 F. Supp. 1322 (1978); Lac Courte Oreilles Band of Lake Superior Chippewa Indians, et al. v. State of Wisconsin, et al. (LCO III), 653 F. Supp. 1420 (W.D. Wis. 1987); Satz, *Chippewa Treaty Rights,* 2; Charles F. Wilkinson, *Blood Struggle: The Rise of Modern Indian Nations* (New York: W.W. Norton, 2005), 153.

26. Ujke, "State Regulation of Lake Superior Chippewa," 162.; Satz, *Chippewa Treaty Rights,* 2; Basil Johnston, *Ojibway Heritage* (Lincoln,NE: Bison Books, 1990); H. James St. Arnold and Welsey Ballinger, eds., *Dibaajimowinan: Anishinaabe Stories of Culture and Respect* (Odanah, WI: Great Lakes Indian Fish and Wildlife Commission, 2013).

27. *LCO III*, 653 F. Supp. 1420.

28. Wilkinson, "To Feel the Summer in the Spring," 380–382; Edmund J. Danzinger, *The Chippewas of Lake Superior* (Norman: University of Oklahoma Press, 1979), 7–8.

29. *LCO III*, 653 F. Supp. at 1424.

30. *Bouchard*, 464 F. Supp. 1322.

31. Satz, *Chippewa Treaty Rights*, 6, 8; Wilkinson, *Blood Struggle*, 153.

32. Satz, *Chippewa Treaty Rights*,13. See also David R. Wrone, "The Economic Impact of the 1837 and 1842 Chippewa Treaties," *American Indian Quarterly* 17, no. 3 (Summer 1993): 329–340.

33. *Bouchard*, 464 F. Supp. 1322; Wilkinson, "To Feel the Summer in the Spring," 383. See also Wrone, "Economic Impact."

34. *Bouchard*, 464 F. Supp. at 1323.

35. Wilkinson, "To Feel the Summer in the Spring," 385.

36. Ibid., 383, 385–386; Ujke, "State Regulation of Lake Superior Chippewa," 163.

37. *LCO III*, 653 F. Supp. at 1428–1429; Wilkinson, "To Feel the Summer in the Spring," 385; Rick Whaley and Walter Bresette, *Walleye Warriors: An Effective Alliance Against Racism and for the Earth* (Philadelphia: New Society Publishers, 1994), 6.

38. *Bouchard*, 464 F. Supp. at 1323; *Lac Courte Oreilles Band of Lake Superior Chippewa Indians, et al., v. Lester P. Voigt, et al. (LCO I)*, 700 F.2d 344 (1983); Satz, *Chippewa Treaty Rights*, 18.

39. *Bouchard*, 464 F. Supp. 1322; Satz, *Chippewa Treaty Rights*, 23.

40. Treaty with the Chippewa (1837), 7 Stat. 536; Donald J. Hanaway, *History of the Chippewa Treaty Rights Controversy* (Madison: Wisconsin Department of Justice, 1989), 1.

41. *Bouchard*, 464 F. Supp. At 1323; *LCO I*, 700 F.2d 344; Satz, *Chippewa Treaty Rights*, 23.

42. Larry Nesper, *The Walleye War: The Struggle for Ojibwe Treaty Rights of Wisconsin's Chippewa Indians in Historical Perspective* (Madison: Wisconsin Academy of Sciences, Arts and Letters, 1991), 45–46. See also Wrone, "Economic Impact," for an estimate of the number of board feet of lumber and an estimated inventory of natural resources acquired by the United States through the Treaty of 1837 and Treaty of 1842.

43. *Bouchard*, 464 F. Supp. At 1323–1324 ; *LCO I*, 700 F.2d at 345.

44. Satz, *Chippewa Treaty Rights*, 38.

45. Ibid.

46. Treaty with the Chippewa (1842), 7 Stat. 591.

47. *LCO I*, 700 F.2d at 346; Wilkinson, "To Feel the Summer in the Spring," 388; Nesper, *The Walleye War*, 45–46.

48. Satz, *Chippewa Treaty Rights*, 45; Danzinger, *The Chippewas of Lake Superior*, 96–97; Zoltan Grossman, "Unlikely Alliances: Treaty Conflicts and Environmental Cooperation Between Native American and Rural White Communities" (Ph.D. diss., University of Wisconsin–Madison, 1992), 542.

49. *Bouchard*, 464 F. Supp. At 1325.

50. Ibid., 1327; Wilkinson, "To Feel the Summer in the Spring," 388; Nesper, *The Walleye War*,46.

51. *Bouchard*, 464 F. Supp. at 1326.

52. See Satz, *Chippewa Treaty Rights*, chap. 4; Great Lakes Indian Fish and Wildlife Commission, "Sandy Lake: Tragedy and Memorial," brochure, http://www.glifwc.org/publications/pdf/SandyLake_Brochure.pdf.

53. *Bouchard*, 464 F. Supp. At 1326–1327; *LCO I*, 700 F.2d at 346; Satz, *Chippewa Treaty Rights*, chap. 4; Nesper, *The Walleye War*, 46; Whaley and Bresette, *Walleye Warriors*, 14–15.

54. *Bouchard*, 464 F. Supp. At 1327–1328; Thomas Vennum, *Wild Rice and the Ojibway People* (St. Paul: Minnesota Historical Society Press, 1988), 259, cited in Satz, *Chippewa Treaty Rights*, 56; Whaley and Bresette, *Walleye Warriors*, 15.

55. *Bouchard*, 464 F. Supp. at 1327; *LCO I*, 700 F.2d at 347; Vennum, *Wild Rice and the Ojibway People*, 259; Whaley and Bresette, *Walleye Warriors*, 15.

56. *Bouchard*, 464 F. Supp. at 1327.

57. Ibid.;*LCO I*, 700 F.2d at 347.

58. *Bouchard*, 464 F. Supp. at 1329; *LCO I*,700 F.2d at 347; Satz, *Chippewa Treaty Rights*, 56–60; Whaley and Bresette, *Walleye Warriors*, 15; Great Lakes Indian Fish and Wildlife Commission, "Sandy Lake: Tragedy and Memorial."

59. Despite contravening orders, Ramsey and his allies continued to press forward with their removal plans because "the purport of this order remains a secret" (*Bouchard*, 464 F. Supp. at 1328–1329).

60. Satz, *Chippewa Treaty Rights*, 67.

61. Ibid.; Nesper, *The Walleye War*, 46; Whaley and Bresette, *Walleye Warriors*, 15–17.

62. *Bouchard*, 464 F. Supp. at 1329–1330; *LCO I*, 700 F.2d at 348; Satz, *Chippewa Treaty Rights*, 67. No formal record of Fillmore's rescission can be found, but the decision is consistent with his handling of Indian affairs, and annuities due in later years were indeed paid at La Pointe. Satz gives significant credit to opposition of white citizens of the region for Fillmore's decision.

63. *Bouchard*, 464 F. Supp. at 1330; *LCO I*,700 F.2d at 348; Hanaway, *History of Chippewa Treaty Rights*, 3.

64. *Bouchard*, 464 F. Supp. at 1330.

65. Ibid.; Satz, *Chippewa Treaty Rights*, 68.

66. *Bouchard*, 464 F. Supp. at 1330.

67. Treaty with the Chippewa (1854), 10 Stat. 1111; *Bouchard*, 464 F. Supp. at 1331; Satz, *Chippewa Treaty Rights*, 69.

68. *Bouchard*, 464 F. Supp. at 1331; Wilkinson, "To Feel the Summer in the Spring," 387; Satz, *Chippewa Treaty Rights*, 68.

69. *Bouchard*, 464 F. Supp. at 1331; Whaley and Bresette, *Walleye Warriors*, 17.

70. Treaty with the Chippewa (1854).

71. *Bouchard*, 464 F. Supp. at 1332; Danzinger, *The Chippewas of Lake Superior*, 182. See also Erik M. Redix, *The Murder of Joe White: Ojibwe Leadership and Colonialism in Wisconsin* (East Lansing: Michigan State University Press, 2014).

72. Wilkinson, "To Feel the Summer in the Spring," 387–388.

73. Ibid., 388; Satz, *Chippewa Treaty Rights*, 69. Two of the six Lake Superior Bands, St. Croix and Sakaogon, remained landless until after the passage of the Indian Reorganization Act in the 1930s because the former was unrepresented at the 1854 treaty council and the latter signed a separate treaty in 1855 that the Senate failed to ratify.

74. Wrone, "Economic Impact," 5.

75. Satz, *Chippewa Treaty Rights*, 79–80; Nesper, *The Walleye War*, 19.

76. Hanaway, *History of Chippewa Treaty Rights*, 4; Satz, *Chippewa Treaty Rights*, 80; Nesper, *The Walleye War*, 49. See also Grossman, "Unlikely Alliances."

77. Wilkinson, "To Feel the Summer in the Spring," 394; Nesper, *The Walleye War*, 49.

78. Nesper, *The Walleye War*, 49.

79. Silvern, "State Centrism," 34.

80. Brian L. Pierson, "Chippewa Treaty Rights Litigation in Wisconsin," State Bar of Wisconsin, http://www.wisbar.org/. See also State v. Doxtator, 47 Wis. 278 (1879); State v. Rufus, 205 Wis. 317 (1931); In re Blackbird, 109 F. Supp. 139 (E.D. Wis. 1901); and State v. Morrin, 136 Wis. 552 (1908).

81. Nesper, *The Walleye War*, 49–50; Larry Nesper, "Twenty-Five Years of Treaty Rights and Tribal Communities," in *Minwaajimo: Telling a Good Story*, ed. LaTisha A. McRoy (Odanah, WI: Great Lakes Indian Fish and Wildlife Commission), 294–297.

82. Nesper, *The Walleye War*, 49–50, 7; Nesper, "Twenty-Five Years of Treaty Rights," 294–297; Grossman, "Unlikely Alliances," 327.

83. Nesper, *The Walleye War*, 49; Nesper, "Twenty-Five Years of Treaty Rights," 294–297; Patty Loew, "Hidden Transcripts in the Chippewa Treaty Rights Struggle: A Twice Told Story," *American Indian Quarterly* 21, No. 4 (Autumn, 1997), 717.

84. Nesper, *The Walleye War*, 50.

85. Ibid., 50–51.

86. Fred Vine quoted in Nesper, *The Walleye War*, 49.

87. Satz, *Chippewa Treaty Rights*, 84–85; *In re Blackbird*, 109 F. Supp. 139 (E.D. Wis. 1901); Wilkinson, "To Feel the Summer in the Spring," 394.

88. Satz, *Chippewa Treaty Rights*, 84–85; Wilkinson, "To Feel the Summer in the Spring," 394; Loew, "Hidden Transcripts," 716.

89. "The Killing of Chief Joe White, 1894: Articles & Court Documents," online facsimile, Wisconsin Historical Society, http://content.wisconsinhistory.org/u?/tp,25923; Redix, *The Murder of Joe White*; Chantal Norrgard, *Seasons of Change: Labor, Treaty Rights, and Ojibwe Nationhood* (Chapel Hill: University of North Carolina Press, 2014), 53–54.

90. In this context, Morrin's citizenship stems from a provision in the General Allotment Act, also known as the Dawes Act, through which those Indians deemed "competent" would receive citizenship and title in fee simple to their assigned individual parcel of reservation lands formerly owned collectively by their nation.

91. Hanaway, *History of Chippewa Treaty Rights*, 4; Silvern, "State Centrism," 42.

92. Hanaway, *History of Chippewa Treaty Rights*, 4; Wrone, "Economic Impact," 329.

93. The precedents included *Blackbird*, *U.S. v. Winans*, or *Worcester v. Georgia*. See Wilkinson, "To Feel the Summer in the Spring," 395.

94. Satz, *Chippewa Treaty Rights*, 85; Silvern, "State Centrism," 42; Wrone, "Economic Impact," 331.

95. Satz, *Chippewa Treaty Rights*, 83; Wilkinson, "To Feel the Summer in the Spring," 395. Rennard Strickland, Stephen J. Herzberg, and Steven R. Owens, "Keeping Our Word: Indian Treaty Rights and Public Responsibilities; A Report on a Recommended Federal Role Following Wisconsin's Request for Federal Assistance" (Madison: University of Wisconsin Law School, April 6, 1990), 4–5; Nesper, *The Walleye War*, 51; Wrone, "Economic Impact," 3.

96. Satz, *Chippewa Treaty Rights*, 85; John B. Lemieux, et al. v. Agate Land Company and City of Superior, 193 Wis. 473–474.

97. Satz, *Chippewa Treaty Rights*, 1.

98. Ibid., 85; Robert C. Nesbit, William Fletcher, and State Historical Society of Wisconsin, *Wisconsin: A History*, 2nd ed. (Madison: University of Wisconsin Press, 1989), 480.

99. State v. Johnson, 212 Wis. 301–313.

100. Ibid.; Satz, *Chippewa Treaty Rights*, 85; Loew, "Hidden Transcripts," 717.

101. Satz, *Chippewa Treaty Rights*, 87; Wilkinson, "To Feel the Summer in the Spring," 395. See also Ronald N. Satz, "After the Treaties: The Chippewa Struggle to Retain Reserved Treaty Rights in the North Woods of Wisconsin," in *Minnetrista Cultural Center and Ball State University. Woodland National Conference: 1991–1992 Proceedings* (Muncie, IN: Minnetrista Cultural Foundation, Inc., 1993), 107–126.

102. Silvern, "State Centrism," 38.

103. Ibid., 44.

104. Norrgard, *Seasons of Change*, 43; McRoy, *Minwaajimo*.

105. Aaron Shapiro, "Up North on Vacation: Tourism and Resorts in Wisconsin's North Woods, 1900–1945," *Wisconsin Magazine of History* 89, no. 4 (Summer 2006): 2–13; Satz, *Chippewa Treaty Rights*, 89; Grossman, "Unlikely Alliances," 326–327.

106. Satz, *Chippewa Treaty Rights*, 89; Wilkinson, "To Feel the Summer in the Spring," 395; John R. Wunder, *"Retained by the People": A History of American Indians and the Bill of Rights* (New York: Oxford University Press, 1994), 107–111.

107. Nesper, *The Walleye War*, 53. For more information on Public Law 83-280, see Carole Goldberg, *Planting Tail Feathers: Tribal Survival and Public Law 280* (Los Angeles: American Indian Studies Center, University of California, Los Angeles, 1997).

108. Satz, "After the Treaties," 114; Satz, *Chippewa Treaty Rights*, 94–95.

109. Nesper, *The Walleye War*, 54; Grossman, "Unlikely Alliances," 327.

110. Loew, "Hidden Transcripts," 718.

111. Ibid.

112. Satz, *Chippewa Treaty Rights*, 89; Nesper, *The Walleye War*, 53; Loew, "Hidden Transcripts," 717; Norrgard, *Seasons of Change*, 1–2.

113. Satz, *Chippewa Treaty Rights*, 116; Wilkinson, "To Feel the Summer in the Spring," 378.

Chapter 2

1. *Lighting the Seventh Fire*, DVD, dir. Sandra Sunrising Osawa (Seattle, WA: Upstream Productions, 1999); Patty Loew, "Hidden Transcripts in the Chippewa Treaty Rights Struggle: A Twice Told Story; Race, Resistance, and the Politics of Power," *American Indian Quarterly* 21 (1997): 717–718.

2. Chris Graef, "Dr. Richard St. Germaine: 'Our Elders Warned Us,'" *News from Indian Country*, n.d.; *ENGAGE: State, Local, and Tribal Government*, dir. Educational Communications Board (Educational Communications Board, 2010); Ronald N. Satz, *Chippewa Treaty Rights: The Reserved Rights of Wisconsin's Chippewa Indians in Historical Perspective* (Madison: Wisconsin Academy of Sciences, Arts and Letters, 1991); Larry Nesper, *The Walleye War: The Struggle for Ojibwe Spearfishing and Treaty Rights* (Lincoln: University of Nebraska Press, 2002); Loew, "Hidden Transcripts," 716.

3. *Chippewa*, like *Indian*, is a term of art reflected in federal law. The federal government recognizes Lac Courte Oreilles, Lac du Flambeau, St. Croix, Red Cliff, Bad River, and Mole Lake/Sakaogon as independent bands of a larger political unit, the Lake Superior Band of Chippewa Indians. They call themselves "Anishinaabe" (plural *Anishinaabeg*), which translates as "the people," or "spontaneous beings." *Ojibwe* is perhaps the most common term in contemporary use, especially in reference to the language. Many scholars have claimed that it is derived from a name used by neighboring peoples who referred to them as "o-jib-weg," in reference to the pictographs they drew on birchbark scrolls, and became corrupted to "Chippewa" by English speakers. See Leon Valliere Jr., "A Brief History of Waaswagoning Ojibweg," in *Memories of Lac du Flambeau Elders*, ed. Elizabeth M. Tornes (Madison: The Board of Regents of the University of Wisconsin System, 2004), 9–76; and Anton Treuer, *The Assassination of Hole-in-the-Day* (St. Paul, MN: Borealis Books, 2011), 217–219. This study will use *Ojibwe* except where quoted source material uses a different term.

4. *Lac Courte Oreilles Band of Lake Superior Chippewa Indians, et al., v. Lester P. Voigt, et al. (LCO I)*, 700 F.2d 344 (1983). Both the Seventh Circuit's 1983 decision and the ensuing litigation carry Voigt's name.

5. Nesper, *The Walleye War*, 68; Rick Whaley and Walter Bresette, *Walleye Warriors: An Effective Alliance Against Racism and for the Earth* (Philadelphia: New Society Publishers, 1994), 18. Some accounts do not include the detail about notifying the DNR in advance, and in one of the most recent accounts from the Tribble brothers themselves, in *ENGAGE*, they tell how they moved their shanty after the wardens had flown overhead.

6. *Lighting the Seventh Fire*; *ENGAGE*; Loew, "Hidden Transcripts," 718.

7. Alan Caldwell, former DPI American Indian Studies Consultant (1984–1991), personal communication with the author.

8. Satz, *Chippewa Treaty Rights*, 94; Nesper, *The Walleye War*, 68; David R. Wrone, "The Economic Impact of the 1837 and 1842 Chippewa Treaties," *American Indian Quarterly* 17, no. 3 (1993): 331; *ENGAGE*.

9. Satz, *Chippewa Treaty Rights*, 94; Nesper, *The Walleye War*, 68; Francis Paul Prucha, *American Indian Treaties: The History of a Political Anomaly* (Berkeley: University of California Press, 1994), 421; Wrone, "Economic Impact," 331.

10. Donald J. Hanaway, *History of the Chippewa Treaty Rights Controversy* (Madison: Wisconsin Department of Justice, March 1989), 1.

11. *LCO I*, 700 F.2d 344.

12. Charles F. Wilkinson, "To Feel the Summer in the Spring: The Treaty Fishing Rights of the Wisconsin Chippewa," *Wisconsin Law Review*, no. 3 (1991): 396.

13. Deborah Shames, ed., *Freedom with Reservation: The Menominee Struggle to Save Their Land and People* (Madison, WI: National Committee to Save the Menominee People and Forests, 1972); Nicholas C. Peroff, *Menominee Drums: Tribal Termination and Restoration, 1954–1974* (Norman: University of Oklahoma Press, 1982); and David R. M. Beck, *The Struggle for Self-Determination: History of the Menominee Indians Since 1854* (Lincoln: University of Nebraska Press, 2005).

14. For more on the Red Power era in Wisconsin, see Patty Loew, *Indian Nations of Wisconsin: Histories of Endurance and Renewal*, 2nd ed. (Madison: Wisconsin Historical Society Press, 2013). For more on the Red Power movement generally, see Joane Nagel, *American Indian Ethnic Renewal: Red Power and the Resurgence of Identity and Culture* (New York: Oxford University Press, 1996); Troy R. Johnson, *The Occupation of Alcatraz Island: Indian Self-Determination and the Rise of Indian Activism* (Urbana: University of Illinois Press, 1996); Paul Chaat Smith and Robert Allen Warrior, *Like a Hurricane: The American Indian Movement from Alcatraz to Wounded Knee* (New York: The New Press, 1997); and Troy R. Johnson, Joane Nagel, and Duane Champagne, eds., *American Indian Activism: Alcatraz to the Longest Walk* (Urbana: University of Illinois Press, 1997).

15. For more on spiritual and educational movements, see Julie Davis, *Survival Schools: The American Indian Movement and Community Education in the Twin Cities* (Minneapolis: University of Minnesota Press, 2013); James Treat, *Around the Sacred Fire: Native American Religious Activism in the Red Power Era* (Urbana: University of Illinois Press, 2007); and Susan Applegate Krouse, "What Came Out of the Takeovers: Women's Activism and the Indian Community School of Milwaukee," *American Indian Quarterly* 27, no. 2 (2003): 533–547.

16. Wilkinson, "To Feel the Summer in the Spring," 397.

17. Ibid.

18. Satz, *Chippewa Treaty Rights*, 93; State v. Gurnoe, 53 Wis. 2d 390, 192 N.W. 2d 892 (1972), quoted in Wilkinson, "To Feel the Summer in the Spring," 397.

19. Ibid.

20. The *Boldt* decision affected the treaty rights of the Hoh, Makah, Muckleshoot, Nisqually, Puyallup, Quileute, Skokomish, Lummi, Quinault, Sauk-Suiattle, Squaxin Island, Stillaguamish, Upper Skagit, and Yakima nations. For more on the *Boldt* decision, United States v. Washington, 384 F. Supp. 312 (W.D. Wash. 1974), aff'd, 520 F.2d 676 (9th Cir. 1975), see Charles F. Wilkinson, *Messages from Frank's Landing: A Story of Salmon, Treaties, and the Indian Way* (Seattle: University of Washington Press, 2000).

21. *United States v. Bouchard*, 464 F. Supp. 1322, 1357–1358 (1978); David Michael Ujke, "State Regulation of Lake Superior Chippewa Off-Reservation Usufructuary Rights: Lac Courte Oreilles Band of Chippewa Indians v. Wisconsin, 653 F. Supp. 1420 (W.D. Wis. 1987)," *Hamline Law Review* 11, no. 1 (Spring 1988): 157.

22. *Bouchard*, 464 F. Supp. at 1349–1350.

23. Ibid., 1352–1361; Satz, *Chippewa Treaty Rights*, 94; Ujke, "State Regulation of Lake Superior Chippewa," 157–158; Zoltan Grossman, "Unlikely Alliances: Treaty Conflicts and Environmental Cooperation Between Native American and Rural White Communities" (Ph.D. diss., University of Wisconsin–Madison, 1992), 327; Barbara Perry and Linda Robyn, "Putting Anti-Indian Violence in Context: The Case of the Great Lakes Chippewas of Wisconsin," *American Indian Quarterly* 29 (Summer–Fall 2005): 610.

24. *Bouchard*, 464 F. Supp. at 1352.

25. Ibid., 1359.

26. Ibid., 1352.

27. Ibid., 1361.

28. Hanaway, *History of Chippewa Treaty Rights*, 6.

29. Wilkinson, "To Feel the Summer in the Spring," 398; Satz, *Chippewa Treaty Rights*, 94; Ujke, "State Regulation of Lake Superior Chippewa," 158–161.

30. *LCO I*, 700 F.2d at 352–353.

31. Ibid.

32. Ibid., 349, 356; Wilkinson, "To Feel the Summer in the Spring," 398; Satz, *Chippewa Treaty Rights*, 94.

33. *LCO I*, 700 F.2d at 361–362; *LCO III*, 653 F. Supp. at 1425; Wilkinson, "To Feel the Summer in the Spring," 398; Nesper, *The Walleye War*, 68.

34. *LCO I*, 362; Wilkinson, "To Feel the Summer in the Spring," 398; Nesper, *The Walleye War*, 68; Perry and Robyn, "Putting Anti-Indian Violence in Context," 610.

35. Wilkinson, "To Feel the Summer in the Spring," 398; Satz, *Chippewa Treaty Rights*, 94; Brian L. Pierson, "Chippewa Treaty Rights Litigation in Wisconsin," State Bar of Wisconsin, http://www.wisbar.org.

36. *LCO I*, 700 F.2d at 363; Wilkinson, "To Feel the Summer in the Spring," 399; Satz, *Chippewa Treaty Rights*, 94; Pierson, "Chippewa Treaty Rights Litigation in Wisconsin."

37. Great Lakes Indian Fish and Wildlife Commission (GLIFWC), *A Guide to Understanding Chippewa Treaty Rights* (Odanah, WI: GLIFWC, 1991), 24; *LCO I*, 700 F.2d at 365; *LCO III*, 653 F. Supp. at 1425; Satz, *Chippewa Treaty Rights*, 94; Pierson, "Chippewa Treaty Rights Litigation in Wisconsin."

38. Satz, *Chippewa Treaty Rights*, 94; Pierson, "Chippewa Treaty Rights Litigation in Wisconsin."

39. *LCO I*, 700 F. 2d. at 365; Satz, *Chippewa Treaty Rights*, 94.

40. Ujke, "State Regulation of Lake Superior Chippewa," 158n32; Nesper, *The Walleye War*, 3.

41. Frank Morris, "Cutting New Paths in Modern America," *Wausau Daily Herald*, November 1, 1987.

42. Satz, *Chippewa Treaty Rights*, 95.

43. Nesper, *The Walleye War*, 71.

44. *LCO I*, 700 F.2d at 342; Lac Courte Oreilles Band of Lake Superior Chippewa Indians, et al. v. State of Wisconsin, et al. (LCO II), 760 F.2d 177, 179 (1985).

45. Nesper, *The Walleye War*, 76.

46. Satz, *Chippewa Treaty Rights*, 94–95.

47. *LCO III*, 653 F. Supp. at 1423–1424.

48. *LCO II*, 179; *LCO III*, 653 F. Supp. at 1423.

49. *LCO II*, 760 F.2d at 179–180; Satz, *Chippewa Treaty Rights*, 95.

50. *LCO II*, 760 F.2d at 182–183; Satz, *Chippewa Treaty Rights*, 95.

51. *LCO II*, 760 F.2d at 182.

52. Ibid., 182–183.

53. Ibid., 183.

54. Wilkinson, "To Feel the Summer in the Spring," 399.

55. *LCO III*, 653 F. Supp. at 1423; Satz, *Chippewa Treaty Rights*, 97; Great Lakes Indian Fish and Wildlife Commission (GLIFWC), *Protecting and Preserving Rights and Resources: Great Lakes Indian Fish and Wildlife Commission 1989 Annual Report* (Odanah, WI: GLIFWC, 1990); GLIFWC, *A Guide to Understanding Chippewa Treaty Rights*; GLIFWC, *Great Lakes Indian Fish and Wildlife Commission Annual Narrative Report Fiscal Year 2009* (Odanah, WI: GLIFWC, 2010).

56. Nesper, *The Walleye War*, 71–75.

57. Ibid., 73; GLIFWC, *Chippewa Treaty Rights: Hunting, Fishing, Gathering on Ceded Territory* (Odanah, WI: GLIFWC, 1987), 2.

58. Nesper, *The Walleye War*, 76.

59. Wilkinson, "To Feel the Summer in the Spring," 408.

60. Nesper, *The Walleye War*, 76.

61. Wilkinson, "To Feel the Summer in the Spring," 377n6.

62. *LCO III*, 653 F. Supp. at 1429; *LCO I*, 700 F.2d at 350; United States v. Winans, 198 U.S. 371 (1905); Winters v. United States, 207 U.S. 564, 576–577; 28 S.Ct. 207, 211; 52 L.Ed. 340 (1908).

63. *LCO III*, 653 F. Supp. at 1429–1430.

64. Ibid., 1429; Satz, *Chippewa Treaty Rights*, 97; Nesper, *The Walleye War*, 89.

65. *LCO III*, 653 F. Supp. at 1429.

66. *LCO III*, 653 F. Supp. at 1424, 1427–1428, 1430; Satz, *Chippewa Treaty Rights*, 97; Nesper, *The Walleye War*, 89.

67. *LCO III*, 653 F. Supp. at 1430.

68. Ibid., 1423–1424, 1430, 1432.

69. Ibid., 1433, 1424, 1427; Satz, *Chippewa Treaty Rights*, 97; Nesper, *The Walleye War*, 89.

70. *LCO III*, 653 F. Supp. at 1432, 1430; Satz, *Chippewa Treaty Rights*, 97.

71. "State to Appeal Ruling on Chippewa Treaties," *Milwaukee Journal*, February 19, 1987; Satz, *Chippewa Treaty Rights*, 97.

72. Lac Courte Oreilles Band of Lake Superior Chippewa Indians, et al. v. State of Wisconsin, et al. (LCO IV), 668 F. Supp. 1233, 1238, 1242 (W.D. Wis. 1987); Satz, *Chippewa Treaty Rights*, 97–98; GLIFWC, *Understanding Chippewa Treaty Rights*.

73. Nesper, *The Walleye War*, 94; Wilkinson, "To Feel the Summer in the Spring," 399–400; Satz, *Chippewa Treaty Rights*, 97–98.

74. *LCO IV*, 668 F. Supp. at 1239–1240; Wilkinson, "To Feel the Summer in the Spring," 399–400; Satz, *Chippewa Treaty Rights*, 97–98.

75. *LCO IV*, 668 F. Supp. at 1241–1242.

76. Hanaway, *History of Chippewa Treaty Rights*, 5; Nesper, *The Walleye War*, 94.

77. Satz, *Chippewa Treaty Rights*, 98.

78. Hanaway, *History of Chippewa Treaty Rights*, 5; Nesper, *The Walleye War*, 94.

79. Hanaway, *History of Chippewa Treaty Rights*, 8.

80. Ibid., 5, 10; Loew, "Hidden Transcripts," 721.

81. Loew, "Hidden Transcripts," 721.

82. Ibid., 721–722. See Nesper, *The Walleye War*, for a detailed account of the efforts to negotiate a settlement with Lac du Flambeau.

83. Nesper, *The Walleye War*, 95.

84. Lac Courte Oreilles Band of Lake Superior Chippewa Indians, et al. v. State of Wisconsin, et al. (LCO V), 686 F. Supp., 227 (W.D. Wis. 1988).

85. *LCO V*, 686 F. Supp. at 228, 233; Satz, *Chippewa Treaty Rights*, 98; Wilkinson, "To Feel the Summer in the Spring," 377; GLIFWC, *Protecting and Preserving Rights and Resources*; GLIFWC, *Understanding Chippewa Treaty Rights*.

86. Lac Courte Oreilles Band of Lake Superior Chippewa Indians, et al., v. State of Wisconsin, et al. (LCO VI), 707 F. Supp. 1034 (W.D. Wis. 1989).

87. *LCO VI*, 707 F. Supp. at 1053–1055.

88. Ibid., 1060; Satz, *Chippewa Treaty Rights*, 98; GLIFWC, *Understanding Chippewa Treaty Rights*.

89. *LCO VI*, 707 F. Supp. at 1057; Wilkinson, "To Feel the Summer in the Spring," 377n8.

90. *LCO VI*, 707 F. Supp. at 1060; Satz, *Chippewa Treaty Rights*, 98.

91. Lac Courte Oreilles Band of Lake Superior Chippewa Indians, et al., v. State of Wisconsin, et al. (LCO VII), 740 F. Supp. 1400, 1401–1402 (W.D. Wis. 1990).

92. *LCO VII*, 740 F. Supp. at 1401–1402, 1413–1427; Satz, *Chippewa Treaty Rights*, 98; Wilkinson, "To Feel the Summer in the Spring," 400; GLIFWC, *Understanding Chippewa Treaty Rights*.

93. *LCO VII*, 740 F. Supp. at 1416; Wilkinson, "To Feel the Summer in the Spring," 400.

94. *LCO VII*, 740 F. Supp. at 1417–1419; Wilkinson, "To Feel the Summer in the Spring," 399.

95. *LCO VII*, 740 F. Supp. at 1418–1419; Wilkinson, "To Feel the Summer in the Spring," 401; GLIFWC, *Understanding Chippewa Treaty Rights*.

96. *LCO VII*, 740 F. Supp. at 1426–1427; Wilkinson, "To Feel the Summer in the Spring," 401; GLIFWC, *Understanding Chippewa Treaty Rights*.

97. Satz, *Chippewa Treaty Rights*, 98.

98. Ibid., 123.

99. Ibid.; Lac Courte Oreilles Band of Lake Superior Chippewa Indians, et al. v. State of Wisconsin, et al., (LCO VIII), 749 F. Supp. 922–923 (W.D. Wis. 1990); Wilkinson, "To Feel the Summer in the Spring," 403.

100. Satz, *Chippewa Treaty Rights*, 98.

101. Ibid., 99.

102. Lac Courte Oreilles Band of Lake Superior Chippewa Indians, et al., v. State of Wisconsin, et al. (LCO IX), 758 F. Supp. 1262 (W.D. Wis. 1991); Satz, *Chippewa Treaty Rights*, 99.

103. *LCO IX*, 758 F. Supp. at 1271.

104. Satz, *Chippewa Treaty Rights*, 99–100; GLIFWC, *Understanding Chippewa Treaty Rights*.

105. Satz, *Chippewa Treaty Rights*, 99–100; Wilkinson, "To Feel the Summer in the Spring," 403; GLIFWC, *Understanding Chippewa Treaty Rights*.

106. Rennard Strickland, foreword to Satz, *Chippewa Treaty Rights*, xii.

107. Loew, "Hidden Transcripts," 716.

108. Satz, *Chippewa Treaty Rights*, 104; Ronald N. Satz, "After the Treaties: The Chippewa Struggle to Retain Reserved Treaty Rights in the North Woods of Wisconsin," *1991–1992 Proceedings of the Minnesota Council for Great Lakes Native American Studies Woodland National Conference* (Muncie, IN: Minnetrista Cultural Center and Ball State University, 1993), 115; Patty Loew and James Thannum, "After the Storm," *American Indian Quarterly* 35 (2011): 161, 172–173; Whaley and Bresette, *Walleye Warriors*, 51, 55–57, 95–96; Nesper, *The Walleye War*, 117.

109. For a thorough study of efforts to inform, educate, and persuade the public, see Lawrence Bobo and Mia Tuan, *Prejudice in Politics: Group Position, Public Opinion, and the Wisconsin Treaty Rights Dispute* (Cambridge: Harvard University Press, 2006), and Patty Loew, "Voices from the Boatlandings in the Chippewa Treaty Rights Dispute: Source Selection and Bias in the Coverage of Two Very Different Newspapers" (master's thesis, University of Wisconsin–Madison, 1992).

Chapter 3

1. Patty Loew, "Hidden Transcripts in the Chippewa Treaty Rights Struggle: A Twice Told Story; Race, Resistance, and the Politics of Power," *American Indian Quarterly* 21 (1997): 713–728; Patty Loew, "Remarks," in *Minwaajimo: Telling a Good Story—Preserving Ojibwe Treaty Rights for the Past 25 Years*, ed. LaTisha A. McRoy (Odanah, WI: Great Lakes Indian Fish and Wildlife Commission, 2011): 186; Patty Loew and James Thannum, "After the Storm: Ojibwe Treaty Rights Twenty-Five Years After the Voigt Decision," *American Indian Quarterly* 35 (Spring 2011): 172.

2. Loew and Thannum, "After the Storm," 161.

3. See, for example, Great Lakes Indian Fish and Wildlife Commission (GLIFWC), *Moving Beyond Argument: Racism and Treaty Rights* (Odanah: GLIFWC, 1989), and Ronald N. Satz, *Chippewa Treaty Rights: The Reserved Rights of Wisconsin's Chippewa Indians in Historical Perspective* (Madison: Wisconsin Academy of Sciences, Arts and Letters, 1991).

4. Rick Whaley and Walter Bresette, *Walleye Warriors: An Effective Alliance Against Racism and for the Earth* (Philadelphia: New Society Publishers, 1994), 48.

5. Jeffery Robert Connolly, "Northern Wisconsin Reacts to Court Interpretations of Indian Treaty Rights to Natural Resources" *Great Plains Natural Resources Journal* 11, no. 1–2 (2006–2007), 136.

6. Richard W. Jaeger, "Lake Scenes Likened to Selma Battle," in *Treaty Crisis: Cultures in Conflict*, ed. Frank Denton (Madison: Wisconsin State Journal, 1990), 38; Elizabeth Brixley, "Churches Caught in Treaty Conflict" in Denton, *Treaty Crisis*, 40; Satz, *Chippewa Treaty Rights*, 102.

7. Satz, *Chippewa Treaty Rights*, 104.

8. State of Wisconsin, Legislative Reference Bureau, *Chippewa Off-Reservation Treaty Rights* (Madison: State of Wisconsin Legislative Reference Bureau, December 1991).

9. Larry Nesper, *The Walleye War: The Struggle for Ojibwe Spearfishing and Treaty Rights* (Lincoln: University of Nebraska Press, 2002), 3; Whaley and Bresette, *Walleye Warriors*, 11. This fishing method gave its name to one of the larger Ojibwe villages in Wisconsin, *Waaswaaganing*, "Place of Fishing by Torch Light," which later French observers translated as Lac du Flambeau (Lake of the Torch). Leon A. Valliere Jr., "A Brief History of Waaswaaganing Ojibweg," in *Memories of Lac du Flambeau Elders*, ed. Elizabeth Tornes (Madison: The Board of Regents of the University of Wisconsin System, 2004), 42.

10. Whaley and Bresette, *Walleye Warriors*, 43.

11. Nesper, *The Walleye War*, 22, 24; STA/Wisconsin Brochure, Wisconsin Department of Public Instruction American Indian Studies Program Files, in possession of the author.

12. Nesper, *The Walleye War*, 77.

13. Lac Courte Oreilles v. State of Wisconsin, 653 F. Supp. 1420, 1432 (W.D. Wis. 1987); Satz, *Chippewa Treaty Rights*, 97; Nesper, *The Walleye War*, 89.

14. Nesper, *The Walleye War*, 78.

15. Ibid., 77–78.

16. Ibid., 27; STA/W Brochure.

17. Satz, *Chippewa Treaty Rights*, 101.

18. Ibid.; Barbara Perry and Linda Robyn, "Putting Anti-Indian Violence in Context: The Case of the Great Lakes Chippewas of Wisconsin," *American Indian Quarterly* 29 (Summer-Fall 2005): 590-625; 598.

19. Satz, *Chippewa Treaty Rights*, 106; Satz, "After the Treaties," 115; Perry and Robyn, "Putting Anti-Indian Violence in Context," 613; Sharon Metz, "Just Keep on Walking," in *Minwaajimo: Telling a Good Story—Preserving Ojibwe Treaty Rights for the Past 25 Years*, ed. LaTisha A. McRoy (Odanah, WI: Great Lakes Indian Fish and Wildlife Commission, 2011): 257-258.

20. Satz, "After the Treaties," 115; Wisconsin Advisory Committee to the United States Commission on Civil Rights, *Discrimination Against Chippewa Indians in Northern Wisconsin: A Summary Report* (Madison: The Committee, 1989), 15.

21. Perry and Robyn, "Putting Anti-Indian Violence in Context," 592.

22. Ibid., 594. Emphasis in original.

23. Satz, *Chippewa Treaty Rights*, 100–101; Nesper, *The Walleye War*, 4; Sharon Metz, "Remarks," in McRoy, *Minwaajimo*, 182.

24. Lac Courte Oreilles Tribal Governing Board and Ad Hoc Commission on Racism in Wisconsin, *Wisconsin's Educational Imperative: Observations and Recommendations of the Ad Hoc Commission on Racism; Indian-White Relations, 1984* (Hayward, WI: Lac Courte Oreilles Tribal Governing Board and Ad Hoc Commission on Racism in Wisconsin, November 30, 1984), 7.

25. Nesper, *The Walleye War*, 4.

26. Rennard Strickland, foreword to *Chippewa Treaty Rights: The Reserved Rights of Wisconsin's Chippewa Indians in Historical Perspective*, by Ronald N. Satz (Madison: Wisconsin Academy of Sciences, Arts and Letters, 1991), xi–xiii.

27. Loew and Thannum, "After the Storm," 172.

28. Satz, *Chippewa Treaty Rights*, 101; Wisconsin Advisory Committee, *Discrimination*, 15.

29. Satz, *Chippewa Treaty Rights*, 101; Loew and Thannum, "After the Storm," 161, 172–173; Brian Pierson, "The Spearfishing Rights Case: *Lac du Flambeau Band v. Stop Treaty Abuse-Wisconsin*," in McRoy, *Minwaajimo*, 226; Zoltan A. Grossman, "Indian Issues and Anti-Indian Organizing," in *When Hate Groups Come to Town: A Handbook of Effective Community Responses* (Atlanta: Center for Democratic Renewal, 1992), 5; Wisconsin Advisory Committee, *Discrimination*, 13.

30. Satz, *Chippewa Treaty Rights*, 102; Perry and Robyn, "Putting Anti-Indian Violence in Context," 617; Dee Ann Mayo, "Remarks," in McRoy, *Minwaajimo*, 281.

31. Satz, *Chippewa Treaty Rights*, 101; Perry and Robyn, "Putting Anti-Indian Violence in Context," 616; Nesper, *The Walleye War*, 22.

32. Satz, *Chippewa Treaty Rights*, 101.

33. Steve Hopkins, "Hayward Is Calm Amid Disputes," in *Treaty Crisis: Cultures in Conflict*, ed. Frank Denton (Madison: Wisconsin State Journal, 1990), 42–43; Nesper, "The Walleye War," 79.

34. Whaley and Bresette, *Walleye Warriors*, 31.

35. Satz, *Chippewa Treaty Rights*, 106; Satz, "After the Treaties," 115; Nesper, *The Walleye War*, 4; Metz, "Remarks," 183; Metz, "Just Keep on Walking," 257; Grossman, "Indian Issues and Anti-Indian Organizing," 5.

36. Whaley and Bresette, *Walleye Warriors*, 31, 37.

37. GLIFWC, *Moving Beyond Argument*, 40.

38. George Hesselberg, "Profile: Dean Crist," in Denton, *Treaty Crisis*, 18; GLIFWC, *Moving Beyond Argument*, 33, 37.

39. Hesselberg, "Profile: Dean Crist," 18.

40. Satz, "After the Treaties," 101–102; Hesselberg, "Profile: Dean Crist," 18

41. Hesselberg, "Profile: Dean Crist," 18.

42. Grossman, "Indian Issues and Anti-Indian Organizing," 12.

43. Hesselberg, "Profile: Dean Crist," 18; Grossman, "Indian Issues and Anti-Indian Organizing," 12; GLIFWC, *Moving Beyond Argument*, 33.

44. Grossman, "Indian Issues and Anti-Indian Organizing," 12. Honor Our Neighbors Origins and Rights (HONOR) led the boycott of Treaty Beer.

45. GLIFWC, *Moving Beyond Argument*, 29; George Hesselberg, "Profile: Tom Maulson," in Denton, *Treaty Crisis*, 8–9; Hesselberg, "Profile: Dean Crist," 18. "The Grand Wizard" is an allusion to the Ku Klux Klan, whose leader is known by that title.

46. Hesselberg, "Profile: Dean Crist," 18.

47. Ibid.

48. Ibid.

49. Whaley and Bresette, *Walleye Warriors*, 51; Satz, *Chippewa Treaty Rights*, 106.

50. Rudolph C. Ryser, *Anti-Indian Movement on the Tribal Frontier*, 2nd ed., Occasional Paper 16 (Olympia, WA: The Center for World Indigenous Studies, 1992), http://nzdl.sadl.uleth.ca.

51. Nesper, *The Walleye War*, 4; Grossman, "Indian Issues and Anti-Indian Organizing," 5–6; Whaley and Bresette, *Walleye Warriors*, 34, 37.

52. Nesper, *The Walleye War*, 117; Grossman, "Indian Issues and Anti-Indian Organizing," 12; Midwest Treaty Network, "Wisconsin Treaties: What's the Problem?" Midwest Treaty Network brochure (1989) in DPI AIS Program Files, in possession of the author; Whaley and Bresette, *Walleye Warriors*, 51, 55–57.

53. Nesper, *The Walleye War*, 117; Midwest Treaty Network, 1989.

54. Midwest Treaty Network, 1989.

55. Ibid.; Jaeger, "Lake Scenes Likened to Selma Battle," 39; Nesper, *The Walleye War*, 117, 118; Grossman, "Indian Issues and Anti-Indian Organizing," 13.

56. Midwest Treaty Network,1989; Nesper, *The Walleye War*, 118; Jaeger, "Lake Scenes Likened to Selma Battle," 39.

57. Nesper, *The Walleye War*, 117.

58. Ibid.; Grossman, "Indian Issues and Anti-Indian Organizing," 13.

59. Jaeger, "Lake Scenes Likened to Selma Battle," 39.

60. Ibid.; Nesper, *The Walleye War*, 118.

61. Jaeger, "Lake Scenes Likened to Selma Battle," 39.

62. Grossman, "Indian Issues and Anti-Indian Organizing," 12.

63. Jaeger, "Lake Scenes Likened to Selma Battle," 39; Grossman, "Indian Issues and Anti-Indian Organizing," 13;

64. Jaeger, "Lake Scenes Likened to Selma Battle," 39.

65. Satz, *Chippewa Treaty Rights*, 115.

66. Ibid.; Grossman, "Indian Issues and Anti-Indian Organizing," 11; Metz, "Remarks," 183; Jaeger, "Lake Scenes Likened to Selma Battle," 39; Metz, "Just Keep on Walking," 257–258; Whaley and Bresette, *Walleye Warriors*, viii.

67. "Lac du Flambeau: Men of the Torches," *Anishinabe: The Chippewa of Wisconsin*, supplement to the *Wausau Daily Herald*, November 1, 1987, 7.

68. Wisconsin Advisory Committee, *Discrimination*, 13; Whaley and Bresette, *Walleye Warriors*, 37.

69. Wisconsin Advisory Committee, *Discrimination*, 17.

70. Satz, *Chippewa Treaty Rights*, 101.

71. GLIFWC, *Moving Beyond Argument*, 7; Loew and Thannum, "After the Storm," 197–198.

72. Wisconsin Advisory Committee, *Discrimination*, 13, Whaley and Bresette, *Walleye Warriors*, 37.

73. Wisconsin Advisory Committee, *Discrimination*, 14; Whaley and Bresette, *Walleye Warriors*, 58.

74. GLIFWC, *Moving Beyond Argument*, 19; Whaley and Bresette, *Walleye Warriors*, 37.

75. GLIFWC, *Moving Beyond Argument*, 5, 43, 44; Nesper, *The Walleye War*, 146; Wisconsin Advisory Committee, *Discrimination*, 13; Whaley and Bresette, *Walleye Warriors*, 107; "Lac du Flambeau: Men of the Torches," 7.

76. Satz, *Chippewa Treaty Rights*, 102; Donald L. Fixico, "Chippewa Fishing and Hunting Rights and the Voigt Decision," in *An Anthology of Western Great Lakes Indian History*, ed. Donald L. Fixico (Milwaukee: University of Wisconsin–Milwaukee American Indian Studies Program, 1987), 498–507; Nesper, *The Walleye War*, 146; Whaley and Bresette, *Walleye Warriors*, 107.

77. Satz, *Chippewa Treaty Rights*, 103; Tom Maulson, "Remarks," in McRoy, *Minwaajimo*, 164; Susan Lampert Smith, "Activists Watch for Peace at Landings: It's Minocqua, Not Managua," in Denton, *Treaty Crisis*, 39.

78. Jaeger, "Lake Scenes Likened to Selma Battle," 38.

79. George Hesselberg, "Profile: George Meyer," in Denton, *Treaty Crisis*, 37.

80. "US Official 'Appalled' by Tapes of Protests During Spearfishing," *Milwaukee Sentinel*, June 2, 1989, quoted in Satz, *Chippewa Treaty Rights*, 103.

81. Maulson, "Remarks," 167.

82. Ibid.

83. Ibid.; Jim St. Arnold, "Social, Economic and Political Issues Panel, Questions, and Comments," in McRoy, *Minwaajimo*, 192.

84. St. Arnold, "Social, Economic and Political Issues Panel," 191–192.

85. Satz, *Chippewa Treaty Rights*, 104; Satz, "After the Treaties," 115.

86. Ibid.

87. Brixley, "Churches Caught in Treaty Conflict," 40.

88. Ron Seely, "Cultures Clash in North," in Denton, *Treaty Crisis*, 26.

89. Brixley, "Churches Caught in Treaty Conflict," 40; Metz, "Remarks," 182–183.

90. Jaeger, "Lake Scenes Likened to Selma Battle," 38.

91. Perry and Robyn, "Putting Anti-Indian Violence in Context," 604–605; Grossman, "Indian Issues and Anti-Indian Organizing," 13.

92. Loew, "Hidden Transcripts," 723; Metz, "Remarks," 182; Perry and Robyn, "Putting Anti-Indian Violence in Context," 604.

93. Perry and Robyn, "Putting Anti-Indian Violence in Context," 606.

94. Loew, "Hidden Transcripts," 723.

95. Hesselberg, "Profile: George Meyer," 37. See also Brian Pierson, "The Spearfishing Rights Case," 225–236.

96. Metz, "Remarks," 182.

97. Satz, *Chippewa Treaty Rights*, 101.

Chapter 4

1. Ronald N. Satz, *Chippewa Treaty Rights: The Reserved Rights of Wisconsin's Chippewa Indians in Historical Perspective* (Madison: Wisconsin Academy of Sciences, Arts and Letters, 1991), 106.

2. Rick Whaley and Walter Bresette, *Walleye Warriors: An Effective Alliance Against Racism and for the Earth* (Philadelphia: New Society Publishers, 1994), 31.

3. Steve Hopkins, "Hayward Is Calm Amid Dispute," in *Treaty Crisis: Cultures in Conflict*, ed. Frank Denton (Madison: Wisconsin State Journal, 1990), 42–43.

4. Ibid.

5. Larry Nesper, *The Walleye War: The Struggle for Ojibwe Spearfishing and Treaty Rights* (Lincoln: University of Nebraska Press, 2002), 76.

6. Ibid., 77.

7. Ibid., 79.

8. Ibid.

9. Ibid.

10. Ibid.

11. Ibid.

12. Ibid., 80–81.

13. Ibid., 81.

14. Ibid.

15. Ibid., 81–82. For more information on the significance of the drum and the songs used, see Thomas Vennum Jr., *The Ojibwe Dance Drum: Its History and Construction* (St. Paul: Minnesota Historical Society Press, 2009).

16. Nesper, *The Walleye War*, 82.

17. Ibid.

18. Ibid.

19. Ibid.

20. Ibid.

21. Ibid.

22. Ibid., 83–84; Tom Maulson, "Remarks," in *Minwaajimo: Telling a Good Story*, ed. LaTisha A. McRoy (Odanah, WI: Great Lakes Indian Fish and Wildlife Commission, 2011), 168.

23. Nesper, *The Walleye War*, 84.

24. Zoltan A. Grossman, "Indian Issues and Anti-Indian Organizing," in *When Hate Groups Come to Town: A Handbook of Effective Community Responses* (Atlanta: Center for Democratic Renewal, 1992), 5.

25. Nesper, *The Walleye War*, 84.

26. Ibid.

27. Ibid.

28. Ibid., 87.

29. Ibid., 88.

30. Ibid., 82.

31. Ibid., 88.

32. Ibid.

33. Ibid.

34. Ibid., 3.

35. Hopkins, "Hayward Is Calm Amid Dispute," 42–43.

36. Ron Seely, "Minocqua Peace Slower to Gel," in Denton, *Treaty Crisis*, 44.

37. Ibid., 44.

38. Hopkins, "Hayward Is Calm Amid Dispute," 43.

39. Nesper, *The Walleye War*, 89.

40. Whaley and Bresette, *Walleye Warriors*, 48.

41. Nesper, *The Walleye War*, 91.

42. Ibid.

43. Whaley and Bresette, *Walleye Warriors*, 43.

44. Ibid., 49; Nesper, *The Walleye War*, 92; Barbara Perry and Linda Robyn, "Putting Anti-Indian Violence in Context: The Case of the Great Lakes Chippewas of Wisconsin," *American Indian Quarterly* 29, no. 3–4 (Summer–Fall 2005): 617.

45. Nesper, *The Walleye War*, 92; Whaley and Bresette, *Walleye Warriors*, 49.

46. Whaley and Bresette, *Walleye Warriors*, 49.

47. Ibid.

48. Nesper, *The Walleye War*, 92.

49. Whaley and Bresette, *Walleye Warriors*, 49; Nesper, *The Walleye War*, 92.

50. Nesper, *The Walleye War*, 92.

51. Ibid.

52. Whaley and Bresette, *Walleye Warriors*, 43.

53. Nesper, *The Walleye War*, 92.

54. Whaley and Bresette, *Walleye Warriors*, 43.

55. Nesper, *The Walleye War*, 92.

56. Ibid.

57. Ibid.

58. Perry and Robyn, "Putting Anti-Indian Violence in Context," 617.

59. Nesper, *The Walleye War*, 92.

60. "Tribe Condemns PARR as Racist," *Lakeland Times*, May 1, 1987, quoted in Nesper, *The Walleye War*, 93.

61. Nesper, *The Walleye War*, 93.

62. Ibid.

63. Ibid.

64. Ibid.

65. "Chippewas Hold Unification Ceremony at Butternut Landing," *Lakeland Times*, May 5, 1987, quoted in Nesper, *The Walleye War*, 93.

66. Jim St. Arnold, "Social, Economic and Political Issues Panel, Questions, and Comments," in McRoy, *Minwaajimo*, 192.

67. Nesper, *The Walleye War*, 99.

68. Ibid., 123.

69. Hopkins, "Hayward Is Calm Amid Dispute," 43; Nesper, *The Walleye War*, 99.

70. Nesper, *The Walleye War*, 90.

71. Ibid., 95–96.

72. Nesper, *The Walleye War*, 95; Richard W. Jaeger, "Lake Scenes Likened to Selma Battle," in Denton, *Treaty Crisis*, 38–39.

73. "Letter to the Editor: Stop Sucking Your Thumbs and Act," *Lakeland Times*, April 8, 1988, quoted in Nesper *The Walleye War*, 96.

74. Grossman, "Indian Issues and Anti-Indian Organizing," 6.

75. Nesper, *The Walleye War*, 100.

76. Grossman, "Indian Issues and Anti-Indian Organizing," 6.

77. Nesper, *The Walleye War*, 99.

78. Grossman, "Indian Issues and Anti-Indian Organizing," 6.

79. Ibid.; Nesper, *The Walleye War*, 99; Great Lakes Indian Fish and Wildlife Commission (GLIFWC). *Moving Beyond Argument, Racism and Treaty Rights* (Odanah, WI: GLIFWC, 1989): 27.

80. Nesper, *The Walleye War*, 105.

81. Ibid., 100.

82. Ibid., 102.

83. Ibid.

84. Whaley and Bresette, *Walleye Warriors*, 60.

85. Ibid.

86. Ibid., 60–61.

87. Nesper, *The Walleye War*, 97; Whaley and Bresette, *Walleye Warriors*, 60.

88. Whaley and Bresette, *Walleye Warriors*, 60–61.

89. Ibid.

90. Ibid.

91. Ibid.

92. Ibid.

93. Ibid., 93.

94. Ibid., 92.

95. Jeff Mayers, "Cultures in Conflict," in Denton, *Treaty Crisis*, 1, 6–7; Whaley and Bresette, *Walleye Warriors*, 92–93.

96. Mayers, "Cultures in Conflict," 7.

97. Ibid.

98. Ibid.; Nesper, *The Walleye War*, 131.

99. Nesper, *The Walleye War*, 132.

100. Whaley and Bresette, *Walleye Warriors*, 94.

101. Nesper, *The Walleye War*, 112–114; Whaley and Bresette, *Walleye Warriors*, 95–96.

102. Nesper, *The Walleye War*, 117, 118.

103. Jaeger, "Lake Scenes Likened to Selma Battle," 39; Maulson, "Remarks," 165; Sharon Metz, "Just Keep on Walking," in McRoy, *Minwaajimo*, 257–258; Grossman, "Indian Issues and Anti-Indian Organizing," 11.

104. Metz, "Remarks," McRoy, *Minwaajimo*, 183; Jaeger, "Lake Scenes Likened to Selma Battle," 39; Sharon Metz, "Just Keep on Walking," in McRoy, *Minwaajimo*, 258; Whaley and Bresette, *Walleye Warriors*, viii; Midwest Treaty Network, "Wisconsin Treaties: What's the Problem?" Midwest Treaty Network brochure (1989) in Wisconsin Department of Public Instruction American Indian Studies Program Files, in possession of the author.

105. GLIFWC, *Moving Beyond Argument*, 20.

106. Patty Loew and James Thannum, "After the Storm: Ojibwe Treaty Rights Twenty-Five Years After the Voigt Decision," *American Indian Quarterly* 35 (Spring 2011): 197; GLIFWC, *Moving Beyond Argument*, 20.

107. GLIFWC, *Moving Beyond Argument*, 19.

108. Ibid., 20.

109. Ibid., 21.

110. Nesper, *The Walleye War*, 121; GLIFWC, *Moving Beyond Argument*, 32, 38; Whaley and Bresette, *Walleye Warriors*, 100.

111. GLIFWC, *Moving Beyond Argument*, 32.

112. Nesper, *The Walleye War*, 121.

113. Whaley and Bresette, *Walleye Warriors*, 95.

114. Nesper, *The Walleye War*, 146.

115. Nesper, *The Walleye War*, 133. Nesper provides an extensive discussion of the disagreements between the Wa-Swa-Gon Treaty Association and the elected tribal leadership in chapters 5 and 6.

116. Nesper, *The Walleye War*, 133–134.

117. Ibid., 133.

118. Satz, *Chippewa Treaty Rights*, 118; Nesper, *The Walleye War*, 130.

119. Nesper, *The Walleye War*, 130.

120. Ibid.

121. Ibid.

122. Satz, *Chippewa Treaty Rights*, 118; Nesper, *The Walleye War*, 131.

123. Wisconsin Advisory Committee to the United States Commission on Civil Rights, *Discrimination Against Chippewa Indians in Northern Wisconsin: A Summary Report* (Madison: The Committee, 1989), 4.

124. Satz, *Chippewa Treaty Rights*, 118; Nesper, *The Walleye War*, 131.

125. Whaley and Bresette, *Walleye Warriors*, 100.

126. Ibid.

127. Nesper, *The Walleye War*, 132; Whaley and Bresette, *Walleye Warriors*, 100.

128. Nesper, *The Walleye War*, 133.

129. Whaley and Bresette, *Walleye Warriors*, 102–103.

130. Ibid., 104.

131. Nesper, *The Walleye War*, 130, 135.

132. Loew and Thannum, "After the Storm," 174.

133. Satz, *Chippewa Treaty Rights*, 119.

134. Nesper, *The Walleye War*, 136.

135. Ibid., 135.

136. Satz, *Chippewa Treaty Rights*, 118; GLIFWC, *Moving Beyond Argument*, 5.

137. Nesper, *The Walleye War*, 136; Whaley and Bresette, *Walleye Warriors*, 107.

138. Whaley and Bresette, *Walleye Warriors*, 107.

139. Nesper, *The Walleye War*, 136.

140. Whaley and Bresette, *Walleye Warriors*, 107.

141. Satz, *Chippewa Treaty Rights*, 118; Loew and Thannum, "After the Storm," 174.

142. Brian L. Pierson, "Remarks," in McRoy, *Minwaajimo*, 170.

143. Satz, *Chippewa Treaty Rights*, 118.

144. Ibid.

145. Ibid.

146. Ibid.

147. Nesper, *The Walleye War*, 137.

148. Ibid.

149. Ibid., 137–138.

150. Ibid., 138.

151. Ibid.

152. Ibid.

153. Ibid., 137.

154. Satz, *Chippewa Treaty Rights*, 118.

155. Nesper, *The Walleye War*, 138.

156. Ibid.

157. Whaley and Bresette, *Walleye Warriors*, 108.

158. Nesper, *The Walleye War*, 138–139.

159. Ibid., 139.

160. Ibid.

161. Ibid.

162. Ibid.

163. Ibid.

164. Ibid.

165. Satz, *Chippewa Treaty Rights*, 118.

166. Nesper, *The Walleye War*, 135; Whaley and Bresette, *Walleye Warriors*, 108–111.

167. Nesper, *The Walleye War*, 135.

168. Ibid., 140.

169. Ibid., 135–149.

170. Whaley and Bresette, *Walleye Warriors*, 111.

171. Nesper, *The Walleye War*, 150; Alton "Sonny" Smart, "Remarks," in McRoy, *Minwaajimo*, 275.

172. Nesper, *The Walleye War*, 150.

173. Ibid., 151–152; Whaley and Bresette, *Walleye Warriors*, 110–111. Bill Means recalls this incident in *Lighting the Seventh Fire*, DVD, dir. Sandra Sunrising Osawa (Seattle, WA: Upstream Productions, 1999).

174. Nesper, *The Walleye War*, 152.

175. Ibid.

176. Ibid.; Whaley and Bresette, *Walleye Warriors*, 111.

177. Ibid., 153.

178. Wisconsin Advisory Committee, *Discrimination*, 4–5.

179. Ibid., 5.

180. Ibid.

181. Frank Denton, "Better Information Is How We Can Help," in Denton, *Treaty Crisis*, 1–2.

182. Ibid., 2.

183. Whaley and Bresette, *Walleye Warriors*, 113.

184. Ibid., 114.

185. Denton, "Better Information," 1; Ronald N. Satz, "After the Treaties: The Chippewa Struggle to Retain Reserved Treaty Rights in the North Woods of Wisconsin," in *1991–1992 Proceedings, Woodland National Conference* (Muncie, IN: Minnetrista Cultural Foundation, Inc., 1993), 115.

186. Satz, "After the Treaties," 116.

187. Ibid.

188. Mayers, "Cultures in Conflict," 6.

189. Patty Loew, "Hidden Transcripts in the Chippewa Treaty Rights Struggle: A Twice Told Story; Race, Resistance, and the Politics of Power," *American Indian Quarterly* 21 (1997): 723.

190. Ron Seely and Jeff Mayers, "North Steps Toward Peace," in Denton, *Treaty Crisis*, 3–4; Metz, "Remarks," 183; Midwest Treaty Network, *1990 Witness Report: Chippewa Spearfishing Season; Violence, Ineffective Law Enforcement, and Racism* (Madison: The Network, 1991), 8; Loew and Thannum, "After the Storm," 174.

191. Seely and Mayers, "North Steps Toward Peace," 4; Metz, "Remarks," 183; Midwest Treaty Network, *1990 Witness Report*, 8.

192. Satz, *Chippewa Treaty Rights*, 121.

193. Midwest Treaty Network, *1990 Witness Report*, 8.

194. Ibid.

195. Ibid.

196. Ibid.

197. Pierson, "Remarks," 172; Loew and Thannum, "After the Storm," 175.

198. Satz, *Chippewa Treaty Rights*, 100; Loew, "Hidden Transcripts," 723.

199. Pierson, "Remarks," 174.

200. Loew, "Hidden Transcripts," 723.

201. Pierson, "Remarks," 172.

202. Loew and Thannum, "After the Storm," 175. For a full discussion of the case, see "The Spearfishing Civil Rights Case: *Lac du Flambeau Band v. Stop Treaty Abuse-Wisconsin*," in McRoy, *Minwaajimo*, 225–236.

203. Maulson, "Remarks," 166.

204. Rennard Strickland, foreword to *Chippewa Treaty Rights: The Reserved Rights of Wisconsin's Chippewa Indians in Historical Perspective* by Ronald N. Satz (Madison: Wisconsin Academy of Sciences, Arts and Letters, 1991), xii.

205. Perry and Robyn, "Putting Anti-Indian Violence in Context," 603.

Chapter 5

1. Veda Stone obituary, *Eau Claire Leader-Telegram*, January 11, 1996; Marie Lynn Mierzejewski, "The Imprint of One Woman: Veda Stone's Influence on Wisconsin Native Americans" (senior thesis, University of Wisconsin–Eau Claire, December 12, 2006), 10–13.

2. Ronald N. Satz, *Chippewa Treaty Rights: The Reserved Rights of Wisconsin's Chippewa Indians in Historical Perspective* (Madison: Wisconsin Academy of Sciences, Arts and Letters, 1991), 94; Brian L. Pierson, "Chippewa Treaty Rights Litigation in Wisconsin," State Bar of Wisconsin, http://www.wisbar.org.

3. Elizabeth Brixley, "Churches Caught in Treaty Conflict," in *Treaty Crisis: Cultures in Conflict*, ed. Frank Denton (Madison: Wisconsin State Journal, 1990), 40.

4. Jeffrey Robert Connolly, "Northern Wisconsin Reacts to Court Interpretations of Indian Treaty Rights to Natural Resources," *Great Plains Natural Resources Journal* 11 (2006–2007): 136; Patty Loew, "Hidden Transcripts in the Chippewa Treaty Rights Struggle: A Twice Told Story; Race, Resistance, and the Politics of Power," *American Indian Quarterly* 21 (1997): 721; George Lipsitz, "Walleye Warriors and White Identities: Native Americans' Treaty Rights, Composite Identities, and Social Movements," *Ethnic and Racial Studies* 31 (2004): 102.

5. Jim Oberly, "Race and Class Warfare: Spearing Fish, Playing 'Chicken,'" *The Nation* (June 19, 1989): 844–845; State of Wisconsin, Legislative Reference Bureau, *Chippewa Off-Reservation Treaty Rights* (Madison: State of Wisconsin Legislative Reference Bureau, December 1991), 16.

6. Lac Courte Oreilles Tribal Governing Board and Ad Hoc Commission on Racism in Wisconsin, *Wisconsin's Educational Imperative: Observations and Recommendations of the Ad Hoc Commission on Racism: Indian-White Relations* (Hayward, WI: Lac Courte Oreilles Tribal Governing Board and Ad Hoc Commission on Racism in Wisconsin, 1984), 8.

7. Members of the commission included chair Veda Stone, chief commissioner, School of Arts and Sciences Outreach, UW–Eau Claire; William Cardy, priest, St. Phillip's Roman Catholic Church; Paul DeMain, advisor to the governor on Indian affairs; Randolph Kahn, B'nai B'rith Jewish Anti-Defamation League; Barbara Morford, Governor's Committee on Equal Rights; Peggy Prueher, Church Women United Board; Mary Reddin, attorney and board member of Wisconsin Civil Liberties Union; Ronald Satz, dean of Graduate Studies and professor of history, UW–Eau Claire; Ursula Schramm, B'nai B'rith; Nancy Stein, professor of sociology, Normandale Community College; and William Wantland, bishop, Episcopal Diocese of Eau Claire.

8. Lac Courte Oreilles Tribal Governing Board and Ad Hoc Commission on Racism in Wisconsin, *Wisconsin's Educational Imperative*, 11.

9. Ibid.

10. Ibid.

11. Ibid., 9, 29.

12. Ibid., 10.

13. Ibid., 5–30.

14. Ibid., 12.

15. Ibid.

16. Ibid.

17. Ibid., 13.

18. Ibid.

19. Ibid.

20. Ibid.

21. Ibid.

22. Ibid., 14–17.

23. Ibid., 14.

24. Ibid., 16.

25. Ibid.

26. Ibid., 17.

27. Wisconsin Advisory Committee to the United States Commission on Civil Rights, *Discrimination Against Chippewa Indians in Northern Wisconsin: A Summary Report* (The Committee, 1989), 17.

28. Ibid., 2–3.

29. Ibid., 1.

30. Ibid., 8.

31. Ibid., 12.

32. Ibid., 15.

33. Ibid., 2.

34. Ibid., 1.

35. Ibid., 21.

Chapter 6

1. *Lighting the Seventh Fire*, DVD, dir. Sandra Sunrising Osawa (Seattle, WA: Upstream Productions, 1999).

2. David W. Saxe, "Theory for Social Studies Foundations," *Review of Educational Research* 62 (Autumn 1992): 260.

3. See Michael W. Apple, *Official Knowledge: Democratic Education in a Conservative Age* (New York: Routledge, 2000); and Michael W. Apple, "The Politics of Official Knowledge: Does a National Curriculum Make Sense?" *Teachers College Record* 95 (Winter 1993): 222.

4. Patricia Albjerg Graham, "Battleships and Schools," *Daedalus* 124 (Fall 1995): 43.

5. Nancy W. Bauer, "Guaranteeing the Values Component in Elementary Social Studies," in *Social Studies Education: The Elementary School*, ed. John Jarolimek (Washington, DC: National Council for the Social Studies, 1967), 43.

6. See Apple, *Official Knowledge*.

7. Ibid., 222.

8. Ibid.

9. See Apple, *Official Knowledge*. Ellen Condiffe Lagemann, "The Plural Worlds of Educational Research," *History of Education Quarterly* 29 (Summer 1989): 183–214.

10. Stephen J. Thornton, "NCSS: The Early Years," in *NCSS in Retrospect*, ed. O. L. Davis (Washington, DC: National Council for the Social Studies, 1996), 1.

11. John Jarolimek, *Guidelines for Elementary Social Studies* (Washington, DC: Association for Supervision and Curriculum Development, 1967), 1; Richard F. Elmore and Susan H. Fuhrman,

"Governing the Curriculum: Changing Patterns in Policy, Politics, and Practice," in *The Governance of Curriculum: The 1994 ASCD Yearbook*, ed. Richard F. Elmore and Susan H. Fuhrman (Arlington, VA: Association for Supervision and Curriculum Development, 1994), 4.

12. Elmore and Fuhrman, "Governing the Curriculum," 5; Jarolimek, *Guidelines for Elementary Social Studies*, 1.

13. Jarolimek, *Guidelines for Elementary Social Studies*, 13; Richard L. Simms, "Pluralism: Historical Roots and Contemporary Responses," in *Racism and Sexism: Responding to the Challenge*, ed. Richard L. Simms and Gloria Contreras (Washington, DC: National Council for the Social Studies, 1980), 12; Lloyd Kendall, "Using Learning Resources in Concept Development," in *Social Studies Education: The Elementary School*, ed. John Jarolimek (Washington, DC: National Council for Social Studies, 1967), 542; Jesus Garcia and Edward Buendia, "NCSS and Ethnic Diversity," in Davis, *NCSS in Retrospect*, 55. See also Michael W. Apple and Linda K. Christian-Smith, "The Politics of the Textbook," in *The Politics of the Textbook*, ed. Michael W. Apple and Linda K. Christian-Smith (New York: Routledge, 1991), 1–21, and Michael W. Apple, *Cultural Politics and Education* (New York: Teachers College Press, 1996).

14. Elmore and Fuhrman, "Governing the Curriculum," 3.

15. US Department of Education, "What is ESEA?," Home Room blog, May 2015, http://blog.ed.gov/2015/04/what-is-esea/

16. Jarolimek, *Guidelines for Elementary Social Studies*, 1.

17. Ibid., 19.

18. Susan H. Fuhrman, "Legislatures and Education Policy," in *The Governance of Curriculum: The 1994 ASCD Yearbook* (Arlington, VA: Association for Supervision and Curriculum Development), 30–31; Jarolimek, *Guidelines for Elementary Social Studies*, 19.

19. Jarolimek, *Guidelines for Elementary Social Studies*, 1.

20. Ibid., 20, 22.

21. Ibid., 20–21.

22. Ibid., 31.

23. Ibid., 28.

24. Christine J. Woyshner, "Notes Toward a Historiography of the Social Studies," in *Research Methods in Social Studies Education: Contemporary Issues and Perspectives*, ed. Keith Barton (Greenwich, CT: Information Age Publishing, 2006), 29.

25. Saxe, "Theory for Social Studies Foundations," 260.

26. Woyshner, "Notes Toward a Historiography," 17.

27. Diane Ravitch, "A Brief History of Social Studies," in *Where Did Social Studies Go Wrong?*, ed. James Fleming, Lucien Ellington, and Kathleen Porter-Magee (Washington, DC: The Thomas B. Fordham Institute, 2003), 1.

28. Ibid., 2; James L. Barth, "NCSS and the Nature of Social Studies," in Davis, *NCSS in Retrospect*, 15–16; John D. Haas, *The Era of the New Social Studies* (Washington, DC: National Institute of Education, DHEW, 1977), 57; Thornton, "NCSS: The Early Years," 3.

29. Haas, *The Era of the New Social Studies* 57.

30. Woyshner, "Notes Toward a Historiography," 27; Herbert M. Kliebard, *The Struggle for the American Curriculum, 1893–1958*, 2nd ed. (New York: Routledge, 1995), 108–110. See also Hazel Hertzberg, *Social Studies Reform, 1880–1980* (Boulder, CO: SSEC Publications, 1981)

31. William H. Watkins, "Thomas Jesse Jones, Social Studies, and Race," *International Journal of Social Education* 10, no. 2 (Fall–Winter 1995–1996): 132. Some scholars, including Saxe, dispute both Jones's role on the committee and the connection between social studies as adopted in 1916 and his earlier work at Hampton.

32. Ravitch, "A Brief History of Social Studies," 3.

33. Jarolimek, *Guidelines for Elementary Social Studies*, 4.

34. Davis, *NCSS in Retrospect*, ii.

35. Jarolimek, *Guidelines for Elementary Social Studies*, 4; Jack L. Nelson and William R. Fernekes, "NCSS and Social Crisis," in Davis, *NCSS in Retrospect*, 91; Thornton, "NCSS: The Early Years," 5.

36. Nelson and Fernekes, "NCSS and Social Crisis," 93. See also Gordon C. Lee, "Government Pressures on the Schools During World War II," *History of Education Journal* 2 (Spring 1951): 65–74.

37. Nelson and Fernekes, "NCSS and Social Crisis," 93.

38. Haas, *The Era of the New Social Studies*, 12; Kliebard, *The Struggle for the American Curriculum*, 226–227; Jeffrey Byford and William Russell, "The New Social Studies: A Historical Examination of Curriculum Reform" *Social Studies Research and Practice* 2, no. 1 (Spring 2007), 40.

39. Kliebard, *The Struggle for the American Curriculum*, 226–227; Haas, *The Era of the New Social Studies*, 12; Hyman G. Rickover, *Education and Freedom* (New York: Dutton, 1959), 154.

40. Kliebard, *The Struggle for the American Curriculum*, 227.

41. Ibid., 229.

42. Haas, *The Era of the New Social Studies*, 20.

43. Fannie R. Shaftel, Charlotte Crabtree, and Vivian Rushworth, "Problem Solving in the Elementary School," in *The Problems Approach to the Social Studies*, ed. Richard E. Gross, Raymond H. Muessig, and George L. Fersh (Washington, DC: National Council for the Social Studies, 1960), 36.

44. Shaftel, Crabtree, and Rushworth, "Problem Solving in the Elementary School," 42.

45. Ibid., 42.

46. Ibid., 44.

47. Barth, "NCSS and the Nature of Social Studies," 10; Robert D. Barth, James L. Barth, and S. Samuel Shermis, *The Nature of Social Studies* (Palm Springs, CA: ETC Publications, 1978), iv–v.

48. John Jarolimek, "Conceptual Approaches: Their Meaning for Elementary Social Studies," in *Social Studies Education: The Elementary School*, ed. John Jarolimek (Washington, DC: National Council for the Social Studies, 1967), 547.

49. William B. Stanley, "Recent Research in the Foundations of Social Education, 1976–1983," in *Recent Research in Social Education: Issues and Approaches*, ed. William B. Stanley, Catherine Cornbleth, Richard K. Jantz, Kenneth Klawitter, and James Leming (Washington, DC: ERIC Clearinghouse for the Social Sciences/Social Science Education, National Council for the Social Studies, and Social Science Education Consortium, 1985), 311; Shirley H. Engle, "Decision Making: The Heart of Social Studies Instruction (1960)," in *Voices of Social Education, 1937–1987*, ed. Daniel Roselle (New York: Macmillan, 1987), 76.

50. Stanley, "Recent Research in the Foundations of Social Education," 311.

51. Jarolimek, *Guidelines for Elementary Social Studies*, 2.

52. Ibid., 8; Jarolimek, "Conceptual Approaches," 535.

53. Jarolimek, *Guidelines for Elementary Social Studies*, 9; Jarolimek, "Conceptual Approaches," 547.

54. Melvin Arnoff, "Introducing Social Studies Concepts in the Primary Grades," in Jarolimek, *Social Studies Education*, 548.

55. Ibid.

56. Bauer, "Guaranteeing the Values Component," 44.

57. Ibid., 46.

58. Jarolimek, *Guidelines for Elementary Social Studies*, 9; Linda S. Lesvik, "NCSS and the Teaching of History," in Davis, *NCSS in Retrospect*, 23; Barth, "NCSS and the Nature of Social Studies," 13; James P. Shaver, "NCSS and Citizenship Education," in Davis, *NCSS in Retrospect*, 37.

59. Haas, *The Era of the New Social Studies*, 74.

60. Ibid., 87.

61. Stanley, "Recent Research in the Foundations of Social Education," 312–313.

62. Robert E. Jewett and Robert B. Ribble, "Curriculum Improvement and Teacher Status," *Social Education* 31 (January 1967): 20, 21.

63. Donald W. Robinson, "Ferment in the Social Studies," *Social Education* (November 1967): 363.

64. Ibid., 361.

65. Haas, *The Era of the New Social Studies*, 37–38.

66. William R. Fielder, "Two Styles of Talk About Values," in Jarolimek, *Social Studies Education*, 36.

67. Robinson, "Ferment in the Social Studies," 362, 363.

68. Fielder, "Two Styles of Talk About Values," 36.

69. Ibid.

70. Lucien Ellington and Jana S. Eaton, "Multiculturalism and Social Studies," in *Where Did Social Studies Go Wrong?*, ed. James Leming, Lucien Ellington, and Kathleen Porter-Magee (Washington, DC: Thomas B. Fordham Foundation, 2003), 70.

71. Fielder, "Two Styles of Talk About Values," 36.

72. See, for example, William W. Savage Jr., ed., *Indian Life: Transforming an American Myth* (Norman: University of Oklahoma Press, 1977); Robert F. Berkhofer, *The White Man's Indian* (New York: Alfred A. Knopf, 1978); Philip J. Deloria, *Playing Indian* (New Haven: Yale University Press, 1998); and Philip J. Deloria, *Indians in Unexpected Places* (Lawrence: University of Kansas Press, 2004).

Chapter 7

1. Linda S. Lesvik, "NCSS and the Teaching of History," in *NCSS in Retrospect*, ed. O. L. Davis (Washington, DC: National Council for the Social Studies, 1996), 26.

2. Ibid.

3. John D. Haas, *The Era of the New Social Studies* (Washington, DC: National Institute of Education, DHEW, 1977), 79.

4. Ibid., 79.

5. Lesvik, "NCSS and the Teaching of History," 24.

6. Nancy W. Bauer, "Guaranteeing the Values Component in Elementary Social Studies," in *Social Studies Education: The Elementary School*, ed. John Jarolimek (Washington, DC: National Council for the Social Studies, 1967), 43.

7. Lesvik, "NCSS and the Teaching of History," 24.

8. John Jarolimek, *Guidelines for Elementary Social Studies* (Washington, DC: Association for Supervision and Curriculum Development, 1967), 9.

9. Lesvik, "NCSS and the Teaching of History," 24; Haas, *The Era of the New Social Studies*, 81.

10. Jack L. Nelson and William R. Fernekes, "NCSS and Social Crisis," in Davis, *NCSS in Retrospect*, 97.

11. Ibid., 97.

12. Ibid., 98.

13. Ibid.

14. Emily Fuller Gibson, "The Three D's: Distortion, Deletion, Denial," *Social Education* 33 (April 1969): 405–409, quoted in Eleanor Blumenberg, "Responses to Racism: How Far Have We Come," in *Racism and Sexism: Responding to the Challenge*, ed. Richard L. Simms and Gloria Contreras (Washington, DC: National Council for the Social Studies, 1980), 35.

15. Rupert Costo and Jeannette Henry, *Textbooks and the American Indian* (San Francisco: The Indian Historian Press, 1970), 7.

16. Michael B. Kane, *Minorities in Textbooks: A Study for Their Treatment in Social Studies Texts* (Chicago: Quadrangle Books, 1970), 10, quoted in Blumenberg, "Responses to Racism," 35.

17. Richard L. Simms, "Bias in Textbooks: Not Yet Corrected," *Phi Delta Kappan* 53 (November 1975): 201.

18. Richard L. Simms, "Pluralism: Historical Roots and Contemporary Responses," in *Racism and Sexism: Responding to the Challenge*, ed. Richard L. Simms and Gloria Contreras (Washington, DC: National Council for the Social Studies, 1980), 13.

19. Blumenberg, "Responses to Racism," 35.

20. Jesus Garcia and Edward Buendia, "NCSS and Ethnic Diversity," in Davis, *NCSS in Retrospect*, 58.

21. Ibid.

22. Haas, *The Era of the New Social Studies*, 80.

23. NCSS Task Force on Curriculum Guidelines, *Social Studies Curriculum Guidelines*, 3.

24. Ibid., 3–4.

25. Ibid., 16.

26. Ibid., 17.

27. Ibid., 19–20; Blumenberg, "Responses to Racism," 31–32. The National Council for Social Studies

was far from alone in its new direction, as several national organizations also advanced policy statements, produced publications, and engaged in professional development and curriculum development to promote multicultural education. These efforts included civil rights organizations and such leading education organizations as the American Association of Colleges for Teacher Education, the Association for Supervision and Curriculum Development (ASCD), the National Education Association, the United Federation of Teachers, and National Council for Social Studies. ASCD engaged leading scholars in the field of multicultural education in its working groups on bias-free tests, and it published two special issues of *Educational Leadership* that focused on multicultural education, in November 1971 and again in April 1974. See Blumenberg, "Responses to Racism," 33.

28. Haas, *The Era of the New Social Studies*, 80.

29. NCSS Task Force on Curriculum Guidelines, *Social Studies Curriculum Guidelines*, 19–20; Blumenberg, "Responses to Racism," 33.

30. The Ethnic Heritage Centers Act of 1972, Title IX, sec. 901; Simms, "Pluralism," 16; Blumenberg, "Responses to Racism," 31.

31. Blumenberg, "Responses to Racism," 31.

32. Ibid.; The Ethnic Heritage Centers Act of 1972, Title IX, sec. 901.

33. Blumenberg, "Responses to Racism," 29.

34. Wis. Stat. § 118.02(c)8.

35. Blumenberg, "Responses to Racism," 33.

36. Eleanor Blumenberg, "Shards from the Splintered Melting Pot in America," *Phi Delta Kappan* (November 1973): 210, quoted in Blumenberg, 1980, 24.

37. Blumenberg, "Responses to Racism," 29.

38. Ibid., 31–32.

39. NCSS Task Force on Ethnic Studies Curriculum, *Curriculum Guidelines for Multiethnic Education*, 5.

40. Ibid., 6.

41. Ibid.

42. Ibid., 8.

43. "Dispositions" is a common term in teacher education and licensing. Professional standards, such as Wisconsin's Teacher Standards, reflect concern for "knowledge, skills, and dispositions." See Wis. Admin. Code PI 34.02.

44. NCSS Task Force on Ethnic Studies Curriculum, *Curriculum Guidelines for Multiethnic Education*, 9.

45. Ibid., 21.

46. Ibid.

47. Ibid., 28.

48. Ibid., 36.

49. Ibid., 24, 28.

50. Ibid., 27.

51. Ibid., 24, 33.

52. Ibid., 29.

53. Ibid., 28.

54. Ibid.

55. Blumenberg, "Responses to Racism," 23; Simms, "Pluralism," 13.

56. Simms, "Pluralism," 16; Blumenberg, "Responses to Racism," 23.

57. James A. Banks, "Multiethnic Education Across Cultures: United States, Mexico, Puerto Rico, France, and Great Britain," *Social Education* (March 1978): 177–185, quoted in Simms, "Pluralism," 16.

58. Beryle Banfield, "Biting the Bullet: Racism and Sexism and the Challenge for Social Studies," in Simms and Contreras, *Racism and Sexism: Responding to the Challenge*, 68.

59. Ibid., 68.

60. Ibid.

61. National Council for Social Studies, "Revision of the NCSS Social Studies Curriculum Guidelines" (Washington, DC: National Council for Social Studies, 1979), 179, quoted in James P. Shaver, "NCSS and Citizenship Education," in Davis, *NCSS in Retrospect*, 39–40.

62. Robert D. Barth, James L. Barth, and S. Samuel Shermis, *The Nature of Social Studies* (Palm Springs, CA: ETC Publications, 1978), 69; William B. Stanley, "Recent Research in the Foundations of Social Education, 1976–1983," in *Recent Research in Social Education: Issues and Approaches*, ed. William B. Stanley, Catherine Cornbleth, Richard K. Jantz, Kenneth Klawitter, and James Leming (Washington, DC: ERIC Clearinghouse for the Social Sciences/Social Science Education, National Council for the Social Studies, and Social Science Education Consortium, 1985), 317.

63. "Human Relations" is one approach to what would later be called "multicultural education." Many schools, including those in Wisconsin, began to create Human Relations programs during this era. This language is also reflected in part of the statutory language in Act 31, Wis. Stat. § 118.19(8) (1989), which addresses teacher education and licensing.

64. Banfield, "Biting the Bullet," 66.

65. Ibid.

66. Ibid., 65.

67. Ibid., 67.

68. Lesvik, "NCSS and the Teaching of History," 29.

69. Ibid., 27.

70. Susan H. Fuhrman and Richard F. Elmore, "Governors and Education Policy in the 1990s," in *The Governance of Curriculum: The 1994 ASCD Yearbook*, ed. Richard F. Elmore and Susan H. Fuhrman (Arlington, VA: Association for Supervision and Curriculum Development, 1994), 59.

71. Ibid., 59–60.

72. Lesvik, "NCSS and the Teaching of History," 28.

73. Stanley, "Recent Research in the Foundations of Social Education, 348.

74. Lesvik, "NCSS and the Teaching of History," 23.

75. See, for example, Lynne V. Cheney, *American Memory: A Report on the Humanities in the Nation's Public Schools* (Ann Arbor: University of Michigan Library, 1987); Diane Ravitch and Chester E. Finn Jr., *What Do Our Seventeen-Year-Olds Know? A Report on the First National Assessment of History and Literature* (New York: HarperCollins, 1987); Allan Bloom, *The Closing of the American Mind* (New York: Simon and Schuster, 1987); and E. D. Hirsch Jr., *Cultural Literacy: What Every American Needs to Know* (New York: Vintage, 1988).

76. James L. Barth, "NCSS and the Nature of Social Studies," in Davis, *NCSS in Retrospect*, 17; American Historical Association, Carnegie Foundation for the Advancement of Teaching, Organization of American Historians, National Commission on Social Studies in the Schools, and National Council for the Social Studies, *Charting a Course: Social Studies for the 21st Century; A Report of the Curriculum Task Force of the National Commission on Social Studies in the Schools* (Washington, DC: National Council for the Social Studies, 1989).

77. American Historical Association et. al, *Charting a Course*.

78. Barth, "NCSS and the Nature of Social Studies," 17.

Chapter 8

1. Michael W. Apple, "The Politics of Official Knowledge: Does a National Curriculum Make Sense?" *Teachers College Record* 95 (Winter 1993): 222; Michael W. Apple, *Official Knowledge: Democratic Education in a Conservative Age*, 2nd ed. (New York: Routledge, 2000); Michael W. Apple, *Ideology and Curriculum*, 2nd ed. (New York: Routledge, 1990).

2. Wis. Const. art. X, § 1; Wis. Stat. § 115, Subchapter II (1989).

3. Wis. Stat. § 118.01(1) (2) (1989).

4. Wis. Stat. § 120.12(14) (1989); Wis. Stat. § 121.02(1) (1989); Wis. Stat. § 121.02(1)(L)1-3 (1989).

5. A. Clark Hagensick, "Purging History in Wisconsin: Promises and Pitfalls," *Wisconsin Magazine of History* 67, no. 4 (Summer 1984): 282.

6. Ibid., 283.

7. Ibid., 283–284.

8. Ibid., 284.

9. Laws of Wisconsin (1927), quoted in Hagensick, "Purging History in Wisconsin," 283–284.

10. Hagensick, "Purging History in Wisconsin," 288.

11. Laws of Wisconsin (1953), chap. 90, quoted in Hagensick, "Purging History in Wisconsin," 283–284.

12. Hagensick, "Purging History in Wisconsin," 292.

13. Ibid.

14. Wisconsin Department of Public Instruction and Wisconsin State Wartime Studies Committee, *The Social Studies in Wisconsin Schools* (Madison: Wisconsin Department of Public Instruction and Wisconsin State Wartime Studies Committee, 1943); Wisconsin Department of Public Instruction and Wisconsin Wartime Studies Committee, *A Challenge to Every Wisconsin Teacher* (Madison: Wisconsin Department of Public Instruction and Wisconsin Wartime Studies Committee, 1942).

15. Wisconsin Department of Public Instruction, *A Conceptual Framework for the Social Studies in Wisconsin Schools* (Madison: Wisconsin Department of Public Instruction, 1964); Wisconsin Department of Public Instruction, *A Conceptual Framework for the Social Studies*, 2nd ed. (Madison: Wisconsin Department of Public Instruction, 1967); Wisconsin Social Studies Curriculum Study Committee, *Knowledge, Processes, and Values in the New Social Studies* (Madison: Wisconsin Department of Public Instruction, 1970), vii; Wisconsin Social Studies Curriculum Study Committee, *Program Improvement for Social Studies Education in Wisconsin* (Madison: Wisconsin Department of Public Instruction, 1977), 18.

16. Wisconsin Social Studies Curriculum Study Committee, *Program Improvement*, 18.

17. Wisconsin Department of Public Instruction, *A Conceptual Framework*, 1st ed., 18.

18. Ibid.

19. Ibid.

20. Ibid.

21. Ibid.

22. Ibid., 19.

23. Wisconsin Social Studies Curriculum Study Committee, *Knowledge, Processes, and Values*, vi.

24. Ibid., vii.

25. Ibid., vi.

26. Ibid.

27. Ibid.

28. Ibid.

29. Ibid.

30. Ibid.

31. Ibid.

32. Ibid.

33. Wisconsin Social Studies Curriculum Study Committee, *Descriptors for Political Understanding: A Guide to Asking Questions About Learning Related to Political Literacy in Wisconsin Schools, K-12* (Madison: Department of Public Instruction, 1976), 10.

34. Ibid., 12.

35. Ibid., 4.

36. Ibid., 4, 10.

37. Ibid., 15.

38. Ibid., 5.

39. Wisconsin Social Studies Curriculum Study Committee, *Program Improvement*.

40. Ibid., 18.

41. Ibid., 19.

42. Ibid.

43. Ibid.

44. Ibid.
45. Ibid.
46. Ibid.
47. Ibid.
48. Ibid., 38.
49. Ibid., 38.
50. Ibid., 40–41.
51. Ibid., 40.
52. Wisconsin Social Studies Curriculum Study Committee, *Descriptors for Anthropology: A Guide to Asking Questions About Learning Anthropology Facts and Concepts in Wisconsin Schools, K-12* (Madison: Wisconsin Department of Public Instruction, 1978), 10.
53. Wisconsin Social Studies Curriculum Study Committee, *Descriptors for Sociology: A Guide to Asking Questions About Learning Sociology Facts and Concepts in Wisconsin Schools, K-12* (Madison: Wisconsin Department of Public Instruction, 1985), 3.
54. Wisconsin Social Studies Curriculum Study Committee, *Descriptors for Understanding United States History: A Guide to Asking Questions About Learning Related to History in Wisconsin Schools, K-12* (Madison: Wisconsin Department of Public Instruction, 1986), 2.
55. Ibid., 9.
56. Ibid.
57. Ibid., 10.
58. Ibid.
59. Ibid., 11.
60. Ibid., 12.
61. Ibid., 14.
62. Ibid., 15.
63. Ibid.
64. Ibid., 16.
65. Ibid., 17.
66. Ibid., 17–18, 19.
67. Ibid., 19.
68. Ibid., 21.
69. Ibid., 23.
70. Francis Paul Prucha, *American Indian Treaties: The History of a Political Anomaly* (Berkeley: University of California Press, 1994), 1.
71. Wisconsin Social Studies Curriculum Study Committee, *A Guide to Curriculum Planning in Social Studies Education*, Bulletin No. 6251 (Madison: Wisconsin Department of Public Instruction, 1986), vii.
72. Myra P. Sadker and David M. Sadker, *Sex Equity Handbook for Schools* (New York: Longman, 1982), quoted in Wisconsin Social Studies Curriculum Study Committee, *A Guide to Curriculum Planning*, xi.
73. Wisconsin Social Studies Curriculum Study Committee, *A Guide to Curriculum Planning*, xi.
74. Ibid., xiii.
75. Ibid., xiii.
76. Ibid., xiv.
77. Ibid., 2–3.
78. Ibid., 2–4.
79. Ibid., 6.
80. Ibid., 7.
81. Ibid.
82. Ibid.
83. Ibid.
84. Ibid.

85. Ibid., 51.

86. Ibid., 54.

87. Ibid., 53–54.

88. Ibid.

89. Wisconsin Department of Public Instruction, *Enacted Bills Relating to Education, 1989 Legislative Session* (Madison: Wisconsin Department of Public Instruction, 1990).

Chapter 9

1. John Jarolimek, *Guidelines for Elementary Social Studies* (Washington, DC: Association for Supervision and Curriculum Development, 1967), 13; Jesus Garcia and Edward Buendia, "NCSS and Ethnic Diversity," in *NCSS in Retrospect*, ed. O. L. Davis Jr. (Washington, DC: National Council for Social Studies, 1996), 55; Richard L. Simms and Gloria Contreras, eds., *Racism and Sexism: Responding to the Challenge* 61 (Washington, DC: National Council for the Social Studies, 1980); Kyle Roy Ward, *History in the Making: An Absorbing Look at How American History Has Changed in the Telling over the Last 200 Years* (New York: New Press, 2006); Joseph Moreau, *Schoolbook Nation: Conflicts Over American History Textbooks from the Civil War to the Present* (Ann Arbor: University of Michigan Press, 2003); Jonathan Zimmerman, *Whose America?: Culture Wars in the Public Schools* (Cambridge, MA: Harvard University Press, 2002).

2. Ward, *History in the Making*, xiii.

3. Charles E. Brown, "Wisconsin Indian Tribes," pamphlet (Madison, WI: State Historical Museum, 1923).

4. William Ellery Leonard, "Acknowledgements—To Charles E. Brown," *The Wisconsin Archaeologist* 25, no. 2 (1944): 64.

5. Albert O. Barton, "Wisconsin's Charles Brown," *The Wisconsin Archaeologist* 25, no. 2 (1944): 51–53; John G. Gregory, "Charles Edward Brown, Early Milwaukee Background," *The Wisconsin Archaeologist* 25, no. 2 (1944): 44.

6. Barton, "Wisconsin's Charles Brown," 51–52; W. C. McKern, "Acknowledgements—To Charles E. Brown," *The Wisconsin Archaeologist* 25 no. 2 (1944): 56; Col. (Chief) Yellow Thunder, "Acknowledgements—To Charles E. Brown," *The Wisconsin Archaeologist* 25, no. 2 (1944): 58–59; August Derleth, "Acknowledgements—To Charles E. Brown," *The Wisconsin Archaeologist* 25, no. 2 (1944): 71–72.

7. Brown, "Wisconsin Indian Tribes," 3.

8. Ibid.

9. Ibid.

10. Ibid., 4.

11. Ibid.

12. Ibid.

13. Ibid., 4–5.

14. Ibid., 5.

15. Ibid.

16. Ibid.

17. Ibid., 5–6.

18. Ibid., 6.

19. Ibid.

20. Ibid.

21. Ibid.

22. Ibid.

23. Ibid.

24. Ibid., 7.

25. Ibid.

26. Ibid.

27. Ibid., 8.

28. Ibid.
29. Ibid.
30. Ibid.
31. Brown, "Wisconsin Indian Tribes," pamphlet (Madison, WI: State Historical Museum, 1927), 1; Charles E. Brown, "Wisconsin Indian Tribes," pamphlet (Madison, WI: State Historical Museum, 1931).
32. Margaret G. Henderson, Ethel Dewey Speerschneider, and Helen L. Ferslev, *It Happened Here: Stories of Wisconsin* (Madison: State Historical Society of Wisconsin, 1949), vii.
33. Ibid., vi.
34. Ibid., 3.
35. Ibid., 159–195.
36. Moreau, *Schoolbook Nation*, 154.
37. Ibid.
38. "Young People Aid in Research into State's History," *Rhinelander Daily News*, December 15, 1955.
39. *Wisconsin State Journal*, July 20, 1947; "Jaunts with Jamie: We Owe Much to Mrs. Mary Ryan," *Milwaukee Sentinel*, July 12, 1966.
40. Mary Tuohy Ryan, "A Friendly Hello!" *Junior Badger History* 1, no. 1 (October 1947): 16.
41. "Jaunts with Jamie: We Owe Much to Mrs. Mary Ryan."
42. "Green Bay Convention," *Badger History* 10, no. 1 (September 1956): 8.
43. Donna Duehr, "The Lake with Short Ears," *Badger History* 1, no. 1 (October 1947): 4–5.
44. John W. Jenkins, "Things to Do," *Badger History* 1, no. 7 (April 1948): 8–9.
45. "The Old Indian Agency House at Portage," *Badger History* 1, no. 1 (October 1947): 8–10.
46. "September in Wisconsin History," *Badger History* 1, no. 1 (October 1947): 13; "October in Wisconsin History," *Badger History* 1, no. 1 (October 1947): 13–14.
47. Marilla Fuszard, "Aztalan," *Badger History* 1, no. 1 (October 1947): 17; Anne Eccles, "The Indian's Land," *Badger History* 1, no. 1 (October 1947): 18.
48. Ryan, "A Friendly Hello!," 16.
49. Ebenezer Williams Junior Historians, "Badger ABC," *Badger History* 1, no. 8 (May 1948): 18–19.
50. Mary Tuohy Ryan, "A Wisconsin Letter for You," *Badger History* 2, no. 3 (November 1948): 1. The initial announcement about Lily Rosa Minoka-Hill, "The Outstanding American Indian, 1947," appeared in *Badger History* 1, no. 4 (January 1948): 14.
51. Mary Burgener, "Thanksgiving: An Appreciation," *Badger History* 2, no. 3 (November 1948): 6.
52. Hester Wolfe, "I Saw the Last of the Foxes," *Badger History* 2, no. 3 (November 1948): 2.
53. Ibid.
54. Ibid.
55. Governor's Commission on Human Rights, "Policy Adopted November 7, 1945," *Badger History* 2, no. 3 (November 1948): 16–17.
56. "Indian Boys and Girls," *Badger History* 2, no. 3 (November 1948): 17.
57. Ibid.
58. Ibid.
59. Ibid.
60. Ibid.
61. Ibid.
62. Ibid.
63. Ibid.
64. Ibid.
65. Mary Tuohy Ryan, "A Wisconsin Letter for You," *Badger History* 3, no. 3 (November 1949): 1.
66. Georgia Kenyon, "Chief Black Hawk in Madison," *Badger History* 3, no. 3 (November 1949): 2–3; Mary Martin, "Black Hawk and Vernon County," *Badger History* 3, no. 3 (November 1949): 14–17; "Black Hawk: A Saukie Brave," *Badger History* 3, no. 3 (November 1949): inside back cover.
67. Ronald Everson, "The Spirit of Early Wisconsin," *Badger History* 3, no. 3 (November 1949): 17–18.
68. Alexius Baas, "The Legend of Monona," *Badger History* 3, no. 3 (November 1949): 4–7.
69. "Indian Boys and Girls Today," *Badger History* 3, no. 3 (November 1949): 3.

70. "A Man of Peace—Beloved by All," *Badger History* 3, no. 3 (November 1949): 8–9.

71. "Q and A About History," *Badger History* 8, no. 3 (November 1954): 5–6; "Menominee Indian Reservation," *Badger History* 8, no. 3 (November 1954): 12–13.

72. "Q and A About History," *Badger History* 8, no. 3 (November 1954): 5–6.

73. Ibid., 6.

74. Ibid.

75. Lac du Flambeau Public School, "Lac du Flambeau Centennial Year, 1854–1954," *Badger History* 8, no. 7 (March 1955): 5–8.

76. Ibid.

77. Ibid.

78. Ibid., 6.

79. Ibid.

80. Ibid.

81. Ibid., 7.

82. Ibid., 8.

83. "Historical Society Adds New Program," *Eau Claire Daily Telegram*, October 20, 1955.

84. Doris Platt, "A Wisconsin Letter for You," *Badger History* 9, no. 3 (November 1955): 1.

85. Ibid.

86. Warren Wittry, "Evidence of Ancient Man in Wisconsin," *Badger History* 9, no. 3 (November 1955): 4–5.

87. Roosevelt School, Grade 5, "It Did Happen Here," *Badger History* 9, no. 3 (November 1955): 22–24.

88. Ibid., 22.

89. Ibid., 22–24.

90. Julie Gunderson, "The Kidnapping of Two Young Wisconsin Pioneers," *Badger History* 9, no. 3 (November 1955): 24–26.

91. Terry Genrich, "The Wisconsin River," quoted in Doris Platt, "To Wisconsin Boys and Girls," *Badger History* 10, no. 3 (November 1956): 1.

92. Marlin Bence, "A Trip to Lac du Flambeau," *Badger History* 10, no. 3 (November 1956): 17.

93. Sally Sauer, "The Lost Partridge Child," *Badger History* 11, no. 3 (November 1957): 8–10.

94. Nelta Oviate Friend, "The Stockbridge," *Badger History* 11, no. 3 (November 1957): 14–16.

95. "The Indian Room—Oshkosh Public Museum," *Badger History* 11, no. 3 (November 1957): 26–27.

96. "A Famous Wisconsin Indian—Red Bird," *Badger History* 12, no. 3 (November 1958): 6–7; "Red Bird Surrenders," *Badger History* 12, no. 3 (November 1958): 7–8.

97. "Wisconsin Indians Today," *Badger History* 12, no. 3 (November 1958): 24.

98. Ibid.

99. Don N. Anderson, "Our Seventy-Second County—Menominee," *Badger History* 13, no. 3 (November 1959): 2.

100. Ibid., 3.

101. Ibid.

102. Thurman O. Fox, "For Your Wisconsin Notebook: Wisconsin Indian History," *Badger History* 13, no. 3 (November 1959): 17.

103. Ibid.

104. Ibid., 18.

105. St. Anthony School, "From Reservation to What?" *Badger History* 16, no. 9 (May 1963): 14.

106. Ibid.

107. Ibid., 15.

108. Ibid.

109. Ibid.

110. Dorothy G. McCarthy, "Chief Yellow Thunder . . . Man of Honor," *Badger History* 17, no. 4 (December 1963), 2.

111. Ibid.

112. Ibid.

Chapter 10

1. Howard Kanetzke, "Fun for Junior Historians," *Badger History* 18, no. 1 (September 1964): 1.

2. Douglas Gorgen, "The Old Man of the Dalles," *Badger History* 18, no. 1 (September 1964): 2–3; "Jim Micha, "The Making of Man Mound," *Badger History* 18, no. 1 (September 1964): 22–25.

3. Bureau of American Ethnology, *14th Annual Report of the Bureau of American Ethnology to the Secretary of the Smithsonian Institution, Part 1* (Washington, DC: Government Printing Office, 1896), 161–238; Frances Densmore, *Chippewa Customs* (St. Paul: Minnesota State Historical Society, 1929); Charles Robinson, "The Legend of Red Banks," *Badger History* 18, no. 1 (September 1964): 10–11. The article does not provide any additional information about the storyteller, but "O-kee-wah" may refer to Margaret Okeewah DeLanglade, daughter of Charles DeLanglade.

4. "A Word About Indians," *Badger History* 19, no. 1 (September 1965): 2.

5. Ibid.

6. Ibid., 3.

7. Ibid.

8. Lorraine Nelson, "The Copper Culture," *Badger History* 19, no. 1 (September 1965): 4–7; Howard Kanetzke, "Indian Effigy Mounds," *Badger History* 19, no. 1 (September 1965): 12–15; Howard Kanetzke, "Aztalan—Wisconsin's First City," *Badger History* 19, no. 1 (September 1965): 16–23.

9. Cathy May, "The Woodland Indians," *Badger History* 19, no. 1 (September 1965): 26–35.

10. Lorraine Nelson, "Black Hawk: A Play," *Badger History* 19, no. 1 (September 1965): 44.

11. Ibid.

12. Niki Smith, "Menominee County—A Modern Experiment," *Badger History* 19, no. 1 (September 1965): 46–51.

13. Ibid., 46.

14. Ibid., 48.

15. Ibid.

16. Ibid.

17. Ibid., 49.

18. Ibid., 50.

19. Ibid.

20. Ibid.

21. Ibid., 50–51.

22. Ibid., 51.

23. "Wisconsin Indians," *Badger History* 21, no. 2 (November 1967): 2.

24. Ibid.

25. Ibid., 3.

26. Ibid.

27. Ibid.

28. Ibid.

29. Elsie Patterson, "The Decorah Family," *Badger History* 21, no. 2 (November 1967): 4.

30. Ibid., 5.

31. Ibid.

32. Ibid., 8.

33. Ibid., 15.

34. Ibid.

35. Ibid.

36. "Words to Learn and Use," *Badger History* 21, no. 2 (November 1967): 16–17.

37. Howard Kanetzke, "Red Bird: Winnebago Chieftain," *Badger History* 21, no. 2 (November 1967): 30.

38. Ibid.

39. Ibid., 35–36.

40. Ibid., 36.

41. Howard Kanetzke, "Agent for the Winnebago," *Badger History* 21, no. 2 (November 1967): 43.

42. Elsie Patterson, "Yellow Thunder," *Badger History* 21, no. 2 (November 1967): 46.

43. Ibid., 49.

44. Ibid.

45. Ibid.

46. Ibid.

47. Ibid., 51.

48. Ibid.

49. Ibid.

50. Lydia Flanders, "Recollections of Yellow Thunder," *Badger History* 21, no. 2 (November 1967): 52–54.

51. Ibid., 54.

52. Robert L. Bennett, "Government and Indians," *Badger History* 21, no. 2 (November 1967): 58.

53. Ibid.

54. Ibid., 61.

55. Ibid., 62.

56. Donald N. Anderson, "Preserving Landmarks," *Badger History* 25, no. 2 (November 1970): 6, 7.

57. Margaret Van Hulst, "The Grignon House," *Badger History* 25, no. 2 (November 1970): 50.

58. Ibid.

59. Ibid.

60. "About Archaeologists and Anthropologists," *Badger History* 25, no. 3 (January 1972): 3.

61. Ibid., 6.

62. Ibid., 8.

63. Peggy Moore, "Indian Rockshelters" *Badger History* 25, no. 3 (January 1972): 12.

64. Jonathan Carver, "Manners and Customs of Indians," *Badger History* 25, no. 3 (January 1972): 16–29.

65. "Wild Rice, Then and Now," *Badger History* 25, no. 3 (January 1972): 57–59.

66. "The Fox Indians in Wisconsin: A Discovery Unit," *Badger History* 25, no. 3 (January 1972): 34.

67. "Indian Medicine," *Badger History* 26, no. 2 (November 1972): 5–9.

68. "William Hamilton: Wisconsin Mining Pioneer and Indian Fighter," *Badger History* 27, no. 1 (September 1973): 39–40.

69. "Puzzles," *Badger History* 28, no. 1 (September 1974): 3.

70. "Chart: Prehistoric Indians of Wisconsin," *Badger History* 28, no. 1 (September 1974): 4–5; "Prehistoric Indian Cultures," *Badger History* 28, no. 1 (September 1974): 6–9; "Woodland Indians," *Badger History* 28, no. 1 (September 1974): 38–49.

71. "The Copper Culture," *Badger History* 28, no. 1 (September 1974): 12–14; "Indian Effigy Mounds," *Badger History* 28, no. 1 (September 1974): 15–20; "Indian Quillwork," *Badger History* 28, no. 1 (September 1974): 50–51; "Birchbark Containers: Mocucks," *Badger History* 28, no. 1 (September 1974): 52–53; "Making a Birchbark Canoe," *Badger History* 28, no. 1 (September 1974): 54–63.

72. "Aztalan," *Badger History* 28, no. 1 (September 1974): 26–37; "Hopewell Indians," *Badger History* 28, no. 1 (September 1974): 21–23.

73. "Indian Effigy Mounds," *Badger History* 28, no. 1 (September 1974): 18.

74. "Hopewell Indians," *Badger History* 28, no. 1 (September 1974): 23.

75. "Aztalan," *Badger History* 28, no. 1 (September 1974): 35.

76. "Three Wisconsin Maps," *Badger History* 28, no. 4 (March 1975): 18–21.

77. "Changes in Indian Life After 1634," *Badger History* 29, no. 4 (March 1976): 2.

78. Ibid., 2–3.

79. Ibid., 3.

80. Ibid.

81. "The Decorah Family," *Badger History* 29, no. 4 (March 1976): 9, 10.

82. Ibid., 17.

83. "Red Bird and Winnebago Lead and Land," *Badger History* 29, no. 4 (March 1976): 18.

84. Ibid., 20–21.

85. Ibid., 24.

86. Howard Kanetzke, "Agent for the Winnebago," *Badger History* 29, no. 4 (March 1976): 31.

87. Ibid.

88. Anne Jordan, "Whose Land? A Story of Black Hawk," *Badger History* 29, no. 4 (March 1976): 38.

89. Ibid., 44.

90. Ibid.

91. Ibid.

92. "Indians Lose Lands in Wisconsin," *Badger History* 29, no. 4 (March 1976): 46–49.

93. "The Picture Gallery," *Badger History* 29, no. 4 (March 1976): 50–55.

94. "Oshkosh and Menominee Lands," *Badger History* 29, no. 4 (March 1976): 56.

95. Elsie Patterson, "Yellow Thunder," *Badger History* (November 1967): 46–51; "Wa Kun Cha Koo Kah, Yellow Thunder," *Badger History* 29, no. 4 (March 1976): 61–64.

96. "Wa Kun Cha Koo Kah, Yellow Thunder," *Badger History* 29, no. 4 (March 1976): 64.

97. Howard Kanetzke, "Soldiers of the Revolution," *Badger History* 29, no. 1 (September 1976): 38.

98. Ibid.

99. Ibid.

100. Ibid.

101. Jane A. Smith, "Place-Names in Wisconsin History," *Badger History* 29, no. 3 (January 1977): 60.

102. Ibid.

103. "Pioneers Come to Wisconsin," *Badger History* 32, no. 1 (September 1978): 2.

104. Gail Van Every, "Pioneering," *Badger History* 32, no. 1 (September 1978): 5.

105. Ibid., 9.

106. "Picture Gallery: Modern Wisconsin Women," *Badger History* 33, no. 1 (September 1979): 42.

Chapter 11

1. John Jarolimek, *Guidelines for Elementary Social Studies* (Washington, DC: Association for Supervision and Curriculum Development, 1967), 13; Jesus Garcia and Edward Buendia, "NCSS and Ethnic Diversity," in *NCSS in Retrospect*, ed. O. L. Davis Jr. (Washington, DC: National Council for Social Studies, 1996), 55; Kyle Roy Ward, *History in the Making: An Absorbing Look at How American History Has Changed in the Telling Over the Last 200 Years* (New York: New Press, 2006); Joseph Moreau, *Schoolbook Nation: Conflicts Over American History Textbooks from the Civil War to the Present* (Ann Arbor: University of Michigan Press, 2003); and Jonathan Zimmerman, *Whose America? Culture Wars in the Public Schools* (Cambridge, MA: Harvard University Press, 2002).

2. Wis. Stat. § 118.03(1)-(2) (1967).

3. Wis. Stat. ch. 40.50 (1953); Wis. Stat. § 118.03(2) (1967); A. Clark Hagensick, "Purging History in Wisconsin: Promises and Pitfalls," *Wisconsin Magazine of History* 67, no. 4 (Summer 1984): 284.

4. Richard F. Elmore and Susan H. Furhman, "Governing Curriculum: Changing Patterns in Policy, Politics, and Practice," in *The Governance of Curriculum: The 1994 ASCD Yearbook*, ed. Richard F. Elmore and Susan H. Fuhrman (Arlington, VA: Association for Supervision and Curriculum Development), 4.

5. Ward, *History in the Making*, xv.

6. Louis G. Romano and Nicholas P. Georgiady, *Exploring Wisconsin* (Chicago: Follett Educational Corporation, 1957); Louis G. Romano and Nicholas P. Georgiady, *Exploring Wisconsin* (Chicago: Follett Educational Corporation, 1967); Louis G. Romano and Nicholas P. Georgiady, *Exploring Wisconsin* (Chicago: Follett Educational Corporation, 1970); Louis G. Romano and Nicholas P. Georgiady, *Exploring Our State, Wisconsin* (Chicago: Follett Publishing Co., 1977).

7. Romano and Georgiady, *Exploring Wisconsin*, 1957, i.

8. Ibid., 4.

9. Ibid., 6.

10. Ibid.

11. Ibid.

12. Ibid., 8–11.
13. Ibid., 9.
14. Ibid., 8.
15. Ibid., 9.
16. Ibid., 8.
17. Ibid., 9.
18. Ibid.
19. Ibid.
20. Ibid., 10.
21. Ibid.
22. Ibid.
23. Ibid., 11.
24. Ibid., 12.
25. Ibid.
26. Ibid.
27. Ibid.
28. Ibid.
29. Ibid., 13.
30. Ibid.
31. Ibid.
32. Ibid., 14.
33. Ibid., 13.
34. Ibid., 14.
35. Ibid.
36. Ibid.
37. See, for example, Nancy Oestreich Lurie and Patrick J. Jung, *The Nicolet Corrigenda: New France Revisited* (Long Grove, IL: Waveland Press, 2009).
38. Romano and Georgiady, *Exploring Wisconsin*, 1957, 15.
39. Ibid.
40. Ibid.
41. Ibid., 17.
42. Ibid., 19.
43. Ibid., 23–24.
44. Ibid., 25.
45. Ibid., 26.
46. Ibid., 29.
47. Ibid.
48. Ibid.
49. Ibid., 30.
50. Ibid.
51. Ibid.
52. Ibid.
53. Ibid., 33–34.
54. Ibid., 74.
55. Ibid., 99.
56. Ibid.
57. Ibid.
58. Ibid., 100.
59. Ibid.
60. Ibid., 101.
61. Ibid.
62. Ibid., 102.

63. Ibid., 111.
64. Ibid., 112.
65. Ibid., 115.
66. Ibid., 118.
67. Ibid., 118–120.
68. Ibid., 116.
69. Ibid., 117.
70. Ibid.
71. Ibid., 123–124.
72. Ibid., 123.
73. Ibid.
74. Ibid.
75. Romano and Georgiady, *Exploring Wisconsin*, 1967.
76. Ibid., 14.
77. Ibid., 16–19.
78. Ibid., 37.
79. Ibid. 38.
80. Ibid., 39.
81. Ibid.
82. Ibid.
83. Ibid.
84. Ibid., 40.
85. Ibid.
86. Ibid., 47.
87. Ibid.
88. Ibid., 48.
89. Ibid., 51.
90. Ibid.
91. Ibid.
92. Ibid., 52.
93. Ibid., 103.
94. Ibid., 124.
95. Ibid., 125.
96. Ibid., 126.
97. Ibid., 135.
98. Ibid., 136.
99. Ibid., 138.
100. Ibid., 139.
101. Ibid.
102. Ibid., 139.
103. Ibid., 143.
104. Ibid.
105. Ibid., 157.
106. Several of the photographs and illustrations have been replaced to reflect the changing times. Some photographs of cargo ships (99) and factories (100) have been updated to reflect changing technology. Others merely offer a different view, such as the updated drawing of the Milwaukee Civic Center (112), the photo of Bascom Hall on the University of Wisconsin–Madison campus (122), and the portrait of the Wisconsin Supreme Court Justices, which replaces a photo of court in session (151). Some illustrations and photographs have been changed to incorporate some African Americans (101) in drawings of football teams and factory workers, in a photograph of the American Motors factory in Kenosha (108), and of a classroom scene where students are running for student government (147).

107. Romano and Georgiady, *Exploring Wisconsin*, 1967, 111.
108. Romano and Georgiady, *Exploring Our State, Wisconsin*, 4–31.
109. Ibid., 26–27.
110. Ibid., 32–53.
111. Ibid., 37.
112. Ibid.
113. Ibid., 38–39.
114. Ibid., 40.
115. Ibid., 41. Other figures featured in this way include Peter Pond (50), Cordelia Harvey (66), Yellow Thunder (70), Ansel Clark (87), John Muir (91), Kate Pelham Newcomb (109), Edward Allis (119), Edna Ferber (138), Margarethe and Carl Schurz (141), Ada James (152), and Belle Case La Follette (167).
116. Ibid., 42.
117. Ibid., 43.
118. Ibid., 44.
119. Ibid., 54–67.
120. Ibid., 62.
121. Ibid.
122. Ibid., 62–63.
123. Ibid., 63.
124. Ibid., 62.
125. Ibid., 68–79.
126. Ibid., 69.
127. Ibid.
128. Ibid.
129. Since the 1780s, the Stockbridge had been living among the Oneidas in New York, and while the Oneidas did re-establish their communities near Green Bay, the Stockbridge did so initially near Kaukauna before another forcible removal further south to Lake Winnebago. By the early nineteenth century, the Munsee were allied with the Stockbridge, and the Stockbridge-Munsee had lands adjacent to the Brothertown near Calumet by the late 1820s. See James W. Oberly, *A Nation of Statesmen: The Political Culture of the Stockbridge-Munsee Mohicans, 1815–1972* (Norman: University of Oklahoma Press, 2005), and Patty Loew, *Indian Nations of Wisconsin: Histories of Endurance and Renewal*, 2nd ed. (Madison: Historical Society Press, 2013).
130. Romano and Georgiady, *Exploring Our State, Wisconsin*, 69.
131. Ibid.
132. Ibid.
133. Ibid.
134. Ibid., 70.
135. Ibid.
136. Ibid.
137. Ibid.
138. Ibid.
139. Ibid., 69.
140. Ibid., 70.
141. Ibid., 72–75.
142. Ibid., 77.
143. Ibid., 78.
144. Ibid., 129.
145. Ibid., 129–133.
146. Ibid., 150–161.
147. Ibid., 154.
148. Ibid., 164.

Chapter 12

1. American Indian Language and Culture Education Board report (1985), Wisconsin Department of Public Instruction American Indian Studies Program Files, in possession of the author.

2. David Wallace Adams, *Education for Extinction: American Indians and the Boarding School Experience, 1875–1928* (Lawrence: University Press of Kansas, 1995), 336; Hazel W. Hertzberg, *The Search for an American Indian Identity: Modern Pan-Indian Movements* (Syracuse: Syracuse University Press, 1971), 36–37, 73–74. For more information on the development of a sense of "Indianness" by boarding school students, see Michael C. Coleman, *American Indian Children at School, 1850–1930* (Jackson: University Press of Mississippi, 1993).

3. Society of American Indians, *Papers Read Before the First Annual Conference of the American Indian Association, Ohio State University, Columbus, OH, October 12 to 15, 1911* (Columbus, OH: Society of American Indians, 1911), 71–72.

4. Ibid., 99.

5. Ibid., 108.

6. Ibid., 105.

7. Ibid., 81; Thelma Cornelius McLester, "Oneida Women Leaders," in *The Oneida Indian Experience: Two Perspectives*, ed. Jack Campisi and Laurence Hauptman (Syracuse: Syracuse University Press, 1988), 110.

8. McLester, "Oneida Women Leaders," 109; Society of American Indians, *Papers Read Before the First Annual Conference*, 81.

9. McLester, "Oneida Women Leaders," 110; Society of American Indians, *Papers Read Before the First Annual Conference*, 81. It is interesting that Parker, the editor of the proceedings, noted the applause received by both Chase and Cornelius, but does not indicate similar approval of his own paper nor the words of other respondents.

10. Hertzberg, *Search for an American Indian Identity*, 36–37.

11. See, for example, Hertzberg, *Search for an American Indian Identity*; Bruce E. Johansen and Barry M. Pritzker, eds., "Society of American Indians," *Encyclopedia of American Indian History* (Santa Barbara, CA: ABC-CLIO, 2008); John W. Larner, "Society of American Indians," *Native America in the Twentieth Century: An Encyclopedia*, ed. Mary B. Davis, (New York: Garland, 1994); and Jeffery R. Hanson, "Ethnicity and the Looking Glass: The Dialectics of National Indian Identity," *American Indian Quarterly* 21 (Spring 1997): 195–209. *American Indian Quarterly* and *Studies in American Indian Literatures* published a special joint issue focused on Society of American Indians. See 37, no. 3, "The Society of American Indians and Its Legacies: A Special Combined Issue of SAIL and AIQ" (Summer 2013).

12. Jonathan Zimmerman. *Whose America? Culture Wars in the Public Schools* (Cambridge: Harvard University Press, 2002), 21.

13. W. H. Thompson, "Are We Victims of British Propaganda? I—Patriots and Propagandists," *Forum* 79 (April 1928): 509, quoted in Zimmerman, *Whose America?*, 21.

14. Zimmerman, *Whose America?*, 22–25.

15. Ibid., 23.

16. Janusz Mucha, "From Prairie to the City: Transformation of Chicago's American Indian Community," *Urban Anthropology* 12, no. 3/4 (Fall Winter 1983): 343.

17. Ibid., 344.

18. "Thompson Will Get Indians' Complaint: In War Paint They Will Go to Tell Mayor of Chicago of Propaganda Against Them," *New York Times*, November 7, 1927.

19. Rupert Costo and Jeannette Henry, *Textbooks and the American Indian* (San Francisco: The Indian Historian Press, 1970), 2.

20. Ibid.

21. Ibid., 2–3.

22. Ibid., 3.

23. Ibid. The statement lists no tribal affiliation for Peters, but provides one for all other signatories.

24. Ibid., 5.

25. Ibid.

26. Ibid., 6; Margaret Connell Szasz, *Education and the American Indian: The Road to Self-Determination Since 1928*, 3rd ed. (Albuquerque: University of New Mexico Press, 1999), 158–159.

27. Costo and Henry, *Textbooks and the American Indian*, 6–7.

28. Ibid., 7.

29. Ibid., 7–8. Henry explains that opposition from "descendants of gold miners" and the Catholic Church led the State Curriculum Commission to table their recommendations before assigning them for "further consideration" to the Statewide Social Sciences Study Committee. By 1970, the commission had yet to act on them.

30. Ibid., 8. Henry briefly describes an incident in Minnesota where "a group of Indian people" successfully challenged the use of a textbook "which degraded the Native people," despite opposition from the American Civil Liberties Union who "resisted the removal of the book on grounds of 'freedom of speech.'"

31. Ibid., 9.

32. Ibid.; Ian Chambers, "The History of Native American Studies at the University of California Riverside," *Indigenous Nations Studies Journal* 2, no. 2 (Fall 2001): 83.

33. Costo and Henry, *Textbooks and the American Indian*, 11; Tony R. Sanchez, "The Depiction of Native Americans in Recent (1991–2004) Secondary American History Textbooks: How Far Have We Come?" *Equity and Excellence in Education* 40, no. 4 (2007): 312.

34. Costo and Henry, *Textbooks and the American Indian*, 11; Sanchez, "The Depiction of Native Americans," 312.

35. Szasz, *Education and the American Indian*, 159; Sanchez, "The Depiction of Native Americans," 312. See also Naomi Caldwell-Wood and Lisa Mitten, "I is not for Indian: The Portrayal of Native Americans in Books for Young People," *Multicultural Review* 1, no.2 (1990): 26–33; Frances Fitzgerald, *America Revised* (Boston, MA: Atlantic Monthly Press/Little Brown, 1979); James Loewen, *Lies My Teacher Told Me* (New York: New York Press, 1995); Tony Sanchez, "Evaluating Native American Trade Books for Accuracy," *TELLing Stories: Theory, Practice, Interviews, and Reviews* 1, no.2 (1997): 4–10; Tony Sanchez, "'Dangerous Indians': Evaluating the Depiction of Native Americans in Selected Trade Books," *Urban Education* 36, no.3 (2001): 400–426; Beverly Slapin, Doris Seale, and Rosemary Gonzales, *How to Tell the Difference: A Guide to Evaluating Children's Books for Anti-Indian Bias* (Berkeley, CA: Oyate, 1996); Annalee Good, "Framing American Indians as the 'First Americans': Using Critical Multiculturalism to Trouble the Normative American Story," *Social Studies Research and Practice* 4, no. 2 (July 2009): 49–66; Ronald A. Jetty, *They're Supposed to Be Sovereign Nations: Hegemony Constructions of Contemporary American Indian Issues in Current United States History Textbooks* (PhD diss., University of Wisconsin, Madison, 1998); G. Patrick O'Neill, "The North American Indian in Contemporary History and Social Studies Textbooks," *Journal of American Indian Education* 26, no. 3 (May 1987): 22–28.

36. Katherine Shanley, "Writing Indian: American Indian Literature and the Future of Native American Studies," in *Studying Native America: Problems and Prospects of Native American Studies*, ed. Russell Thornton (Madison: University of Wisconsin Press, 1998), 137.

37. Lawanna Trout, "Native American History," in *Teaching American History: New Directions*, ed. Matthew T. Downey (Washington, DC: National Council for Social Studies, 1982), 96.

38. Ibid., 103.

39. Ibid.

40. Ibid., 104.

41. Ibid.

42. Ibid., 93.

43. Ibid.

44. Szasz, *Education and the American Indian*, 159.

Chapter 13

1. Elmer L. Davids Sr., "Our People—Past, Present and Future: The Stockbridge–Munsee Band of Mohican Indians," address delivered at the American Indian Chicago Conference, June 1961, Arvid E. Miller Historical Library/Museum, Bowler, Wisconsin.

2. Shelley Oxley, *The Stockbridge-Munsee Tribe: A History of the Mahican and the Munsee Indians of Wisconsin* (Rhinelander, WI: Rhinelander School District, 1981); Wisconsin Woodland Indian Project, *The History of the Hochungra People (Winnebago Tribe) of Wisconsin* (Rhinelander, WI: Rhinelander School District, 1981); Shelley Oxley, *Keepers of the Fire: The History of the Potawatomie Indians of Wisconsin* (Rhinelander, WI: Rhinelander School District, 1981); Shelley Oxley, *The History of the Oneida Indians* (Rhinelander, WI: Rhinelander School District, 1981); Shelley Oxley and Ernie St. Germaine, *The Anishinabe: An Overview Unit of the History and Background of the Wisconsin Ojibway Indian Tribe* (Rhinelander, WI: Rhinelander School District, 1981); Shelley Oxley, *The Anishinabe: Bad River; A Unit on the History of the Bad River Band of Lake Superior Ojibway Indians* (Rhinelander, WI: Rhinelander School District, 1981); Shelley Oxley, *The Anishinabe: Lac Courte Oreilles; A Unit on the History of the Lac Courte Oreilles Band of Lake Superior Ojibway Indians* (Rhinelander, WI: Rhinelander School District, 1981); Ernest St. Germaine, *The Anishinabe: Lac du Flambeau; A Unit on the History of the Lac du Flambeau Band of Lake Superior Ojibway Indians* (Rhinelander, WI: Rhinelander School District, 1981); Shelley Oxley, *The Anishinabe: Mole Lake; A Unit on the History of the Mole Lake Band of Lake Superior Ojibway Indians* (Rhinelander, WI: Rhinelander School District, 1981); Shelley Oxley, *The Anishinabe: Red Cliff; A Unit on the History of the Red Cliff Band of Lake Superior Ojibway Indians* (Rhinelander, WI: Rhinelander School District, 1981); Shelley Oxley, *The Anishinabe: St. Croix; A Unit on the History of the St. Croix Band of Lake Superior Ojibway Indians* (Rhinelander, WI: Rhinelander School District, 1981); Shelley Oxley, *The History of the Brotherton Indians* (Rhinelander, WI: Rhinelander School District, 1981).

3. Wisconsin Woodland Indian Project, *American Indian Dance Costumes* (Rhinelander, WI: Rhinelander School District, 1982); Robin Carufel, *Winnebago Applique* (Rhinelander, WI: Rhinelander School District, 1982); Wisconsin Woodland Indian Project, *Corn: The Gift of the American Indian People* (Rhinelander, WI: Rhinelander School District, 1982); Wisconsin Woodland Indian Project, *American Indian Foods* (Rhinelander, WI: Rhinelander School District, 1982); Wisconsin Woodland Indian Project, *Porcupine Quillwork on Birchbark* (Rhinelander, WI: Rhinelander School District, 1982); Wisconsin Woodland Indian Project, *Indian Dwellings* (Rhinelander, WI: Rhinelander School District, 1982); Wisconsin Woodland Indian Project, *Music of the Woodland Indians* (Rhinelander, WI: Rhinelander School District, 1982); Wisconsin Woodland Indians Project, *Methods of Travel and Migration Among the American Indians* (Rhinelander, WI: Rhinelander School District, 1982); Wisconsin Woodland Indians Project, *Names and Maps Tell a Story of Wisconsin* (Rhinelander, WI: Rhinelander School District, 1982); Wisconsin Woodland Indians Project, *Beadwork: Beadwork Design of American Indians* (Rhinelander, WI: Rhinelander School District, 1982); Wisconsin Woodland Indians Project, *What Is an Indian?* (Rhinelander, WI: Rhinelander School District, 1982); Wisconsin Woodland Indians Project, *The Web of the Creator: Basketry* (Rhinelander, WI: Rhinelander School District, 1982); Wisconsin Woodland Indians Project, *The Uses of Birchbark* (Rhinelander, WI: Rhinelander School District, 1982); Wisconsin Woodland Indians Project, *Eagles* (Rhinelander, WI: Rhinelander School District, 1982); Wisconsin Woodland Indians Project, *The Moccasin Game* (Rhinelander, WI: Rhinelander School District, 1982); Wisconsin Woodland Indians Project, *Bijpindjiganaong: The Bone Game* (Rhinelander, WI: Rhinelander School District, 1982); Wisconsin Woodland Indians Project, *Harvesting Manomin* (Rhinelander, WI: Rhinelander School District, 1982).

4. American Indian Language and Culture Education Board (AILCEB), *American Indian Education in Wisconsin*, Bulletin No. 5913. (Madison: Wisconsin Department of Public Instruction, 1984), 1.

5. AILCEB, *American Indian Education in Wisconsin*, 1; American Indian Language and Culture Education Board report (1981), Wisconsin Department of Public Instruction, American Indian Studies Program Files (hereafter DPI AIS Files), in possession of the author.

6. The law was enacted as Chapter 346 and later renumbered as Wis. Stat. § 115, Sub. IV (1979); AILCEB, *American Indian Language and Culture Education Board*, 3.

7. AILCEB, *American Indian Language and Culture Education Board*, 1, 3; AILCEB, *American Indian Education in Wisconsin*, 1.

8. AILCEB, *American Indian Education in Wisconsin*, 1.

9. Wis. Stat. § 115; AILCEB, *American Indian Language and Culture Education Board*, 2.

10. AILCEB, *American Indian Language and Culture Education Board*, 2.

11. Wis. Stat. § 13.83 (3) (1982). The American Indian Study Committee had its origins in the Menominee Indian Study Committee, which operated from 1957 to 1974 to address issues related to Menominee termination. The Native American Study Committee, which operated from 1976 to 1980, was its successor. The American Indian Study Committee operated from 1982 to 2000, before being succeeded by the Special Committee on State-Tribal Relations.

12. American Indian Study Committee, Wisconsin Legislative Council, *Summary of Proceedings*, December 13, 1983, Madison, WI, 11–12. Metz (D-Omro) represented the Ninetieth Assembly District from 1975 to 1986. She later helped to found the treaty rights advocacy organization Honor Our Neighbors Origins and Rights (HONOR) and served as its first executive director.

13. American Indian Study Committee, *Summary of Proceedings*, Dec. 13, 1983, 12.

14. American Indian Study Committee, Wisconsin Legislative Council, *Summary of Proceedings*, July 20, 1984, Lac Courte Oreilles Reservation, Hayward, WI, 3–4.

15. Ibid., 4.

16. Ibid., 4–5.

17. Ibid., 6.

18. Ibid.

19. Ibid., 6–7.

20. Ibid., 7.

21. Ibid.

22. Ibid. Emphasis in original.

23. Ibid.

24. AILCEB, *American Indian Education in Wisconsin*, 4.

25. Ibid.

26. Ibid.

27. Wis. Admin. Code PI 3.01 (37) (1980); Wis. Admin. Code PI 3.07(7)(a) 13-15 (1980).

28. AILCEB, *American Indian Education in Wisconsin*, 57.

29. Ibid., 63.

30. Lac Courte Oreilles Tribal Governing Board and Ad Hoc Commission on Racism in Wisconsin, *Wisconsin's Educational Imperative: Observations and Recommendations of the Ad Hoc Commission on Racism: Indian-White Relations* (Hayward, WI: Lac Courte Oreilles Tribal Governing Board and Ad Hoc Commission on Racism in Wisconsin, 1984), 12.

31. Ibid.

32. Ibid., 13.

33. Ibid.

34. Ibid., 16.

35. Ibid., 17.

36. Ibid., 13.

37. AILCEB, *Report on the Status of Indian Education in the State of Wisconsin* (Madison, WI: 1985), 1.

38. Ibid., 2.

39. Ibid.

40. Ibid.

41. Ibid., 3.

42. Ibid.

43. Ibid., 2.

44. Ibid., 3.

45. Ibid., 4.

46. Ibid.

47. Ibid.

48. AILCEB, *The 1985–1987 Biennial Report on the Status of Indian Education in the State of Wisconsin* (Madison, WI: 1988), 1.

49. American Indian Study Committee, *Summary of Proceedings*, Dec. 11, 1990, 5.

50. AILCEB, *The 1985–1987 Biennial Report*, 4.

51. Ibid., 11.

52. Alan J. Caldwell, Presentation Before the Wisconsin American Indian Study Committee, State Capitol, Feb. 1, 1988, DPI AIS Program Files, in possession of the author.

53. Ibid., 1–2.

54. Ibid., 2.

55. Ibid.

56. Ibid.

57. Ibid., 3–4.

58. Ibid., 3.

59. Ibid.

60. American Indian Study Committee, Wisconsin Legislative Council,*Summary of Proceedings*, February 29, 1988, Oneida Reservation, Oneida, WI, 7.

61. Ibid.

62. Ibid.

63. Ibid.

64. Ibid.

65. Jo Deen B. Lowe, state/tribal liaison, to GLITC Board of Directors and Other Interested Parties, memo, June 12, 1989, 1, DPI AIS Program Files, in possession of the author.

66. Ibid.

67. Ibid.

68. Ibid.

69. Ibid., 2.

70. Wisconsin State Legislature, Legislative Reference Bureau, Assembly Amendment 1 to Senate Bill 31. LRBb1646/2. Page 24, line 139.

71. Steve Schultze, "Budget Calls for Classes on Indians," *Milwaukee Journal*, June 28, 1989.

72. Ibid.

73. Ibid.

74. Wisconsin State Legislature, Legislative Reference Bureau, Conference Amendment 1 to Assembly Amendment to 1989 Senate Bill 31. LRBb1821/2. Pages 2–3, lines 34–36.

75. Wis. Stat. § 115.28(17)(d) (1989).

76. Ibid.

77. Wis. Stat. § 118.19(8) (1989).

78. Wis. Stat. § 121.02(1)(h) (1989).

79. Ibid.

80. "Alan Caldwell," in D. C. Everest Area Schools, *Native Nations of Wisconsin: Sharing Their History, Culture, and Traditions* (Weston, WI: D. C. Everest Area Schools Publications, 2009), 102.

Chapter 14

1. American Indian Study Committee, Wisconsin Legislative Council, *Summary of Proceedings*, August 18, 1989. Bad River Tribal Building, Odanah, WI, 5.

2. Ibid., 6.

3. Ibid.

4. Ibid.

5. Ibid.

6. Ibid.

7. Ibid.

8. Ibid., 7.

9. Ibid.

10. Ibid.

11. Ibid.

12. Ibid., 8, 16.

13. Ibid., 10–11.

14. Ibid., 11.

15. Ibid., 15.

16. Ibid.

17. Ibid., 16.

18. Ken De Foe, First American Prevention Center, testimony to American Indian Study Committee, Friday, August 18, 1989, Odanah, WI. Courtesy of David Lovell, Legislative Council Staff.

19. Ibid.

20. Ibid.

21. Ibid.

22. American Indian Study Committee, *Summary of Proceedings*, Aug. 18, 1989, 6.

23. Ibid., 16–17.

24. American Indian Study Committee, Wisconsin Legislative Council, *Summary of Proceedings*, December 12, 1989, Madison, WI, 6–7.

25. Ibid., 9.

26. Ibid., 7.

27. Ibid.

28. Ibid.

29. Ibid., 8.

30. Ibid., 9.

31. Ibid.

32. Ibid., 9–10.

33. Larry Nesper, *The Walleye War: The Struggle for Ojibwe Spearfishing and Treaty Rights* (Lincoln: University of Nebraska Press, 1999), xiii.

34. American Indian Language and Culture Education Board (AILCEB), *The 1987–1989 Biennial Report on the Status of Indian Education in the State of Wisconsin* (Madison, WI: AILCEB, 1990), 1.

35. Ibid.

36. Ibid., 3.

37. Ibid., 1.

38. Ibid., 3.

39. Ibid., 1.

40. Ibid., 3.

41. Ibid., 4.

42. Ibid., 5.

43. Ibid., 5–6.

44. Ibid., 5.

45. Wisconsin Department of Public Instruction (DPI), "Appendix E: The Status of Indian Education in the State of Wisconsin," in *The 1989–1991 Biennial Report* (Madison, WI: DPI, 1992), 64.

46. Ibid.

47. Ibid., 63.

48. Ibid.

49. Ibid.

50. Ibid.

51. Ibid., 75.

52. Ibid.

53. Ibid.

54. American Indian Study Committee, *Summary of Proceedings*, December 11, 1990, Madison, WI, 4, 5.

55. Ibid., 4.

56. Ibid.

57. Shelley Hadley and David Trechter, *Wisconsin Education Act 31 2014 Administrator and Teacher Survey*, Survey Center Research Report 2014/6 (River Falls, WI: University of Wisconsin River Falls, 2014) at http://www.wiea.org/uploads/files/Act-31-Survey-Executive-Summary-Final-June-2014.pdf.

Conclusion

1. Ronald N. Satz, *Chippewa Treaty Rights: The Reserved Rights of Wisconsin's Chippewa Indians in Historical Perspective* (Madison, WI: Wisconsin Academy of Sciences, Arts and Letters, 1991), xv.

2. Ibid., xv.

3. Denise Kohout, email messages to author, August 8 and August 10, 2017; Connie Ellingson, email message to author, August 10, 2017.

4. Frances de Usabel and Jane A. Roeber, *American Indian Resource Manual for Public Libraries*, Bulletin No. 92429 (Madison: Wisconsin Department of Public Instruction, 1992).

5. Wis. Stat. §115.28(17)(d) (1990); Ronald N. Satz, Anthony G. Gulig, and Richard D. St. Germaine, *Classroom Activities on Chippewa Treaty Rights*, Bulletin No. 92150 (Madison: Wisconsin Department of Public Instruction, 1991).

6. Ronald N. Satz, *Classroom Activities on Wisconsin Indian Treaties and Tribal Sovereignty*, Bulletin No. 96156 (Madison: Wisconsin Department of Public Instruction, 1996).

7. DPI American Indian Studies Program Files, 1989–1991; Alan J. Caldwell and J P Leary, "Looking Back at 20 Years of Act 31," presentation at National Indian Education Association Annual Convention, Milwaukee, WI, October 23, 2009.

8. Wis. Stat. § 121.02(1)(h) (1990).

9. Wisconsin Media Lab, "ENGAGE! State.Tribal.Local.Government," http://wimedialab.org/series/engage-state-tribal-local-government-series; Patty Loew, *Native People of Wisconsin*, 2nd ed. (Madison: Wisconsin Historical Society Press, 2015); Bobbie Malone and Kori Oberle, *Wisconsin: Our State, Our Story*, 2nd ed. (Madison: Wisconsin Historical Society Press, 2016).

10. "WisconsinAct31.org in PK–16 Education," University of Wisconsin–Madison School of Education, www.wisconsinact31.org.

11. Wis. Stat. § 118.19(8) (1990).

12. Wis. Stat. § 118.01(c)7-8 (1990).

13. See J P Leary, "The American Indian Studies Summer Institute: Professional Development for Culturally Responsive Teaching and Learning," in *Narrowing the Achievement Gap for Native American Students: Paying the Educational Debt*, ed. Peggy McCardle and Virginia Berninger, (New York: Routledge, 2015), 79–89.

14. Wisconsin Department of Public Instruction, "Wisconsin Education Standards (20 Standards)," 1989, https://dpi.wi.gov/sites/default/files/imce/cal/pdf/wi-edstds.pdf; Wis. Stat. § 121.02(1) (a)-(t) (1990).

15. Wis. Stat. § 121.02(1)(h) (1990); Wis. Admin. Code PI 8.01(2)(h)3 (1990); Wis. Stat. § 121.02(1)(L) (1990); Wis. Admin. Code PI 8.02(2)(L) (1990).

16. Wis. Admin. Code PI 8 (1994), https://docs.legis.wisconsin.gov/code/register/1994/466b/insert/pi8.pdf.

17. Sue Grady, email message to author, August 2, 2017; "DPI Changes Would Cut 100 Jobs," *Wisconsin State Journal*, February 13, 1995.

18. Wisconsin Department of Public Instruction, "History—Wisconsin's Model Academic Standards for Social Studies," https://dpi.wi.gov/social-studies/standards/history.

19. Patricia Velde Peterson, "What is Measured is Treasured: The Impact of the No Child Left Behind Law on Nonassessed Subjects," *Clearing House* 80, no. 6 (July–August 2007): 290; Alfie Kohn,

"Testing Emphasis Crowds Out Teaching of Core Subjects" *USA Today*, September 4, 2001; J P Leary, "No Child Left Behind, High Stakes Testing, and Implications for American Indian Studies in Wisconsin," presentation at the Wisconsin Indian Education Association Annual Conference, Wisconsin Dells, WI, April 2, 2004. See also Gahan Bailey, Edward L. Shaw, Jr., and Donna Hollifield, "The Devaluation of Social Studies in the Elementary Grades," *Journal of Social Studies Research* 30, no. 2 (2006): 18–29; M. Gail Jones, Brett D. Jones, and Belinda Hardin, "The Impact of High Stakes Testing of Teachers and Students in North Carolina," *Phi Delta Kappan* 81, no. 3 (November 1999): 199–203; and Alfie Kohn, "Emphasis on Testing Leads to Sacrifices in Other Areas" *USA Today*, August 21, 2001.

20. Shelley Hadley and David Trechter, "Wisconsin Education Act 31: 2014 Teacher and Administrator Survey Report," June 2014, http://www.wiea.org/uploads/files/Act-31-Survey-Executive-Summary-Final-June-2014.pdf, 3.

21. Ibid., 3–4.

22. Carol Juneau and Denise Juneau, "Indian Education for All: Montana's Constitution at Work in Our Schools," *Montana Law Review* 72, no. 11 (Winter 2011): 114.

23. Ibid., 118.

24. Montana Office of Public Instruction, *Indian Education for All*, http://opi.mt.gov/programs/indianed/IEFA.html#gpm1_1; Montana Office of Public Instruction, "Indian Education Summit—A Call to Action," October 2004, http://www.opi.mt.gov/pdf/indianed/IESummit/indianeducationforall.pdf; Bobby Ann Starnes, "Montana's Indian Education for All: Toward an Education Worthy of American Ideals," *Phi Delta Kappan*, 88, no. 1 (2006): 186. For detailed discussions on Indian Education for All, see *Phi Delta Kappan*, 88, no. 3 (Nov. 2006).

25. Denise Juneau and Mandy Smoker Broaddus, "And Still the Waters Flow: The Legacy of Indian Education in Montana," *Phi Delta Kappan*, 88, no. 3 (Nov. 2006): 196; Juneau and Juneau, "Indian Education for All," 120.

ACKNOWLEDGEMENTS

As I complete this project, I am reminded that no one accomplishes such an undertaking on their own. I am profoundly grateful to those who shaped me as a person, taught me as a student, and helped me to develop as a scholar. This project grew out of my work at the Wisconsin Department of Public Instruction. When the time came, it became my dissertation in the Educational Policy Studies department at the University of Wisconsin–Madison. With the encouragement of colleagues and students, it has grown beyond that initial inquiry to become *The Story of Act 31*.

I am grateful to my former colleagues at DPI, particularly the members of the Equity Mission Team and Content and Learning Team. Barbara A. Bitters, DPI's "unofficial archivist," shared files from her time as section chief of the Bureau of Exceptional Education Programs and as director of the Equity Mission Team that were essential for the later portions of this book. The late Barbara Thomas, AILCEB staff member, was a valued colleague at DPI, and our long ago discussions echoed throughout the writing process. Sue Grady, former director of the Content and Learning Team and former special assistant to the superintendent, provided important guidance about policy matters, fielded complex questions on short notice and with quick turnaround, and provided encouragement throughout the process. Rebecca Vail, director of the Content and Learning Team, and Denise Kohout, director of human resources at DPI, provided valuable guidance in tracking down information on staff positions and budget allocations. I am especially grateful to have worked with Connie Ellingson, the only DPI staff member to have worked with all of the American Indian Studies consultants. She is the institutional memory of the program, a thoughtful advisor, capable assistant, and good friend. Social studies consultant Kris McDaniel, and my successor, David O'Connor, ably carry on this work and have gracefully fielded my "quick questions."

This project began as my dissertation in the Educational Policy Studies program at UW–Madison. My dissertation advisor, William J. Reese, capably and compassionately guided me through that process. He, along with his fellow historians of education, Michael Fultz and Adam R. Nelson, provided deep insights, cautions, and sound ideas for developing that manuscript into this book. My committee also included two scholars whose research greatly informs my own, Patty Loew and Larry Nesper. They generously shared sources, stories, leads, questions, and words of encouragement. Other faculty members at UW–Madison, Michael W. Apple, Patricia Burch, Carl Grant, and Michael Olneck, also profoundly shaped my thinking about education policy and the politics of teaching and learning. I was also fortunate to work with Doug Kiel, Libby Tronnes, and the late Skott Vigil, doctoral students in history who comprised my "Dissertators Anonymous" group.

My colleagues and students at the University of Wisconsin–Green Bay have actively contributed to this project as well. In First Nations Studies, I want to acknowledge Lisa Poupart, Forrest Brooks, Anne Gretz, Portia Skenandore-Wheelock, and Kayu Brooks. My predecessor at UWGB, Rosemary Christensen, was also very generous in sharing her time, expertise, and experience working on education policy. I also want to thank the elders-in-residence in the Education Center for First Nations Studies, Selma Buckwheat, Shirley Barber, Carol Cornelius, Napos, Richie Plass, Bernadine Vigue, Richard Ackley, and Susan Daniels, for their commitment to community, dedication to our shared work, sense of humor, and support for me as a teacher, scholar, and human being. This book would not be what it is without their willingness to talk things through, raise questions, share teachings, and otherwise visit over coffee and tea.

I am fortunate to work with supportive colleagues at UWGB. My faculty mentor, David Voelker, along with colleague Lisa Poupart, read every word of every draft of my dissertation. David's critical feedback, encouragement, and ongoing willingness to discuss this project and broader issues of historical research and writing have greatly improved the revised manuscript. During the revision process, I received valuable feedback on chapter drafts from colleagues Jon Shelton, Alison Staudinger, and Kim Reilly. My colleagues in education, particularly Tim Kaufman and Christin DePouw, helped me to keep the narrative grounded and alerted me to new scholarship in the field. Research librarian Bekky Vrabel was instrumental in my newspaper research and was always ready to help track down additional sources.

My students at UWGB have been crucial to this project. My spring 2012 First Nations and Education Policy students Kate Bennett, Melissa Brooke, Rob Fish, Donald Keeble, Todd Klakowicz, Chris Lamont, Kevin Maulson, Ann Miller, and Jackie Wawiorka shared the joy and pain of this dissertation like few others. In Spring 2015, I was fortunate to teach a capstone seminar on Act 31. These students read my dissertation as part of a research process culminating in policy briefings to State Superintendent Tony Evers. I greatly appreciated their enthusiasm, wit, and insightful, candid feedback, even about "the boring chapter." Their projects built upon my initial research, highlighted new sources and perspectives, and informed my own revisions. Many thanks to Emily VerHaagh, Danielle Van Boxtell, Kendall Sherman, Lizz Peterson, Donald Keeble, Emma Berg, Megan Jones, Kai Pyle, Danielle Karl, and the late David Metoxen. This book is better because these students were my teachers. I promised them all their names would go in the book, so now they have to read it.

Colleagues and friends from around the country sustained my morale, provided flashes of insight, and served as a profound challenge to the notion of isolated scholarship. I am grateful for their friendship, words of encouragement, phone calls, emails, Facebook posts, and live and in-person conversations. I am particularly grateful to Jay Dew, Brad Raley, Jacki Rand, Bryan Brayboy, Susan Faircloth, David Beaulieu, Ricardo Torres, Cary Miller, Heather Ann Moody, Debra Barker, Xong Xiong, Bert Zipperer, Laurie Frank, Richie Plass, and Lily Antone-Plass. All of these connections highlighted others and served as reminders that all is connected, all is related, and that everything happens for a reason.

I was fortunate to work with and learn from several people discussed in these pages, and their influence has profoundly shaped this project. The late Alan Caldwell, who helped to enact Act 31 through his position at DPI, his role on AILCEB, and his service to WIEA, became my mentor and my friend. The late Dorothy W. Davids and the late Ruth Gudinas serve as incredible role models for anyone seeking to remain "useful" as a scholar deeply engaged in meeting the needs of practitioners and supporting tribal communities. Dorothy's efforts as a member of AILCEB and the American Indian Study Committee helped to enact Act 31. Ruth was a staunch ally to Native people, and her American Indian Tribal Governments curriculum was one of the first pieces disseminated to schools to address the new requirements. My father-in-law, Gordon Thunder, has made service to Indian Country and the Ho-Chunk Nation his life's work. Veda Stone was a mentor to generations of Native college students, including me. Sharon and Tom Metz, founders of HONOR and the HONOR Resource Center, have been involved with this work dating back to Sharon's service in the legislature and Tom's role as a classroom teacher. Perhaps no one has shaped me more as a scholar than the late Ronald N. Satz, the most challenging teacher I ever had, who taught me about Act 31, insisted that I apply to the DPI American Indian Studies Program, and co-founded the American Indian Studies Summer Institute with me in 1997.

Each year we held the American Indian Studies Summer Institute, I learned profound lessons from the participants, presenters, and staff. It would be nearly impossible to identify or adequately acknowledge all that I learned from my summer institute family, including Ron Satz, Alan Caldwell, Rosemary Christensen, Lisa Poupart, Barbara Munson, Christine Munson, Cathy Caldwell, Adrienne Thunder, Nehomah Thundercloud, Sharon Thom-Fredericks, Lyn Skenandore, Samantha Greendeer, Clif Morton, Bert Zipperer, Lance Kelley, Richie Plass, DeLanna Studi, Carol Amour, Leroy Cardinal, Andrew Gokee, Barbara Miller, Crystal Tourtillott, Brian Jackson, Matthew Stewart, Waubano, Audrey O'Kimosh, Tom Metz, Dorothy Davids, Ruth Gudinas, Connie Ellingson, Forrest Brooks, and Kalanaketskwas Nicole Brooks. It is from this group of people and our collective realization that implementation had become disconnected from its roots that the need to relearn and retell the story of Act 31 became the focus of my research.

My family has shaped the person I am, reinforcing the value of education, encouraging me along the way, and instilling in me the qualities needed to persevere. They also contributed to this project more directly. My parents, Wally and Sheila Leary, and my sister, Sarah Leary, willingly read drafts, tracked down sources, and made sure I took time to eat. My dad helped me with a major reorganization of the manuscript. My grandparents, Anita and Howard Leary, provided a place to stay, space to write, and the best company. Their place has always been home to me, and I wrote much of the dissertation and this manuscript at their kitchen table and on their back porch. Words cannot do justice to express their contributions nor my gratitude for their ongoing support.

My greatest debt of gratitude is to Adrienne Thunder, my wife, my best friend, and my companion for over twenty-five years, who shared the sacrifices that go along with an undertaking like this. She is herself a visionary thinker, outstanding writer, and professional educator in her own right. It would be impossible to identify all the ways that she influenced me, but her insights, observations, challenges, and questions improved my work, and me as a person, in ways both great and small. This book, my scholarship in general, and my life as a whole, are much better because of her. My accomplishments clearly reflect all that I have learned and received from this brilliant woman.

Lastly, I wish to express my gratitude to the Wisconsin Historical Society Press. This project grew out of a strong working relationship with Kathy Borkowski from my time at DPI. Kate Thompson was instrumental in reconceiving the dissertation as a book, and Carrie Kilman served as the first editor. I am especially grateful to have worked with editor Sara Phillips, who brought this project to fruition. Her content knowledge, thoughtfulness, ability to smooth the academic edges off of my writing, and project management skills are unmatched.

INDEX

ABOUT THE AUTHOR

J P Leary is an associate professor of humanities, First Nations studies, and history at the University of Wisconsin–Green Bay. He is also a member of the graduate faculty in education and a faculty affiliate with the Professional Program in Education Center for First Nations Studies. He served as the American Indian Studies Consultant at the Wisconsin Department of Public Instruction from 1996 until 2011. Leary earned a master's in American history from the University of Oklahoma and a PhD in educational policy studies from UW–Madison.

SHERI ANN DOLFEN, WISCONSIN HISTORICAL SOCIETY